designing
knitwear

designing

knitwear

Deborah Newton

The Taunton Press

Cover photo: Cathy Carver

© 1992 by The Taunton Press, Inc.

First printing: March 1992
Printed in the United States of America

A THREADS Book

THREADS® is a trademark of The Taunton Press, Inc., registered in the U.S.
Patent and Trademark Office.

The Taunton Press, 63 South Main Street, Box 5506, Newtown, CT
06470-5506

Library of Congress Cataloging-in-Publication Data

Newton, Deborah.
    Designing knitwear / Deborah Newton.
       p.   cm.
    "A Threads book."
    Includes bibliographical references and index.
    ISBN 0-942391-06-3
    1. Knitting.   2. Design.   I. Title.
TT820.N555   1992   91-36451
746.9'2 — dc20   CIP

To my mother and father,
Evelyn and Charles Newton,
who led me to books.

*A*cknowledgments

*O*ver the years, the best part of my job has been working with fellow knitters. Without their skills and enthusiasm, I would surely not have begun or finished this project. I am very grateful to my dear friends Patricia Yankee, Barbara Khouri, Ethel Wood, Hilary Sweigart, Lisa Tamura and Mary Andrews, who helped me with the knitting and with many other tasks for this book. My thanks also to the other wonderful knitters who have helped me in the past: Judy Davis, Brenda McClosky, Judy Furlong, Diana Jackson and Janet D'Alesandre, whose knowledge of yarns and ability to track them down has been invaluable.

For early influences, I am indebted to Barbara Walker for her impeccable knitting books and to costume designer Barbara Matheson, who, for many years, shared her vast garment construction experience with me.

For access to museum collections, I thank Jean Druesedow and Kimberly Fink of the Costume Institute of the Metropolitan Museum of Art in New York, and Susan Anderson Hay and Pamela Parmel of the Museum of the Rhode Island School of Design in Providence. Also thanks to Margot Schevill of the Haffenreffer Museum of Anthropology in Bristol, Rhode Island.

I offer a special thank-you to the many individuals who answered questions and offered their support during the course of writing this book. Only a lack of space prevents me from naming them all. For an expert introduction to the knitting machine, I am indebted to Susan Guagliumi of Studio by White, VWS, Inc. Thanks too to Anne MacDonald and Claire Phillips for photo suggestions and to the ever-generous Pat Chew and Kristin Nicholas of Classic Elite Yarns for an abundance of materials. I am grateful to Bill Rice for allowing us to shoot some of the photography in his studio. Thanks to Robert Lilly of Unger Yarns for permission to include the fulled vests in Chapter 8, which were originally designed for this company. Thanks to Theresa Gaffey for helping me check the instructions for all the garments; to Joe Rossi for the make-up; and to my sister, Regina Newton Orio, and Susan Moore, Anthony Fratus, Betsy Levine, Margery Winter and Roberta Houllahan for their considerable support and contributions.Thanks to my brother, Jason Newton, and to my friends who also patiently posed for photos: Michael Cafferty, Helen Cottrell, Jessie Davis, Risa Gilpin, Gail Harrison, Louanne Skorupa, Pamela Parmel, Carol Pilkington, Heather Rigny and Rebecca Wood.

Invaluable to me were the many companies and their representatives who contributed materials for projects and swatches in the book: Susan Bates; Berger Du Nord; Bernat Yarn and Craft; Berroco, Inc.; B. Blumenthal and Co., Inc.; Brunswick Yarns; Cascade Yarns; Classic Elite Yarns, Inc.; Crystal Palace Yarns; Evergreen Enterprises; Ironstone Warehouse; Lanas Margarita, Inc.; Lane Borgosesia; Laninter Corp.; Plymouth Yarn Company; Renaissance Yarns; Reynolds Yarns, A Division of JCA, Inc.; Silk City Fibers; Simpson/Southwick Co.; Westminster Trading Corp.; and William Unger & Co.

A special thank-you to my dear friend, photographer Cathy Carver, whose marvelous eye and very hard work helped create the wonderful images in this book. It is always a pleasure to work with such a professional.

Special thanks too to everyone in the book department at The Taunton Press for their hospitality, patience and unflagging enthusiasm. I am especially grateful to my art director, Deborah Fillion, for getting involved early in the process to help work out some of the visual concepts in the book and for creating a visually exciting design for the book.

Much of the credit for this book should go to my editor, Christine Timmons. She epitomizes the best in editorial guidance, combining clear-headed organization with creative vision and a true love for the book-making process. I am deeply grateful for her eye-opening suggestions, her patience and her delightful wit, all of which helped me to enjoy a very difficult task.

And to Paul Di Filippo, the most generous person of all, my love and deepest thanks.

Contents

Learning to See

*t*en years ago, when I was a novice designer, the lack of available information on knitwear design frustrated me thoroughly. I searched for direction in numerous knitting books but found only descriptions of standard garment shapes and instructions for how many stitches to cast on for a given width. Although these guidelines were useful, I wanted much more information. What about the subtleties of fit? How to shape a complicated garment? How to use color successfully? And, as elusive to me as anything, where do ideas and inspiration come from?

Armed with these questions, I began investigating design on my own, starting with simple shapes and plain fabrics. Because I was very interested in knitting techniques, my early projects were often inspired by traditional knitted garments. I also became interested in knitted designs from the past and collected them for inspiration for detail and silhouette.

As time passed and I became more adept, I began to refer to books beyond the realm of knitting. Books about drawing helped me un-

derstand color relationships. Studying illustrations in all kinds of books helped me develop my cartoon-like sketching style. Books on embroidery offered inspiration for new patterns. Books on sewing helped me learn about garment construction and shaping. I also began to look closely at all kinds of clothing, from garments in fashion magazines to historical pieces in museum collections to vintage and ethnic clothing. From all these sources, I adapted garment shapes and details to use in my knitwear designs, testing new ideas with new projects.

Although I was not aware of it as a novice designer, I now realize that learning to design successfully is largely a process of learning to see. This may seem an oversimplification, but it really isn't. Learning to see is about getting to the very basic nature of things and learning to identify their specific qualities. For anyone who wants to explore visual ideas and make connections among them, looking carefully and really seeing has to be an ongoing activity.

Facing page:
An enlarged detail of a circuit board might serve as the basis for a colorwork pattern with metallic yarns.

I don't want the notion of learning to see to seem vague or difficult. In fact, just the opposite is true—nothing could be simpler or less complicated if you proceed step by step. Nor do I want learning to see to seem an out-of-reach pursuit, only within the realm of the "creative" personality. It's a skill that anyone can easily learn.

Before I began to design, I didn't really see what surrounded me. Like many of us in this fast-paced culture, which inundates us with images on TV and in books and magazines, I looked at a multitude of things every day in a very cursory, distanced way. I took in an over-all impression, without absorbing the details.

Happily, with my interest in design came an awakening of my sight. This was a very gradual process, which I was unaware of at first. But, with my goal of becoming a designer in mind, I began to scrutinize everything more carefully. Soon I found myself actively involved in seeing things more clearly. I no longer saw only the whole but also the parts making up that whole. I saw shapes and silhouettes, pattern and background. I saw all kinds of texture and unusual color combinations. Everything came under my design scrutiny—even, for example, the gridwork at a bus stop, whose patterning I could use in my work.

To learn to see more clearly, you have to focus your mind on visual details. This process must entail some questioning on your part, at least at the outset. The goal of this questioning is to identify the details, character and components of what you see. For example, you might ask, what are the qualities of what I'm looking at? What is it made of? What are its proportions? Which feature is dominant, and does it obscure less obvious qualities? Is the color combination pleasing or jarring? Why? Is the surface interest due to texture, color or a reflective shine? Is the patterning bold or delicate? Will I remember this object, or will it make no impression on me at all?

Such questions may seem silly at first, but they are important because they will help you initiate a dialog with yourself and force you to become actively involved in what you see. After a while this questioning becomes more or less automatic.

This timelessly appealing, close-fitting cardigan from a 1904 knitting pattern shows that even the simplest fabric can be quite effective when paired with an interesting shape and handsome details. (Photo courtesy of the Library of Congress.)

Designed Expressly for "Stitches."
SWEATER MADE OF 8-FOLD BEAR BRAND ZEPHYR GERMANTOWN, WITH TAM O' SHANTER OF THREE RABBIT ANGORA WOOL
For Description See Pages 2 and 3

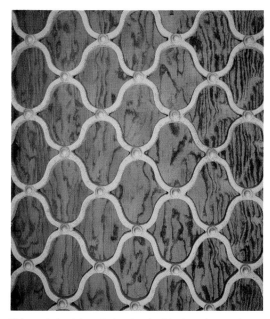

This metal gridwork, backed with tinted wood, could inspire a graceful, curving diamond pattern, knitted in a solid color on a soft, variegated background. Bobbles or buttons where the lines intersect might add detail.

These 16th-century knitted ecclesiastical garments use patterns in different ways. The garment at right combines a textured knit/purl pattern with gold stranded colorwork. The sleeveless garment's graphic pattern has a bold, modern look. (Metropolitan Museum of Art. Garment at right: Frederick C. Hewitt Fund, 1914; sleeveless garment: Fletcher Fund, 1946.)

This detail of a dress by Emilio Pucci reminds me of 1960s Op Art and is a wonderful combination of color and graphics. I'm intrigued by the way the ruffly motif expands outward from the corner and how the fine black lines outline the areas of the sophisticated color combination.

You may ask as you read this, out of everything that passes by, what is it that I'm supposed to look at? What am I looking for? It's often useful to begin looking at familiar things. If you're an avid knitter, you probably already see the craft of knitting quite clearly because you're interested in it. Perhaps you can easily recognize pattern stitches because you have trained your eye to identify their basic qualities. But do you compare patterns, noting their similarities and differences? Do you understand the techniques used to form similar fabrics? What do you see when you look at knitted fabrics from the past?

And what about the world beyond knitting? Do you look at woven fabrics with the same interest as knitted fabrics, or do you pass them by? What about garment shapes—are you familiar with any kinds of ethnic or historical clothing, or only the kinds of garments you and your family wear? Does fashion with all its permutations fascinate you, as it does me? What colors stimulate you—why? When you

Inspiration for knitwear design can come from nonknitted fabrics and garments. For example, the geometric shapes, bold color combinations and embellishments in these wonderful ethnic fabrics could be readily adapted to knitwear. From left to right: a cross-stitched Mexican shawl, a Turkish kilim and an embroidered Indian skirt embellished with shisha mirrors.

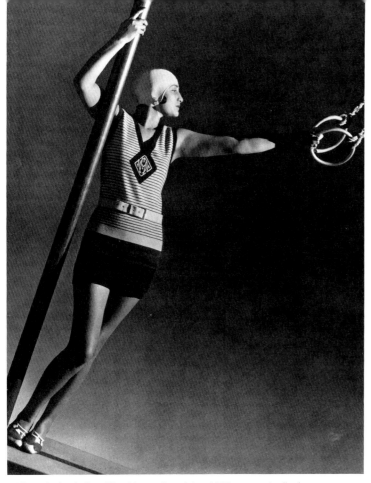

Although the knitted bathing suits of the 1930s seem bulky by our standards, they still offer inspiration for today's garment designs. (Photo by George Hoyningen Huene, Frederick R. Koch collection, Harvard Theatre Collection.)

Start simply, by looking carefully at a few familiar things each day as if you'd never seen them before. Then make a point of scrutinizing things you've never seen before. Through improved sight, you will gain a greater appreciation of the shape, color and texture of the world—and you will lay the groundwork for becoming a designer.

designing, or making choices

We're all familiar with the results of design—witness the multitude of objects that surround us in our culture. But it seems to me that the act of designing itself is one of the most invisible activities in our world. We see and use thousands of designed items, but rarely do we know how they were conceived or what idea sparked their creation.

In order to write about knitwear design, I had to think a lot about design in general. To design means to make something, starting with an idea and ending with a finished product. Some design is based on function, or fulfilling a need. Think of the basic paper clip—pure function. At the other extreme, some design is purely for delight or decorative effect. I always think of jewelry as the most ornamental of all design forms. But more often than not, good design combines both function and looks.

Knitwear design also involves taking an idea and making a finished product based on that idea. What makes designing knitwear different from designing other clothing is the nature of the fabric itself. Knitted fabrics generally have more stretch than woven fabrics, a characteristic that you can subdue or enhance by your choice of yarn, needle size and pattern. You also need to choose an appropriate garment shape and finishing techniques for your knitted fabric. I've found that managing all of these choices does not happen magically. Instead, I think that designing successfully requires creating a plan and testing that plan before making the final product.

To many people, the process of designing knitwear seems difficult and inaccessible. Some knitters may feel that it's beyond them and consequently never bother to try. I think the traditional invisibility of the design process is what gives designing its mystique. In fact, designing knitwear is very straightforward if you approach it slowly and systematically.

look at an illustration in a magazine, can you describe the artist's style—is it like a cartoon? A copy of an old master? A computer-like drawing? When you visit a museum, what attracts you? Can you describe it? If you see something puzzling, do you turn away, or do you take the time to identify your response before moving on to something else? When you go to the bookstore or a library, do you wander into unfamiliar sections, or visit the same shelves every time?

These questions are meant to help you think about your "viewing habits." Clearly, no two individuals look at the world in the same way, nor are they drawn to the same things. Your background, interests, heritage and where you live, among other things, all influence what you choose to focus your sight on and how you see. But whatever your visual focus, a conscious effort to broaden the way you look at things will add immeasurably to your daily experience and quickly sharpen your vision.

My first sweater design (far right), created in 1977, was a dropped-shoulder pullover, decorated with the simplest possible depiction of a tree. My fourth sweater and first published design (near right), completed in 1982, was inspired by Aran texture and took an entire year, working off and on, to design and knit.

I've already mentioned that the route into design is learning to see. More specifically, in order to design knitwear, you must learn to make choices based on what you see. These choices can be few and very simple—you could even alter just one or two elements of an existing design as a way of beginning to make choices—or these choices can be numerous and complex. But remember that a design need not be complex to be successful. The best designs, whether simple or complicated, are well thought out and visually interesting.

I used to think that the more I knew about knitting, the better designer I would be. I know now that this is not entirely true. Knitting skills certainly provide a strong foundation for design, and they allow you to pursue more complicated designs with success. But knitwear design is really less a question of technique than an issue of observing and then carefully making and executing choices based on your observations. The novice knitter can design as successful a sweater as the expert.

One of the keys to learning to design is to base your initial designs on what is familar to you. You could, in fact, design hundreds of successful sweaters without ever going beyond traditional knitting patterns and basic shapes. I'm not embarrassed to wear the first pullover I ever designed, which really couldn't be simpler (see the sweater at right in the photo above). It is decorated at the lower edge with simple, triangular pine trees, which I still find quite effective. I did misjudge the neckline, making it too wide, but I solved the problem by picking up stitches from the inside and working a large turtleneck collar, which I found improved the design. I learned quite a few good lessons from this garment—that simple graphics can be very effective, that a boxy shape is comfortable, functional and, above all, easy to plan. And, perhaps the most important of all, I learned that a mistake can be turned into a positive feature of a garment.

Early in my design career, I made two important decisions—"promises" to myself—that have served me well. I decided, first, always to start with an idea that truly excites me and, second, to make each design look as good as it possibly could. These may seem like obvious

The graphic combination of pattern on pattern in this old photo immediately stirred my design sight. I can envision several fabrics and garment shapes based on these summer dresses. Photo, The Bettmann Archive.)

This print of a French peasant girl in traditional dress, from a book from the 1930s (*Les Costumes Régionaux de la France*, published by Pegasus Press), might inspire a knitted sampler of floral patterns, worked in the rich colors of her outfit — or it might help me devise a new style of sketching.

design potential. First, I see two wonderful, eye-catching graphic patterns. Could they be adapted to knitted fabric? How would I best capture the patterns? Perhaps I could swatch to come up with a striped pattern. The more complicated pattern might require charting — would I align it sideways or up and down, as shown in the photo? What about combining the striped pattern with the graphic one? What type of garment shape would I use? What season would I design it for, and what would my yarn choice be? A knitted dress is an interesting concept that I haven't thoroughly explored. What an interesting raglan — it makes good use of the striped patterns. And what is that area of puffy fabric at the sides of the striped dress? A ruffle? A ruched panel? How would it look knitted?

I hope the above paragraph conveys a little of the confusion that prevails at the outset of the design process, even for an experienced designer. I know that something will come out of this initial inner dialog, but at this point I don't know exactly what it will be. If I want to get the process underway, I need to harness my excitement and start to make choices that will bring one major idea to the fore. I might store the other ideas away or put them on hold only until I've finished the current project.

Since there are so many choices to make when designing, it's necessary to develop a process to organize and deal with the flow of ideas. Without a system, most people lack focus and tend to drift from one idea to another without finding a way to connect them.

This book represents the design process I've worked out over the years and upon which I still rely both for professional work and when I'm designing and knitting purely for pleasure. (I also find this system very useful for nonknitting projects.) If you've not yet established your own system for designing, I hope you'll borrow the information in these pages and use it to help you you devise your own methods of design. This information cannot be swallowed and immediately absorbed overnight. It must be used to be understood. You'll also want to explore this information in your own way, adding to the process a large dose of curiosity about your own interests and a good measure of patience.

goals, but, especially in the case of the latter, it's sometimes tempting to settle for results that are not quite right, particularly when you are struggling with a new idea. To ensure that I keep my promises to myself, I stop working on a project when I feel tired or frustrated, and resume after getting some distance from the material. I always choose the most appropriate material and the best that I can afford. I never settle for less. And I always try to take the time to iron out all the questions and difficulties I have with a project before beginning to knit. In addition, I keep a file of visual images to simulate and inspire me.

Because designing often requires sifting through many ideas before settling on one. I would like to share with you my initial train of thought when I see something interesting. Above is a black-and-white photo that seized me the second I saw it. Obviously it has nothing to do with knitting, but I see in it a lot of

My *design* process

My design system is based on the need to have both a clear, detailed idea of what each design will look like before it is knitted and a way of accurately and efficiently recording the information needed to produce the design. In order to sell my designs to magazines and yarn companies, I realized that I also needed a strong presentation. And, as my list of clients grew and I could no longer knit every design myself, I found I needed an easy, foolproof system of instruction that I could give to other knitters and which they could follow without mistakes. The system I developed meets these various needs and also breaks up the work of designing into small, easily managed parts. Ultimately, any design system you develop should, I think, enable you to see and test all the aspects of a project before you begin to knit.

My design process has four basic phases: inspiration, swatching, capturing the design on paper and keeping records. In the inspiration phase, an idea starts to percolate in my mind. The idea can come from anywhere. I might be inspired by something knitterly, like a traditional pattern stitch. I might decide I want to shape a garment in an unusual way. Or I might have several ideas that I want to combine in a single garment. Although getting ideas is exciting, I'm always very confused during this phase of the design process because I'm uncertain about how to proceed.

The only way I get out of my confusion is to take up yarn and needles and begin to swatch. During this phase, I try to take advantage of my initial enthusiasm—time wears it thin—to gain momentum with an idea. With my inspiration in mind, I choose a variety of yarns and begin to experiment with them. (Of course, I could choose just one yarn and struggle to make it work for my idea, but then I'd have nothing to compare it to.) For me, swatching is the most crucial stage of designing knitwear because I always want the best possible fabric to express or support my idea. Why settle for a commomplace fabric when, with a little patience, you can have an outstanding one?

I always experience a loss of confidence during the swatching phase because swatching is difficult work. And, although I fight the urge, I often anticipate too much and allow myself to develop an image of what I want the swatch to look like, rather than waiting to see how it actually turns out. This may seem confusing because I've already said that you need to begin with an idea in mind. Well, that's true, I think, but you also need to keep a loose rein on that idea. Sometimes your yarn combined with the stitch pattern you're using will produce an entirely unexpected result, perhaps better than your original notion, and off you'll go in a totally new direction.

I try numerous swatches, changing needle size, yarn, stitch or color pattern, or some combination of changes, until I've produced a fabric that I'm happy with. Once that happens, I begin to capture the design on paper. I find this phase of the design process invigorating. My energy has returned, I'm excited with the fabric, and I'm anxious to figure out what will show it off to best advantage. Since I'm always intrigued with what my garment will look like, I now spend very enjoyable time sketching the possible variations and variously combining or subtracting details. When I like the rough results, I make a more careful, studied drawing, including all of the design details. I take notes about the fabric to help me remember how it was made. If I've devised a new stitch pattern or combined patterns in an unusual way, I chart these patterns with symbols before I forget what I've done.

With my swatch and final sketch in hand, I note the gauge of my fabric. I return to any preliminary charts I may have saved to refine the pattern so that it's easy to follow. Because I'm always concerned with fit and shaping, I spend a great deal of time charting the silhouette and size of my project on graph paper. If I've planned areas of pattern for my garment, I work out their placement on this chart for best visual effect.

Finally, I chart the entire garment on a large sheet of graph paper, using one square for each stitch. This chart lets me see at a glance the whole knitted piece and forces me to consider every aspect of the design. I plot any stitch patterns on this large chart and note all the increases and decreases on the appropriate rows. I mark checkpoints on the chart where problems could arise, so that I can keep an eye out from them. Along the way, I question myself constantly—have I thought out all the details? This chart serves well as a final instruction, whether for me or my fellow knitters, but I usually also write a complete set of instructions to accompany this chart.

The last phase of my design process, record keeping, is a by-product of the previous steps. After the garment is done, I gather and put away all the swatches and charts for future reference, jotting notes about the design's effectiveness. I may return to this material at a later date for various reasons. I might want to repeat or alter a shape or pick up a finishing detail that worked well in the past. I might reuse or vary a pattern graph. And sometimes, when I feel I'll never have another idea again, I look back through my records to be inspired anew by an old design.

You might find my planning process time-consuming — and it is. But it avoids many problems down the line, and time is actually gained in the knitting. Because of all of this planning, in half a dozen years of working with knitters and producing hundreds of garments, I can proudly say that the knitting has had to be ripped out only a couple of times.

Do I feel that my process eliminates spontaneity or play? On the contrary. My process may be structured, but I try to take my time with each phase, exploring all possibilities before coming to a conclusion. It's true that occasionally I'll have a revelation during the knitting of the garment, at which point I may change my plans or I may hang on to this new information for use in a later design.

Although I usually follow the order described above, a design will sometimes develop according to its own order. That is, I may chart a garment shape before swatching a fabric for it, or start swatching with an intriguing yarn before I have any idea of what I'll do with it. But, no matter where I start or how I proceed through the process, I always pass through all the design phases and end up with a firm visual representation of the project. I try to enjoy the testing phase, considering as many approaches as possible. And I love the sketching, as you, too, can learn to do. But after the experimenting is over, I like to lock my ideas into place. Over the years, I have come to enjoy the process of designing as much as the knitting itself.

How to *U*se this book

This book is intended to give you a design system to borrow partly or entirely until you develop your own. Because the book's focus is design rather than technique per se, I've included technical information only when it relates specifically to design issues. If a technique I mention is fully described in numerous other references, I have not reiterated this basic information in my design discussion. Hence, if you come across an undescribed technique that's unfamiliar to you, please consult one of the books listed in the Bibliography on pp. 258-260.

Each of the chapters in this book deals with a separate area of design. Chapters 2 through 5 deal with the fundamental issues of design — yarn; fit and silhouette; designing with basic knit and purl stitches; and color and graphics. Chapters 6 through 8 — "The Comfortable Classics," "Themes & Samplers," and "Dressmaker Details & Finishing Techniques" — address more complicated areas of design and build upon the material that is presented in the earlier chapters.

You can use the book in linear fashion, as a sort of study course, reading from beginning to end and gradually acquainting yourself with the cumulative steps in my design process. Or, if you're interested in a particular topic — for example, color — you can enter the book at that point and work forward, backward or in any order you like through the other chapters. I've made a point of presenting the material in each chapter so that it can stand alone at the same time that it relates to what precedes and follows it. Whether you want to use the book systematically or dip in and out for inspiration and information, I hope you'll find it a valuable reference for all your design work.

Throughout the book you'll notice recurring elements related to my design process with such titles as "Capturing the Design," "Avoiding a Tangle," "Swatch Project" and "Designer Notebook." In "Capturing the Design," you will find information on numerous tools and techniques for getting your design onto paper — from making schematic drawings to learning how to sketch. In "Avoiding a Tangle," you'll learn how to sense trouble before it starts and head off problems at the pass. In addition to the regular attention paid to swatching in each chapter, many chapters include a "Swatch Project" that precedes the final project. In these swatch projects, I've made use of the test swatch for the final project as an element of that project—for example, as a pocket or shoulder pad—or as the basis for an accessory like a hat or purse. Although it's not always possible to do so, whenever I can I like to find a use for a swatch that often takes a great deal of energy and time to create.

Each chapter ends with a project whose design is based upon some of the main issues in the chapter. In some cases, I've also offered an alternative design to show you how I explore ideas in several ways. The "Designer Notebook" records my inspiration for the design, along with the project's swatches and some of my notes, sketches and other records. With the project, you'll also find full written instructions and all the schematics and charts you need to make the garment if you want. Rather than duplicating my designs, however, I encourage you to use my instructions as general guidelines and alter the patterns in some way to personalize them for yourself. By doing this, you'll begin to make valuable design decisions. For each of your projects, I also encourage you to keep a notebook of your own, which will serve as an automatic record-keeping system to which you can refer in the future.

Finally, as a kind of afterword to each chapter, I've included a section called "What if…?" This is my way of recalling some of the issues in the chapter and reopening the design decisions I made in the final project. Here, you'll find suggestions on different approaches to the designs or design ideas presented in the chapter. The point of "What if…?" is the question mark. After completing any project, I always question myself on the success or failure of the design, improvements I might make in it and other directions I might explore with it. I find this a very productive process, which often yields the point of departure for the next project. You, too, may find it helpful to ask "What if…?" whenever you complete a project.

At the end of the book, you'll find a brief, very personal addendum entitled "Pushing the Limits." After years of designing and exploring the design process, and after the challenging task of completing this book, I'm ready now to move on to something new. I'm ready to push beyond the limits of traditional knitwear design, and this addendum presents some thoughts about where I want to go next.

At this crossroads, I feel some of the same confusion I felt when I first began designing. Certain things I am sure of—for example, I

know that I'll continue to use the design process that has helped me in the past. But, having acquired this discipline, I now look forward to experimenting in a less structured, more free-form fashion. It's time for me to ask myself what I can do with knitwear design that I haven't done before, perhaps starting by using new methods and unusual knitting materials. While pursuing this new avenue, I will nonetheless continue to study past fashion and the work of other designers, like Elsa Schiaparelli, one of my favorites. And having explored many complex projects in the past, I look forward to returning to the simple knitting ideas, to begin again, seeing them with new eyes.

For me, putting together this addendum has served as a way of taking stock and clarifying some of my current goals. In some ways, those goals are just as much a "design project" as any of the garments I created for this book, and I'll likewise get to them step by step.

I hope you'll join step with me in the following pages on the path into the design process and that you'll find it as rewarding as I do. I also hope that this book help will you see potential in the familiar and draw inspiration from the unusual. Above all, I hope this book leads you to design with confidence, ease and great pleasure.

This crocheted shawl and glove set from the 1930s, attributed to French designer Elsa Schiaparelli, uses unusual metallic strands to create a dramatic eveningwear combination. (Museum of Art, Rhode Island School of Design; gift of the Estate of Edith Stuyvesant Vanderbilt Gerry.)

2 Designing with Yarn

*t*his chapter is about yarn. More precisely, it's about getting actively involved with yarns as a designer. For many knitters and designers, yarns themselves are irresistible. Their brilliant colors and intriguing blends of fiber and texture beckon endlessly, but finding potential in even a great-looking yarn can be a real challenge. A beautiful skein of yarn, as you may already know, does not always produce a wonderful knitted fabric. On the other hand, a plain, undistinguished yarn sometimes knits up into an unexpectedly luxurious material.

When I first began designing, yarns confused me thoroughly. Why weren't all yarns of the same weight interchangeable? Even yarns of the same fiber didn't react in the same way when knitted. One wool yarn produced a firm, crisp fabric, while another wool yarn of the same weight gave me a buttery, almost limp material. One smooth yarn looked good in almost any pattern I tried, while a comparable yarn yielded handsome results only in the simplest stitch.

Often I bought enough yarn for a sweater, only to find that what I thought the yarn would do was impossible. Like many knitters, I would be deceived by the skein of yarn itself, envisioning the wonderful effects it would produce before I had even worked with it.

My disappointments led me to adopt a new, more active way of dealing with yarns. If a yarn intrigued me, I would knit at least one swatch, or sample, with it before allowing myself to imagine what I might do with it. Usually after the first swatch, I would change needle size to get a different gauge and try different patterns with the same yarn. I would produce a number of swatches, and only after creating a fabric that pleased me would I start a project. In other words, I had learned to let the yarn show me what it wanted to do or what it did best before committing it to a project.

Capturing the design

Making a good swatch

Knit swatches of each yarn you're considering for a project with at least two different sizes of needles to see how the fabric is altered by the change. Don't feel that you have to knit with the "proper" needle size for a given yarn, that is, the one suggested on the yarn's label. It's not essential to aim for the suggested gauge. Instead, knit a swatch that looks and feels good to you, which you'll find by experimenting with various needle sizes. Do not, however, change needle size within the same swatch (unless this is intended to be a feature of the fabric). Work a separate swatch with the same number of stitches for each different size of needle.

With regard to the swatch's size, the larger it is, the more information it will reveal. I suggest knitting a 5-in. to 8-in. square so that you can really see the fabric and let it drape and move. Make an educated guess about how many stitches to cast on. In order to produce flat, uncurling edges on the swatch, knit the edge stitches—the first and last couple of stitches on every row—regardless of the stitch pattern you're using for the rest of the swatch.

Swatches can be blocked to even out stubborn irregularities in the fabric. Blocking, however, is not always necessary and is largely a matter of personal taste. It should be used only to enhance a fabric. However, if you plan to block your final project, you must also block the swatch. You can do so by wetting or steaming the swatch, depending on its fiber content (see the chart on p. 230 for full instructions).

A swatch is a valuable resource and should be kept for reference. For this reason, I always tag my swatches with labels noting needle size, yarn and pattern-stitch source.

Experimenting with yarns can be one of the most exciting aspects of knitwear design, especially if you approach the process without preconceived plans or biases. Sometimes this is easy, but at other times it takes perseverance. You need to forget about how you would like a yarn to perform, and let go of your attachment to favorite fibers. Be willing to spend time with new yarns, learn to "read" what they reveal, and you'll move from yarn to fabric to design with greater success.

Throughout the book I use the word *fabric* to describe the knitted swatches and the material of the garments in the projects at the end of each chapter. It's important to get used to the fact that, for every knitwear design, wearable or not, you are first creating a knitted fabric, and this fabric must really suit the project you have in mind, in weight, texture, drape and general appearance. Remember, any design is the result of all the preliminary choices you make—perhaps the most important of which is yarn selection.

Swatching

Before discussing different types of yarns and fibers, it's useful to get acquainted with yarns by jumping right into the swatching process. Even if you're an experienced knitter, you should still find this a valuable exercise; it may help change the attitudes that you've developed toward certain yarns and offer up some new ideas.

The act of swatching requires only a minimum of concentration and a small amount of yarn, yet it yields enormous rewards. Swatching with new yarns can rejuvenate your creative powers and make you look anew at the familiar. Maybe you've avoided this kind of experimentation in the past because it seemed too easy, or conversely because it seemed like a difficult stumbling block. But swatching serves as an invaluable testing ground for a yarn and is the tangible proof of what it can produce. The swatching process is intended to provoke and answer questions about the yarn, and should always begin the design process.

The importance of swatching, however, extends beyond the initial selection of yarn. Once you've begun to think about a design, swatching enables you to test out all aspects of this design—for example, the colorwork or stitch pattern, or the way you envision trimming an edge. Even though the swatching process may seem awkward at first, as you gain more experience with it, you'll find it an invaluable tool that's crucial for designing knitwear.

To start the swatching process, first assemble a mixed group of yarns, which might include the following: a familiar yarn that you've enjoyed in the past, a yarn you find attractive but haven't yet knitted with, a very fine yarn, a very heavy one and one that you personally find unattractive and might otherwise avoid.

I suggest working two swatches with each yarn in a simple stockinette fabric (that is, knitting one row, purling one row and repeating this sequence). Work the first swatch with the size of needle indicated on the yarn's label (if you don't have the label, just use the needle size you expect would be suggested for this yarn). Then knit the second swatch with a much larger or smaller needle to produce an exaggerated effect, whether looser or tighter. In each case, cast on enough stitches so that you end up with a piece of fabric that's large enough to handle and look at, not just a skinny strip the size of a wristband. For other suggestions on making a good swatch, see the sidebar on the facing page.

Once you've gathered your yarns and have in mind these simple directions, close this book and work the swatches. Even if this process seems a waste of time, force yourself to do it anyway. Forget about gauge and the fact that the knitting may look different from anything you've ever done before. Simply create a variety of knitted fabrics.

When you've finished swatching (and this may take more time than you expect), you can analyze your swatches as a designer. What does the swatch look like? Does it have a unique appearance? If so, what are the reasons? Which side of the swatch is more attractive? Why? Does the smooth side of the fabric enhance the yarn, or does the bumpy side seem more interesting?

Now think about how the fabric feels and behaves. Is it soft and limp, or dense and stiff? Does it have drape and body? Does it resemble fabric you've knitted in the past? Or does it seem odd for a knitted fabric—if so, choose a word to describe it. Is it flimsy? Papery? Does it feel like cardboard or perhaps like plastic?

About the swatches in this book

Throughout this book you'll see dozens of swatches of different knitted fabrics. Some swatches show only one pattern, others combine several patterns, and still others incorporate edgings. The various groupings of swatches sometimes show similarities among patterns and at other times point out their differences. I've used a wide range of yarn types for these swatches to show how various yarns affect the knitted fabric.

When these swatches were photographed, I made sure that the pictures would show both some of the edges of the swatches and the little irregularities that are characteristic of hand-knitted fabrics. You'll note that some of the swatches curl slightly and that some have little bumps or ripples due to the combination of pattern and yarn. Some have been blocked, to be sure, but even so, I made sure not to flatten the life out of them. What I hope you'll realize as you look through these photographs is that each swatch is a real, vital fabric with unique characteristics that need to be considered when designing knitwear.

Compare the pairs of swatches knitted with the same yarn. What contrasts have been created by changing needle size? Does one swatch seem better than the other in terms of tension and gauge? In other words, does it show off the yarn to its best advantage?

Finally, what could you envision using each fabric for? Are any suitable for clothing? Accessories? If not, why? Stretch your imagination if the swatch seems alien to you, and try to picture it as something, or at least ask yourself what it reminds you of. Not all swatches or yarns are destined to yield a successful project. However, each yarn does hold some information that can be unlocked only by actually working with it. And swatching with any yarn will help you gain experience and give you a point of comparison for future swatching and decision making for each new design.

Various fibers lend different qualities to knitted fabrics. In the upper left group, the top swatch, made of Icelandic wool, produces a dense fabric, while the fuzzy alpaca and smooth merino wool swatches beneath have more drape. At lower left, the brown all-linen swatch is coarser and stiffer than the soft cotton/linen-blend swatch atop it. At upper right, the rayon/nylon-blend swatch (at bottom) is stiff and has a rather plastic sheen, while the all-rayon swatch (on top) is limp, soft and natural-looking. At lower right, the lustrous silk fabric on top has more drape than its grainy, coarse silk cousin.

Inside *Yarns*

When I first started designing, I knew next to nothing about how yarns were made or what they were made of. Since then, I've read a lot about fibers and seen how yarns are spun. I've also designed hundred of knitted garments and have seen how almost every type of yarn reacts in a variety of knitted fabrics. Reading about yarns can help you make design decisions, but nothing can replace the actual experience of working with them, which is why I began this chapter by asking you to jump into swatching. Now that you've done that, you may find it useful to look more closely at the various fibers used for yarns.

As a professional, I've worked with a tremendous range of yarns, from exquisitely light lambswool to a synthetic that squeaked as it moved across the needle. The best yarns are wonderful to knit with, and I encourage you to use them. But don't necessarily avoid yarns that are more difficult to handle—synthetics and novelties have their place too. In many ways, I've learned more about designing and problem solving from less resilient yarns than from very manageable, traditional wools. Mind you, I'm not suggesting that you rush out and buy a slew of unmanageable yarns. But do occasionally buy a ball of an unusual yarn and try to produce an interesting fabric with it. You'll find that you'll deal better with your favorite yarns by gaining experience with more difficult ones.

Handknitting yarns are divided into those made from natural fibers and those made from synthetics. Natural fibers, like wool, silk and cotton, come from a wide variety of animal and vegetable sources; except for being cleaned and spun into yarn, they are more or less unchanged from their natural state. By contrast, synthetic fibers are manufactured, rather than just processed. Some synthetics, like rayon, are made from a natural base of cellulose, usually from trees or woody plants. Other man-made fibers, like acrylic or nylon, are derived from a chemical base.

There are various ways of spinning fibers into yarn, and each produces a differently textured strand. Loosely twisting the fibers into a strand produces a soft, lofty yarn, while twisting tightly produces a stiff, less yielding strand. The strand can be twisted to the right (Z-twist) or to the left (S-twist), and the direction of the twist subtly affects the surface of the yarn and the knitting. A single strand (called a "single," or "ply") can, in turn, be twisted with one or

In these swatches, knitted from plied or twisted yarns, you can see how the texture of the strand affects the fabric. From left to right, a mohair yarn loosely twisted with a synthetic strand with fine thread 'hairs;' a flat, synthetic ribbon twisted with a firm, slubbed yarn; a plied wool with tweed flecks; a shiny mercerized cotton with a cabled twist; a synthetic cord twisted with a slubbed mohair blend.

more similar or different strands to create a plied yarn. The plies can be loosely or tightly twisted, or variously handled to produce a wide range of effects, from smooth yarns that highlight pattern stitches to bouclés, slub yarns and novelty yarns that usually obscure patterns.

When a loose twist, which allows fibers to expand, is combined with a fluffy fiber, like some cottons or mohair, or with a naturally elastic fiber, like wool, the resulting yarn "fills in" the small spaces in the knitting between stitches and rows. This kind of yarn makes a spongy, full-bodied fabric, even when worked on large needles. On the other hand, when any fiber, whether elastic or firm, is tightly spun, it tends to have a more string-like appearance when knitted and will not "fill in." Using a smaller needle with tightly spun yarns helps to avoid what I call a "fishnet" appearance in the fabric.

The point is to be aware that the structure of each yarn creates a certain texture in the strand, which will, in turn, contribute to the texture of the knitted fabric. If you're not already familiar with the structure of yarns, try pulling apart the yarn ends hanging from the swatches you made and see if you can determine how the structure of a given strand affects the texture and surface of the knitted fabric.

Even though I've worked with a large variety of yarns, I've not yet worked with some intriguing fibers that are generally less accessible to knitters. Among these are fibers from the llama, which I've read are coarser and less silky than the fibers from its cousin, the alpaca. I'd also like to try qiviut, the soft, cashmere-like fiber of the musk-ox, from the arctic regions of North America. Less appealing to me are the luxury fibers of the guanaco and vicuña, wild animals from South America that must be killed for their fibers to be gathered.

Animal fibers and filaments

There are many animals whose hair or fibers are used to create yarn, and technically the term **wool** applies to all of these fibers. In fact, however, most knitting yarns designated as "wool" come from sheep fibers. Animal fibers vary greatly from one another, ranging in length from under an inch to many feet, and, in texture, from silky to coarse and hairy. Whatever their source or characteristics, lengths of a given animal fiber or hair, called staple lengths, are made into yarn by spinning or twisting them together into strands.

STRUCTURE OF VARIOUS FIBERS AND FILAMENTS

Coarse wool   Fine wool   Alpaca   Cashmere   Silk   Cotton   Linen   Acrylic

When you visit a yarn shop, you'll see many different yarns labeled as wool. Although all such yarns obviously derive from sheep, their labels rarely indicate the specific source of the fiber, that is, the breed of sheep. And even if the labels told you the source of the wools, in most cases you probably would find little difference among them. Some breeds, however, do produce very distinctive wools, which are identified on the label, and these types of wool are worth looking for. The lofty Icelandic wools, for example, are very warm and soft. The slightly hairy Shetland wools are delightfully light and airy (it's not real Shetland yarn if its label calls it "Shetland type"). Wool from the merino sheep is considered the finest in the world—look for it if you want silky, elastic yarn. And all the wools I've ever tried from New Zealand—where sheep seem to be a national treasure—were wonderful.

I love wool because it rarely poses problems in knitting and always enhances a design. It has no equal. Wool is springy and stretchy, the very qualities we prize in a knitted fabric. It also insulates and is warm, though a lightweight variety can be cool in summer. And because of the fibers' physical structure, specifically their central channel, it dyes easily and retains color well. Also, because wool can hold up to one-third of its weight in water before beginning to sag, it is great for functional all-weather garments. At the other extreme, smooth, refined wools can create the dressiest of garments that cling provocatively or drape softly.

Many knitters avoid wool because most types of wool cannot be machine washed without shrinking. In the shrinking process, the scaly outer layer of wool fibers, which looks like the surface of a pinecone, expands when wet. When these wet fibers are also agitated and abraded, as they are when machine washed, the scales interlock and the fibers open up, loft and lose their elasticity.

Shrinking a knitted fabric usually occurs unintentionally. However, it's entirely possible to shrink a knitted fabric on purpose to produce the characteristic felt-like, extra warm and water-resistant fabric that results. The controlled, intentional shrinking of a fabric is called "fulling" and requires some careful advance planning on the designer's part to produce a final fulled garment the size and shape desired. For a slightly fulled effect, completed garment sections or assembled garments can be steamed or immersed in water and mild soap, and gently washed without abrasion. For more extreme, overall fulling of the fabric, warm water and soap are combined with abrasion. (For a more detailed description of the fulling process, see p. 231, and for a close-up look at fulled fabric, see pp. 246-247.)

Often slight fulling occurs in the underarm area of a knitted garment, due to the combined abrasion and perspiration from wear. To avoid underarm fulling, be sure to make the armhole deep enough to keep the fabric away from the underarm (see also pp. 47-52 for more information on designing armholes).

Generally speaking, most wool yarns should be washed by hand (though they can also be dry cleaned). Some wool yarns are now treated with a "Superwash" process, which coats the individual fibers and enables them to resist fulling and shrinking. If you're interested in trying to full a Superwash wool, test a few different brands by fulling a swatch of each. Some of these yarns will produce an uncharacteristically stiff fabric when fulled, while others seem to resist fulling altogether.

Wool from the **alpaca,** a member of the camel family from South America's upper Andes Mountains, is shinier and silkier than sheepswool and is known for its strength. Available in a lovely range of natural colors—ivory, grey, deep brown and warm caramel (my favorite)—alpaca fibers knit into a heavy, less drapable fabric than sheepswool; it usually hangs with gravity, rather than blousing. Unless firm edges and seams are planned to support the weight of the fiber, alpaca sweaters may stretch out of shape. This hairy fiber also tends to flatten textured patterns and blur any subtle distinctions.

Mohair is spun from the long, shiny hair of the Angora goat. This fiber is springier than wool, long-wearing, lightweight and warm, and suited to both inner- and outerwear. A fine, thread-like strand of mohair can knit into a diaphanous, spiderweb fabric (see the photo at right on p. 198), which would yield the ultimate sweater for a summer evening. At the other seasonal extreme, many curly or bouclé mohair yarns resemble fur and can knit up into wonderful cool-weather jackets (see the photo on pp. 68-69).

The most obvious quality of knitted mohair garments is that they look larger than they are—that is, the hairs extend above the surface of both sides of the fabric, creating the illusion of bulk. Because of the fuzzy surface, more ease (space between the fabric and body) is required than usual for a good fit (see pp. 43-45). Bold pattern stitches and garment shapes suit mohair, as do simple designs that emphasize the qualities of the fiber. Some curly or bouclé mohair yarns even resemble fur when knitted (see the "fur" trim in the photo of my 1920s-inspired coat on p. 153).

Angora yarn, made from the long hair of the Angora rabbit, is fuzzy and smooth, and finer and more slippery than mohair. Since it's expensive, use it in small quantities for accent or blended with another fiber.

I get my favorite angora from a local spinner who breeds English Angora rabbits. The rabbits' hair is so long that the animals look like big clouds. Although she usually combs the

I'm fascinated by yarns that mimic fur. After finding the photo at right of Edward, Prince of Wales, cloaked in an ermine-collared robe for his 1911 investiture, I decided to knit my own 'ermine' collar and cuffs (above) to dress up an old machine-knit cardigan. I used handspun angora yarn with extra-long hair and knotted tufts of black mohair to complete the effect. In keeping with the royal theme, I replaced the sweater's plain buttons with rhinestone ones. (Photo at right: UPI/Bettmann Newsphotos.)

fibers from the rabbits before spinning, she occasionally delights me by spinning directly from the rabbit (which causes no harm or pain to the animal), holding the lovely creature in her lap.

Cashmere comes from combing the undercoat of the cashmere goat and is softer and lighter than wool but doesn't hold up as well. **Camelhair** is also soft and warm but less durable than wool. Both of these fibers are used in classic lightweight yarns, often blended with sheepswool for strength and to cut expense. Nonetheless, they are both still expensive yarns, so use them for luxury items.

Silk is made from a long thread secreted by the silk moth caterpillar to form a cocoon. Unlike short-staple animal fibers, silk is one continuous filament that must be carefully unwound before it can be spun.

Silk makes the most elegant of all yarns—beautiful because of its luster, its ability to hold brilliant color and its drape. Silk fiber is warm, strong and resilient—and scarce and expensive as well.

Silk yarns are very seductive, yet they can be difficult to work with. Even though most silk yarns seem firm and do not appear to stretch during knitting, they nevertheless tend to "grow" and lengthen in the finished fabric (see how I've handled this problem with my silk kimono-like garment on p. 165). If you want to work with silk, be sure to swatch first, and choose another yarn if this growth will adversely affect your design. You may find it preferable to work with yarns blended with silk and other fibers.

Vegetable fibers

Yarns made from vegetable fibers—principally cotton and linen—have become increasingly popular and fashionable, in large part because they fill a niche in the yarn market between seasons. For the novice and expert designer alike, these yarns offer a broad range of brilliant colors and texture for cooler warm-weather fabrics. They will never replace the versatility of wool, but they do have their merits. Although you'll most likely choose a yarn made from animal fiber if you want elasticity, insulation and longevity, you may well opt for a vegetable-fiber yarn or blend if you're looking for easy care and coolness.

Cotton yarn is produced from the seed hair of the cotton plant. Although cotton is usually considered the summer equivalent of wool, it does not perform at all in the same way. Cotton is heavier and far less elastic than wool and often needs to be knitted with a very small needle to keep the ribbed areas "springy." Cotton softens and loses body with wear, though washing tends to firm it up again. Wool and cotton blends—of which there aren't enough—combine the best of both fibers and are perfect for trans-seasonal garments (see the Designer Notebook project on pp. 99-104).

There is a wide range of cotton yarns available to the hand knitter. Most notable perhaps are the shiny, mercerized cottons in brilliant, clear colors. Strong, fine-gauge cottons—especially those with a firm, cabled twist, which knit up into crisp fabrics—make long-wearing garments that are well worth the knitting investment. And there are many summer novelty cottons to explore, from soft, fluffy yarns that knit into a terrycloth-like fabric to crisp, crinkled yarns that look like straw or basket material when knitted.

Although cotton yarns have wonderful qualities, they also produce heavy fabrics that are weighty in warm weather and which tend to stretch with wear. To avoid such problems, work these heavier yarns with a smaller needle than you would for a wool yarn of the same weight. Also keep the size of your garment to a minimum when working with cotton yarns that yield a gauge of four or fewer stitches to the inch. To do this, consider short silhouettes with short sleeves or no sleeves at all.

Pure **linen** yarn is made of the bast, or strong woody fiber, of the flax plant. A 100% linen yarn is extremely inelastic and is, in fact, so difficult to work with that I once had to turn down a commission in it. I prefer linen yarns blended with another fiber, which are easier to knit and produce a more comfortable fabric. Unbleached, flax-colored linen is beautiful when tinted, which allows the original barklike color of the plant to emerge.

Synthetic fibers

Many knitters have no use for synthetic yarns because they're not natural fibers and so are less comfortable to wear. If you belong to this camp, consider an occasional defection. Synthetic yarns are varied and often decorative, though of course they should not be used to the exclusion of natural fibers.

Rayon challenges the definition of "natural fiber." It is manufactured from natural cellulose found in plants or from its chemical substitute. Because it is man-made—that is, manufactured rather than just processed—it is considered synthetic, even when made from natural cellulose. However, knitted rayon fabric has what I'd call a natural "feel."

Originally called "wood silk" or "artificial silk" because of its sheen and luster, rayon yarn is seldom found unblended. It is most often paired with vegetable fibers and is intended for summer use, though occasionally it finds its way into a wool blend, to which it adds sheen and drape. What attracts me most about rayon is the way it dyes and holds a wide range of bright colors.

Acrylics come straight from the test tube to your knitting needles. Nylon yarns are derived from polyacrylonitrile—a substance whose name I cannot even pronounce—and are available under various trade names like Orlon™ and Acrilan®. At their most deceitful, these yarns look and feel like wool, while in their natural state, they resemble plastic. Available in a wide range of colors, most acrylic yarns are virtually indestructible, except when exposed to a flame. The one advantage of acrylics over many other yarns is that they can be machine washed and dried.

Although I like to poke fun at acrylics because I associate them with plastic, they do have their place. In a blend, they lend strength; and, as the stuff of children's garments, they wear like iron. They also play an important role in what I affectionately call the Dime Store School of Needlework, which is usually worked in garish colors, sold at bazaars and ranges from covers for toilet-paper rolls and coat hangers to embossed potholders and wacky afghans. While many purists are dismayed at the knitted and crocheted items produced by the Dime Store Knitters, I think they represent a whimsical area of American folk design.

Novelty and specialty yarns

There is a host of novelty and specialty yarns to choose from; these yarns may or may not contain some of the fibers I've already mentioned above. Many knitters, myself included, use the term *novelty* to describe a yarn with an interesting surface texture. Like a classic smooth yarn, a novelty can be plied with multiple strands, but the strands are twisted in such a way that one or more of them curls,

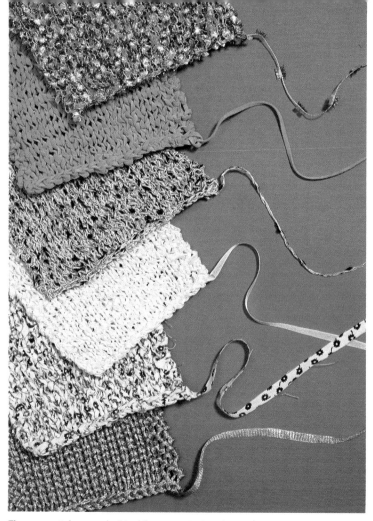

These swatches are knitted from nontwisted novelty or specialty yarns. From bottom to top: a flat, tubular nylon ribbon; a flat strip cut from woven cotton fabric; a woven rayon ribbon; a chained synthetic strand; a flat strip cut from synthetic suede; a tiny woven synthetic strand with 'eyelash' extensions.

shortens up or otherwise sits unusually in the finished strand. The strand's texture can also be produced by traditionally twisting plies that are themselves textured with fiber curls, tails, bumps or intermittent slubs.

Specialty is a term I use to describe a yarn or strand (they're not all made from fibers) that is not specifically marketed for hand knitters. Some specialties are functional; others are purely decorative. Some must be relegated to small areas or details on a garment because they would be too heavy or uncomfortable if worked over the entire garment. You may need to stretch your imagination to use some of these specialty yarns successfully. Yet precisely because they're unusual yarns that present a challenge, they can help you develop your learning-to-see skills (see Chapter 1).

For metallic effects, you can use yarn or materials from less likely sources. For this swatch I alternated stripes of a slubbed metallic yarn and a soft, red wool, which produced a ripply fabric (see p. 26 for some hints on working ruched fabric). The decorative bow is knitted with stiff trim bought at a fabric store; the whimsical necklace is worked with a length of keychain from the hardware store.

Metallic yarns are among my favorite specialties. Although these yarns look like metal, most of them are made of plastic film that has been treated to look like metal. Those that actually use metal generally wrap a metallic strand around a soft fiber filament, or core. One such example, Lurex®, can be quite lurid (as its name suggests) if not used with a little discretion. I find metallics great fun for creating special effects and details, but they don't produce particularly comfortable fabric unless they are blended with softer fibers.

One functional specialty yarn is **elastic yarn,** which is meant to be knitted in with another yarn (like cotton or linen) that lacks elasticity to lend it stretch. However, I've found that this extra strand, no matter how fine or stretchy, usually just stiffens up the fabric. Consequently, I prefer to sew this strand into the back of the knitted fabric.

In addition to the yarns regularly sold in knitting stores, don't overlook other types of yarns. **Coned yarns** used by weavers are often less expensive than yarns that have been packaged for knitting. However, occasionally coned yarn has not had its twist set with a finishing process and will produce a bias slant to the fabric when you knit with it. To determine if the coned yarn you want to use biases, you'll need to work a swatch.

Yarn that biases can usually be treated. First, wind it into skeins and wet it. Then slip rods through the top and bottom loops of the skeins, and hang the top rod up and weight the bottom rod on each end in order to keep the skeins taut. After allowing the skeins to dry thoroughly, check again for biasing by swatching.

If you find that a bias slant remains, you need not abandon the yarn. Despite the fact that most designers avoid yarns that bias, be adventurous and consider such yarns and the fabrics they produce a design challenge. On the facing page is a simple diagram that shows what happens when two bias pieces of fabric are sewn together into a tube with their right sides facing out. However, if you sew these bias pieces together with one right-side-out and the other wrong-side-out, the tube and the angle of its seams become different. To see the results of this change, arrange two pieces of paper "cut on the bias" in this way. How might you incorporate this feature of bias fabric into a design? When thinking about this, remember that some knitted lace patterns also have a bias slant (see the photo at right on p. 198 for a design incorporating this feature).

Also consider working with **cotton embroidery floss** and **wool tapestry yarns** (Persian or crewel types) when you need a small amount of yarn for color or detail. And think about knitting with **fabric strips,** which you can cut yourself or buy already cut. The effect of knitted fabric strips is similar to, but much coarser than the effect of knitted ribbon-type yarns. And strips cut on the bias will stretch to create a thready, raveled surface. Traditional American rag rugs could provide inspiration for an interesting knit garment using fabric strips.

Leather, suede and **fur strips** can also be knitted. Depending on the thickness of the strips and the needle size used, the fabric can be dense, or soft and open.

SEWING BIAS FABRICS INTO A TUBE

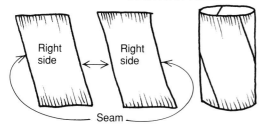

Sewing two pieces of fabric with right sides facing out produces a tube with diagonal seams.

Cords and **ropes** can be used to knit non-wearables. Keep in mind that the larger the strand, the more obvious its structure in the finished piece. One fiber artist I know of produces dramatic results by knitting large strands of rope with broomstick "needles."

Fishing line and **dental floss** are familiar to those who knit them in to reinforce the heels of socks, but you may be able to think of a more decorative design application. Also look to hardware, electronics, dressmaker, and art-supply stores for unusual knitting materials. Strip electrical wiring to see what lies beneath the surface. Try knitting braid intended for sewing trim. And how about working a necklace from a length of key-chain cord by simply casting on a row of stitches and then binding them off on the next row (see the photo on the facing page). In short, try knitting with any flexible strand you find that you can cast on your needles. Don't be hesitant—exploring is at the heart of designing.

Yarn weights

As a designer, you'll need to consider yarn weight when you have a specific project in mind. Below, I've grouped yarns by the weight of the strand, but I can only generalize about the weight of the finished fabrics they'll produce. Only swatching will tell you this. I've indicated the various names by which the yarn type is commonly known, but these rarely tell you anything about the yarn itself. I've also indicated the type of garments commonly associated with certain yarn weights, but remember that these are only guidelines.

Fine yarns, often called fingering, baby or sportweight yarns, conventionally yield from 6 to 8 stitches to the inch on needles ranging from size 5 down to size 2 (see pp. 29-30 for a discussion of calculating gauge). Usually these yarns are plied and are frequently used for gloves, mittens and baby clothes because they're generally lightweight and flexible. Baby yarns in this category are also often machine washable. Shetland yarns, which come in a wide range of beautiful clear and heathery colors, are often available in this weight. There are also many fingering-weight luxury yarns, like blends of wool and silk, camelhair or cashmere. Fine-gauge cottons, traditionally associated with crocheted doilies and knitted coverlets, can also be used for handsome, lightweight knitted garments. Few novelties, however, are available in this weight.

Don't shy away from fine yarns because you think they're time-consuming to knit. You can often work them on larger needles at a looser gauge. Generally speaking, these yarns offer excellent yardage for their weight.

Medium-weight yarns generally yield from 4 to 6 stitches to the inch on size 6 to size 8 needles. Often referred to as worsted, Saxony, Germantown or double-knitting-weight yarn, medium-weight yarns are perhaps the most versatile of knitting yarns and are available in a wide range of fibers and types, including many novelties. I find them suited to a variety of garments for both adults and children, from traditional sweaters and pullovers to heavy outdoor coats. They are also often good for baby clothes and are great for blankets and afghans because they're not too heavy.

Heavyweight yarns, called bulky or chunky yarns, are generally worked on size 9 to size 15 needles and usually yield a gauge of from 2 to 4 stitches to the inch. These yarns have limited use—mostly for heavy sweaters and coats or for very weighty blankets—and their bulk allows only for simple garment structures. Care must be taken not to work them too firmly, or they will create stiff, board-like fabrics.

Yarns for all seasons

The basic seasonal rule is simple: warm fibers for winter, cool ones for summer. But also think about designing garments that pass easily from one season to another. Lightweight wool, mohair or silk are all great for transseasonal sweaters, either spring or fall, especially when worked loosely or in openwork patterns. And cotton lends a sporty, youthful look to traditional winter sweaters.

For an interesting contrast, combine summer yarns in the same sweater with more insulating ones. Metallic yarns might remind you of the winter holidays, but a light touch of brass

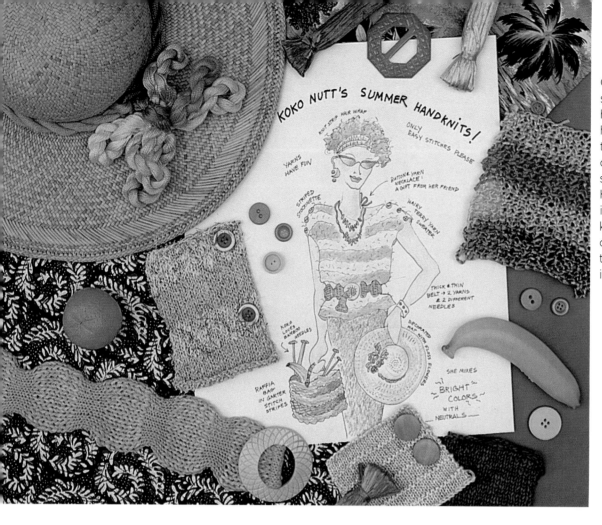

Over the years, sketching has helped me create a host of characters to wear my designs. Here my summertime friend Koko Nutt is inspired by simple knitted patterns, colorful yarns, bold textures and interesting buttons.

would add an interesting highlight to a linen or rayon summer sweater. The idea is simply to begin to look at and use yarns in new ways.

Some die-hard wool addicts have no patience at all with summer yarns. And I can sympathize—there are a lot of undistinguished summer yarns marketed every year to fill in between seasons. But there are also some wonderful summer yarns in fabulous colors and with interesting textures. These yarns might never give you the satisfaction of a long-wearing wool, but they can provide texture and are fun to work with. My friend Koko Nutt (see the photo above) reminds me that designing is not all serious!

Whatever your seasonal concerns are, always search for the best materials you can afford. It's a simple fact that good materials contribute to good design. If you're not crazy about a yarn, don't buy it just because it happens to be on sale. If a yarn doesn't set off a spark of excitement for you, your project will probably reflect your lack of inspiration.

Designing with Yarn

Designing with yarn is about making beautiful fabric that suits the project you have in mind. If you're a novice designer and nervous about the decisions involved in creating an entirely original design, why not begin gradually? Start by substituting the yarn called for in an existing pattern.

Working a new yarn in a familiar pattern can completely change the character of the garment. I'm always excited when a knitter successfully works one of my designs in a yarn different from the one I've chosen. Sometimes, however, a change of yarn can compromise the design and fail to show it off to best advantage. The way to know this ahead of time is—you guessed it—by swatching.

I cannot emphasize enough how important a tool swatching is for a designer. Whatever the nature of your design project, the preliminary step should always be swatching. And the swatches you create should excite you. Don't settle for a swatch that seems just okay. Aim for beautiful.

The first step in designing with yarn is to acquaint yourself with the yarns you want to work with — the fibers they're made of and the kind of fabric they'll produce when knitted. If you love the look of a single strand in the skein, you need not always hide it in the knitted fabric. You can display the strand by working elongated stitches, knitting in loops, or knotting or tying fringe along the edge or surface of the fabric. (The Bibliography on pp. 258-260 lists books with instructions for these techniques.)

In addition to simply substituting a yarn, think about creating your own new yarn by combining two or three strands into one. The simplest way to do this is to knit two strands of the same yarn together, doubling the weight of the strand. Whenever I can't find a yarn in particular weight that I want, I double a finer yarn. Often I'll work the body of a garment with a heavy, double-strand fabric and the edgings or details with the fine, single strand. Whenever I do this, I always test this combination first on my swatch.

When doubling a strand, don't expect that all the qualities of the original yarn will necessarily be retained. Sometimes a double-strand fabric feels completely different from a fabric worked with a single strand. Your fabric will also be more uneven than were the two strands twisted together since they'll occasionally separate slightly in the knitting.

You can also combine totally different yarns to make a special blend. Try mixing a plain, functional yarn with a more decorative one. Or combine a fine strand with a heavier one to lend a bit more detail and interest to the knitted surface. Be aware that you can also pur-

chase very fine strands of yarns, sometimes called "mixers," that have slubs or other dots of texture at intervals. When combined with another strand, they add interest without weight or changing your gauge.

When you mix two different yarns together, do not wind them into the same ball. The heavier yarn will knit up faster than the fine one, leaving you with a tangled mess. I find it much easier just to knit the strands from two individual balls.

In addition to mixing yarns to make up a new strand, you can also mix different types and weights of yarns within a given fabric. You can approach combining yarns either by trying to control the fabric you produce — in which case you'll want to swatch carefully to test how yarns of different weights and fibers mix — or by working yarns of different weights in random, patchwork fashion. The latter may cause drastic changes in width and weight throughout the fabric and make it difficult to design with, but all designers should nonetheless indulge in this random knitting at one time or another. You're likely to end up with an odd-shaped piece of fabric with uneven edges and maybe a wavy surface that refuses to lie flat. But knitting this way can be terribly exciting and liberating. If you want to put your resulting piece of work to use, make it become a curious scarf. Or it might become the starting point for a special one-of-a-kind garment. The purpose of this sort of knitting, however, should be the sheer pleasure of doing it and the knitting experience you gain—you need not produce a functional garment or object. I suggest hanging this fabric up on your bulletin board. Sew beautiful buttons on it just for fun. Play with it and enjoy it.

As a designer, however, you'll generally need a fabric that's more predictable in order to create garments of a certain size. Happily, you can mix a variety of yarns and still create a more even, predictable fabric by repeating geometric patterns—stripes, checks, triangles and so on. It's easiest to work a pattern of simple stripes that regularly alternates heavy and light yarns in basic stockinette, reverse stockinette or garter stitch. The repeated stripe sequence may produce an edge that's a little wavy, but it will be predictably so. To minimize the waviness, you can do one of two things. Knitting the fine yarn on larger needles than it normally calls for produces a looser fabric—whose look you may not like with the tightly knit heavier-weight stripe. You could also increase stitches before working the fine yarn on smaller needles and then decrease stitches to work the heavier yarn. To decide how to design the stripe sequence, test it by swatching.

A knitted, ruched fabric like the one in the photo on p. 22 resembles seersucker and alternates a flat, smooth band with a looser, "ruffled" one. To work ruched fabric, knit one band with a fine yarn on a very small needles and the other with a heavier yarn and large needles. I've had the best results working these bands in stockinette stitch with smooth yarns, which produces a very clean break between them and highlights their difference. When you swatch for this effect, remember that you're aiming for exaggeration in each band—very tight for the fine yarns and soft and loose for the heavy one.

If you mix more than two yarns in a project, it's easier if they're of similar weights. If they aren't, you might have to change needle size between the areas or increase or decrease stitches to maintain the same gauge within the piece. You'll find more about this on pp. 34-35, where the project for this chapter mixes a wide variety of yarns of different types and weights.

Beginning to design in two dimensions

I began my knitting career with potholders. For years, from childhood to my late teens, I knitted only flat garter-stitch potholders. At best, my designing was confined to sewing two potholders together to make a pullover for a doll. Now I wish I had been more creative—potholders could have been the swatches that led me to larger rectangles.

DESIGNING WITH 2-D SQUARES AND RECTANGLES

SCARF

SHAWLS

TIE

CLIP-ON BOW TIE

BELT

BOW

POT HOLDER

AFGHANS

RUG

PLACEMATS

EYEGLASS CASE

PILLOW

CURTAINS

EDGINGS

TO SEW ON

BLANKET

PURSES

ALL SORTS

When designing with simple patterns, consider how a new type or color of yarn will merge with the old yarn. In the stockinette swatch at the left of the photo, there is a clean break between colors. In the more textured reverse-stockinette swatch at right, the old color of yarn is carried up into the new section, creating a soft, blurred edge to the stripes.

Introducing new yarns in garter-stitch fabric produces a clean break between colors in the swatch at left and a blurred break, similar to that in reverse-stockinette fabric, in the swatch at right.

Two-dimensional projects are a good place to begin designing and learning to combine swatch and gauge information, with measurements and simple graphing techniques. Some 2-D projects are so familiar that they're almost invisible—scarves, placemats and, yes, pot-holders. But what a design challenge to revitalize them! Shawls are wonderful, easy projects, especially if they're kept to a simple rectangular shape. Think as a designer would, and try to conceive of ways to revitalize this familiar garment. Similarly, consider ways to inject life into blankets, afghans, curtains, rugs and belts. On a larger scale, you might contemplate a wall hanging or hammock project, and consider using unconventional yarns for each.

There are no standard measurements for 2-D objects. Simply choose a size that seems appropriate to you, or borrow measurements from another flat piece, perhaps a scarf or even a towel or pillow case. These existing shapes and sizes offer a point of departure for your decision making. When planning shawls and scarves, I often cut a large piece of woven fabric, trimming it down until I find a size I feel is right. If my test fabric is similar in weight to my swatch, I can also anticipate how the full-size project will drape.

Designing with simple pattern stitches

Simple pattern stitches like stockinette, reverse stockinette and garter stitch focus attention on the yarn itself, and this is the place to start when you're ready to add the design decision of pattern to the choice of yarn. A really dramatic yarn like a highly textured novelty almost designs the fabric itself and needs no complicated patterns, which would probably be obscured by the yarn. A simple yarn can also benefit from simple patterns.

Don't take these simple pattern stitches for granted because you've knitted them so often in the past. You could spend an entire design career working them with different yarns, making a different fabric every time.

Garter stitch is the easiest knitted fabric of all to make. You knit every stitch in every row, which causes the rows to crowd together, creating bumpy, horizontal ridges and forming a thick fabric. Each corrugated ridge is formed by two rows of knitting, and no matter what yarn or needle size you use, both sides of the fabric look the same. Garter-stitch fabric lies perfectly flat, without curling at the edges.

One curious characteristic of garter stitch is that it usually has as many stitches per inch of width as it does ridges per inch of length. If you cast on and knit 20 stitches and you work 20 ridges (that is, 40 rows), you'll have knitted a perfect square. This feature has inspired many people, most notably master knitter Elizabeth Zimmermann, to design seamless garter-stitch garments.

Your progress with garter stitch will be slow. It takes more rows to knit a length of garter-stitch fabric than the same length of most other patterns, except perhaps some slip-stitch patterns (see pp. 180-183). Because of this, garter stitch takes more yarn than you'd expect.

I use garter stitch mainly for warmth, working it in lofty wools. It makes the best fulled wool fabric I know of and is totally impervious to wind and weather (see the sidebar on p. 231). You need to experiment with needle size when working garter stitch to get the right density for your project. Working garter stitch on a smaller needle than normally called for with a given yarn or with a very heavy yarn tends to make the fabric dense and weighty. If you would like a more drapable fabric, use a larger needle size than the yarn usually calls for. By using summer fibers on a slightly larger needle than suggested, you'll create an open material. By coupling a fine-weight wool with a very large needle, you'll produce a gossamer garter-stitch fabric, which is lovely for shawls.

Be careful with garter stitch. Because of its weight, it tends to widen and stretch with wear. A springy wool yarn will hold the fabric's shape well, but a less resilient fiber will eventually stretch out of shape. The edges of garter stitch tend to waver if they're not trimmed or enclosed in a seam. For a firmer edge, slip the first stitch of every row, as if to purl, with the yarn in back.

Stockinette stitch (made by knitting one row and purling the next) is perhaps the most commonly used of all stitch patterns. When worked with even tension, the surface of stockinette is smooth and looks like rows of evenly lined up little letter Vs. The regularity of stockinette really enhances a fine, smooth, full-bodied yarn and will tame a wild novelty. When worked in a yarn with body and fullness, stockinette drapes and is springy. But if the yarn is inelastic, worked with too large a needle and does not fill in the spaces between the stitches, the fabric will be unattractive. With a slinky or limp yarn, or with some synthetics that lack body, the surface tends to be irregular.

Stockinette does not naturally lie flat but tends to curl at the edges. You can block it to flatten it slightly, but it really needs to be edged with something firm to hold it in place. Ribbed fabrics or flat knit/purl patterns are good for edging (see pp. 91-95).

Reverse-stockinette stitch is the purl, or wrong side, of stockinette stitch. This pattern yields the bumpy texture of garter stitch without its thickness. The bumps on the surface of reverse stockinette are broad and much less refined than the Vs on the other side of the fabric. The pebbly surface accentuates textured and hairy yarns and tends to become irregular with a yarn that does not fill in.

Be sure to swatch to check the drape and body of a given yarn in reverse stockinette. My favorite use for this stitch is as a trim, allowing it to roll, as it will naturally, and form a crisp edge (see p. 92).

When you change yarns at the beginning of a row of a stockinette or garter-stitch stripe, you'll produce a clean break between colors. Changing yarns at the beginning of a reverse-stockinette row, however, produces a somewhat "blurred" break between colors since the back of the stitches shows in both interlaced rows (see the photos on p. 27). For a clean break in reverse-stockinette or garter stitch, work a knit row in the new color on the right side and then resume the pattern stitch. For a blurred break on the right side of garter-stitch stripes, attach a new yarn at the start of the wrong-side row that completes the alternate-colored stripe.

Capturing the design

Once you're satisfied that your swatch is just right, you're ready to move on to the more technical work of capturing your design, that is, putting your knitting plan on paper. This involves calculating the gauge of your knitting, plotting the size and shape of your project on graph paper and estimating the amount of yarn you will need.

Calculating gauge

Calculating gauge means figuring out how tightly or loosely your knitting is worked and consequently how many stitches and rows you get to the inch with your yarn and pattern stitch. Knowing stitch gauge is crucial when you're planning projects that need to fit. You can't be sure that your garment pieces will come out to the needed width if you haven't correctly read your gauge from the test swatch and cast on the required number of stitches. Row gauge is less important than stitch gauge, especially when working in a simple allover pattern stitch, since the length of a garment can usually vary a bit. Nonetheless, calculating your row gauge will help you figure out how many pattern repeats will fit in a certain length of knitting.

Designing knitwear is largely about making beautiful fabric, regardless of the gauge specified for a specific yarn by its manufacturer. The suggested gauge on a yarn's label may not be the most effective gauge for that yarn. I suggest therefore that you always try working a yarn with several needle sizes, choose the fabric that you like best and then determine the gauge of that swatch.

Before calculating your gauge, block your swatch if you plan to block the final garment. Otherwise, your gauge measurement will be inaccurate. Then, with the swatch laid flat, mark with pins two points in the center of the swatch at least 4 in. apart and on the same row. Traditional gauge rulers often suggest calculating gauge over 2 in., but the fewer stitches you measure over, the less accurate your gauge will be. For example, you might find that working a swatch in worsted-weight yarn yields a gauge of 21 stitches over 4 in., or 5¼ stitches per inch. Obviously it's easier and more accurate to measure one full stitch at the end of the 4-in. span rather than a half-stitch at the 2-in. point. Additionally, because your tension may vary from one side of the swatch to the other, you'll aver-

This group of swatches, each worked over 30 stitches, shows a wide range of yarn weights and the very different gauges and fabrics they produce. From bottom to top: a Shetland lace-weight wool makes a gossamer fabric at 7 stitches per inch. A plied fingering wool yields a similar gauge but a denser fabric. A plied worsted-weight wool, working up at 5 stitches per inch, and a heavier, twisted wool, with 3½ stitches per inch, both yield soft, wearable fabrics. The wool roving creates a heavy, dense fabric at 2½ stitches per inch.

Work a swatch at least 5 in. square to establish your gauge (the number of stitches per inch). With a smooth fabric like the swatch at right, measure and mark a 4-in. span with pins. Then count the number of stitches between pins and divide by four to arrive at your gauge. With a curly fabric whose stitches may be obscured, as in the swatch at left, you can sew yarn marker lines within which to measure.

age out these irregularities by measuring over more stitches and more accurately establish your real gauge.

Once you have positioned your pins on the swatch, count the number of stitches between them (a clear plastic ruler will let you see the swatch beneath). Dividing the number of stitches by the number of inches between the pins gives you the stitches per inch. For example, if I count 28 stitches in 4 in., my stitch gauge is 7 stitches to the inch.

To calculate the row gauge, similarly measure over a vertical distance of at least 4 in. Then divide the number of rows by the number of inches in your measurement, which gives you the number of rows per inch. For example, if I count 24 rows in 4 in., my row gauge is 6 rows to the inch. If you have a sequence of stripes, you may prefer to measure each individual stripe, or you may want to calculate the gauge from the whole sequence of stripes.

Once you've established your gauge, use this number for all calculations for your project, even if it's a fraction like 3¾ stitches per inch. Don't fudge or round your gauge up to an even number for the sake of convenience. If you work with a gauge other than what is actually in your swatch, you'll pay for it later with an ill-fitting garment. (See also pgs. 86-88, 130-132 and 200-201 for further information on stitch multiples and gauge.)

When working a garment, it's a good idea to begin with a sleeve and recheck your gauge after about 8 in. If your gauge doesn't match that of your swatch, you can fairly easily adjust your sleeve and also adjust your calculations for the body and other pieces of the garment.

Graphing, or charting, your pattern

After you've established your gauge, use graph paper to plot the size and shape of your project. Even with a simple 2-D project in which size isn't crucial, plot out the shape you want in order to see the proportions of the piece. Get used to plotting out and visualizing the component pieces of your project on a grid—but use a pencil so you can easily make changes.

When plotting shapes, let one square of your graph paper represent one inch, as I have done in the schematics throughout this book. As a note to yourself, write the desired width measurement below the piece and its length to one side. Then record your stitch and row gauge on the chart. To establish how many stitches to cast on for each section of the garment, multiply the width of the cast-on lower edge of each section by your stitch gauge. To establish how many stitches to increase or decrease to accommodate the garment shaping, measure the widest or narrowest point on the garment and again multiply by your gauge. Note these figures next to the appropriate sections.

If the row gauge will affect your fabric, multiply the number of rows per inch by the length of each section and similarly record this number on your graph paper. If you have a repeating sequence, see if your length accommodates full repeats. If not, you may need to shorten or lengthen your garment to fit in full repeats. If the repeat needs to be centered or fall at a certain spot on the garment, you'll need to plot where it begins and ends on the schematic. If possible, draw any pattern or other graphics right on the graph to help you envision the surface of the piece.

The graphed plan for your project is both a visual tool and your knitting instructions. Add to it any other relevant information—note your needle size, attach your yarn label, record yardage and so on—to make it a complete record of the project. If you make any changes as you knit, alter the graph accordingly, and note anything you think useful to describe your decision-making process.

Estimating yarn needs

Commercial knitting patterns always indicate the amount of yarn needed. When you create your own designs, you'll have to estimate how much yarn you need. This can be difficult if you're working with an unfamiliar yarn or a new garment shape. Yardage amounts noted on the yarn label are helpful in determining yarn needs, but they are only a guideline since every yarn takes up differently in the knitted fabric. For example, a hairy yarn fills in the spaces between stitches more than a smooth yarn, and hence you might need less yardage of the hairy yarn—though not necessarily less weight—than you would of a smooth yarn of the same gauge to produce the same size piece of fabric. Most knitters don't mind having yarn left over from a project, but running out in midproject is a cruel fate—especially when you have made design decisions you would hate to alter.

How do you know—or intelligently guess—if you'll have enough of a yarn that may be costly or difficult to get more of? There are no definitive formulas for estimating yarn needs, only some general guidelines. First, when you have a project in mind, look for similar garments in magazines or pattern books—or this book for that matter—and check the amount of yarn called for in the instructions. If you want to change a pullover into a cardigan, you'll need only enough extra yarn to make the front

bands—approximately 2 oz. to 4 oz. If you want to make long sleeves out of a short-sleeve pattern, you'll need only 4 oz. to 6 oz. more, unless your projected lower sleeve is especially wide. Adding a wide or long ribbed turtleneck to a jewel-neck sweater will take a surprising amount of yarn—often half or the full amount needed for a single sleeve. To add details like pockets or a collar, increase the amount of yarn needed by 2 oz. to 4 oz. Adding extra length to a sweater may take 4 oz. to 8 oz. more.

Changing patterns also affects yarn needs. Knit/purl patterns will take few ounces more than will stockinette for the same sweater. An allover pattern that drastically changes the gauge, however, can take from 6 oz. to 12 oz. more. Lace patterns often take about 4 oz. less than stockinette for the same sweater, especially if the garment is to be severely blocked. And for textured or cabled patterns, add from 6 oz. to 12 oz. more yarn.

When knitting colorwork patterns or color graphics, you'll have to decide the proportion each yarn occupies in your project and calculate accordingly. It's easy to assess proportions and calculate for graphics, but Fair Isle patterns take a little more work. Work a swatch in your Fair Isle pattern and look carefully at it. Try to determine the proportionate weight that each color occupies in the pattern and then calculate your yarn needs accordingly.

If you have questions about yarn needs, ask your yarn-shop personnel, who have had lots of experience with these calculations. It's always better to buy more yarn than you need and return unused balls to the store. Often when you're purchasing yarn to start a project, yarn shops will set aside extra skeins of the yarn (for a reasonable period of time) to ensure against your running out. This service is usually free.

When you complete a project, always record how many yards of yarn you used (multiply the number of skeins by the yards in each, which will be indicated on the label). Keeping such records will enable you to make better estimates of future yarn needs.

When you knit with yarns that are not readily available or with unconventional knitting materials that don't readily convert to regular yarn yardage, it's especially important to find a way to estimate your yarn needs before beginning your project. One direct approach is to work a swatch of a given dimension, rip it out and measure the yardage used. (If you do this, photocopy your swatch before ripping it out to keep a record of its size and texture.) Alternatively, you can tie markers along a length of your yarn at intervals of several yards before you begin swatching. When you've finished a good-sized swatch, the markers will show exactly how much yarn you've used for a given number of inches.

Swatch project & designer notebook

I love making swatches. For me, they're perfect little objects that I enjoy completing for their own sake. I like to touch them, decorate them and stare at them for inspiration. I have received such a positive response to my swatches over the years that I've been encouraged to continue making them.

I began the Swatch Project by working many small swatches, each in a different yarn. These led me to design a larger striped swatch that combined all of the yarns. I was able to use this large swatch for a small evening purse, lined with woven fabric and decorated with a twisted cord and glass bead buttons.

I have very little patience with designers who don't get to know their materials and refuse to experiment with swatching. Once I heard a designer boast about the fact that she rarely swatched. I chose not to speak, but her designs did so eloquently — the fabrics were bland and pedestrian.

Although I like swatching for swatching's sake and for enjoyment, the practical side of me is pleased when I'm able to turn the swatch into something useful — for example, a pocket for a garment or a collar or cuff. I know that everyone doesn't share my love of swatching, and the process can be tedious, especially when a yarn is slow to reveal its good side. If you dislike swatching, try making it more palatable by planning a small project that will also serve as your testing ground.

Alternatively, you might try incorporating your swatch into your finished project — for example, as a pocket or, folded in half diagonally if the swatch is square, as a shoulder pad. I've tried to do this as often as possible with the designs in this book. Sometimes you'll need to stretch your imagination to use your swatch, and other times you'll find that it just isn't practical or possible to incorporate the swatch into the final garment. Then you'll simply need to resign yourself to swatching as a necessary prelude to a project.

For me, every project begins in a different way, with a different point of departure. Occasionally I might have a garment in mind before beginning to swatch, but I try to keep the notion vague and not to lock myself into any final image of the garment until I've had a chance to swatch. At first I play around with a few different needles and yarns to find an interesting fabric, often thinking just a little about the project I have in mind. After some combination of yarn and needles clicks with me, I set to swatching in earnest to get a good fabric that I like. As I swatch, the project often becomes clearer in my mind, and I fashion an image of it with the fabric in mind.

More often than not, I begin with only the desire to create an interesting swatch. While writing this chapter, I thought it would be interesting to combine a variety of different yarns to create interesting texture. I wasn't thinking about what I would do with the fabric — that would come later.

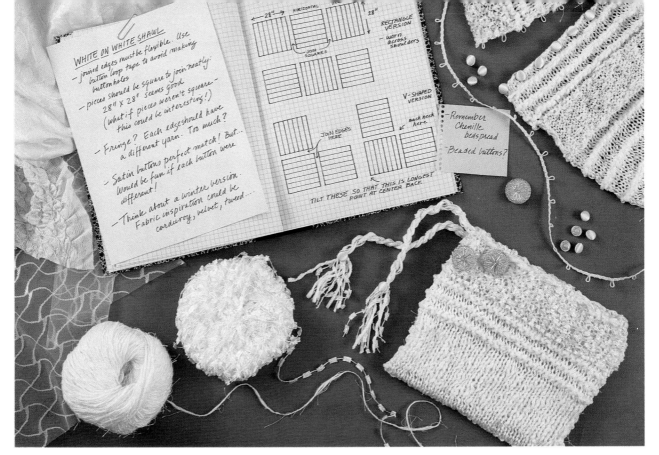

While I was thinking about texture, I went to my local fabric store. I couldn't pass a display of bridal materials without buying a small piece of each. Something about them caught my eye—all white, in different weights and with different drapes. I was especially attracted to the white-on-white materials, which juxtaposed matte and shiny areas of pattern. I fell in love with a sheer, ruched machine knit, whose ruffly surface was created by an elastic thread woven in at intervals. (I made a note to myself to try this in hand knitting.)

As I studied these materials, other white fabrics came to mind—the chenille bedspread I had as a child, thick terry towels, crisp summer seersucker, the net-like tulle in ballerina tutus that brought back memories of working with theater costumes.

This bit of nostalgia evoked by the bridal display made me decide that I wanted to create my own knitted white-on-white fabric. So I assembled a variety of white novelty yarns. I didn't worry about compatible weights. I just wanted to see what kinds of knitted fabrics they would create. I chose a soft ribbon, a shiny "eyelash" yarn, a thick chenille, a nubby novelty and a cotton blended with a shiny synthetic hairy fiber. I knitted a swatch in each, aiming for the best needle size and drape. Inspired by the bedspread, I worked single garter-stitch

chenille ridges on a ribbon stockinette-stitch background. The hairy cotton was too lightweight in comparison to the others, so I worked another swatch double-strand.

I played around with the swatches, lining them up next to each other until I found a sequence I liked. I decided that combining them in stripes would be the easiest approach to this fabric because of their different weights. Having decided upon the sequence, I plotted the gauges for each stripe on a chart, which allowed me to figure out how many increases or decreases would be needed between stripes to keep the edges of the fabric even. This chart, in turn, became the instructions for a large, 8-in. swatch that combined all the patterns. The decorative fabric in the swatch turned out to be heavy and drapey, and the next step was to decide what kind of design it would be suited to. Because of its fiber content, color and sheen, the fabric was inappropriate for everyday wear. But it seemed perfect for a very simple shawl that could be worn on holidays and special occasions.

The swatch itself was just the right size to make an evening purse to match the shawl. I folded it in half and sewed the sides. Then I lined it with one of my inspirational fabrics and twisted lengths of the yarns together to make a beautiful drawstring cord.

Assembled are some of the yarns, notions and fabrics that inspired my shawl (see the photo on p. 35), as well as a couple of pages from my Designer Notebook.

To begin working out my shawl, I plotted a rectangular shawl shape on graph paper. Hmm…how could I vary this 2-D surface? If I divided the shawl into three squares, I could join the pieces so the stripes would run in different directions. I thought about sewing the squares together but decided that solution was too pedestrian for this glamorous piece. My mind jumped back to the bridal department in the fabric store, and I thought of the flexible buttonhole tape sold for use with little satin-covered bridal buttons. Could I button the sections together? I was excited!

If I sewed the tape on different edges, I could button the pieces together in different ways and change the shawl, as my mood dictated, from a basic rectangle to a more triangular shape. I played with this idea on graph paper and decided I was really pleased by it. Finally I calculated the length and width of each square, repeating the pattern established in the swatch, and arrived at the design of the shawl you see on the facing page.

Yarns in this book

For each project in the book I list the yarn type and fiber I used, along with yardage and gauge information. In addition, I describe the drape and thickness of the fabric I created. Since this book is about knitwear design, my yarn choices are meant to inspire, just as the projects are. I don't want you to feel obliged to use the same yarns I chose. Try taking the initiative as a designer and choose a new yarn for the project that suits your design interests. Remember that when substituting a new yarn, you need not find one that has the exact same yardage, only one that's similar. Matching gauge is more important.

If you're bewildered at the thought of altering my design or using it as inspiration, don't despair. Believe it or not, I'm very confused when I begin any project—after all, designing is about making decisions that gradually move toward the moment when you can begin to knit. If you want to alter the design but are having trouble getting started, try looking at the "What if…?" section that ends each chapter.

Instructions for three-part shawl

This shawl is made of three knitted squares that button together in two ways to form either a large rectangle or a V shape. If you prefer, you can eliminate the buttonhole tape and buttons and permanently sew the squares together. As an alternative to sewing, you can pick up stitches for the second square along an edge of the first square, and for the third square along the edge of the second.

I used five different white yarns—a chenille, a ribbon, an "eyelash" yarn, a nubby yarn and a hairy yarn—which are listed below. Feel free to make substitutions for any of these yarns, but be sure to swatch to obtain the best gauge for your selection of yarns.

FINISHED MEASUREMENTS
Each of 3 parts measures 28 in. square.

MATERIALS
• Chenille: 3 skeins of Rowan's "Chunky Cotton Chenille" from Westminster Trading (100% cotton; 3½ oz = 153 yd).
• Ribbon: 9 tubes of "Glacé" from Berroco (95% rayon, 5% polyester; 1¾ oz = 75 yd).
• "Eyelash" yarn: 3 balls of Pingouin's "1920" from Laninter (85% viscose, 15% polymide; 1¾ oz = 82 yd).
• Nubby yarn: 3 balls of "Dante" from Berroco (65% rayon, 27% cotton, 8% nylon; 1¾ oz = 90 yd).
• Hairy yarn: 3 balls of Pingouin's "Fresque" from Laninter (45% cotton, 30% linen, 25% polymide; 1¾ oz = 123 yd).
• 1 pair each knitting needles sizes 6, 9 and 10, or sizes to obtain gauge.
• Approx 70 satin-covered buttons from B. Blumenthal.
• Approx 1¾ yd buttonloop tape from B. Blumenthal.

Gauge

- With ribbon and chenille yarns in striped sequence: 16 sts equal 4 in., with size 10 needle.
- With nubby yarn, in St st: 20 sts equal 4 in., with size 6 needle.
- With hairy yarn, with 2 strands held tog in rev St st: 14 sts equal 4 in., with size 10 needle.
- With "eyelash" yarn, in rev St st: 16 sts equal 4 in., with size 9 needle.
- To save time later, take time to swatch and check your gauge.

Patterns

St st: k RS row, p WS row.
Rev St st: p RS row, k WS row.
Narrow striped sequence (over any number of sts): * With ribbon: k 1 row, p 1 row. With chenille: k 2 rows. Rep from * 2 more times. Then, with ribbon: k 1 row, p 1 row.
Wide striped sequence (over any number of sts): * With ribbon: (k 1 row, p 1 row) twice. With chenille: k 2 rows. Rep from * 2 more times. Then, with ribbon: (k 1 row, p 1 row) twice.

Notes

- Beg each stripe with a RS row and end with a WS row.
- When changing yarns, work any incs or decs evenly spaced on 1st row of new section.

Individual Squares

- Make 3 squares, working pats in order and to lengths indicated on chart.
- You can pick up sts for 2nd square along an edge of 1st square, and for 3rd square, along an edge of 2nd.

The finished shawl, inspired by a variety of white fabrics, uses a range of novelty yarns and buttons together in three sections. The heavy material of the shawl has a luxurious drape that creates a very dressy effect.

FINISHING

Weave in all ends. Then, if you want to button squares tog, pin a length of buttonloop tape evenly along WS of desired edge, so that loops extend slightly beyond edge. Allow an extra ½ in. at each end to turn under. Sew tape in place with a needle and thread. Count buttonloops, then sew same number of buttons along adjoining edge. If you prefer, you can eliminate buttons and buttonhole tape and sew squares tog.

NOTE TO SCHEMATICS:

The schematic at right is hand-written, as you would do for your own designs. All other schematics in this book are typeset for ease in reading.

SCHEMATIC FOR EVENING PURSE

1 square = 1 in.

SCHEMATIC FOR THREE-PART SHAWL

Make three squares as follows:

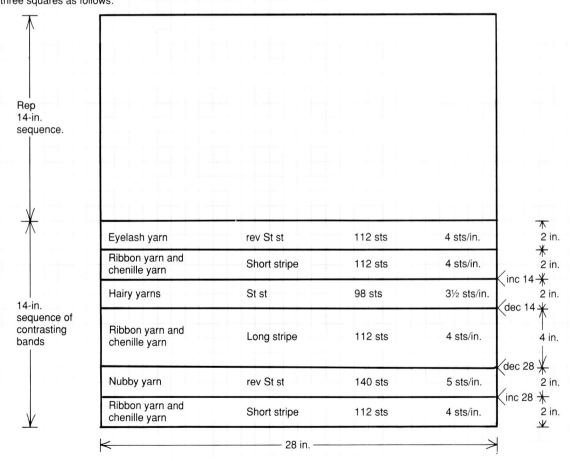

Eyelash yarn	rev St st	112 sts	4 sts/in.
Ribbon yarn and chenille yarn	Short stripe	112 sts	4 sts/in.
Hairy yarns	St st	98 sts	3½ sts/in.
Ribbon yarn and chenille yarn	Long stripe	112 sts	4 sts/in.
Nubby yarn	rev St st	140 sts	5 sts/in.
Ribbon yarn and chenille yarn	Short stripe	112 sts	4 sts/in.

Rep 14-in. sequence.

14-in. sequence of contrasting bands

← 28 in. →

1 square = 1 in.   Beg each contrasting band with RS row.

WHAT IF...?

Whatif I worked the Shawl's squares in different colors?

← giant hood

What if I used the squares to form a garment — smaller squares would be best

↑ loose, boxy garment

Many smaller squares to make a square shawl

odd-shaped combination of squares

3 Fit & Silhouette

Perhaps the most challenging aspect of designing knitwear is learning how to make a garment fit. The simplest sweater or dress can merely drape the body in fabric but not conform to it; a more complex garment may mimic the figure in an almost architectural way. Whatever you hope to design, you'll need to coordinate the garment's structure with the body beneath it in order to get a good fit.

Many things affect fit, and all need to be considered in designing a garment. First, of course, the wearer's body measurements must be taken into account. Also important are fabric weight; the garment's silhouette, structure (how the individual pieces are shaped to work together) and function; and the wearer's need for comfort. Fashion also affects fit in that it presents a continually changing silhouette for the designer to consider.

I learned very gradually about this difficult area of design. In the beginning, I turned to knitting books for help. They described simple garments and basic sleeve types and necklines. Helpful, yes. But limited, because beyond these patterns, I didn't find any discussion of the fundamental issues involved in achieving a good fit. I did occasionally find formulas to follow to get measurements for good-looking classic garments. But useful as these formulas were, they were rigid, and each sweater had the same basic shape as the last.

In my early days of designing, I also ran headlong into difficulties never mentioned in knitting books. What was I to do, for example, if I wanted a good-fitting silhouette that was bulkier than the classic sweaters these books described? What if I wanted a deeper armhole than suggested for my size? How would this affect my sleeve? If I departed from the books' prescribed guidelines, how was I to calculate where the waistline would fall in a fitted sweater? Why was it that exactly the same sweater knitted in several different yarn weights fit differently each time? These books left so much unsaid.

The books also discussed hand knits as if they belonged to an isolated area of clothing with no relationship to any other garment. To get a basic understanding of fit, I began to look beyond the knitting shelves in the library for books on sewing, couture, tailoring and ethnic garments. These texts often shed light on dark areas. They made me think about what hand knits have in common with other types of clothing as well as what makes them unique.

I also began to look carefully at all kinds of clothing. I studied ready-to-wear garments in stores, vintage clothing, and costumes and historical pieces in museums. I compared hand knits to machine knits. I looked for details, necklines and sleeve shapes. I measured and recorded. I scoured magazines for the fashion architecture of the season. I even found myself distracted by clothing in leisure moments—did you ever notice the way a sleeve is set into a baseball uniform?

I made a great leap forward once I had defined the basic considerations that go into making a garment: First, the garment has to be made out of something, that is, a material or *fabric*. Second, the garment can be narrow or wide or somewhere in between, and variously shaped—this is its *silhouette*. Third, the pieces of a garment can be arranged and sewn together in a number of ways within this silhouette—this arrangement is the garment's *structure*. Finally, I realized that the coordination of all these elements is crucial to getting a good *fit* in the garment.

With each new project I designed, I tried a new combination of these basic elements. Reusing measurements that had worked for me before, I would try a familiar silhouette with a different-weight yarn and a different structure. Or I would try new silhouettes—or perhaps just a new element like a sleeve—working in a fabric that I had used in the past. Of course, my experiments didn't always work, but when I was successful, I put the new-found information to work in another design and gradually accumulated a body of information from which I could selectively draw.

Hundreds of knitted garments later, my experience has shown that there is no single formula with which you can magically produce a wide range of garment types. The process of designing is not as straightforward as that. But I've devised a flexible design process for myself that systematically leads me through the crucial issues of fabric, silhouette, structure and fit, which must be addressed each time you design a garment. For this reason, you'll find these concerns mentioned again and again throughout this book. While you're learning to design and creating your own design system, I suggest you borrow the guidelines below to help you get started. You'll find there's still plenty of room in this system to express yourself and make your own choices about how a garment looks and fits.

My design process entails the following steps:

1. Getting acquainted with the needs and tastes of the person for whom I'm designing;

2. Swatching and choosing a fabric for the project;

3. Exploring garment shapes through sketching;

4. Deciding upon a silhouette;

5. Establishing actual body measurements;

6. Establishing ease;

7. Deciding upon the garment's basic structure; and

8. Charting the garment and useful body points.

The order of these steps is flexible, and you can approach them in any way that suits you or your project. You can work through them sequentially, work several at a time or double back to refine a given element in light of decisions made later down the road. As you gain more experience, you'll probably find yourself juggling all of these concerns simultaneously. Whatever their order, each step is important and must be considered to produce a successful design.

Swatching, the first concrete step in the design process, is discussed at length in Chapter 2 (see pp. 14-15). In Chapter 6, there's an illustrated discussion of learning to sketch your designs (see pp. 164-168). And in this chapter, you'll find addressed how to coordinate silhouette and size, establish body measurements and ease, decide upon the garment's structure and chart your design.

Perhaps the best person to begin designing for is yourself. You already know how various garments in your wardrobe—knitted and nonknitted—fit. You know which are the most comfortable, which are flattering and which should be sent to the thrift shop! Knowing what you like and what fits well is the first step in successfully designing a new garment for yourself. And, when you design for yourself, you're never without your model.

There's also much to be learned about fit and design in general by creating knits for other people. I suggest trying hard to design what other people want rather than trying to impose your style on them. Not only will you please the wearers, you'll also learn a lot about design in the process. Although it may be easier to design for someone with a body type similar to your own, don't let this be a determining factor. Whether you design for women, men or children, you need to learn the basic issues for each. Whenever you start designing for a new body type, be sure to choose a project that interests you and to begin with a simple garment. In deciding whom to design for, choose someone who is, above all, patient and available for measuring and fitting sessions.

Once you've decided upon your model and are acquainted with his or her taste about garments and fit, you can begin exploring the fabric for the design. It's important always to swatch at the outset of the design process—even if your design is inspired by a special shape or structure rather than the fabric itself—since fabric significantly affects fit. All designs look wonderful in the mind's eye and sketched out on paper. But until you have a good swatch—the stuff the actual garment will be made of—your design is only an idea. I cannot stress this enough. You may, in fact, need to work many swatches before settling on the best fabric for your project (see the sidebar on p. 14 for suggestions on making a good swatch). But once you've selected your fabric, you're ready to begin shaping it into a garment.

Start by looking again at the swatch. Flex it, stretch it, take time to let it speak to you. Let it tell you something about what it would contribute to a garment. Remember that the knitted fabric supports the garment silhouette and structure. Soft, stretchy fabrics suit close-fitting garments and garments designed to drape. A stiff, inflexible fabric might ruin a sweater designed to drape and be close-fitting, but it would be perfect for a more structured garment. If you were planning a coat that flared at the lower edge, a firm fabric would contribute to the structure and fit, but a softer fabric might cause the coat to droop and sag.

How do you move from swatch to garment design? How do you decide what kind of garment that will be? For me, this transition always begins by sketching (see pp. 164-168), which then moves me into charting. The kind of design you create also depends on your knitting skill level, your interests and personality, and the fabric you select. You may be a daring designer—dying to attempt an unusual silhouette or passionate about experimenting with color or novelty yarns. Or you may be more cautious—a classicist with a penchant for detail and a love of traditional yarns and natural fibers. Or, like myself, you may see yourself as a little bit of both. Above all, it's important to chase the ideas that excite you.

I suggest that novice designers begin by designing very basic garment shapes before moving on to more complex ones. Don't attempt too much too soon, or your difficulties may discourage you. Also, at the beginning, take on only one design project at a time. Choose a good yarn, swatch in simple patterns and plan well before you begin to knit. Make every attempt to solve the problems you encounter along the way and to finish every design you begin, even if it falls short of your expectations. There is not much to learn from a sweater that stays unfinished in your knitting bag.

Establishing *Silhouette & size*

The term *silhouette* refers to the basic outline of a garment, that is, how the garment clings to, falls from or stands away from the body. These basic silhouette types, shown in the drawing on p. 42, are termed *close-fitting*, *classic* and *oversized* or *exaggerated*.

A close-fitting, body-conscious silhouette mimics the body or closely conforms to it. Usually a garment that clings needs to be shaped with more attention to specific body measurements than does a looser style. Because of the fabric's inherent stretch, a close-fitting knit has more ease of movement than a similarly styled woven garment. In a heavyweight knitted fabric, a close-fitting silhouette may look tailored. In a lighter-weight fabric, this silhouette can have a blouse-like effect.

BASIC GARMENT SILHOUETTES

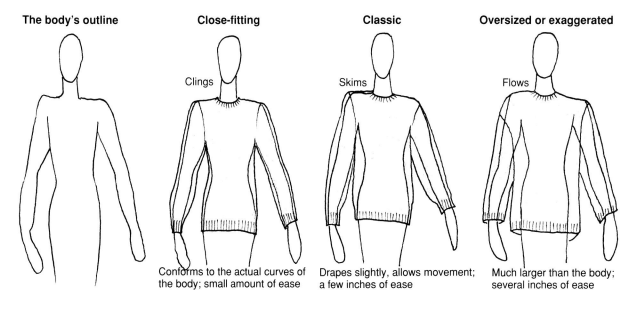

The body's outline | **Close-fitting** | **Classic** | **Oversized or exaggerated**

Clings

Skims

Flows

Conforms to the actual curves of the body; small amount of ease

Drapes slightly, allows movement; a few inches of ease

Much larger than the body; several inches of ease

A classic, loose-fitting silhouette skims the body with only enough extra fabric for the garment to drape slightly, rather than cling. This silhouette can be worked successfully in any fabric weight and allows for ease of movement. Sports clothing usually has a classic fit, as do most traditional sweaters.

An oversized or exaggerated silhouette intentionally includes extra fabric, either to accommodate bulk underneath (for example, as a coat would do) or to create a more dramatic visual effect. In a heavy fabric, an oversized silhouette might have the look of a luxurious fur coat. In a lightweight fabric, a larger garment could flow and drape.

If you have trouble envisioning what silhouette is, look through magazines for examples of garments, both knitted and nonknitted, and group them according to the categories mentioned above. The garment's construction, or structure, is not important—just its outline.

As you refine your design sense, you'll realize that there are sweaters that fall somewhere between these three basic silhouettes. And more sophisticated sweaters can have "hybrid" silhouettes. For example, a trapeze-shaped jacket fits close around the shoulders but is loose and full at the lower edge. Conversely, a wide, exaggerated shoulder line may be balanced by a waistline that conforms to the body.

You'll also find that silhouette is often influenced by the garment's function. When I design garments for work or sport, I aim for an outline that fits the body just loosely enough to allow for movement. When I design for fashion or fun, when ease of movement is not the primary concern, I might exaggerate the silhouette, allowing extra fabric for drama, or I might make the silhouette of such garments narrower to accentuate the wearer's slimness.

It may seem odd at first, but garments need not be the only source of inspiration for silhouette ideas. As an exercise in imagination, try thinking about unexpected shapes that could inspire thoughts about silhouette. I think immediately of the three-dimensional forms that are presented at the beginning of every drawing book. Can you relate a ball, a cone (either point up or point down) or a cube to your thoughts about garments? How about a clipped poodle or strangely shaped topiary hedges? And the egg cup that sits on your kitchen shelf? Recently I saw an asymmetrical pair of sunglasses, with one eye section larger and more shapely than the other, which made me think about a change in silhouette that had never occurred to me before. How about a garment that clings on one side of the body and drapes from the other?

HYBRID SILHOUETTES

Trapeze

Wedge shape

Close-fitting body and lower sleeve; exaggerated upper sleeve

Close-fitting upper body; classic sleeve, with exaggerated lower edge

Oversized shoulder; close-fitting sleeve and wrist; exaggerated lower edge and cuff

Oversized upper body; classic fitted sleeve; close-fitting hip

Size, body measurement and ease

I feel compelled to introduce the term *size* only because it is so commonly associated with garments. But in the clothing industry, the term refers to a system of standard sizing, and, as a designer of one-of-a-kind garments, the word means little to me.

There are many sizing systems, and all vary slightly. The garment industry uses one set of average measurements for given sizes, and sewing and knitting books, magazines and patterns all offer variations on this system. Each of these systems nonetheless presents more or less the same standard, give or take ½ in. here and there. A woman's standard size 10, for example, specifies a 32½-in. bust, a 25-in. waist and a 34½-in. hip. However, it's obvious that women who share the same size can vary greatly in height, weight and body shape. Any standard size chart should therefore be considered as ideal rather than real.

Although standard size systems provide only very general sizing guidelines, you may find them helpful, as I once did, if you're just beginning to design. The sizing charts found in sewing and pattern books present the important body points that you need to consider when designing and acquaint you with the relationship of the body's parts. In addition to the familiar bust, waist and hip measurements, you will often find on these charts back-neck-to-waist and cross-shoulder measurements (see the drawing on p. 45). It's interesting to note the increment, or difference in inches, between

Try to imagine this delightfully shorn poodle wearing a garment — one whose silhouette varies from one area to another. (Photo, UPI/Bettmann Newsphotos.)

sizes to get a sense of how bodies vary. Generally speaking, there are more changes in width than length from one size to another. These charts also point out the measurement differences between men and women, which is especially useful when planning unisex garments. For example, if I were planning a garment that could be worn by both a man and a woman, it would need to accommodate the larger size of the man but still have a sleeve length that could be worn by a woman.

Since individual bodies vary so greatly in shape, a designer needs to move beyond standard sizing once it's understood and individually work out the sizing for each new design. The size of each knitted piece making up the garment must be based on the wearer's actual body measurements, the type of fabric to be used and the desired silhouette. Whenever I design, I always refer to the wearer's actual body measurements and suggest you do the same. If you can, forget the word "size" altogether and replace it in your design vocabulary with actual body measurements.

In addition to body measurements, you also need to account in your design for *ease*, that is, the amount of extra fabric allowed beyond body measurements. Ease ensures that you achieve a comfortable fit and your desired silhouette. Ease is decided upon after body mea-

surements, silhouette and fabric weight are known. In a lightweight fabric, a close-fitting garment may need no extra ease beyond the body measurements. The same garment worked in a heavy yarn, however, would need at least 2 in. extra to make it fit well and produce the same effect. If the garment is to be body-hugging, like a leotard, it should measure 1 in. or 2 in. less than the body. A classic, loose-fitting garment in a medium-weight fabric requires 4 in. to 8 in. extra ease beyond the body measurements. And an oversized sweater will need to be as much as 12 in. to 15 in. larger than the body beneath it. Remember, however, that ease varies with the size of the wearer. A small woman requires much less ease for a classic garment than a large man does.

Remember, too, that with a heavy fabric or a hairy one, like mohair, the inner measurement of the garment is smaller than its outer measurement. Hence, you'll need a little more ease with such fabrics than you would for a smooth, lightweight fabric. Once you've decided upon a silhouette and a yarn, refer to the ease chart below for a suggested amount of ease to add to the bust or chest measurement.

Ease is most crucial at the bust or chest, and this automatically adds width to the hip measurement if the garment is unshaped at the sides. Ease should also be added to the cross-

Ease Chart

Inches of ease to be added for given silhouettes and fabric weights according to body measurements

Fabric weight	Tight to close-fitting			Classic to slightly oversized			Oversized to exaggerated		
	light	medium	heavy	light	medium	heavy	light	medium	heavy
Bust/chest 32 in.	-1 to 1	0-2	1-3	3-5	4-6	5-7	7+	8+	9+
34-36 in.	0-2	1-3	2-4	4-6	5-6	6-8	8+	9+	10+
38-40 in.	0-1	1-3	2-4	4-6	5-6	6-8	8+	9+	10+
42-44 in.	1-2	2-4	3-5	5-7	6-8	7-9	9+	10+	11+
46-48 in.	2-4	3-5	4-6	6-8	7-9	8-10	10+	11+	12+

Note: All numbers are approximate. The plus symbol (+) indicates that you may exceed this figure.

IMPORTANT BODY MEASUREMENTS FOR DESIGNERS

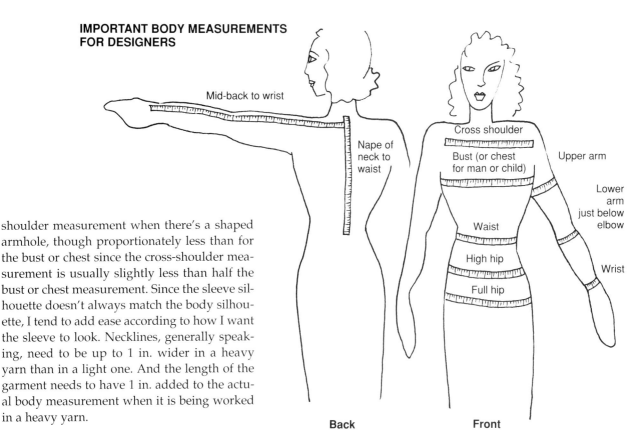

Mid-back to wrist

Nape of neck to waist

Cross shoulder

Bust (or chest for man or child)

Upper arm

Lower arm just below elbow

Waist

High hip

Wrist

Full hip

Back   **Front**

shoulder measurement when there's a shaped armhole, though proportionately less than for the bust or chest since the cross-shoulder measurement is usually slightly less than half the bust or chest measurement. Since the sleeve silhouette doesn't always match the body silhouette, I tend to add ease according to how I want the sleeve to look. Necklines, generally speaking, need to be up to 1 in. wider in a heavy yarn than in a light one. And the length of the garment needs to have 1 in. added to the actual body measurement when it is being worked in a heavy yarn.

Taking body measurements

Whenever you take body measurements, always use a flexible tape measure. When taking your own measurements, enlist the help of another person to ensure accuracy. Stand straight, and wear lightweight clothing. For circumference measurements—around the bust, hips, arms and so on—be sure the tape measure loosely encircles the widest point and lies flat without shifting its horizontal position. For measuring lengths, allow the tape to fall loosely, as fabric would, in order to avoid planning pieces that are too short.

Bust or chest The most important body measurements for a good fit are those for the bust or chest and across the shoulders (see the drawing above). This upper-body area is the point from which a garment hangs and the arena for much of the body's movement. If a garment doesn't fit well in this area, the armholes and sleeves will also be problematic, and the look of the entire garment will be thrown off. Measure at the bust point, or fullest part of the bust, which is usually at 8 in. to 9 in. below the shoulder.

The bust or chest, with ease added, often sets the body width of a nonfitted sweater. If you're planning a simple sweater, like one with a dropped shoulder, this measurement may be all you need to plan the body of a garment. If your garment will be long, remember also to consider the hip measurement.

Cross-shoulder width The width of your garment at the shoulder affects not only the garment's look and fit but also the shaping of the armhole and sleeve. For a structured, fitted garment, the cross-shoulder width should be similar to the body width. When working in a lightweight yarn, make the cross-shoulder measurement the same as the body measurement. For medium-weight and heavyweight fabrics, add respectively 1 in. or 2 in. of ease. For a looser, more casual garment, make the cross-shoulder measurement 2 in. to 6 in. wider than the body, depending on the fabric weight and body width. As you will see later in this chapter, this measurement is related to the way a cap sleeve is shaped.

Waist and hip The waist and hip measurements are less crucial than the bust or chest for the average garment that falls straight from the shoulder and ends in the high hip area. For fitted garments, however, the waist measurement is crucial. For long sweaters or jackets, the hip measurement is important, especially if it is larger than the bust. The same amount of ease should be added to the waist as is added to the bust/chest measurement for comfort.

Since the width of the garment body will be set by the bust/chest measurement, you often will not need the hip measurement. However, if the actual hip measurement is larger than the bust, make sure that the width of the garment body accommodates both bust and hip.

Take the hip measurement closest to the point where the bottom of your garment will hit. This may be what I call the full hip, or the widest part of the hip, which is generally 7 in. to 8 in. below the waist. Or the garment edge may fall at the high hip, approximately halfway between the full hip and waist. Whenever I take someone's measurements, I routinely record these two hip measures.

Lengths I find it useful to record a few body lengths. Often I don't need them, but they nonetheless help me envision the body's geography (see also the sidebar on p. 60). Most important is the back-neck-to-waist measurement, which is especially useful when planning fitted garments. I also find it helpful to know where the fullest point of the bust or chest (called the bust point on women) occurs on the torso—usually 8 to 9 in. below the shoulder—as well as where the waistline falls. Both of these measurements are important for deciding where shaping should occur in a fitted garment.

Another important length is from the center-back neck over the shoulder to the wrist. I use this measurement as a check for sleeve length. That is to say, by subtracting half of the cross-front measurement of the garment body from this total length, I am left with what my total sleeve should measure. For a simple sleeve without a cap, like a dropped shoulder, this is the total length. For a sleeve with a cap, this measurement reflects both the height of the cap plus the sleeve length from the wrist to the

beginning of the cap shaping. If you are measuring a sleeve on an existing garment, be sure that you measure it along its centerline, perpendicular to the lower edge of the wrist or cuff; never measure along the side edge, which is usually shaped.

deciding upon garment structure

A garment's *structure,* or construction, is the assembly of parts that create the silhouette, or outline. I see the parts of a garment as puzzle pieces that must neatly fit together to create the silhouette's shape. There are many ways to structure a garment, and you must choose those that best produce the look and/or fit you're after. On pp. 47-59 you'll find sections dealing with the different structural elements of a garment, what they look like, how they fit the body and how to plan them. But first, here's an overview of how I work out a garment's structure (see the drawing on the facing page for clarification of the terms associated with garment construction).

To ensure good looks and good fit, each area of a garment requires special attention. I begin by generally addressing the individual parts making up the garment body. Then I gradually refine each section until the garment is completely planned.

The most important structural details of a garment occur above the armhole. These include how the sleeve meets the body and how the neckline and shoulders are shaped. Also important is the shaping of the sleeves and the body below the armholes.

No matter how complex my project will be, I always begin by envisioning the body section of the garment as a shapeless tube, which will gradually be altered to accommodate armholes, sleeves, neckline, shoulders and, if for a fitted garment, waist. Having already established my silhouette, I add ease to the bust/chest measurement to settle the basic width of this body tube. Next I plot this tube on graph paper, usually beginning with a view of the front. Reminding myself of my fabric weight, I establish the armhole depth for the garment, based on the width of the sleeve and the way it will join the body. At the same time, I establish the cross-front measurement.

Next I plot the sleeve, deciding the width at the upper arm first, since this is related to the armhole depth. Sleeve length and cap shaping must be considered together, with the width at the lower sleeve figured last. Finally I return to the body again to plot the neckline and shape the shoulders.

Sometimes I proceed in another order when planning the different areas. Often I plan the neckline and shoulder shaping first, especially if the neckline is the focus of the garment or if the sleeve affects the neckline shaping, as it would with a saddle-shoulder or a raglan sleeve (see pp. 52-54). Since all of the areas of the garment are somewhat interrelated, I often move back and forth between them, sketching in rough lines and then returning to refine my plans.

Joining sleeve to body

The most crucial decision for any garment design is how the sleeve joins the body. There are many ways to work this join, and each will produce a different look and fit. Sleeves unshaped at the upper edge, such as dropped-shoulder and indented sleeves, create a boxy look and fit. Alternatively, the sleeve's upper edge can be shaped into a cap and joined to a shaped armhole. This adjustment eliminates fabric bulk at the underarm area and creates a range of fit possibilities from loose to body-conscious. Whereas some sleeve caps join the garment only at the armhole area, raglan and saddle-shoulder sleeves extend over the shoulder and affect the fit of the neckline. Dolman sleeves are knitted as extensions of the garment body and often have no shoulder seams, which causes them to be fuller and drape more than other sleeves.

No matter what type of sleeve/body join you decide upon, three interrelated measurements must be established: cross-shoulder width, sleeve width at the upper arm and armhole depth. In some cases, you'll also need to decide the height of the sleeve cap. Getting the appropriate measurements for these areas ensures that your sleeve will interlock neatly with the body and give you the look you want. I first consider these measurements separately, settling on a rough figure for each based on the silhouette and fabric weight. Then I consider how the measurements work together, and I refine the figures based on the characteristics of the sleeve join I've chosen.

TERMS ASSOCIATED WITH GARMENT CONSTRUCTION

The schematics for this simply shaped garment body and two different sleeves cannot possibly represent all garment types, but they serve to point out crucial measurements for garment design and construction.

Finding the correct relationship between these figures can be easy for the dropped-shoulder joins and a real challenge for cap-sleeve joins. Don't be surprised if you find it confusing. After much experience, I still find this the most demanding area of garment construction. Charting a schematic is a big help here, since it allows you to see the garment pieces. I often cut out my charted sleeve and hold it up, paper doll-style, next to the armhole in the charted body schematic (see p. 226 for a related example of my paper-doll cut-out method). Although the paper bears no similarity to fabric, it nonetheless helps me see how the areas relate. (See also the sidebar on charting on p. 60).

Simple sleeves

The simplest join between sleeve and body is found in the T-shaped garment. This garment has an unshaped tube for a body and uses one of three types of sleeve—a dropped shoulder, indented or dolman—unshaped at the upper edge where it joins the body. Garments with such simple sleeves are comfortable to wear if they're carefully planned, but they do not conform to the body because they have little, if any, armhole shaping.

SIMPLE SLEEVES

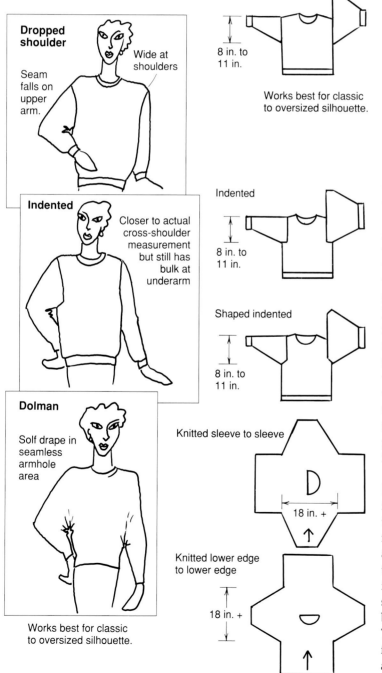

Dropped shoulder

Seam falls on upper arm.

Wide at shoulders

8 in. to 11 in.

Works best for classic to oversized silhouette.

Indented

Closer to actual cross-shoulder measurement but still has bulk at underarm

Indented

8 in. to 11 in.

Shaped indented

8 in. to 11 in.

Dolman

Solf drape in seamless armhole area

Knitted sleeve to sleeve

D

18 in. +

Knitted lower edge to lower edge

18 in. +

Works best for classic to oversized silhouette.

Dropped-shoulder sleeve The most basic unshaped sleeve is the dropped shoulder, which has both an unshaped armhole and an unshaped sleeve top. The entire sleeve is a simple rectangle or trapezoid joined to form a tube, which is, in turn, attached to the body tube of the garment. Because there is no armhole shaping, this garment is very wide across the upper body, causing the sleeve/body join to drop over the upper arm—hence its name.

The dropped shoulder is easy to make and assemble. It is commonly found in traditional sweaters worked in the round. It has a casual, unconstructed look, well suited to sportswear.

Yet as popular as it is, the dropped-shoulder style has some drawbacks. First, there is usually some bulk at the underarm because of the lack of armhole shaping. Second, it is not well suited to close-fitting silhouettes in which the body tube sits uncomfortably close to the underarm. (For such garments, I prefer the indented sleeve, discussed below, which produces a similar look and greater comfort.) The dropped-shoulder sleeve is best used for either classic, loose-fitting silhouettes or exaggerated ones, both of which stand away from the body.

To establish the appropriate measurements for a dropped-shoulder sleeve, first determine the body width and hence the cross-shoulder width. Then choose a sleeve width you like with the body tube; half of this width automatically sets the armhole depth. For a classic, loose-fitting to slightly oversized silhouette, the ideal sleeve width for the average-sized woman is 16 in. to 20 in., and for the average-sized man, 18 in. to 21 in., depending on the fabric weight and actual body size. The sleeve can be wider, but additional fabric adds bulk to the underarm area. In an exaggerated silhouette, almost any sleeve width is possible, since the garment's body will hang far enough away from the underarm to drape rather than cling.

Indented sleeve The indented sleeve is a refinement of the dropped-shoulder sleeve. Here, too, the sleeve top is unshaped, but the garment body has a squared-off underarm, created by binding off a small section, usually 1 in. to 3 in. on either side. When joined, the seam falls closer to the actual cross-shoulder measurement of the body, eliminating some of the bulk associated with the dropped shoulder. The sleeve thus needs to be a bit longer than for the dropped-shoulder garment to fill in the area carved away from the body tube.

I've often encountered confusion among knitters as to how the sleeve is inserted into this armhole. Before seaming the sleeve, the bound-off top is sewn to the vertical part of the armhole. Then a small section of upper-sleeve edge is sewn to the bound-off body section where they meet. The sleeve is finally seamed.

The indented sleeve creates the visual impression of narrower shoulders. It lends a slightly more structured look to the garment and is best suited to classic, loose-fitting and more oversized silhouettes, though it can be used for close-fitting silhouettes with a fairly wide sleeve. Since it brings the seams in toward the body, it is a better choice for women and children with narrow shoulders than for men, whose shoulders are usually wider. All the guidelines for establishing the armhole depth and sleeve width for the dropped-shoulder sleeve (see the facing page) apply to the indented sleeve as well.

A variation, the shaped indented sleeve, gives a slightly more refined fit in the armhole and allows a bit more ease of movement. Rather than eliminating stitches at the base of the armhole all at once, as for the indented sleeve, a slope is worked by gradually decreasing stitches at each underarm until the desired cross-front measurement is reached. The top corners of the sleeve are similarly sloped rather than squared off. This variation is really the first step toward creating a sleeve with a fitted cap (see p. 52). To determine the armhole depth and width, use the same guidelines as for the dropped-shoulder sleeve (see the facing page).

Dolman sleeve Unlike sleeves that are worked separately, the dolman is worked together with the body in one piece. It is best knitted flat, and the front and back are then seamed from wrist to waist. (Although a dolman sleeve can be knitted in the round from bottom to top, the large sleeve extensions make this awkward.)

The absence in the dolman sleeve of a real armhole seam eliminates underarm bulk and allows the fabric to drape. When the dolman is exaggerated so that the armhole depth extends down to the waist, the sleeve is usually termed a "batwing."

The dolman sleeve looks best on classic, loose-fitting or slightly oversized silhouettes, which have enough fabric to create the drape associated with the style. Here, the armhole depth should be in the neighborhood of 9 in.

to 12 in. and can extend as deep as the waist if you want a full look. The dolman also works well in a close-fitting silhouette if the fabric is lightweight and the armhole depth is at least 8 in. to 9 in. for the average woman. In any case, for the sake of comfort, plan to keep the fabric comfortably out of the underarm area. This style is well suited to soft fabrics, which emphasize the drape. It works well for jackets or coats needing a sleeve soft and full enough to accommodate clothing underneath.

The dolman sleeve can be knitted in two ways, which orient the knitting differently. In the first method, the knitting begins at the lower edge of the garment front (or back), continues over the shoulder and ends at the bottom edge of the garment's other side. When the knitting on the first side reaches the point at which the sleeve is to begin, extra stitches are gradually cast on for it. Once the knitting reaches the same point in the other half of the garment, the extra stitches are gradually bound off to complete the sleeve. Since this method of working the dolman sweater orients the knitted fabric in the sleeve in the same vertical direction as the fabric in the body, be sure you like the effect it produces. The fabric in this type of dolman has little stability over the shoulders—it tends to widen and stretch with the weight of the body and sleeve, causing a sloppy look. To avoid this, the front and back of the garment can be worked separately from the lower edge to the shoulder and joined at the shoulder line by a seam. The drawback of this solution, however, is that this shoulder seam, even though structurally sound, can be unsightly, since it runs down the center of the sleeve. A solution to this problem is to seam only the shoulder area and graft or weave the sleeve sections together. (For more on grafting, see the drawing on p. 94.)

The second approach to knitting a dolman is to work from sleeve to sleeve. This orients the knitted structure of the fabric in the body section horizontally rather than vertically. The knitting begins at the lower edge of one sleeve and continues up the sleeve until the desired length has been worked. Stitches are then cast on for the front and back. Once the body, including the neckline, is worked for its full width, the stitches for front and back are bound off and the second sleeve is knitted from the top to the lower edge. With the fabric running from side to side, the shoulder on this type of dolman tends to be firmer, but the body may not drape as nicely.

To keep the front and back of the garment from sagging, use a yarn that has some body. Also anchor the body with a firm border or rib at the lower edge, and generally avoid garments that are longer than high hip. I prefer to knit a dolman from the lower edge of the body since I think that method produces a better drape in the body part of the garment. (For three easy dolman-sleeve garments, see the Designer Notebook on pp. 66-72.)

Shaped sleeves with a cap

In contrast to a simple sleeve, a shaped sleeve conforms more closely to the actual lines of the body. This sleeve is created by carving fabric out of the armhole area so that the cross-shoulder measurement of the garment is the same as, or close to, that of the body. In addition, the top of the sleeve is shaped to accommodate the curve in the armhole, resulting in what is known as the sleeve cap. When this rounded cap joins the shaped armhole, all of the underarm bulk associated with the more geometric T-shapes is eliminated.

I struggled through many projects before I understood the logistics of successfully producing this type of fitted sleeve. It always presents a potential problem: a sleeve cap that's too big or too small for the armhole. If the measurement around the sleeve cap is larger than the measurement around the armhole, its fullness must be eased in in order for the sleeve to fit into the armhole. A large sleeve cap can result in a puffy, gathered look, which may or may not be the desired effect. On the other hand, if the cap measures less than the armhole itself, the result is a tight, restricted armhole. The best fit is achieved when the distance around the cap measures 1 in. to 2 in. more than the armhole so that it can be eased in slightly, allowing a comfortable margin of ease for movement.

With a shaped armhole, the depth can be up to 2 in. to 3 in. less than for a dropped shoulder. The armhole shaping can begin relatively close to the underarm itself, since the curve creates a more comfortable opening than for the deeper and more squared-off types of sleeves.

There are three types of caps that can be worked on sleeves: gathered or pleated, fitted and shallow. For each of these sleeves, you'll need to establish certain measurements to set up the shaping for the armhole and cap. In the body of the garment, you'll need to set up the cross-shoulder measurement and armhole depth according to your chosen silhouette. In the sleeve, you'll need to plan the cap height and width at the uppermost edge. These cap measurements cannot be made final without referring to the armhole depth and the sleeve width at the upper arm.

Even when you plan your cap sleeve ahead of time, you may find it needs adjustment during the knitting. Remember that you can measure around the cap in progress to see if you're approaching the measurement needed for the cap to fit neatly into the armhole—this may occur sooner than you had planned. If this happens, don't bind off all of your stitches at once, but decrease more rapidly over the next few rows to create a slightly curved edge at the top of the cap.

If you decide you like the shape of the finished cap but find the armhole a bit too large, you can either rip out a couple of rows at the shoulder to accommodate the cap (provided this doesn't affect fit) or rip out a few rows of the cap and reshape it by working some decreases at the very top. Conversely, if the cap is too small, you can add a few rows at the shoulder to accommodate it or rip the last several shaping rows in the cap, add several rows to the height of the cap and then reshape the very top of it. If you stray from your original plan, be sure to note the changes on your schematic drawing for the next time you design a similar sleeve/body join.

Gathered or pleated cap   In the gathered or pleated cap, the sleeve cap is exaggerated in size in order to provide the extra fabric needed for gathering or pleating. These full-capped sleeves are less difficult to work than fitted sleeves because they require less precision in matching armhole to sleeve. However, the caps have a very distinctive look, which is not suitable for every design. I always associate a gathered cap with a Victorian blouse and an almost frilly look. A pleated cap produces a more tailored look, which is nice for women's garments but is rarely used for menswear, and then only for very stylized designs.

A gathered or pleated cap is best suited to a close-fitting or a classic, loose-fitting silhouette in lightweight to medium-weight fabrics. The fullness in the cap tends to widen the silhouette, making the shoulders look broad. A

SHAPED CAP SLEEVES

Gathered or pleated cap

Gathered   Pleated

Works best for close-fitting to classic silhouette.

B

Gathered

Ungathered

C = 7 in. to 10 in.

C

A

Pleat   Pleat

B

B   B

C

C = 6 in. +

(The narrower the sleeve at upper arm, the higher the cap height.)

(The narrower the sleeve, the higher the cap height, or the pleats will be very small.)

Fitted cap

Works best for close-fitting to classic silhouette.

A

B

C

C = approx ⅔ of A

Key

A = armhole depth
B = cap measurement + slight ease
C = cap height

For good fit, measurements A and B should be approx the same, with any excess occurring in the cap.

Shallow cap

Works best for classic to oversized silhouette.

A

B

C

C = 2 in. to 4 in.

1 square = 1 in.

narrow cross-front measurement will keep the weight of the extra fabric in the cap closer to the body and off the upper arm. The armhole should be curved gradually to meet the desired cross-front measurement.

To establish the cross-shoulder measurement for this sleeve, you can generally use the guidelines presented below for the fitted cap. The cap height can vary, according to the look you are after. The taller the cap, the fuller the sleeve. To work the cap, divide in half the stitches that need to be eliminated at each armhole. Bind off the first half all at once, then decrease the remainder gradually, usually one stitch every

right-side row. In a medium-weight fabric, the armhole depth should be about 7½ in. for a small woman, 8½ in. for an average-sized woman and 9½ in. for a large woman. Add another 1½ in. to these measurements if you're working with heavyweight fabrics, and subtract ½ in. for lightweight fabrics.

The shaping in the cap varies, depending on the width of the sleeve at the upper arm. If the sleeve is close-fitting, the cap may need to be taller or have smaller pleats to yield enough fabric for a puffed effect. This tall, narrow cap will necessarily be somewhat square. On the other hand, if the sleeve is very wide at the upper arm, the cap will be broader, with a more gradual curve. The higher the cap in a gathered sleeve, the more pronounced the puffed effect will be. A square cap is usually pleated because it has no curve to fit into the armhole. The curved cap can be either pleated or gathered.

Fitted cap   A shaped sleeve with a fitted cap follows the actual lines of the body. The sleeve cap smoothly fits the armhole without gathers, mimicking the meeting of arm and body. This sleeve style is best suited to the more body-conscious close-fitting and classic silhouettes. If used with a roomier silhouette, the cap can be kept from collapsing by using a shoulder pad.

The fitted cap is the trickiest of all to plan. I've ripped out many, and in the process come up with these general guidelines for fitted caps:

1. The fitted cap works best when the sleeve and body share the same silhouette and ease. For example, a classic, loose-fitting body works well with a classic-fitting sleeve. A close-fitting body and an oversized sleeve would be a less successful match.

2. The cross-shoulder measurement should be close to the actual body measurement. When you want a broader shoulder line, as I often do, work the first third of the armhole shaping to conform closely to the body, and then gradually widen the armhole for the last two-thirds of it. If you choose a fuller silhouette at the shoulder, you may need to use a shoulder pad to fill in the extra width.

3. A direct relationship exists between the armhole depth and the sleeve width: the sleeve should be approximately twice as wide as the armhole is deep, plus or minus 1 in. For example, a 15-in. to 16-in. wide upper sleeve provides the right amount of fabric to form a cap that fits well into an 8-in. deep armhole.

4. The cap height should be about two-thirds of the armhole depth. For instance, for a 7-in. deep armhole, the cap should be about 4¾ in. tall. For an 8-in. deep armhole, it should be about 5½ in. tall, and for a 9-in. deep armhole, about 6 in. tall.

5. The width at the top of the cap should be 4 in. to 6 in., depending on the sleeve width.

6. Half of the stitches assigned to each armhole are usually bound off in one step. The remainder are decreased gradually—on every right-side row in medium-weight to heavy-weight yarn, and on every other right-side row in lightweight yarn.

7. The armhole shaping in the body should be duplicated at the beginning of the cap shaping. After this, the cap may be shaped in a variety of ways, but your aim should be to reach the cap width within the rows necessary to reach the cap height. For the average cap in a medium-weight yarn, decrease one stitch on each side until the cap is 1 in. to 1½ in. short of the top. Then bind off either two or three stitches from each side (or a combination of both) until you reach the desired width at the top or the desired height.

You'll find that there are always exceptions to the above guidelines, especially when you start designing more sophisticated garments whose silhouette varies from body to sleeve. Nonetheless, these guidelines should help you work successfully with most fitted-cap sleeves.

Shallow cap   I often use what I call a sleeve with a shallow cap to create the casual look of a dropped shoulder without the bulk of extra fabric under the arm. Set into a deep, slightly shaped armhole, this sleeve is generally quite wide at the top, and its cap is short. The shallow capped sleeve is suited only to oversized garments. It is perfectly suited for men's garments, in which a more fitted cap would grab uncomfortably around the armhole.

Sleeves connected to the neckline

There are two types of sleeves that pass over the shoulder and become part of the neck edge: saddle-shoulder and raglan sleeves (see the drawing on the facing page). The most obvious characteristic of the saddle shoulder is its strap of fabric that emerges from the top of the sleeve and passes over the shoulder to form a section of the neckline. The width of the top of the strap also contributes to the armhole depth.

Saddle-shoulder sleeve   The saddle shoulder is a very comfortable style to wear and can be worked in any silhouette. It is often used because it can visually extend a pattern in the sleeve toward the neckline. The saddle strap can be designed to be narrow and discreet, or as a wide, bold accent (see the photos on pgs. 144, 169 and 171 for examples of garments that use this detail).

My favorite saddle shoulder is structured with a steep angle at the armhole, connecting the underarm to the outer shoulder. This armhole stops approximately 2 in. short of the de-

SADDLE-SHOULDER AND RAGLAN SLEEVES

Saddle shoulder

Raglan

Simple saddle shoulder

(The wider E is, the deeper the neck depth will be.)

A and B measure the same.

Front and back are the same.

More refined saddle shoulder

Back neck

Front neck

Simple raglan

Straight cap top

Back neck

Front neck

Front and back raglan measure the same.

More refined raglan

Angled cap top

Back armhole

Back neck

Front neck

Front armhole

Back cap

Front cap

Back armhole and back cap measure about 1 in. to 1½ in. more than front armhole and front cap, respectively.

1 square = 1 in.

Key
A = armhole measurement
B = cap measurement
C = shoulder width
D = saddle-strap length
E = saddle top
For good fit A must equal B, and C must equal D.

---

sired armhole depth on both front and back. I slope the shoulders at this point. Then I continue on the back-neck stitches until this extension of the back is as deep as half the width of the strap. At the top of the sleeve, I work the shaping for a shallow sleeve cap before extending a 4-in. wide strap at the top of the sleeve. The sides of the strap are then sewn to the sloped shoulders.

Any other sleeve type, except the dolman, can have a saddle extension. Follow the guidelines for the previously mentioned sleeve types to establish cross-shoulder width, armhole depth, sleeve width and cap height. To add a saddle strap to a sleeve, decide upon the width of the band, then subtract half of it from each armhole at the front and back. Since the strap will emerge from the top of the sleeve or cap,

center it within the section normally bound off. The strap length should be the same as the width of one shoulder.

If the shoulder strap is wide (more than 2 in.), the back neck will be too low for a good fit. There are a couple of ways to deal with this problem. After the shoulder sloping is complete, you can continue working the back-neck stitches to raise the back-neck extension half the width of the shoulder strap (as with my favorite saddle shoulder mentioned above). Or you can work a portion of each strap across the back neck and join them at center back.

For a different effect, the shoulder shaping can occur in the strap rather than in the body. Bind off the shoulder stitches in one step. Decrease gradually at each edge of the shoulder strap for a total of ¾ in. to 1 in. on each side.

For a more refined fit at the neck edge, you can slope the very end of the strap, beginning the shaping at the edge closest to the front neck. Also, the back can be slightly higher than the front at the shoulder line.

For this more refined saddle-sleeve garment, the neckline needs to be shaped only slightly, if at all, in the front. The wider the strap, the less neckline shaping is necessary because half the strap becomes the side of the front neck. Likewise, if the strap top is narrow—that is, about 1 in. wide—the front-neck shaping may need to begin at an earlier point in the body of the garment.

Raglan sleeve The unique appearance of the raglan sleeve is a popular design in knitwear. The seam that joins body and sleeve creates a diagonal line that runs from the underarm to the neck edge. To shape the body, decreases are spaced evenly from the underarm to the neck edge. Similar decreases on the sleeve form a triangular-shaped sleeve cap.

The raglan is a comfortable style that can be adapted to almost any silhouette, with the body and sleeve silhouettes usually matching one another. A raglan armhole needs to be about 1½ in. to 2 in. deeper than a fitted cap sleeve so that there is no pulling along the seams. This style is well suited for heavy garments or those worked with somewhat inelastic yarns because the seams support the weight of the upper body. Raglan garments are perfectly adapted to circular knitting, which eliminates the need for seams in the armhole area.

The raglan line itself may be straight or shaped, but in either case both the cap and sleeve top must share the same number of rows, so that the pieces can be sewn together neatly or that the garment can be worked circularly. The raglan line, above the initial armhole bind-off, which is usually 1 in. to 2 in. wide, is often worked in a straight line, with decreases in both body and sleeve plotted at regular intervals. Alternatively, for decorative purposes, the raglan line can be curved or angled. In this case, the sleeve top can share the same shaping as the curved or angled raglan line. In yet another variation, the body and sleeve top can be shaped differently. This would happen if the silhouette varied from sleeve to body, which would mean that more frequent decreases would need to be worked in one of the two pieces to eliminate width.

Raglans are tricky to design. I do most of my planning for them on graph paper first to help me envision how all of the pieces fit together. I draw in a rough armhole depth, making it about as deep as for a cap since the finished raglan top will add a bit more depth, and then I sketch in the neck width. After that, I angle the body and sleeve top as I want to for the raglan lines.

For the width of the sleeve top for a crew neck, I aim for 1 in. to 3 in. If it's much bigger than this, the neckline will be too large. The neckline itself must be shaped slightly in the front piece only. If the finished sleeve top is about 3 in. wide, the front neckline needs less shaping in order to fit. The neckline should be started about ½ in. to 1 in. below the final decrease for the raglan. Likewise if the sleeve top is narrow (about 1 in. wide or less), the front-neck shaping may need to begin 1½ in. to 2 in. before the raglan shaping is complete.

For a more refined fit, I like to work the back armhole 1 in. higher than the front. Then, when the raglan line on the sleeve top matches the front, I begin to bind off gradually from the front edge in order to match the armhole depth of the back. This creates a nice curve in the neckline from the front to the back.

The one fitting problem I see over and over again with raglan styles is that the garment is made too narrow above the armhole to cover the shoulders comfortably. The result is a cone shape above the underarm. To avoid this problem, I always measure around the shoulders and upper torso at what will be the midpoint of the armhole. I know that the combined width of my garment pieces at this point should total this measurement plus a couple of inches of ease. This is easy to check if you have charted the pieces.

The sleeveless garment

Vests and other sleeveless garments may be quick to knit, but they're a challenge to design. This type of garment can be worked in any silhouette. But to avoid a boxy look and get a better fit, plan to shape the armholes slightly.

The armhole depth of a sleeveless garment must provide enough room for movement and accommodate any edging that's added to stabilize the armhole edge. If you curve the armhole even slightly on a sleeveless garment, the fit will be markedly better.

Shape the armhole according to the silhouette you choose, considering any edging that you might add. Remember that an edging will usually add 1 in. to 1½ in. to each side of the cross-shoulder measurement and raise the underarm area by the same amount. Thus, for a fitted look, you may want the cross-shoulder measurement and edging to match the actual cross-shoulder measurement of the body. I think vests look and fit best if they don't interfere with clothing underneath. This is to say that the finished armhole, with edging, needs to be about ½ in. to 1 in. deeper than if you were planning a fitted-cap sleeve for a close-fitting to classic-fitting silhouette. Oversized vests don't need enormously deep armholes to fit well, unless that's the look you want, since the width of this garment will cause it to sit comfortably away from the body.

Other sleeveless garments that will be worn alone can have a shorter armhole depth than that needed for vests. For a simple woman's shell with a curved armhole, the finished armhole depth, with edging, can be the same as that for a fitted-cap sleeve. Sleeveless tops with an extended shoulder—also called a cap sleeve—benefit from the same armhole depth as (or just slightly less than) for a fitted-cap sleeve and from a gradual slope at the shoulders to keep the armhole from flaring. Cutaway armholes that slant toward the neckline, which are best used in a close-fitting silhouette, should be ½ in. to 1 in. shorter than the cap-sleeve fit.

Sleeveless garments can also be worked with raglan or saddle shoulders. A saddle strap alone, added to join front to back at the shoulders, can be a nice detail (see the Aran vest in the photo on p. 169). A raglan line in the body of a sleeveless garment creates a halter look, which should be reserved for a close-fitting silhouette. For this variation, the front and back are not joined together but are held in place at the neckline edge by a circular band or cord.

Creating the neckline

The neckline is often the focal point of a garment because it frames the face. If designed well, the neckline also contributes to a good fit in the shoulders and hence to the overall fit and look of the garment.

There are numerous possibilities for shaping the neckline, and each can be worked with or without a collar. The four basic types of necklines, discussed on pp. 57-58, are the bateau, or boat, neck, which sweeps straight across the neck from shoulder to shoulder; the square neck; the scooped neck; and the V-neck. Each of these necklines can be varied by widening or deepening and is usually finished off with ribbing or another edging.

Most often a collar is an extension of the edging at the neck, but almost all collars can also be worked separately and sewn on. For a close-fitting collar like a turtleneck, you'll want a flexible join to the body, and hence it's always preferable to pick up stitches for this collar. Although collars work best with the smooth lines of the scooped neckline, they can be added to almost kind of neckline, with the possible exception of the boat neckline. You'll find more about this in the various sections below; for additional information on special collars and on lapels, see pp. 220-227.

I've often thought that there is an inverse relationship between neckline and silhouette to be considered when designing. That is to say, the more close-fitting the silhouette, the wider and larger its neckline can be. And conversely, the more exaggerated the silhouette, the more the design benefits from a close neckline. Of course, this does not mean that body-conscious sweaters should never have a close, fitted neckline, or that oversized sweaters cannot handle a wide neck. My point is that the close-fitting garment gets support from the body and can easily accommodate a large or wide neckline, while an oversized sweater looks sloppy and unstructured with a wide neckline that doesn't help support the garment's weight. In fact, in an exaggerated sweater, the body almost swims beneath the fabric, and a closer neckline can contribute to a much better fit.

PLOTTING NECKLINES, ALLOWING FOR RIBBED EDGES
(suggested widths for average-sized woman)

Bateau, or boat

A = 9 in. to 10 in.

Ribbed upper edges of front and back are seamed together at shoulders to leave comfortable opening.

A = 9 in. to 10 in.

Untrimmed edges are folded to inside to create a slightly curved boat neck.

A = 9 in. to 12 in.

For a more sophisticated boat neck, slope the shoulders over 2 in. to 3 in. before binding off the neck stitches.

Square

A = 6 in. to 8 in.
B = 3 in. to 4 in.
C = 1 in.

Classic square neck with narrow edging has slight shaping at back neck.

A = 8 in. to 10 in.
B = 5 in. to 6 in.
C = 2 in. to 3 in.

Wide square neck has a wide edging for a better fit. Back neck can be squared off or slightly curved, with shaping beginning below shoulder.

A = 6½ to 7 in.
B = 4 in. to 6 in.
C = 1 in.

Sweetheart neckline has a narrow back neck, with a wider front neck that has sloping or curved sides.

Scooped

A = 6½ in. to 7½ in.
B = 2½ in. to 3½ in.
C = 1 in.

Classic crew has scooped neckline with slight shaping at back neck. A mock turtle or turtleneck could be added.

A = 8 in. to 10 in.
B = 4 in. to 5 in.
C = 1 in. to 2 in.

Wide portrait neckline has back-neck shaping that begins below shoulder. If rib is any wider than that shown here, or if rib is added, decreases should be worked at shoulder to conform to body.

V-neck

A = 6½ in. to 7½ in.
C = 1 in.
D = 8 in. to 10 in.

Classic V begins shaping close to armhole depth, with slight shaping at back neck. Bottom of V can be squared off, with ribbing overlapped or butted together (see p. 98).

A = 8½ in. to 9½ in.
C = 1½ in. to 3 in.
D = 11 in. to 13 in.
E = 1 in. to 3 in.

Exaggerated V needs wider back neck or V will be too steep. Slight back-neck shaping begins before shoulder shaping, especially if rib is wide.

Key
A = neck width
B = front-neck depth
C = back-neck depth
D = V depth
E = rib width

I've also noticed that the wider the neckline, the less depth it needs in order to fit well. A very wide neckline that approaches the shoulder will need little depth—and perhaps no shaping at all—to fit. However, a very narrow neckline needs much more depth (up to 3 in. to 4 in., usually at the front) to allow the head to pass through. If a neckline is extremely close, a button opening will help give enough room for the head to pass through. A wide, deep neckline may need an edging to draw it closer to the body.

Edgings are an important element in the final appearance of the neckline. They can stabilize the neck and ensure a better fit if they are worked with smaller needles than those used for the body of the garment. Also consider the width of the edge as you design. A wide border or edging can make a neckline smaller than you envisioned; a narrow edging might leave you with a roomier fit and look. You also need to figure into your design enough room around the neckline, both front and back, to accommodate the edging.

When you're designing the neckline, a tape measure and a piece of yarn can be invaluable. You can drape the yarn around the neck in various ways to simulate different necklines and try out various neck widths and depths. Then use the tape measure to capture the widths and depths at front and back. Transfer these measurements to your schematic and plot the curves within them (see the sidebar on p. 60).

Bateau, or boat, neck   The bateau, or boat, neck is the simplest neckline of all and, in fact, is not really a shaped neckline. The straight upper edge of front and back are simply joined at each shoulder, allowing an opening for the head. This type of neckline can be adapted to any silhouette, but really works best if the garment isn't too heavy, since the neckline will stretch out of shape. It looks trim and geometric with a close-fitting garment and lends a casual look to a larger silhouette, but it goes best with a classic-fitting garment.

The boat neck is easy to vary. An untrimmed head opening can be turned in and sewn to the inside, which produces a scooped effect. Or the upper front and back edges can be overlapped rather than sewn at the shoulders, joining the sleeve with a double thickness at the edge of the shoulder. (You can, of course, sew the overlapped areas together too, if you want.) If you overlap the shoulders, add extra depth in the armhole area to accommodate this overlap. The greater the overlap, the smaller the neck opening will be. The best-looking boat necklines are ribbed or edged for firmness.

The bateau neckline is the only one whose width you really don't need to worry about ahead of time. When the front and back sections are done, just sew the shoulders up (or overlap them) until they fit comfortably and leave a large enough opening for the head.

Square neck   The square neckline is easy to plan and knit, and it can assume a variety of different looks. Wide and shallow, it resembles a boat neck. Deep and narrow, it becomes unusual and dramatic. In general, a square neckline looks best when the finished edge falls somewhere between the edge of your neck and the middle of your shoulder. The "sweetheart"

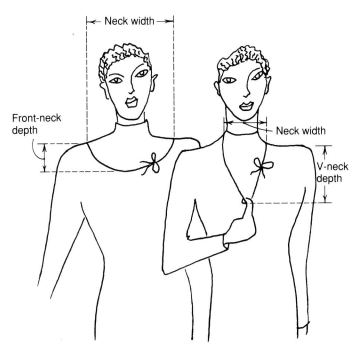

HOLDING A STRING AROUND NECK TO FIND CURVE AND DEPTH OF NECKLINE

neckline is a variation on the square neck, with the sides of the neck edge slanted to join a narrow back neck.

The square neck is the next step up in difficulty from the bateau. A square neckline is easy for beginners, especially if the body of the garment is being knitted in a complicated pattern. The other shaped necklines require more complex decreasing, which would be difficult to work with patterned knitting. With the square neck, you just bind off the necessary width in the center of the piece and continue knitting straight at either side until you reach the shoulder line. I am also fond of mitering the corners of a square neckline, using an interesting rib or flat edging to lend detail to this simple neck. (For more information on mitering and trims, see p. 98.)

Scooped neck   The scooped neckline is perhaps the most common and best-fitting of all necklines since it follows the natural curves at the base of the neck. The classic crewneck is a close-fitting scooped neck that most closely conforms to the body and works well with any silhouette. This neckline can be widened and deepened to frame the face and neck gracefully. The scooped neckline is perhaps the most useful because it forms the basis for so many different kinds of collars (see pp. 220-224).

Whatever the overall width of the scooped neckline, the center third of it is usually left unshaped, with the shaping curves starting on either side of this center section. I try to plan the neckline so that its curves are gradual, ending as close to the shoulder line as possible, to ensure a smoother visual line and a better fit. As with the square neck, use a draped piece of yarn and your tape measure to help you envision the best line. Then take the width and depth measurements and plot the curves on your schematic.

Ribbed edges on scooped necklines can be continued to form higher collars. On a close-fitting neckline, work straight for 3 in. to 4 in. for a mock turtleneck, or for 6 in. to 8 in. for a regular turtleneck. On a wider neckline, you can form a funnel-type collar. Pick up stitches as for a standard edging, but work decreases at two or three points at each shoulder at regular intervals to conform more closely to the body. When you reach the width necessary for a regular turtleneck, continue straight for the desired length. For very wide necklines that have 2 in. to 3 in. of ribbed edges, you may also want to work about 1 in. of decreases on either side at the shoulder area so that the rib lies flat and does not flare.

V-neck   The V-neck is easy to plan, comfortable to wear and traditionally associated with sports clothing. It is often plotted to the same depth as the armhole. But it can also be exaggerated for effect to an exceptionally deep V nearing the waistline. Or it can be made very shallow and wide, and might occur on the front and/or back for a design suited to the drama of an evening sweater. A V-neck usually comes to a point but can also have a squared-off lower edge, from 1 in. to 3 in. wide.

The V-neck works well in any silhouette, provided it can be anchored at the back neck and prevented from riding back on the shoulders. Especially in an oversized silhouette, the back neck should be narrow enough to provide this stability since the front doesn't really conform to the body. When a V-neck garment (or

even a deep scooped neck) rides back or does not fit well, it is usually for one or more of the following reasons:

1. The neckline is too wide and the sweater swims around the neck, constantly changing position;

2. The back neck of the garment has been bound off in one step and is not shaped slightly to conform to the back of the wearer's neck;

3. The back neck is too deep to provide stability at the front. The ideal back-neck shaping begins at the shoulder line, with the beginning of the shoulder shaping;

4. There is no shoulder shaping, causing a poor fit in this area. (For more information on the third and fourth problems above, see the next section on refining fit.)

A finished V-neck, with edging, fits best if the back neck is as wide as the base of the neck itself or no more than 1 in. from the base of the neck on either side. To determine your measurements, use a piece of yarn and a tape measure (as described on p. 57). Be sure to test your V-neck in schematic form, both to check the width of the edged neckline and to see how much the edging will raise the finished V. Try to plan your V-neck decreases so that they end close to the shoulder line—one detail that makes me cringe is a V-neck that ends high up in mid-chest! And like the square neck, the V-neck can be dressed up by working an interesting miter at its point (see the Bibliography on pp. 258-260 for basic information on mitering corners).

Refining the fit   Often back-neck and shoulder shaping can be used to refine a garment's fit. I shape the back neck of almost every garment I design, unless I'm planning a very high neckline. This little refinement allows the back neck to conform to the body and significantly improves the fit of the garment. If the back neck is unshaped, the fabric will bubble up and away from the body at this point.

I bind off the back-neck section in steps to create a slight curve. Some knitters prefer to keep these back-neck stitches on a holder, reserved for the edging. I prefer to pick up the back-neck stitches into the fabric along a bound-off edge. The resulting firmness, coupled with the slight curve, creates a back neck that fits better and keeps its shape.

This shaping involves binding off roughly the center third of the neckline stitches first, in one step, then equally binding off the remaining stitches on either side in two or more steps. For a close-fitting neckline, the back-neck shaping should begin at the same time as the shoulder shaping (see below). For a back neck that's deeper and wider, bind off 3 in. to 4 in. of central stitches at the necessary point below the shoulder. The wider the neckline ribbing, the deeper the back-neck depth must be to accommodate the ribbing (for example, for a 2½-in. rib, the back-neck depth should be at least 2 in.). To plot a gentle curve, plan the steps so that they decrease in size as you approach the shoulder line.

Shaping the shoulders adds immeasurably to good fit by allowing the garment to follow the slope of the natural shoulder line. With dolman, saddle-shoulder and raglan sleeves, shoulder shaping is planned at the same time as the sleeve and neckline. With other sleeves, the shoulder shaping is worked out when the neckline is planned.

Shoulder shaping is easy in sweaters where the sleeve is separate from the neckline. The wider the shoulders of the garment, the greater the slope of the shoulders should be. To bind off each shoulder section in steps, bind off one section of stitches (constituting one step) at the beginning of each shoulder edge or on every other row. For the average shoulder section measuring 3 in. to 6 in. wide, bind off the stitches in three steps. For a shoulder less than 2½ in. wide, bind off in two steps, and for a shoulder larger than 6 in. to 7 in. wide, bind off in four steps.

You can achieve a more sophisticated, less bulky fit in a T-shaped dolman sleeve, where both front and back are worked from the lower edge, by shaping it from the wrist to the neckline, as was done with the coral jacket shown at left in the photo on pp. 68-69. After the stitches for the sleeve have been cast on and the piece worked to the desired wrist depth, the sleeve stitches are gradually bound off over the length needed to complete the armhole depth.

In a saddle-shoulder garment, you can work the shoulder shaping in the body section, or you can decrease along either side of the saddle itself to taper it. The only kind of shoulder shaping necessary in a raglan may be a dart worked at the center of the triangular cap, and this is needed only if the cap is too wide at this point and makes the neckline too large.

*d*esigning to fit real people

Over the years I've designed knits to fit the typical fashion model, whose measurements are actually far from average. She is usually long and lean—generally at least 5 ft. 8 in. tall with a bust measurement of about 34 in. The worst fitting problem she presents, since I never actually meet her, is that I never know her real arm length! When I design for people with less than "perfect" figures—which is most of us, including me—I need to take variations in lengths and widths into account. For example, some people have very narrow shoulders, while others are unusually wide at this body point. For larger women, the hips are often a bit wider than the bust. And arm length varies greatly from one person to the next.

Since it's clear that not all bodies are the same, it's important, first, to study the measurements of the person for whom you're designing and really look at the proportions of the body. Are the hips much larger or smaller than the chest or bust? Is the person short-waisted or very long in the torso? Does he or she have very narrow shoulders, extremely long arms or any other features that seem out of proportion?

Ask the person what he or she finds comfortable. Fit and comfort are very personal matters. Some people like a close, trim fit, but others prefer an oversized or slouchy, pajama effect. And some details completely unrelated to fit, like pockets, can be incorporated into the design if your "model" wants.

Attention to construction details is crucial for creating a comfortable garment. The boundaries of a garment are always important. Be sure that the sleeve length will not fall uncomfortably over the hand. And pay attention to the bottom edge of the garment. If you're designing a classic pullover sweater, the ribbed lower edge at the hip should be full enough to cling gently. If the person for whom you're designing is wide-hipped, you may want to increase the number of ribbed stitches to eliminate stretching. If the person is slim-hipped, you may need to use 10% to 20% fewer ribbed stitches in order to achieve a bloused effect.

If you're designing a more shapely garment for a woman and want an hourglass effect, think about widths and lengths in order to determine the correct position for a fitted waistline. Refer to the back-neck-to-waist measure-

SKELETON CHART

Shoulder

Center

Key

Widths
① = ½ bust or chest
② = ½ waist
③ = ½ high hip
④ = ½ full hip
⑤ = cross-shoulder front

Lengths
⑥ = back neck to waist
⑦ = waist to high hip
⑧ = high hip to full hip
⑨ = shoulder to bust point

Cap-sleeve pullover (schematic plotted over woman's skeleton chart)

Mid-back to wrist

Sample measurements for average-sized woman

Bust	36 in.
Waist	28 in.
High hip	32 in.
Full hip	36 in.
Cross shoulder	14 in.
Back neck to waist	17 in.
Waist to high hip	3½ in.
Waist to full hip	7 in.
Shoulder to bust point	10 in.
Mid-back to wrist	28 in.

Classic, loose-fitting silhouette; mid-weight fabric with 4 in. of ease

Dropped-shoulder pullover (schematic plotted over man's skeleton chart)

Mid-back to wrist

Sample measurements for average-sized man

Chest	40 in.
Waist	34 in.
Hip	41 in.
Cross shoulder	18½ in.
Back neck to waist	21 in.
Waist to full hip	8 in.
Mid-back to wrist	34 in.

Hybrid silhouette, combining classic, loose-fitting lower edge with exaggerated upper body; mid-weight fabric with 8 in. of ease

1 square = 1 in.

Capturing the design

Making and using a skeleton chart

Just as I wouldn't set out toward an unfamiliar destination without a map, I hate to design and start knitting a sweater without first visualizing the garment and the relation of its parts to the body beneath it. Over the years I've learned to map out on graph paper the points of the body in a skeleton chart like the one at left. Then I plot the pieces of the garment over the same chart so that I can see how these pieces relate to the body. At left you'll see two types of garments plotted over two different body types. These charts can't possibly mimic the three-dimensional body, but the points of reference help me visualize the design's details and check proportion.

To make a skeleton chart, refer to actual body measurements. Then:

1. Draw a line down the center of the chart.

2. Plot the body's length from back neck to waist on the central line, making each graph-paper square represent 1 in. Below the waist, plot the length to the high hip.

3. Plot the cross-front measurement at the shoulder line. Divide the bust or chest measurement in half and plot this width at the point at which it falls below the shoulder. Plot half the waist and half the hip where they fall on the central line.

With the body's landmarks plotted on the chart, you can begin planning and plotting the garment atop it. Deciding silhouette, then ease, allows you to set the parameters of the garment body pieces. Then you can gradually alter this chart to include armholes, neckline and any other refinements. The sleeve can be depicted in various ways. I like to extend it to the side of the body section to help visualize its connection to the body. Once you have devised a chart for a certain silhouette and fabric weight, you can refer to it again to help plan other designs. For additional information on charting patterns within a schematic, see the sidebar on pgs. 86-88.

ment (see the sidebar on the facing page). Plan to leave an inch above and below the waist un-shaped to create a gentler curve. Even if you want a fitted waist, you still need to add ease to the waist measurement, often the same amount as for the bust.

When the figure is less than perfect, remember that ease is the key. A tight garment won't make you look slimmer. Dark colors and vertical stripes do have a slimming effect, and using either in the yoke, shoulder and neckline area draws attention away from bulk in the body. But this is again a matter of taste. Many heavy women have told me that they are perfectly comfortable with their size and prefer to wear colors and shapes they like rather than be enslaved to a set of slimming guidelines.

When designing sweaters for men, you'll find that you can use the same basic shapes as for women. Generally, a classic to slightly oversized silhouette provides a comfortable fit and appearance for men.

Since the average man tends to have wider shoulders than a woman, a simple dropped shoulder usually offers a good fit. If the man's shoulders are narrower than average, then shape the armhole slightly.

Sleeve width for men should be conservative—a wide sleeve looks clumsy because of the wide shoulders. For the average, classic sweater, a 20-in. upper sleeve is sufficient.

Longer sweaters are somewhat difficult for most men to wear since they make it hard to get at the pants pockets. Extra length should be reserved for jackets, folk-inspired garments or adventurous nonclassic styles. A classic look for cardigans and pullovers is achieved when the lower edge falls no lower than 5 in. or 6 in. below the waist. Generally, the neckline for a man should be an inch or so wider than for a woman but need not be deeper than the average 2½ in. to 3 in. used for a woman's garment.

Borrowing information from a sweater that fits

I often refer to other garments, including nonknits, to get a sense of how certain measurements create a certain fit. I can be inspired by an entire silhouette or simply want to borrow a detail—like the measurements of a special neckline. If you have a sweater that fits you well, you can use it as the basis for creating a new design. Although woven-fabric garments don't stretch as knits do, they provide a point of departure by supplying measurements.

To recreate the silhouette of your favorite sweater, begin by charting the garment's outline on paper. You can reproduce the garment in a yarn of the same weight or translate it into a new fabric weight. In the latter case, you need to consider ease. If the original garment is lightweight and you want to use a slightly heavier fabric, add 1 in. to 2 in. of ease in the body and a bit less in the sleeve to keep the same fit. Conversely, if the original garment is worked in a heavy fabric and you want to use a lighter fabric, subtract ease from the silhouette measurements.

*a*voiding a tangle

Fixing a sweater that doesn't fit

Whenever a knitted garment doesn't fit, you must analyze what went wrong. If your shaping did not work, then the only real option is to rip out the knitting, replan the design and rework the shaping. However, if a sweater is generally too small or big, there are ways to alter the pieces to produce the necessary fit.

One of the first sweaters I designed introduced me to the problem of sweater pieces that are too small. I had worked a design with a sleeve that was much too narrow. A very complex panel was centered on the sleeve so I was reluctant to rip it out. A nonknitting friend suggested that I simply knit a narrow strip and sew it on to widen the sleeve. I chose a small cable, which worked well visually with the pattern on the sleeve, but I could have worked a simple strip of stockinette. Sewn along the seam, my add-on strip lent the necessary ease I had neglected.

Adding on strips works well only if the shaping of a garment is fairly simple. If the armhole or cap shaping is complex, adding pieces may just complicate the fitting issues. So instead of adding a full strip along the body, you can alternatively add a triangular gusset to the body at the seamline, with the widest part positioned at the underarm and the point tapering into the body. If you have not yet made the sleeve, then increase the armhole measurement to match the new

(continued on p. 62)

After you have finished plotting the parts of your garment on graph paper, the next step is to assign the stitch and row counts to the different areas based on the gauge of your fabric. You will also need to plan increases and decreases to recreate the shape of the individual pieces. On the facing page is a chart of some sample equations that will acquaint you with this process. Remember that stitch counts usually have to be altered slightly to accommodate pattern repeats, provided the change does not alter the silhouette.

(continued from p. 61)

measurement of the body. If the sleeve is already made, open up the seam at the armhole 4 in. to 6 in. and add a mirror-image gusset to the underarm area. If your garment is circularly knitted, you'll need to machine stitch (on both the body and sleeve) two parallel lines 4 in. to 6 in. long on either side of where the underarm seamline would ordinarily fall. Then cut an opening between the stitched lines and sew the added gusset in place.

There may be times, of course, when nothing short of ripping out will make the garment really fit. However, you should not rip out indiscriminately until you've analyzed exactly what the problem is. For example, with a cap-sleeve garment, an upper-body fit that's too tight may be due to one of several reasons. Start questioning yourself about the problem area: Is the cross-shoulder measurement too narrow? Do the armhole seams fall where the chest and arm meet? If this width seems fine, then your sleeve cap may be too narrow (perhaps your upper-sleeve width is a bit skimpy too?). If the body seems fine, then try altering the sleeve alone. On the other hand, if the cross-front measurement seems narrow, then you may need to alter only this area. The point is, don't rip out the sleeve — or any section of the knitting — until you're sure that it's necessary.

Another reason for problems in the upper body is a poor fit in the neckline. Sometimes this is just due to an edging that's too tight, not to the actual shaping of the neckline. Always take out any edging first, try on the garment and see if the problem still exists. If not, redo your edging, adding more stitches for greater ease. If the neckline still does not fit, try to envision a solution. If it seems too narrow or not deep enough, baste around the material where you'd like the new line to fall, undoing shoulder seams if necessary to check the new width. Redraw your schematic to capture your new shaping.

If instead of being too small, your knitted pieces produce a sweater that swims on you, you can try seaming the sweater pieces together a few stitches in from either edge. This will reduce width, but the resulting bulky seam might be uncomfortable and stiff.

Another way to fix a mistakenly oversized sweater is to cut away the excess material. If you cringe at the thought of this unknitterly act, try cutting your swatch first. Pin or, better still, baste the pieces together to the desired measurements to test fit. When you're sure of your new seamlines, mark them. With a short machine stitch, sew in the center of one stitch over from the marked line. Sew a second line right next to the first, approximately a stitch over

(follow a vertical line in the knitting). Cut the knitting one more stitch over from the second machine-stitched line to remove the excess fabric. With the double line of stitching, the edges are now locked in place.

Cutting away excess fabric works best with a simple pattern stitch and simple garment shape. If you eliminate shaping at the armhole by your new cutting lines, you may need to readjust your upper sleeve for a better fit.

I've used the machine-stitch-and-cut method for altering necklines as well. Once I knitted a fine-gauge lace dress for a magazine and was asked to change a simple bateau neckline to a scooped neck. Although I would have preferred to reknit the lace, there was not enough time. So I ripped out the straight upper row on front and back, and shaped the back neck and shoulders. On the front, I shaped the shoulders only, to either side of my desired neck width. I basted the shape of the front neck into the solid lace section, machine stitched above it, then cut out the excess fabric. I added the edging as if the neckline had been shaped by knitting it. (See p. 140 for an example of cutting both the sleeves and the neckline on a circularly knit garment.)

CALCULATING STITCH AND ROW COUNTS FOR GARMENT AREAS

Calculating stitches (sts) for widths and rows for lengths

St gauge = 5 sts per in.
Row gauge = 6 rows per in.

To calculate width of cross front (A), cross back (B), cross shoulder (C), neck (D), lower sleeve (E) and upper sleeve (F): Multiply width of area by st gauge to get number of sts needed to yield width. For example, if cross front (A) equals 20 in., 20 in. x 5 sts per in. = 100 sts.

Width of area x st gauge = total W sts

To calculate sleeve length (G), body length (H), armhole depth (I) and neckline depth (J): Multiply length of area by row gauge to get number of rows needed to yield this length. For example, if armhole depth (I) equals 10 in., 10 in. x 6 rows per in. = 60 rows.

Length of area x row gauge = total L rows

Calculating increases (incs)

To calculate increases to widen a piece equally on two sides (as for a sleeve): Subtract number of sts in width at narrowest point (N) from number of sts at widest point (W) to get total number of sts to be increased. Then divide total number of sts by 2 to get sts to be increased on each side. For example, if N is 20 and W is 60, 60 – 20 = 40, and 40 ÷ 2 = 20. Therefore 20 sts are to be increased on each side.

W sts – N sts = total incs

Total incs ÷ 2 = sts increased on each side

Calculating increase interval

To plot increases within a certain length (as for increases along the length of a sleeve): Divide number of rows (L) by number of incs for one side to get interval at which incs occur. For example, if L is 80 and there are 20 incs to be worked on each side, incs should occur every fourth row (80 ÷ 20 = 4).

L rows ÷ incs (one side) = interval of incs

Note: If interval is an odd number, for example, 3, double it to yield an even number (3 x 2 = 6), divide that even number into two even-numbered sections (2 and 4) and plan to work an inc on each side alternately every second and fourth row.

Calculating decreases (decs)

To calculate decreases to narrow a piece equally on two sides (as for armhole shaping): Subtract sts in narrower measurement (N) from those in wider measurement (W) to get total sts to be decreased. Then divide the total by 2 to get sts to be decreased on each side. For example, to calculate decs for armhole shaping, if cross shoulder has 60 sts and cross front has 90 sts, 30 sts total will need to be decreased (90 – 60 = 30). Dividing this total by 2 yields 15 sts to be decreased on each side of armhole (30 ÷ 2 = 15).

W sts – N sts = total decs

Total decs ÷ 2 = sts decreased each side

Key
A = cross front
B = cross back
C = cross shoulder
D = neck width
E = lower sleeve
F = upper sleeve
G = sleeve length
H = body length
I = armhole depth
J = neckline depth
L = number of rows in given length
N sts = stitches at narrowest width
W sts = stitches at widest width

Dividing body width for shoulders

To divide body width into separate sections for working shoulders: Subtract sts for neck width (D) from total sts in cross shoulder (C) to get total number of shoulder sts. Then divide this total by 2 to get number of sts to be worked for each shoulder. For example, if cross shoulder has 80 sts and neck width has 30, 80 – 30 = 50, and 50 ÷ 2 = 25.

Note: The shoulder sts can be divided into three or four sections in order to plan shoulder slope.

Cross-shoulder sts – neck sts = total shoulder sts

Shoulder sts ÷ 2 = sts for each shoulder

To begin, I start with a detailed schematic that indicates all lengths and widths of my garment design. By multiplying these lengths and widths by my gauge, I can assign stitch counts to the widths and row counts to the lengths. Then I calculate the stitches that will need to be increased or decreased within the shaped areas. Finally I figure the interval at which the increases or decreases will occur in the rows.

The equations in the chart on p. 63 should help you understand this process. For garments with more complicated shaping than those shown, the calculations are similar. Just move systematically from one area to another. For additional guidelines on shaping for sleeves, necklines and shoulders, see these individual sections in the text above.

SKELETON CHART FOR FULL FIGURE

Mid-back to wrist

Cross shoulder

Bust

Waist

1 square = 1 in.

Hip

Try a classic, loose-fitting silhouette, with mid-weight fabric and 4-in. ease added to hip measurement, which is larger than bust measurement.

Sample measurements for full-figured woman	
Bust	49 in.
Waist	41 in.
High hip	51 in.
Full hip	56 in.
Cross shoulder	18 in.
Back neck to waist	16 in.
Waist to high hip	3½ in.
Waist to full hip	7 in.
Shoulder to bust point	10 in.
Mid-back to wrist	30 in.

$d$esigning for special figures

When designing for a special figure, use the same process as you would for any other figure, that is, measure the body, establish ease and structure for your chosen silhouette, then tie all the ends together by charting. At the same time, you also need to acknowledge what is unique about this special figure and what preferences or needs the person may have with regard to the garment's fit and function. Below are some hints from my experience with designing for heavy women and expectant mothers. I have not yet designed for physically challenged people with special needs, but I'm fairly sure the process would be essentially the same.

Designing for the full figure

When designing for a heavy woman or man—that is, a woman with a bust or hip measurement of 42 in. to 50 in. or more, and a man with a chest measurement of 46 in. or more—the goal is still to achieve the best fit possible. There are some slimming visual tricks possible, like using dark colors and vertical patterns, but these serve only to enhance, not substitute for, good fit. In addition to the regular concerns of fit, there are two special considerations when designing for the full figure. First, the garment should be designed to eliminate unnecessary bulk, which means choosing a silhouette and structure with that in mind. Second, measurements should be carefully analyzed to determine which body points to use for establishing widths within the garment.

With regard to silhouette for the larger figure, it's important to add enough ease for the garment to skim, rather than cling to, the body. This eliminates the close-fitting silhouette and points toward the classic to slightly oversized range as more appropriate. I think exaggerated garments can be fine for the larger women, but they should be made of a firm, lightweight to medium-weight fabric.

Lightweight yarns make wonderful fabrics for heavy women because they are not at all bulky, but some knitters may find them tedious to work with for large garments. I would eliminate heavy yarns for full figures for all but short coats and jackets. I've found instead that soft, smooth, worsted-weight yarns drape well and contribute to a smooth line.

With any silhouette, it's important to choose a structure that produces a refined fit around the armhole. Don't design a dropped-shoulder garment for a full figure, since it would make a heavy woman look even broader across the shoulders than she actually is and add uncomfortable extra fabric at the underarm. Choose one of the more body-conscious sleeves, like the fitted cap or raglan. A dolman sleeve can also be attractive if it is shaped at the upper and lower sleeve to eliminate bulk. I've also successfully used the shallow cap sleeve—its wide upper sleeve paired with a deep armhole fits a heavy figure well. The shallow cap sleeve also works well in a saddle-shoulder version.

To plan your garment pieces, analyze the wearer's measurements carefully. Most important, compare the bust and hip measurements. (For the latter, I use the point on the hip where the lower edge of the garment hits.) Take the larger of these two measurements and add ease to establish the width of the body of the garment. On a full figure, you'll often find that the hip is the larger of the two measurements.

Accommodating the hip, however, may result in an excess of fabric in the upper body. When this happens, look to armhole shaping to reduce bulk rather than shaping the sides of the sweater to make the body narrower. For a cap sleeve, measure across the shoulders where the body meets the arm and then add 1 in. to 2 in. to each side. You don't particularly want a wide cross-shoulder in the garment, but because the body is wide, a very narrow cross-front might create an armhole shaped too extremely for a cap to fit well. As a guideline, aim for the armhole shaping to occur over a width of 3 in. to 4 in. Armhole depth for a 48-in. to 52-in. finished bust for a classic fit and shallow cap should measure from 11 in. to 13. in.

To work the armhole shaping, begin by binding off 1½ in. to 2 in. and continue decreasing as for the average sweater. This means your shaping will occur over more rows. For a raglan style, make the initial bind-offs at the armhole a bit wider than average—2 in. to 3 in. each side—before raglan shaping begins.

Sleeves for the larger woman usually need to be a bit shorter than average because the body of the garment is wider. Because wide garments tend to look boxy, use a slightly longer body length (coupled with good armhole shaping) to offset this effect.

Consider the edges of the garment carefully. A tight ribbing is fine at the wrist, but that at the lower edge of the garment should be looser to prevent cutting into the body at the hip or waist. To make the looser ribbing, simply work it on larger needles than those used for the wrist ribbing or, better still, increase the number of stitches used for the ribbing.

The best way to ensure a good fit for a heavier-than-average person is to make a preliminary mock-up garment before beginning to knit. I make this test garment of commercially machine-knitted fabric, based on actual body measurements or those taken from a garment that fits fairly well. I alter the mock-up as necessary to create the best fit, paying special attention to the cross-shoulder and armhole areas (for more detailed information on making a mock-up, see the sidebar on p. 218).

Designing maternity wear

A sweater for an expectant mother needs to accommodate growth throughout the pregnancy. Because the sweater will need to be much larger than average, a lighter weight yarn may be desirable. A deeper than average armhole with a shallow sleeve cap will help avoid bulk at the underarm (see the preceding section, "Designing for the full figure"). More important than anything is to allow ease so that the sweater will drape rather than cling.

Designing a maternity sweater can be a real challenge. Because the sweater requires a lot of knitting, it's good to consider a style that can be worn after the baby is born, too. A knitted poncho or cape would be appropriate for anyone, but suited also for a pregnant woman. Traditional peasant smocks might inspire you to think about a garment that falls from the shoulder or from a yoke. A more fashionable approach might be to design a trapeze shape, with a wide lower edge and narrower shoulders. A ribbed or pleated fabric that would drape on a smaller figure but expand for a pregnant one would make the garment more versatile. Allow the maximum ease at the bustline. A deep armhole will allow for movement even if the weight gain is greater than expected.

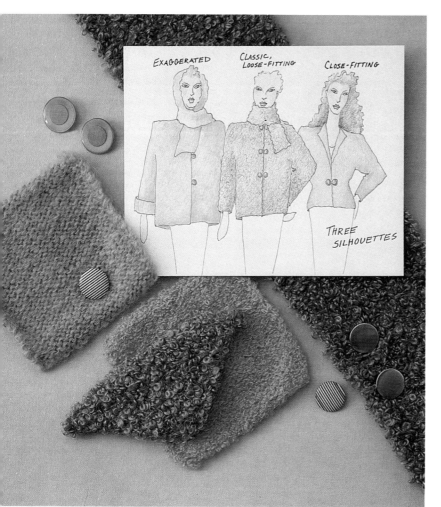

Included in my Designer Notebook are my swatches, among them the blue one folded on the diagonal and sewn to make a shoulder pad; the blue scarf; and my sketch for three simple jackets, each with a different silhouette.

Swatch project & designer notebook

Before I began to swatch or even think about choosing yarns for the project to end this chapter, I asked myself, "What single design could deal with all the issues of fit and silhouette presented in these pages?" After much thought, I realized that I really needed to present three garments, each with a different silhouette. To simplify matters, I decided to make each a variation on a theme, using similar fabrics of the same weight.

To keep my focus on fit and silhouette, I decided my three garments would be extremely simple. I settled on the idea of a thick mohair that would have an interesting texture and some body and which would need very little finishing at the edges — fabric that would be perfectly suited to simple jackets.

I hoped that my swatching would yield something that could be used in the garments themselves. And after acquainting you in the last chapter with schematic instructions for a flat, two-dimensional project (the shawl), I wanted in this chapter to adapt the schematic format to a three-dimensional garment design, relating it to body measurements. With this instructional format, you can vary the directions, if you like, to create your own jacket designs.

With these decisions made, I began swatching. I worked a couple of 8-in. square swatches for each of the yarns I was considering for the jackets, exploring the same stitch gauge and approximate weight in each. I swatched in three mohair yarns, using large needles. Working with the first yarn, a curly mohair in a pretty coral, I decided I wanted a thicker fabric than a single strand would yield and tried knitting two strands held together. Reverse stockinette gave me a soft, thick, subtly textured fabric. Next I tried the heaviest of the three yarns: a lupine blue bouclé that yielded a more deeply textured, fur-like fabric, which also looked best in reverse stockinette. Last I swatched a hairy plain mohair in striking chartreuse. I also used this yarn double-strand in reverse stockinette stitch, which created a thick, hairy fabric.

Since my mohair fabrics seemed well suited to jackets, I thought immediately of using the swatches as shoulder pads. Shoulder pads are useful for any type of sleeve or silhouette in which you want to fill extra space in the shoulder area, as you would with coats and jackets. A shoulder pad can produce a discreetly rounded look in a garment with narrow shoulders or a wide-shouldered silhouette à la Joan Crawford. A pad can also raise the shoulders and thereby shorten sleeves that are a bit too long. Keep this in mind when planning the sleeve length, and add ½ in. if you expect to use shoulder pads.

To make my swatches into the simplest of shoulder pads, I folded each square in half diagonally, then sewed together its edges. In my dolman-style jackets, the pad would be pinned in to check its fit and then sewn to the shoulder seam. (For information on more shapely shoulder pads, see p. 235.)

With my mohair swatches, I wanted to design three very simple garments to reflect the three basic silhouettes discussed in this chapter. I decided to try something I had never done before: I planned each garment to be made from four identical pieces — well, almost identical, since the two front and the two back sections are mirror images of one another).

Using my skeleton chart (see the sidebar on p. 60), with ease added for heavy fabrics, I plotted one-quarter of an exaggerated, boxy dolman-sleeve garment. The only attention I paid to the body beneath was to choose an appropriate sleeve length and to plan the section to cover the hip. This exaggerated silhouette would become the basis for the two more refined silhouettes.

By narrowing the body and shaping the under sleeve I arrived at the design for my simple, classic, loose-fitting silhouette. Finally, for a close-fitting garment, I further shaped the body and upper sleeve. Since length would not affect silhouette for any of these garments, I decided, for the sake of variation, to shorten the two closer-fitting jackets.

I tried to match up each silhouette with the best fabric for it. I decided the least dense chartreuse fabric would drape nicely in the largest garment. The blue swatch was the

Hints on designing coats & winter-weight jackets

It's difficult to design good knitted coats and winter jackets. The most frequent complaints I hear are that they're too heavy and apt to stretch, or that they're not warm enough. Deciding how to get around these issues presents a real design challenge. I hope that my hints below, which cover the four basic areas of concern for these garments, will help you design better coats and jackets.

Fabric

• All coat and jacket fabrics should have body, be firm and never sag.
• Use a yarn made primarily of insulating fibers and one that has stretch, or "memory" — the more memory, the better. My favorite coat and jacket yarns are mohair, doubled for a dense, yet fluffy fabric with a lot of body; any stretchy or resilient wool worked in a firm pattern stitch; and wool knitted and fulled to resemble felt (see p. 231).
• Choose a needle size for your yarn that produces a firm fabric.

Silhouette

• Choose a silhouette to accommodate the fabric you plan for your design and the clothing you'll wear beneath it. Most winter-weight jackets will require an oversized or exaggerated silhouette.
• Add at least 10 in. of ease in the body and up to 6 in. in the cross-shoulder area (see the chart on p. 44).
• Avoid tight ribbing that draws in the lower edges of the body and sleeves and which may crush clothing beneath.
• If you're worried that a knee-length or longer coat will be too heavy, shorten the design to jacket length at the hip or slightly shorter.
• A successful jacket can be made as short as waist length for a cropped effect.
• A double-breasted coat or jacket — or one that wraps — adds extra warmth in the chest area.

Structure

• To lend support to the weight of a coat or jacket, divide the back into two pieces, joined by a center seam.
• Firm shoulder seams also help support the garment's weight.
• Raglan seaming, with or without a sewn dart at the center of the sleeve cap, helps distribute weight in the upper body.
• Shoulder pads help carry weight and give structure in a design with a wide upper body.
• Lining a coat with a lightweight lining material helps reduce wear and stretch in the seat area (see p. 234).

Details

• Keep the size and scale of the coat or jacket in mind when choosing details. A small collar or tiny pockets on a big coat, for example, may look awkward.
• Coats and jackets offer opportunities to use bold details like big lapels, large pockets, belts and huge buttons. Have some fun when you design these garments.

thickest and seemed best suited to the classic silhouette. The soft coral fabric was perfect for the body-conscious silhouette.

Because of the identical four-piece pattern parameters I had set for myself, I knew that some fitting refinements I usually insist on would be lost. First, the four-piece construction would eliminate neck shaping. I would have to plan the best width for each neckline or allow the fronts to open slightly to accommodate the shape of the body at this point. (On the chartreuse jacket, I decided to work a simple collar by knitting an extension on the stitches allocated for the neckline area.) Since no extra fabric was allowed at the center-front edges, the front sections would have to butt together, rather than overlap. To accommodate this design, I needed to choose an appropriate closure and decided upon simple button loops, knitted separately and then attached. I also wanted to firm up the edges of each garment in the simplest way. Ribbing was out—it would get lost in the curly yarns. Testing various edgings on my swatches, I found that I could simply turn in the edges of all the fabrics and sew them down, forming a firm, almost invisible ridge. This would be most useful at the front edges, where stretching would be inevitable.

These simple jackets need only a schematic (see the drawings on pgs. 70, 71 and 72) for instructions. The stitch counts and lengths are all plugged in, and reflect the stitch and row gauges of the different fabrics. The sleeve area indicates the cast-on and bound-off steps, which I planned to be worked within the lengths shown. Along the shaped sides of the coral jacket, I indicated where each increase and decrease should occur. For details about the yarns and my finishing, see the actual directions.

After my garments were done, I decided that the boxy chartreuse jacket looked better without shoulder pads, so I made pads and sewed them along each shoulder seam of the other two jackets. Even for these jackets, the pads are, of course, optional.

With the garments complete, I decided to add a simple accessory to winterize the two larger jackets. With the lupine yarn, I knitted a scarf that could be worn separately or sewn to the back neck of the jacket. I then worked a slightly longer scarf in the chartreuse mohair and sewed one of my swatches to the midpoint of the scarf so it could be used as a hood.

Instructions for dolman-sleeve jackets

These simply shaped jackets with minimal finishing are easy to make.

SIZE
Each to fit 34 (36, 38, 40)-in. bust.

FINISHED MEASUREMENTS (AFTER SEAMING)

Oversized chartreuse jacket
Finished bust at underarm: 48 (50, 52, 54) in.
Length: 29½ (30, 30½, 31) in.

Classic, loose-fitting lupine jacket
Finished bust at underarm: 42 (44, 46, 48) in.
Length: 25½ (26, 26½, 27) in.

Close-fitting coral jacket
Finished bust at underarm: 38 (40, 42, 44) in.
Length: 23 (23½, 24, 24½) in.

NOTES FOR ALL JACKETS
• All 3 are worked in heavyweight rev St st fabric. Each is knitted in 4 pieces, with the 2 pairs of front and back pieces mirror images of each other.
• An extra st has been added to each edge for seaming and finishing edges. Measurements do not include these sts.
• Dolman sleeve is worked at same time as body. To check sleeve length, measure yourself from center back to wrist and compare figure to schematic measurement. If your body measurement is same or less than schematic, work chart as shown. If your measurement is more, multiply difference by st gauge to arrive at extra number of sts to be added to those on schematic. When casting on for sleeve, add extra sts to last cast-on step. At shoulder line, bind off extra sts with 1st step.

These three simple mohair jackets, each with a different silhouette, all have variations on a dolman sleeve.

CHARTREUSE JACKET

MATERIALS
- 22 (24, 26, 28) balls "La Gran" from Classic Elite, (74% mohair, 13% wool, 13% nylon; 1½ oz = 90 yd) in chartreuse #6535.
- 1 pair size 11 knitting needles, or size to obtain given gauge.
- 4 buttons, 1½ in. wide.
- Optional scarf: 7 balls of "La Gran."

GAUGE
- 20 sts and 30 rows equal 8 in. in rev St st with 2 strands held tog and size 11 needle.
- To save time later. take time to swatch and check your gauge.

NOTES
- With 2 strands of yarn held tog, cast on number of sts shown on chart for chosen size. Work in rev St st (p RS rows, k WS rows) to lengths indicated.

- For right back and left front, cast on sleeve sts at beg of RS row. For left back and right front, cast on sleeve sts at beg of WS row. When each piece is complete, sl 11 (12, 12, 13) sts to a yarn holder for neck, bind off rem 58 (58, 60, 60) sts.

FINISHING
Sew back pieces tog at center. Sew fronts to back at shoulders along bound-off edges, leaving neck sts on yarn holders. Sew lower sleeve and side seams.

Collar: With RS facing, beg at right-front neck, sl neck sts from yarn holders to RH needle. Turn, then beg with a p row, work in rev St st for 4 in. Bind off.

Lower edges of body: Allow fabric to roll to WS slightly and sew in place.

Front and lower sleeve edges (shorten sleeve if necessary): Turn a small amount of fabric to WS and sew in place. Sew 4 buttons evenly spaced along left front, 1 in. over from edge.

Button loops (make 4): With 2 strands held tog, cast on 8 sts, then bind off on next row. Sew on right front, opposite buttons.

Optional hood scarf: Cast on 22 sts and work in rev St st for 60 in. Bind off. Turn edges to WS, as for jacket, and sew in place. Along 1 long edge of scarf, mark center 24 in., then pin this section evenly around 3 sides of 8-in. gauge swatch and sew in place to form back of hood.

CHARTREUSE JACKET

26½ (27, 28, 28½) in.

Slip 11 (12, 12, 13) sts to holder for collar.

Bind off 58 (58, 60, 60) sts.

Silhouette: exaggerated
Fabric weight: heavy
Ease: 14 in.

To fit bust size 34 (36, 38, 40) in.
Finished bust measurement: 48 (50, 52, 54) in.

11 (11½ 12, 12½) in.

Bust

29½ (30, 30½, 31) in

Cast on 37 sts.

Waist

18½ in.

Hip

Cast on 32 (33, 35, 36) sts.

12 (12½, 13, 13½) in.

1 st has been added to each edge for seaming and finishing; measurements do not include these sts.

Gauge: 20 sts / 30 rows = 8 in.
One square = 1 in.

LUPINE BLUE JACKET

MATERIALS
- 23 (25, 27, 29) balls "Cleo" from Classic Elite, (74% mohair, 13% wool, 13% nylon; 1¾ oz = 28 yd).
- 1 pair size 10½ knitting needles, or size to obtain given gauge.
- 8 buttons, 1½ in. wide.
- Optional scarf: 5 balls of "Cleo."

GAUGE
- 20 sts and 28 rows equal 8 in. in rev St st with size 10½ needle.
- To save time later, take time to swatch and check your gauge.

NOTES
- For each piece, cast on number of sts shown on chart for chosen size. Work in rev St st (p RS rows, k WS rows) to lengths shown, working shaping as indicated.
- For right back and left front, cast on a step of sleeve sts at beg of every RS row; then, when sleeve depth is reached, bind off all sts at beg of RS row. For left back and right front, cast on a step of sleeve sts at beg of every WS row; then, when sleeve depth is reached, bind off all sts at beg of WS row.

FINISHING
Sew back pieces tog at center. Sew fronts to back at bound-off shoulder edges, leave 7½ (8, 8, 8½) in. for back neck. Sew lower sleeve and side seams.

Lower edges of body: Allow fabric to roll to WS slightly and sew in place.

Front, neckline and lower sleeve edges (shorten sleeve length if necessary): Turn a small amount of fabric to WS and sew in place. Sew 4 buttons evenly spaced on EACH front, 1 in. over from edge, so that when fronts meet, buttons are paired.

Figure-8 button loops (make 4): Cast on 20 sts, then bind off loosely on next row. Join to form a ring, then twist into an "8" shape and use ends to sew at center to hold in place; do not cut ends. With jacket edges butted tog, sl over a pair of buttons, then sew center of button loop to right front.

Optional scarf: Cast on 22 sts and work in rev St st for 44 in. Bind off. Turn edges to WS, as for jacket, and sew in place. Scarf may be worn separately or sewn along back-neck edge.

LUPINE BLUE JACKET

Silhouette: classic fit / slightly oversized
Fabric weight: heavy
Ease: 8 in.

To fit bust size 34 (36, 38, 40) in.
Finished bust measurement (after seaming): 42 (44, 46, 48) in.

1 st has been added to each edge for seaming and finishing; measurements do not include these sts.

Gauge: 20 sts / 28 rows = 8 in.
One square = 1 in.

CORAL FITTED JACKET

MATERIALS

• 13 (15, 17, 19) balls "Sharon" from Classic Elite, (74% mohair, 13% wool, 13% nylon; 1½ oz = 90 yd) in Coral #2588.
• 1 pair size 10½ knitting needles, or size to obtain given gauge.
• 2 buttons, each 1¾ in. wide.

GAUGE

• 20 sts and 30 rows equal 8 in. in rev St st with 2 strands held tog and size 10½ needle.
• To save time later, take time to swatch and check your gauge.

NOTES

• With 2 strands of yarn held tog for each piece, cast on number of sts shown on chart for chosen size.

Work in rev St st (p RS rows, k WS rows) to lengths shown, working shaping as indicated.
• Dec at edges as follows: at beg of RS rows p1, p2tog-b; at end of RS rows, work to last 3 sts, p2tog, p1.
• Inc at edges as follows: at beg of RS rows p1, M1; at end of RS rows, work to last st, M1, p1.
• For right back and left front, cast on a step of sleeve sts at beg of every RS row; then, when sleeve depth is reached, bind off a step at shoulder at beg of every RS row. For left back and right front, cast on a step of sleeve sts at beg of every WS row; then, when sleeve depth is reached, bind off a step at shoulder at beg of every WS row.

FINISHING

• Sew back pieces tog at center. Sew fronts to back at bound-off shoulder edges, leave 7 (7½, 7½, 8) in. for back neck. Sew lower sleeve and side seams. Turn in and sew lower front sleeve and neckline edges as for lupine jacket, shorten sleeve if necessary.
• Sew 1 button on each front at waist level, 1 in. over from edge. Make and attach figure-8 button loop as for lupine jacket, except cast on with 2 strands held tog.

CORAL JACKET (RIGHT BACK AND LEFT FRONT SHOWN HERE)

Silhouette: close-fitting
Fabric weight: heavy
Ease: 4 in.

To fit bust size 34 (36, 38, 40) in.
Finished bust measurement: 38 (40, 42, 44) in.

27½ (28, 28½, 29) sts

Bind off 27 (28, 29, 31) sts.

Bind off 11 sts, 4 times.

11   11   11   11

5 (5½, 6, 6½) in.

45 sts

5   5   5   5   5   5   5   5   5

Cast on 5 sts, 9 times.

Increase 1 st every 1 in., 5 times.

Decrease 1 st every 1 in., 5 times.

11 (11½, 12, 12½) in.

Bust

23 (23½, 24, 24½) in.

12 in.

Waist

Cast on 26 (27, 28, 30) sts.

1 1 1 1 1 1 1 1 1

Hip

9½ (10, 10½, 11) in.

1 st has been added to each edge for seaming and finishing; measurements do not include these sts.

Gauge: 20 sts / 30 rows = 8 in.
One square = 1 in.

WHAT IF...?

What if I combined different silhouettes in the same garment, based on my three mohair jackets?

Close-fitting top

Full bottom section gathered into top.

Oversized upper body

Lower body tapers to close fit.

Asymmetrical look— fitted on one side.

and loose on the opposite side.

Designing with Knit & Purl

4

*r*ichly textured knitted fabrics do not necessarily call for complex stitches. The simplest stitches possible, smooth knits and bumpy purls, can be used side by side or in various combinations to produce wonderfully textured fabrics for garments.

The family of knit/purl patterns evolves from the basic fabrics discussed on pp. 27-28: garter stitch, stockinette and reverse stockinette. Ribbing is probably the most familiar knit/purl fabric, but there are many other such patterns based on the textural differences between knits and purls. Knit/purl fabrics can be essentially flat, thick and dimensional, or rippled and pleated; their surface can be subtly pebbled or boldly patterned.

Because these patterns are all based on a common pair of stitches, they combine easily with one another and work well on a background—or divided by panels—of stockinette, reverse stockinette or garter stitch. All knit/purl patterns are easy to knit, and they produce crisp, clean, elegant fabrics suitable for any type of garment.

Although you're probably already familiar with the basic techniques of working knit/purl patterns, you may not have considered them from the designer's point of view. To begin looking at these patterns with a fresh eye, first, be aware that knit/purl patterns fall into two basic categories: those that are essentially flat and those that are more three-dimensional.

Flat knit/purl patterns, like seed stitch, basketweave, traveling lines, blocks and brocades, produce fabrics that drape well. The effect of these patterns is crisp, quiet and refined, and always reminds me of classic menswear fabrics. More dramatic flat patterns are produced by mixing large areas of smooth knits, which catch the light, with areas of bumpy purls, which cast slight shadows.

In very dimensional knit/purl patterns, like ribbing, welts and pleats, the knit and purl stitches are strategically placed to create a push/pull effect in the fabric. In ribbing, the knit and purl stitches are alternately arranged in vertical columns; in welts, they're positioned

Worked in smooth yarns, these swatches show different arrangements of knit/purl patterns. The beige swatch has a diamond border at the lower edge, framed by three-dimensional, reverse-stockinette ridges and topped off by a deeply ribbed fabric, which could be used to shape a garment. The gold swatch features panel patterns, and the teal swatch, an isolated motif on a stockinette background. The mauve swatch shows an allover pattern that distributes texture evenly across the fabric.

can be inserted into an allover pattern or worked side by side with the same or other panels. When panels are worked side by side, each strip tends to retain its individual identity rather than linking up to form an allover pattern. When used as a horizontal border, a panel can set up an interesting visual step between a pattern at the lower edge of a garment and the body fabric, or it can mark the beginning of a separate yoke.

If you look carefully at allover and panel patterns, you'll see that some are symmetrical and others, asymmetrical. Symmetrical repeats are visually balanced and have a beginning, center and end. The center portion of these patterns is the repeated sequence, with the beginning and end, mirror images of one another. In asymmetrical patterns, there may be a discernible beginning, middle and end, but the two end patterns will not mirror one another. Characteristics like these are useful to notice when you're designing or combining patterns.

Flat knit/purl patterns are best worked in crisp, smooth yarns that clearly define the stitches and create contrast between the knits and purls. Crisp cottons and cabled, or tightly twisted, wools are among my favorite yarns for knit/purl patterns. Yarns with matte surfaces are usually a sure bet, and shiny mercerized cottons add a special luster to purl stitches. It's a good idea to stay away from novelty yarns that draw attention to themselves, since they will blur, rather than define, the stitches. Likewise, avoid hairy yarns like mohair, wools that are soft or limp, and yarns blended with a soft fiber like alpaca. All will produce a beautiful drape but very little stitch definition. If you have your heart set on a particular soft yarn, however, experiment with needle size to find one that will help define the stitches.

With the more dimensional patterns, you can choose from a wider range of yarns since the fabric's 3-D aspect will stand out more than the knit/purl patterning itself. Most yarns can be used, but a yarn with memory, like a springy wool, will both reinforce the dimension of the surface and point up the contrast between knit and purl stitches. A hairy yarn like mohair will blur the stitch definition. And a heavy, inelastic yarn like many cottons will eventually flatten the patterning with wear. To be sure of your choice, take time to swatch before beginning your garment.

in neighboring horizontal bands; and in pleats, they're usually configured in repeating, interlocking triangles.

Both flat and dimensional knit/purl patterns can be worked as an allover fabric, a panel pattern or an isolated motif. Both can also serve as edgings, and dimensional patterns can also replace complicated increases and decreases to draw in and shape the body of a garment.

An allover pattern is made up of a single unit that repeats to form a continuous, unbroken surface. Panel patterns are self-contained repeats, usually worked in a vertical strip, though they can also be used horizontally. A single multiple of any allover pattern can be used to form a panel, and it can be nicely isolated from adjoining patterns by adding a few extra plain stitches on either side of it. A panel

Flat patterns usually need little or no blocking. And though I don't like to flatten 3-D fabrics by blocking them, I find that careful steaming can "set" and emphasize their pattern. However, I block only when I'm sure that steaming will not harm the fiber and, of course, I always block a swatch first (see the blocking chart on p. 230).

A Sampler of my favorite knit/purl patterns

The best way to get acquainted with the knit/purl family of patterns is to survey them in a knitting dictionary (see the Bibliography on pp. 258-260). If you look through old knitting magazines and pattern brochures, you may run across additional knit/purl patterns that never made their way into knitting dictionaries. The photographs in these sources—or engravings in the case of many 19th-century knitting and needlework magazines—will give you a general idea of what a pattern looks like and how the stitches are aligned, but they will not tell you much about the actual nature of the knitted fabric. In order to find out how your yarn, pattern and gauge mix, you must work a swatch.

Most dictionaries have row-by-row instructions for each pattern. Others have charted directions that are even easier to follow. In addition, most sources note how many stitches and rows form the basic unit of a pattern, that is, the pattern repeat. This information is essential for designing. Without it, you know neither the number of stitches nor the number of rows needed to work one or more pattern repeats within a given width and length of fabric. This is the same information you'll need to work out designs with any stitch pattern, not just knit/purl patterns, and you'll also need it to combine different knit/purl patterns in one garment (see also the sidebar on charting on pp. 86-88).

Below is a sampler of my favorite knit/purl patterns. I've started with the flat knit/purl patterns because they're the easiest to design with, and I've ended with the more challenging 3-D patterns.

Seed stitch

Seed stitch, or seeding, is one of the simplest knitting stitches there is—only stockinette and garter stitch are simpler. Seed stitch alternates on every row a single knit stitch with a single purl, creating a checkerboard arrangement and requiring only one simple line of instruction: p1, *k1, p1; repeat from *. If your row has an even number of stitches, just work (k1, p1) across the first row and (p1, k1) across the second row and continue this pattern to align the stitches correctly.

This pattern is my all-time favorite. It's perfectly flat and has a texture that I never tire of. Worked in a smooth yarn, seeding can be crisp and elegant. Knitted in a more textured yarn, it produces a "choppy," rustic effect. In either yarn, seeding yields a very firm stitch, with a tighter row gauge than either of its parents (according to my version of the knitting family tree, garter stitch begat stockinette stitch and reverse stockinette—and seed stitch is their perfect first-born!).

Seed and block patterns are the simplest of the knit/purl family and often look good knitted with textured yarns. At right, seed stitch shows up well in both a fuzzy ivory alpaca/wool blend (top) and gold wool-blend novelty (bottom). At left, the blocks in the gold swatch (top) are outlined in garter, unlike the other two, which alternate knit and purl blocks.

Basketweave patterns can change dramatically by simply varying the proportion of their elements. The subtlest version (purple swatch) is formed of bands of 1x1 ribbing, divided by two stockinette rows. The pink swatch at lower right is formed of a 2x4 rib divided by two stockinette rows. The grey swatch simply alters the proportions of the seed-stitch bands and vertical stockinette strips in the rose swatch at upper right.

Block patterns

Block patterns regularly alternate groups of knit stitches with groups of purl stitches, producing an essentially flat fabric. The blocks of knits and purls can have the same number of stitches, or they can be unbalanced (for example, a block of two knit stitches can alternate with a block of three purls). The blocks can be worked to be almost square, tall and narrow, or short and wide.

The simplest block pattern is really seed stitch (see the previous discussion). The next simplest is moss stitch, which alternates knit and purl stitches every other row and produces a little more surface dimension than seed stitch: (Rows 1 and 2: * k1, pl; repeat from *. Rows 3 and 4: * p1, k1; repeat from *. Repeat rows 1-4.) There are hundreds of other larger block patterns that vary the size of the individual blocks, but all produce flat, crisp fabrics.

Block patterns form simple, yet striking allover flat fabrics, which drape well. These patterns are often reversible and tend to have less regular edges than seeding, which means they benefit from an edging or trim. They can also be used as an accent, a border or a panel to divide more complex patterns.

Block patterns are child's play for the designer. You can plan them out on knitter's graph paper (see p. 88), or you can simply cast on and experiment. Even the beginning designer will find it easy to come up with a beautiful fabric by combining various block patterns with stockinette and reverse stockinette. Block patterns are not at all difficult to knit and design, since they almost always share the same gauge (see pp. 29-30).

Since block patterns evolve naturally from ribbings (see pp. 81-83), you may want to try beginning a swatch with a rib pattern and changing the rib into a block pattern. For example, set up a 3x5 rib, work it for a few rows, then knit the purl stitches and purl the knit stitches. Continue for a few rows before changing the stitches again.

Seed stitch is at its most beautiful when worked as an allover fabric. Because it's both reversible and perfectly flat, it's suitable for scarves, lapels, collars or any area of a garment where both sides are likely to be seen. When used as an allover fabric, seed stitch often doesn't need to be edged since it remains crisp and even at the edges. If I do decide to add an edging, I usually choose one of the simple, discreet trims like a single-row bind-off or a reverse-stockinette-stitch roll (see pp. 91-96 for more information on trim).

Seeding is equally attractive when worked in small units as an accent. I suggest trying horizontal bands of seeding to divide patterns or dropping blocks of seed stitch onto a flatter surface like stockinette. It doesn't take much seed stitch to accent a fabric. Even two seed stitches in a panel can pep up a simple surface. You might also try using seed stitch as a background for cabled patterns instead of the usual reverse stockinette, though seeding does tend to flatten out the cables.

Traveling-line and brocade patterns are among my favorites. The two blue patterns at right are examples of traveling lines. The brocade patterns at left all have highly textured surfaces that play light against dark (from left to right: the pattern worn by Charles I on the day of his execution, a beautiful Bavarian pattern, and the hybrid traveling-line brocade I created by knitting from a weaving chart for an undulating twill pattern).

Basketweave patterns

Basketweave knit/purl patterns lend the impression of bands weaving in and out of the surface of the fabric. They are outgrowths of block patterns but have more depth and are generally not reversible (though the wrong side is usually interesting). The blocks in basketweave are staggered like brickwork and are usually divided by "mortar" of a single band of another simple pattern like stockinette stitch.

The simplest basketweave pattern alternates one knit stitch with one purl stitch for two rows, followed by two rows of stockinette stitch. Then the position of the knits and purls is reversed for the next two rows, and so on. My favorite basketweave pattern involves staggering larger blocks of basketweave (four knit stitches divided by two purl stitches, knitted for four rows) and working the bands in between only two rows deep.

Like block patterns, most basketweave patterns share the same gauge. Try designing your own basketweave patterns by experimenting with different sizes of blocks or different divider patterns. Even if your pattern no longer resembles basketweave, you may like the result, or the basic structure may inspire something altogether new.

Traveling lines

Traveling lines can be straight, diagonal or zigzag. They can also be curved or irregular, but the effect is often less successful. The simplest, most effective line is formed of purl stitches worked on a stockinette ground. This line almost pops off the fabric, whereas a knit-stitch line on a sea of purls tends to get eaten up. Lines can be worked with a single stitch, wider bands of knit/purl patterns or groups of seeding or blocks.

There are several ways to make subtle lines on smooth or textured fabrics without creating a 3-D ribbed effect. The simplest straight line can be made by working a column or row of single garter stitches on stockinette. A raised line can be worked on a field of reverse stockinette by knitting a single stitch on the wrong (knit) side and knitting into the back of the same stitch on the right (purl) side.

If you're knitting diagonal lines, the purl (or knit) stitches composing them can move a stitch to the right or left on the contrasting ground every row, every other row or every fourth row. The more often the line shifts position on the ground, the steeper its angle will be. If the pattern shifts irregularly, the line will waver. I adapted the pattern in the taupe swatch in the photo above from a weaving chart for a pattern known as an undulating twill.

When a knit stitch is twisted, either by knitting or purling into the back of it, it tightens up and produces crisp patterning on a reverse stockinette background. Using fairly elastic yarns, like the smooth wool/cotton blend in the swatch at left, further enhances the pattern's crispness, though even when worked in a soft, fluffy wool, like the swatch at right, the twisted-stitch pattern is well defined.

Traveling lines need not all be straight. Chevrons and zigzags are outgrowths of diagonal lines that change direction after a given interval. These truncated diagonal lines work well in panels; they can also be used as dividers between other patterns.

Traveling-line patterns form flat fabrics and mix well with other knit/purl patterns. Single-stitch lines can form simple accents for other patterns or subtle allover fabrics. Wider traveling lines form striking allover fabrics and combine well with other bold patterns.

Try designing these patterns on graph paper, beginning with easy diagonal lines. Start by plotting a single purl-stitch line on a stockinette background. Then try adding lines of different widths, or plotting a band of seed stitch to move alongside the first purl line.

When you swatch to test your graphed design, don't be afraid to experiment. You may decide to change the direction of the lines halfway through the swatch. If you like the look of your newly designed lines, alter your original chart to reflect the pattern's change.

Brocade patterns

A traditional woven brocade fabric has a raised surface of patterning, produced by introducing into the warp and weft of the ground cloth one or more supplementary pattern yarns. Brocade patterning can be worked with contrasting colors or using the same color as the background. In the latter case, the brocade sets up a lovely matte/shiny contrast between the pattern and the background.

All knit/purl patterns feature raised textures and could be referred to as brocade knits (though, instead of having a matte/shiny surface like their woven counterparts, knit/purl brocades play dark and light areas against one another). However, I reserve the term *brocade* for knit/purl fabrics with complex combinations of texture. In many cases, these brocade patterns combine several small patterns or incorporate motifs formed of simpler patterns. They may feature sophisticated angular shapes or be less well-defined patterns in which the contrast of stitches creates a shadowy surface on the fabric.

The grey swatch in the photo on p. 79 comes from the knitted shirt worn by Charles I on the day of his execution in 1649. For me, this momentous occasion makes the pattern more intriguing. Could you use it to inspire a design? A brocade pullover with a red turtleneck—too macabre for you?

Twisted-stitch patterns

Some of the traditional knit/purl patterns feature single knit stitches that have been twisted by working into the back of the stitch, which tends to compress the stitch and give it a tight, crisp V-shape. The purl side of the stitch looks much the same as it does when the knit stitch is untwisted.

I love patterns that feature these twisted knit stitches, many of which originated in Germany. These individual twisted stitches are not to be confused with the family known as twist stitches (see pp. 183-185), in which two stitches "twist," or change position with each other. Since both types of patterns tend to tighten the stitches, however, they do resemble one another and therefore work well in combination.

Twisted knit stitches can be substituted for plain knit stitches, especially when they appear on a background of reverse stockinette. Stockinette can be twisted if you want more texture, but it will be stiffer than if worked plain.

Ribbing

Ribbing is one of the simplest of the knit/purl family of patterns. This very dimensional fabric is produced by regularly juxtaposing a column of knits with a column of purls. The knit ribs tend to pull forward while the purl ribs settle back in the surface, resulting in a corrugated fabric with a lot of horizontal elasticity.

The most common ribbings are evenly balanced, alternating one or several knit stitches with the same number of purls—for example, a 1x1 or 2x2 rib. But the number of stitches in the knit column can vary from that in the purl column, and the knits can also be twisted, cabled or worked in some other decorative fashion. (Twisting a 1x1 rib for firmness is often suggested, but I find that this separates the columns and that the ribbing tends not to wear as well as when it's untwisted. Nonetheless, a twisted rib harmonizes well in a garment featuring twisted stitches.) The width of the columns of knit and purl stitches affects the fabric's stretch: the wider the ribs, the less the fabric draws in. Patterns that combine narrow panels of stitches are the most elastic.

Ribbing need not always be vertical. If you move over one stitch every four rows when working a 2x2 or a 3x3 rib (narrow ribs work best), you'll produce diagonal ribbing. This fabric is a bit less elastic than its vertical counterpart, so be sure to use smaller needles than you would for regular ribbing if you want to use it for a firm edging.

Many knitters think ribbing is only for the bottom, neck or wrists of a garment, but ribbing can be both decorative and functional and need not be relegated to the edges of a garment. It can serve as an allover fabric, an interesting contrast to other stitch patterns or as a means of shaping a garment. Because I want to emphasize the versatility of ribbing patterns, let's look first at using them in places other than the edges of a garment. (For a discussion of ribbing as edging, see pp. 93-95.)

Ribbing, both straight and diagonal, can be used very effectively as an allover fabric if the yarn, the silhouette and the garment structure are carefully considered. To choose a suitable yarn, keep in mind that a springy yarn will emphasize the ribbed quality of the fabric, and a less elastic yarn will allow the fabric to drape more. Ribbed patterns tend to be heavier than flat knit/purl fabrics because they squeeze more stitches into a given space. So be sure the yarn is not too heavy and that the needles are

Ribbed and welted patterns form 3-D fabrics with great elasticity, especially when worked in wool, as in these swatches. Clockwise from upper left: narrow welts aligned side to side, as they might be in a garment; less elastic, blue diagonal and green textured ribs that work well for allover fabrics; a pair of ribbed fabrics that are useful for drawing in the lower edges of a garment; and wide welts forming accordion-like folds.

average size for the yarn used, especially if you're knitting a very large garment. Mohair yarns are lovely for allover ribbing since they can be worked on somewhat large needles and produce an airy, lightweight fabric. I have also used a worsted-weight cotton in a large ribbed garment, which, to my surprise, turned out to be very wearable, albeit heavy (I made sure to incorporate a strong shoulder seam to support the weight).

RIBBING AND WELTING: MULTIPURPOSE FABRICS

Ribs as allover fabrics

Wide ribs form drapier fabrics.

Flat ribs with little depth add strong vertical lines to a garment.

Use narrow ribs for a close fit.

Ribs to shape areas of a garment

To draw in yoke

To tighten waist

To shape sides of a garment

Welts as allover fabrics

In garments worked side to side

Wide welts form looser, drapier fabric.

Welts at edges form strong horizontal lines.

Narrow welts draw fabric in toward body.

Sleeve worked side to side

Welts for shaping and detail

Welts create peplum effect if waist is cinched.

Welts worked side to side nip in waist and lower edge.

Ribbed fabric can be used with any garment structure or silhouette, but it is perhaps best suited for close-fitting garments or for use in areas of a garment you want to draw in. Tight ribbings (1x1 or 2x2) are a natural for close-fitting garments or areas that need to cling. A wider rib will cling less tenaciously and create drape and soft folds. Wide ribbed patterns that combine a very narrow rib with one at least 1 in. wide cling very little and should be regarded as flat fabrics that will add a strong vertical line to a garment.

When an allover ribbed fabric is planned, checking gauge is important because the garment may draw in more than you expect. To check gauge, first swatch with the yarn to decide how you want the fabric to look and drape on the body. Remember that an allover fabric looks best when it has enough ease to allow the ribs to fold up, even if slightly, rather than be stretched flat. Even for a close-fitting garment, a ribbed fabric should not be stretched to its limits.

Once you determine the width of the ribs and whether you want the fabric to cling to, loosely drape over or stand away from the body, you're ready to establish your gauge. Measure the gauge on the swatch held as you expect the fabric to be used. That is, if you plan a deeply ribbed fabric for a loose or oversized silhouette, do not stretch the swatch when checking gauge. If you intend the fabric to stretch slightly on the body, then stretch the swatch slightly and pin it in position before measuring gauge. And if you want to use the ribbing as a flat fabric rather than a 3-D fabric, then block the swatch flat before measuring its gauge.

Be aware that you'll need a great deal of yarn for a deeply ribbed garment that doesn't cling. I would estimate that any allover-ribbed garment would take up to one-third to one-half more yarn than if would worked in stockinette.

Ribbing can also be used to shape areas of a garment and eliminate complex increasing or decreasing. For example, ribbing used at the waistline or along the sides of the body below the armholes can produce an hourglass effect or simply slim the silhouette. Extending ribbing at the waistline to just under the bustline creates an empire effect. Incorporating a ribbed yoke on a garment with heavy sleeves can help keep the shape in the upper body. In effect, ribbing can serve the function of tucks and darts to shape a garment (for a discussion of tucks and darts, see pp. 212-214).

If you want a fabric to resemble allover ribbing but without the stretch and weight of the real McCoy, hunt through your pattern dictionaries for some of the lovely fakes. The patterns from the brioche rib family lack the elasticity of true ribbing and cannot be used in place of shaping, but they do have ribbing's characteristic thickness and vertical lines. For another ribbed look in a lighter-weight fabric, use slipped stitches on a stockinette surface to create vertical lines. These patterns will not work very well as trim, so confine them to the body of a garment. Finally, ribbed fabrics (and the welted fabrics discussed below) can be embellished, once completed, with smocking.

Welts

Welts are alternating horizontal ridges of stockinette and reverse stockinette stitch (that is, the horizontal equivalent of ribbing), which resemble corrugated cardboard laid on its side. The fabric tends to curl and shorten from the ridges, just as ribbing tends to make the fabric narrower, but welts are less elastic than ribbing. The choice of whether to use welts or ribbing depends simply on the orientation in which you want the pattern to lie and the direction in which you want to knit the garment. For example, a dolman knitted side to side (see

the drawing on p. 48) could use welts for its "ribbed" edges in the body section, though not in the sleeves.

The knit/purl ridges in welted fabric can be worked on the same number of rows, producing a balanced effect that's identical on both sides, or on a different number of rows. The narrower the ridges, the springier and more accordion-like the fabric will be. The wider the ridges, the flatter and softer the fabric will be, and the more drape it will have.

Ridged fabrics tend to draw up and have a tight row gauge, a characteristic that can be used to advantage in designing a garment. For example, by inserting a ridged panel into a smooth fabric for a ruched effect, you might design a sleeve as depicted in the drawing at far right on the bottom of the facing page. Welts also serve as a fine surface for smocking. Vertically knitted side to side, ridged fabrics can resemble pleats for collars, cuffs and peplums. If you substitute ridges for a reverse-stockinette background with cable patterns, you'll achieve an even more richly textured surface (see p. 189).

Small groups of welts can be used as accents or horizontal dividers between patterns. Because of the differing row gauges between patterns, however, they should not be used in a vertical panel alongside flat patterns—unless, of course, you want the welted section to be shorter than the others. When used as an allover, horizontally aligned fabric, welts tend to weigh down and become flat. If you anticipate stretching, block your swatch to stretch it out before checking gauge. The fabric can be used with the welts oriented vertically for an almost pleated effect. In this case, measure gauge as you would for elastic allover ribbing, allowing the fabric to draw in as you would like to see it on the body.

Welts can also be used for shaping, though not as effectively as ribbing. If the body of a garment is worked side to side, welts can be plotted at the waistline area or at the beginning and end of the pieces to draw them in. If you short-row the stockinette areas to create triangular sections, a side-to-side welted garment could assume an interesting trapeze shape. This same technique could be used to shape a peplum.

Pleats or wavy effects are produced by working an allover fabric of interlocking triangles of knits and purls. The swatch at top features the well-known Pilsner pleats, which incorporate eyelets and work well for pleated peplums and cuffs, especially when knitted in a fine yarn. The swatch at bottom shows the fluted-rib pattern in a very elastic wool/mohair blend.

Pleats and wavy fabrics

There are two ways to form pleats in a knitted fabric. One involves a simple combination of knit/purl patterns and the other, the use of carefully placed slipped stitches (see pp. 212-213 for information on slip-stitch pleats). Both methods are easy to work, but they produce pleats that look and hang differently. Knit/purl pleats are soft and resemble textured ribbing, whereas slip-stitch pleats have crisp folds, which look like ironed-in creases in the fabric.

In the small group of knit/purl patterns that form pleated fabrics, a single panel is repeated across the width of the fabric. Within each panel, there are interlocking triangles, or less frequently diamonds, of knits and purls. The push/pull effect of the knit and purl areas forms a fold at the juncture of each panel. For a very pretty pleated fabric that also incorporates eyelets, see the well-known Pilsner, or pennant, pleats (so called because they are formed by interlocking triangular flags) in the photo at bottom left.

Knit/purl pleats can be used effectively in garments and work well when they're allowed to fold up in all but close-fitting silhouettes. Be sure to provide enough ease for the folds to occur, or the fabric will tend to flatten up against the body.

Skirts are an obvious place to use pleats. They can also fall from the ribbed waist of a jacket or sweater and create a flared peplum. In a fine, crisp yarn, you might try to simulate the pleated front of a tuxedo shirt.

I've found that most medium-weight to lightweight yarns work well for pleated patterns. I prefer fine yarns because they squeeze more pleats into a given area. A crisp wool yarn yields a well-defined pleat, whereas a softer or hairier yarn will form limper folds. Like ribbing, an allover pleated fabric is heavier than a flat fabric and requires care in choosing a yarn that will help keep the garment's shape. Wool is the best, and heavy fibers like cotton are the least effective.

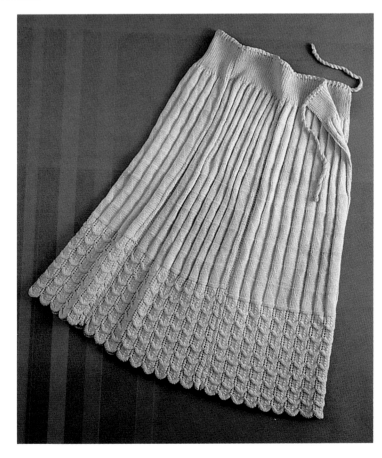

This hand-knitted petticoat features knit/purl Pilsner pleats; a ribbed waistband, threaded with a twisted cord; and a lace flounce that incorporates reverse-stockinette ridges. (Metropolitan Museum of Art; gift of Mrs. Alfred Kramer, 1937.)

To swatch for pleated fabric, work a larger swatch than you would for a flat pattern. Allow for at least four or five pleats in the swatch so you can really see how the finished fabric will look and drape. When you measure for gauge, allow the fabric to fold and pleat as it will in the finished garment. If you flatten the fabric to measure gauge, you will not allow enough ease in your garment for the pleats to form.

In addition to pleated patterns, there are some knit/purl patterns that use different geometric configurations of knits and purls to form ripply, wavy fabrics. When I began knitting, I inadvertently stumbled onto one of these when devising a pattern formed of interlocking parallellograms. On paper, there was no indication of the 3-D nature of the pattern, but it all became apparent when I began to knit (those were the days when preliminary swatching was not a part of my repertoire). The resulting ripply fabric draped in peculiar fashion and was ill-suited to the close-fitting vest I was knitting, so I was forced to flatten the pieces by wet blocking them.

After this experience, I stuck to traditional folded pleats, which work much better for garments (and I also started to swatch before beginning to knit!). An interesting design task would be to explore the various possibilities for combining diamonds, triangles or parallelograms in regular allover formations to compare the results.

*d*esigning with knit/purl patterns

To begin designing with knit/purl patterns, think first about swatching to produce an effective fabric. After you have a successful swatch in hand, you can turn to your garment idea and consider gauge and how your patterns will fit into the garment's structure.

There are several ways to begin designing an interesting knit/purl fabric. You can place a single purl (or knit) graphic motif on a simple stockinette (or reverse-stockinette) background. You can repeat a small knit/purl motif to form an allover pattern (if you are starting from scratch, the charting techniques on p. 87 will help you envision the new pattern on paper before you swatch). Or you can combine traditional patterns with one another or with patterns of your own invention.

Small isolated knit/purl graphics are easy to design. At top is a Celtic motif interpreted by Barbara Walker in textured purl stitches on a stockinette background. At lower right is a moss-stitch star, often seen in traditional guernsey sweaters and to which I once added bobbles at the star's points to transform it into a sheriff's badge. At lower left is a pine tree motif I designed with twisted knit stitches on a reverse-stockinette background.

Isolated graphic motifs

Isolated knit/purl graphic motifs, whether pictorial or abstract, are often beautiful—though not always. Sometimes a motif simply does not translate into knit/purl. Generally speaking, the bolder, more linear and straight-edged a motif is, the more successful the translation. The best contrast for graphic motifs is produced by using purl stitch, seed stitch or small block patterns on a smooth stockinette ground, but knit-stitch motifs on a reverse-stockinette background are also very effective.

In the photo above are some examples of graphic images that translate well into knit/purl. The six-pointed star, a traditional motif worked in a moss-stitch pattern on a plain background, is easy to enlarge or reduce. Other angular shapes, like the pine tree in the neigh-

Allover knit/purl graphics can be as simple as a group of garter-stitch lines, like those in the swatch at left, or more complicated patterns, like those in the swatch at right. For the latter swatch, I first knitted a single diamond to decide the motif's size and shape, then repeated it on graph paper to form an allover pattern.

Charting

A knitter's chart is the equivalent of a symphony conductor's score. The assembly of stitch symbols carefully plotted on paper enables the knitter to orchestrate and produce the charted garment. Charts are used to record the stitches in a particular pattern and also to create schematics, which capture the shape and size of garment pieces for a given design. If you want to design or alter a pattern, record one you've seen in another garment or simply rid yourself of following tedious row-by-row instructions, you'll need to know how to chart.

There are many systems for charting patterns, but all are based on plotting stitch symbols on a grid. I'm fond of the systems devised by Barbara Walker in her book *Charted Knitting Designs* (see the Bibliography on pp. 258-260). Many of Walker's symbols look like the stitch or knitting maneuver they represent, which makes her charts easy to follow.

The symbols used in this book are fairly standard. These charts may look confusing to the newly initiated, but there's no simpler way to follow or record patterns, once you've become familiar with the grid and the symbols themselves. The best place to begin learning about charting is with simple knit and purl patterns. (See p. 192 for some examples of charted lace patterns, pp. 200-201 for information on charting a garment stitch by stitch, and pp. 124-128 and pp. 130-131 for a discussion of charting colorwork patterns.)

With regard to the symbols, I use an empty block to represent a knit stitch and a horizontal dash for a purl stitch. For a twisted knit stitch, I use a "V."

(continued on p. 88)

boring swatch, work well for pictorial graphic motifs. I designed the pine tree first on graph paper, plotting parallelograms flanking a central stem, and then found when knitting it that twisted stitches lent a crispness to the motif, which I worked on a reverse-stockinette background. For more information on graphics and patterning, see pp. 118-128 and pp. 193-195.

To work out a graphic motif and capture the image without distortion, chart it on proportioned knitter's graph paper with the proper stitch-to-row ratio (see the sidebar at right for more information on charting). Draw a basic outline and shade the stitch blocks that are to be purled to fill in the shape. Once you have plotted the motif, swatch it to make sure you like the actual fabric.

You can also use simple horizontal lines as graphics, forming them either with a ridge of reverse stockinette or a ridge or two of garter stitch. These lines can be very effective if interestingly placed on a garment. Narrow stripes make a stronger visual impact when used in groups rather than singly. One of the most striking knitted fabrics I've seen had isolated garter ridges spaced at various intervals. On the other hand, a strategically placed, wide textured stripe in seed stitch or basketweave might be all you need to spark up an otherwise plain garment.

You can use vertical lines for graphics too, working columns of stockinette on a reverse-stockinette background or sections of twisted-stitch ribs or regular ribbing. These graphic lines, whether vertical or horizontal, need not extend the full length or width of the fabric. They can be worked to whatever length your

USING KNIT AND PURL SYMBOLS

Charting King Charles Brocade pattern

Extra st ⟍ ⟵ 12-st rep ⟶

Knit and purl symbols

□ = k on RS rows;
   p on WS rows

⊟ = p on RS rows;
   k on WS rows

v̄ = k into back of st on RS rows;
   p into back of st on WS rows

1 square = 1 in.

Plotting King Charles Brocade (KCB) on a schematic

1. Schematic with allover KCB dividing evenly into st count:

Gauge: 6 sts = 1 in.
20 in. x 6 = 120 sts
KCB = multiple of
   12 sts + 1 st

⟵ 20 in. ⟶

2. Schematic with allover KCB dividing unevenly into st count:

Gauge: 6 sts = 1 in.
21 in. x 6 = 126 sts
KCB = multiple of
   12 sts + 1 st

1 square = 1 in.

⟵ 21 in. ⟶

3. Schematic combining allover KCB with vertical panel pat:

Gauges:
KCB: 6 sts = 1 in.
Panel: 13 sts = 2 in.

2 in.   2 in.
13 sts   13 sts

⟵ 25 ⟶
sts

⟵ 6½ in. ⟶ ⟵ 6½ in. ⟶
         ⟵ 21 in. ⟶

To plot KCB as allover pat, divide st count by st multiple:
120 sts ÷ 12-st rep = 10 even reps.

Since pat has multiple of 12 sts plus 1 st, add 1 st to balance pat (extra st will not affect garment's fit):
120 sts + 1 st = 121 total sts.

To plot KCB as allover pat on wider garment section, again divide st count by st multiple:
126 sts ÷ 12-st rep = 10 reps + 6 extra sts.

To work with partial rep, chart pat, divide extra sts in half and place them to either side of a complete rep. Then, to balance pat and make it beg and end in same place, place extra st to one side of rep (here placed on far left)—127 total sts. (More complex pats may require several sts added to make them beg and end in same place.)

If allover KCB is interrupted by two 2-in. wide panels and has a 4-in. wide center section, two full KCB reps, or 25 sts, will fit evenly into center section. Since 6½-in. panels cannot evenly accommodate full KCB reps, plot pat and extra sts so that pat begs and ends in a pleasing way. Refer to Example 2.

Note: Unlike KCB, panel pat, charted below, is self-contained and cannot be made narrower or wider.

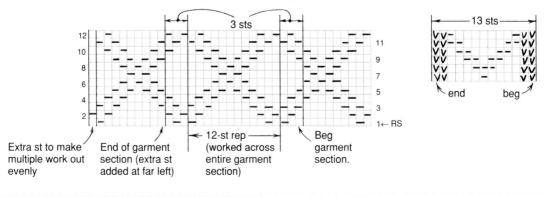

Extra st to make multiple work out evenly

End of garment section (extra st added at far left)

⟵ 12-st rep ⟶ (worked across entire garment section)

Beg garment section.

(continued from p. 86)

Graph paper, of course, can be used for the basic grid for charting. But since most graph paper is plotted with square blocks and the knitted stitch is really rectangular—or wider than it is tall—the rows of the actual knitted fabric will be slightly more compressed than they appear on the charted version of the pattern. Thus, you may want to use special knitter's graph paper to maintain the correct proportion of stitches to rows (see Sources of Supply on pp. 257-258). If you're working with dimensional ribbed or pleated fabric, charts will be of little help in visualizing the fabric, however, and you'll need instead to rely on swatching. And since I depend so much on swatching to help me see all my fabrics, I find that square-grid graph paper is fine for general use.

Beginning to learn to read and work with charts may be a little confusing. To do so, you must envision the chart as representing the right side of the fabric. If you're knitting flat on straight needles, the odd-numbered rows represent rows worked with the right side of the fabric facing you. The even-numbered rows represent rows worked with the wrong side of the fabric facing you. Read the right-side rows from right to left (starting with Row 1 at the bottom of the chart) and the wrong-side rows from left to right—just as you would knit them. (Note that odd-numbered rows need not always be right-side rows. If it suits your purposes to work the first row of the chart as a wrong-side row, then simply read the odd-numbered rows from left to right and the even-numbered rows from right to left.)

Because the chart represents the face of the fabric, right-side rows are worked as shown and wrong-side rows must be worked with the stitch opposite that shown. That is, each stitch charted as a knit stitch in a wrong-side row should actually be purled rather than knitted, and each stitch charted as a purl should be knitted. Knitters new to charting may find this tricky to follow at first, but it will quickly become old hat.

If you're knitting in the round on circular needles, working from a chart is even easier since the right side of the knitting always faces you. Read each row of the chart from right to left, just as you would knit, returning at the end of each row to the right of the chart to begin the next round. Always work the stitch shown by the symbol, without "converting" it for wrong-side rows. Knit/purl patterns are the simplest to chart, with all rows shown. For some patterns, however, only right-side rows are shown if wrong-side rows are all worked the same.

Sometimes you can take inspiration for knit/purl patterns from other kinds of needlework charts, like those used for embroidery. But since the distinction between knit and purl is often subtle in the knitted fabric, these charts generally work best for colorwork translation. For the best translation of knit/purl patterns, look for patterns that will contrast large areas of dark and light. Charts that feature intricate details will probably translate into grainy, blurred fabrics.

Once you've learned to chart and work with a single pattern, you'll need to learn to plot patterns onto the schematic (see the drawing on p. 87). Whether you want to plot a single pattern or several patterns and arrange them horizontally or vertically on the garment section, you must first determine the garment's width and plot it in schematic form. The patterns must then be plotted into this width, and they may or may not fit evenly with full pattern repeats. If they don't fit evenly, which is often the case, you'll be left with a partial repeat of the pattern. In this case, you'll need to add or subtract stitches to make the calculations work out evenly—provided this doesn't affect your garment silhouette—or you'll need to adjust the positioning of the pattern within the garment section. You can either work the partial repeat at both sides of the garment section or just at one side if the pattern is small and has no distinct center portion.

If you're using different patterns in a horizontal arrangement, you'll need to consider each pattern separately and work the calculations described above for each. If you're using different patterns arranged side by side in vertical panels, consider each pattern separately and work the calculations above for each pattern within its given panel width.

If you're having trouble with the calculations, take time to chart the individual patterns to get better acquainted with them and see how they can be broken, if need be, for a partial repeat. In effect, deciding how to plot patterns within a schematic involves give and take between the garment size and pattern repeat. You have to juggle both a bit to find a happy medium that sacrifices neither your silhouette nor the look of the pattern.

Although charting knit/purl combinations on graph paper helps you visualize these pattern marriages, charts cannot substitute for swatching. What you think is very successful on paper may not work out as well when actually knitted. Hence, charting goes hand in hand with swatching.

extend the full length or width of the fabric. They can be worked to whatever length your overall graphic or design calls for.

Graphic lines combine nicely with other patterns and often serve as a good bridge between patterns. If you want to use them to divide patterns, swatch to be sure the lines do not blur into the surrounding patterns. For example, a garter-stitch ridge may need a plain stockinette row before and after it to appear crisp. If you want to add touches of texture to the motif or to the background, you can insert a dot of purl or garter stitch at selected points.

In addition to serving as an isolated graphic, a small knit/purl motif can often provide the basis for an allover pattern. The easiest way to move from a single motif to allover pattern is simply to repeat the motif across the fabric. If the graphic itself is crisp, chances are that it will produce a successful allover pattern, but swatch to be sure. If you want each individual motif in the pattern to retain its individuality (which you often will with pictorial graphic images), divide the motifs with a few plain stitches to keep them from blurring together. Conversely, you may sometimes want a slight overlap with geometric motifs that begin and end in the same way.

To experiment with an allover pattern, make several photocopies of the motif you've chosen, then cut out the copies and arrange them in different ways until you like the configuration. Try arranging them in a checkerboard or staggered basketweave alignment. You might also try a half-step effect, arranging the motifs in panels, staggered side to side, rather than on top of each other. Instead of plotting the motifs close together, you may choose to leave some space between them. When you've settled on an effective arrangement, tape or paste the pieces together, chart the arrangement again if necessary and swatch from the finished chart.

Combining knit/purl patterns

Even the beginning knitter will find it easy to combine knit/purl patterns in the same fabric. Sometimes this can be done while swatching, without any prior planning. At other times, a little preliminary work with graph paper will help you develop a slightly more complicated combination. If you're looking for a real challenge, you might try designing an abstract mixture of patterns, like the one I devised in the photo on p. 74).

FORMING CHECKERBOARD PATTERNS

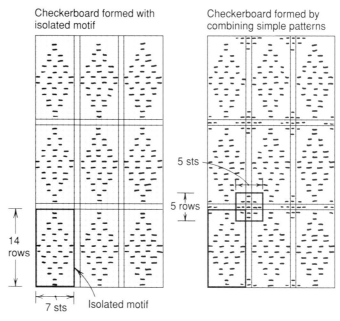

Checkerboard formed with isolated motif

Checkerboard formed by combining simple patterns

5 sts

5 rows

14 rows

7 sts

Isolated motif

ARRANGING SMALL PATTERN REPEATS

Basic square-grid repeat

Horizontally staggered repeat

Half-drop repeat

USING PHOTOCOPYING TO WORK OUT PATTERN ARRANGEMENTS

Horizontally staggered repeat

Half-drop repeat

Knit/purl patterns can be combined in many ways. The coral swatch is a traditional checkerboard of ribs and welts. The lavender swatch at lower left shows the easiest way to combine patterns —arranging them horizontally and dividing them by bands of reverse stockinette. The purple swatch at upper left is a Bavarian pattern combining small knit-two/purl-two blocks with reverse-stockinette ridges in a diagonal arrangement. You could easily change the look of this pattern by widening the ridges or by substituting another pattern for the blocks.

Row gauge, too, should be considered when plotting patterns in vertical panels. Generally speaking, row gauge is an issue only when you're combining flat patterns with more dimensional ones. If one panel has fewer rows in the repeat than its neighbor, the fabric will draw up in this section, which is best to avoid. Sometimes, however, this distortion can be used as a design feature. If you mix the "long" and "short" patterns in checkerboard fashion, for example, the distortion will balance out in the overall fabric.

As with a checkerboard made of a single repeating motif (see the drawings on p. 89), you can vary the arrangement of a checkerboard composed of many different patterns. These fabrics are interesting to design. The checkerboard blocks can be plotted as squares or rectangles, and they can be arranged in a square-grid format, staggered horizontally or positioned in a half-drop repeat. If you select patterns with similar gauges, you'll produce an even surface. If you mix patterns with different gauges or combine a flat pattern with a more dimensional one, the fabric you create may have an interesting, uneven surface. The easiest way to create a block formation is to mix a pattern with a small repeat with a larger

one, allowing the larger repeat to dictate the size of the blocks, as shown in the purple swatch in the photo at left.

Patterns can also be combined in diagonal groupings. Creating diagonal combinations is more complex than designing vertical or horizontal arrangements, but the same principles apply. Two patterns (or more, if you're adventurous) are alternated across the fabric, with both moved consistently one or more stitches over to the left or right every row or every few rows, depending on what looks best. Diagonal movement works best with simple patterns. I would suggest combining seed stitch or one of the smaller block patterns with smooth stockinette. To plan the movement, it's helpful to chart these combinations. Here, as with the checkerboard effect, patterns with different gauges tend to balance each other out in the overall fabric, as you can see in the swatches in the photo above left.

Mixing knit/purl patterns with other fabrics

Knit/purl patterns obviously combine well with each other since they share textural elements, and they also blend nicely with cable and twist-stitch patterns. In addition, they can offer a pleasing contrast when combined with the more substantial of the eyelet and lace patterns (for more on eyelet and lace patterns, see pp. 190-193).

Knit and purl techniques can add texture to colorwork too—more about this in the next chapter. For a change of texture in stranded colorwork pattern, try departing from the usual stockinette stitch and using knit/purl patterns in reverse stockinette or garter stitch. And

USING KNIT/PURL EDGINGS IN MANY WAYS

Narrow edgings

Wide edgings

Tight rib

Loose rib

Different edgings combined in same garment

One dozen miters in the mitered-corner jacket

Curved edges

Trim-less

Edges allowed to curl

when looking for new ways to use garter stitch, don't overlook Barbara Walker's nubby mosaic patterns as possible mates (see *Mosaic Knitting* in the Bibliography on pp. 258-260).

For the ultimate in contrast, mix fabrics worked with novelty yarns with those worked in knit/purl patterns in crisp, smooth yarns. For example, you might edge a fuzzy mohair cardigan with borders of well-defined seed stitch, worked in a crisp yarn. Or try a graphic approach (see pp. 118-128), combining classic knit/purl patterns with areas of shiny, nubby or hairy novelty fabrics.

Edgings & *t*rims

No group of patterns is more useful for trimming and finishing edges than the knit/purl family. An edging, whether narrow or wide, serves to protect the main fabric of a garment, holding it in place and preventing unnecessary stretching. It also draws the eye to the boundaries of a garment and thus becomes an important design feature. A bold edging can enliven

an otherwise nondescript garment, and a small, discreet edging can provide a valuable line of emphasis for an interesting main fabric.

An edging can refine, reinforce or alter a basic silhouette. It can hug the body and draw in the bottom edge, wrist or neck of a garment; or it can be worked the same width as the garment to preserve the silhouette's basic lines. It can also be worked to flare out decoratively, providing three-dimensional contrast to the main fabric.

For a close-fitting, hard-working edging, ribbing reigns as the best choice since it retains its elasticity for a long time. Other less stretchy, flat patterns can also be used.

In order to draw an edge in, the edging pattern generally must be worked with fewer stitches than the garment body. Deciding how many fewer stitches depends on the garment's silhouette and the edging pattern chosen. Since flat fabrics don't stretch like ribbed ones, you will need to calculate differently for each one. If the garment is oversized, you will need far fewer stitches than are used in the body—with ribbing, this could be up to 20% fewer stitches.

These are three of my favorite quiet edgings, barely noticeable, yet useful for stabilizing the edges of a fabric: from left to right, reverse-stockinette-stitch roll, the 'no edging edging' and Elizabeth Zimmermann's I-cord edging.

If the garment is classic and loose-fitting, you may need to decrease the number of body stitches by only 5% to 10% for the edging. If you're designing a close-fitting garment, you may want decrease only a couple of stitches or perhaps work the edging on the same number of stitches as the body—or even add a few—in order to prevent the ribbing from looking too stretched out.

If you want the edging to hang rather than draw in and continue the line established in the garment body, you can take one of two approaches: First, you can work a ribbed edge over extra stitches and/or use a larger needle than you normally would. Second, you can work a flat edging pattern on smaller needles than you would generally use for that pattern and on 5% to 10% fewer stitches than are used in the body. (All flat edgings tend to stretch a bit with wear, so reducing the number of stitches helps ensure that the edge will maintain the line of the silhouette.)

Quiet edgings

There are three particularly "quiet" trims that stabilize the edge of a fabric but do not draw attention to themselves: reverse-stockinette-stitch roll, what I call the "no-edging" edging, and I-cord. These edgings are great for a tailored garment and for de-emphasizing edges and drawing attention to the fabric or garment structure. They are best added after the garment is completed.

The **reverse-stockinette-stitch roll** is produced by knitting a few rows of reverse stockinette, which curl under to form a narrow, rolled edge. Worked on a smaller needle than the main fabric, this trim holds its shape well,

especially in a more elastic yarn, and is a great favorite of mine. To work this edging, pick up stitches along the edge in question, using the same ratio as for the no-edging edging above. Then knit one row, purl one row and bind off in knit on the next row.

The **no-edging edging** is a discreet trim produced by picking up one row of stitches and promptly binding off these stitches on the next row. Sometimes I slightly vary this edging by knitting one row before binding off. I discovered the no-edging edging when making a seed-stitch jacket that needed just a bit of stability to keep the edges from stretching. This is a clean, crisp edging that works best on flat-textured fabrics.

For the average fabric, I generally pick up along a cast-on or bound-off edge, one stitch for every stitch in the edge. Along side edges, I usually pick up three stitches for every four rows, and a few more stitches when the row gauge is tight.

The **I-cord** (or "idiot cord") is another restrained but beautiful edging, which is the invaluable invention of master knitter Elizabeth Zimmermann. This edging, which resembles tubular piping, can be used to join two garment pieces or as decorative edge trim. It can be knitted separately and applied, worked around the edge of a piece or, with a garter-stitch fabric, worked as the fabric is knitted. (For information on making I-cord, see Zimmermann's *Knitter's Almanac* in the Bibliography on pp. 258-260. See also p. 232 for a discussion of bias binding and picot as edgings.)

Bolder trims

In addition to 3-D ribbed, ruffled and pleated edges, many flat knit/purl patterns —like folded-back stockinette, garter stitch, seed stitch, moss stitch, and small block patterns—can be used for a substantial edging. Ribbed edgings make the garment warmer and longer-wearing, but all add an interesting design detail.

Whether narrow or wide, flat knit/purl edges generally retain their firmness for a long time. Almost all of these trims can be knitted in at the lower edges as the garment is worked. Although it's more work to add these trims later, you can sometimes achieve a firmer, more tailored look by picking up stitches and working the trim, then binding off on the assembled pieces. You can easily work buttonholes into most of these trims.

Because stockinette stitch curls at the cast-on edge, it is not used often at the edges of a garment. However, a **folded-back stockinette hem** makes a nice, flat, double-thickness edging. To form a flat fold across the width of a stockinette fabric, purl an entire right-side row —or knit a wrong-side row—at the point where you want the fold to occur.

To add hems on cast-on or bound-off edges, with the wrong side of the fabric facing you, pick up one stitch in the back loop of each stitch along the row, then purl the next row and decrease 10% to 15% of the stitches. (If you're knitting with a finer yarn than that used in the main fabric, there's no need to decrease stitches.) Work the hem to the desired length. Then, instead of binding off, sew the edge down stitch by stitch.

Garter stitch produces a thick, noncurling edge, which works well for a chunky border to match a heavy fabric. I like garter-stitch edges best when they're worked in elastic wools. With cottons and synthetics, garter stitch tends to become flaccid. This edging doesn't curl, but it will stretch with wear and flare out. To prevent stretching, use a needle two sizes smaller than that used for the main knitting and 5% to 10% fewer stitches than for the main knitting.

Buttonholes disappear nicely into the ridges of garter trim. And garter can be easily striped by working every other ridge in a contrasting color. When thinking about garter-stitch edging, I always consider a mosaic pattern, which shares the same qualities as garter stitch and incorporates color as well (see p. 182 for mosaic slip-stitch patterns).

Knit/purl patterns can be used to form bold trims at the edges of a garment. Clockwise, from bottom left: a deep ribbing, a flat 2x2 check, garter-stitch bands and a flat knit/purl pattern.

Garter stitch can be knitted in at the beginning of a piece or picked up and added later. When picking up a garter-stitch edging along a garter-stitch fabric, pick up one stitch for every ridge. On a fabric with a less dense row gauge, pick up two of every three rows. When picking up along a bound-off or cast-on edge, I usually pick up four stitches for every five stitches in the body, or just skip one every 1 in. to 1½ in.

Any flat knit/purl pattern can be used as an edging, but the most effective and long-wearing are the small textured ones like **seed, moss and block-pattern edgings.** While they do not stretch like garter stitch, they must be worked densely enough to withstand wear. Thus, for these patterns, use a smaller needle than you would to work the main body and pick up 5% to 10% fewer stitches than in the main knitting, or about four for every five stitches.

Every knitter knows the value of firm **ribbing** at the edges of a garment for stability and elasticity. Ribbed edges will cling, allowing a looser fabric in the garment body to drape. When combined with a yarn that has stretch and memory, ribbing holds its shape better than any other knitted fabric.

Coping with ribbed trouble

If you're unhappy with a knitted-in ribbing after your garment is complete, or if the ribbing is worn or frayed, you can remove it and add new ribbing. To do this, first cut the yarn at the middle of the row immediately above the ribbing or edging. Then unravel the strand, side to side if you're working flat, or round and round if you're working on circular needles, in order to separate the ribbing and body. Slip the loops from the body section onto a separate needle.

You can then knit new ribbing downward on the body stitches and bind them off. However, since a bound-off edge will always be less flexible than a cast-on edge, I prefer to knit a separate ribbing, working in the same direction as the original knitting, and graft the ribbing and the body together. Grafting can be used to join other sections of the garment too and always produces a stretchy, invisible join. If you have a different number of stitches in the ribbing and body, increase or decrease on the last rib row to make them the same before grafting.

I admire the many knitters who graft pieces together with ease, following diagrams. Unfortunately I have always had difficulty translating what I see in a grafting diagram to the work in my hands. I fumbled for years until I ran across a method described in an English-language special edition of the French publication *Mon Tricot* called "Knit and Crochet." For all of you who

share my problem, here is a description that uses knitterly terms and requires you to insert the yarn needle into only one stitch at a time.

Weave in all ends on your pieces so they don't get tangled with the grafting yarn. Arrange the two pieces to be grafted in your lap or on a table, just as they are to be joined, with the right side of the fabrics facing you, and the knitting needles positioned horizontally with the points to the right. With a blunt tapestry needle threaded with a long piece of yarn and beginning at the right edge, take one stitch from each needle alternately as follows:

Step 1: Insert needle purlwise into 1st st on front needle, draw yarn through st, leaving st on needle.

Step 2: Rolling back needle slightly away from you, insert needle knitwise into 1st st on back needle, draw yarn through st, leaving st on needle.

Now repeat the following four steps to join the remaining sts:

Step 1: Insert needle knitwise into 1st st on front needle, draw yarn through and sl st off needle.

Step 2: Insert needle purlwise into new 1st st on front needle, draw yarn through st, leaving st on needle.

Step 3: Insert needle purlwise into first st on back needle, draw yarn through and sl st off needle.

Step 4: Insert needle knitwise into new 1st st on back needle, draw yarn through st, leaving st on needle.

I discovered that my friend Pat Yankee uses this method too. When teaching it to her students, she repeats, "Knit off, purl on [front needle], purl off, knit on [back needle]…" —a useful rhyme that corresponds to the four steps above.

GRAFTING

Use grafting to join two open rows of knit sts with a third row. Once the steps described above are completed, the grafted yarn will look like a stockinette row.

Back needle

Front needle

Most knitters agree that a thick ribbed edge looks much better than one stretched to its limit. Yet I often see ribbings at the lower edges of garment that look skimpy, as if too few stitches were used. I also see ribbed borders on cardigans and necklines that look stretched out, almost as if they had been blocked.

There are several ways to make a ribbing seem luxurious at all the edges of your design. Although some knitters feel it's unnecessary, I think it's a good idea to swatch in the ribbing of your choice, and measure the gauge over the swatch slightly stretched, just as you want it to be on the body. For very elastic ribbing, choose a pattern with small ribs, like a 1x1 or 2x2. For ribbing that encircles the body, consider the garment's silhouette and the wearer's body measurements at the points where the ribbing will fall. Use your gauge swatch to help you decide the proper number of stitches so that the garment will either hang or cling gently, but not tightly, at these points. Also, remember that, if need be, you can run a length of elastic thread at just the top of the ribbing to help it cling to the body.

For ribbing along cardigan openings or other vertical areas, pick up more stitches than you would if using a flat knit/purl edging (say, four stitches for every five rows, or even five for every six rows). You might think this ribbing would tend to flare out along a buttonhole band, but if you bind off firmly, you'll find that it lies flat and looks thick. At the neckline edge, I also pick up more stitches than used in the body along bound-off edges, usually five stitches for every four in the body. If the neckline is close-fitting, I don't bind off too firmly. The edge may flare a little, but I steam the rib slightly (if the fiber can take it) and flatten it with my fingers.

Ribbing can also be worked to twice the desired length and folded to the inside to form a double-thickness trim (see the edge of my kimono-like garment on p. 165). At a neckline, where you need stretch, either bind off very loosely with a larger needle or sew the edging down stitch by stitch. If a folded ribbing is worked on a smallish needle with a springy yarn, it will not flare, but remember that it will be thick. Thus, you may want to knit it over slightly fewer stitches than I've recommended for single-layer ribbing, especially if you are using an inelastic yarn.

Welted patterns can make interesting ridged edgings. Knitted in at the lower edges of a garment, they provide a strong horizontal line, perhaps best suited to a slender figure. For a narrow welted neckline edging with just a few ridges, pick up as you would for a flat edging. A longer edging produces a stovepipe neckline that will tend to fold up like an accordion.

Welting can also be worked separately, then sewn on to resemble a bulky ribbing. I like to use welting this way because I can work the ridges in contrasting colors for a bright effect that resembles corrugated ribbing (see pp. 119-120 for more about color in ribbing).

Three-dimensional edgings flare, ruffle or pleat. They can be dramatic like a Pierrot collar or as discreet as a small bracelet, but, above all, they're fun. These edgings can serve as collars or cuffs or for peplum effects. A narrow ruffle can be very pretty along the buttonhole edge of a cardigan, provided it's not too heavy or wide. If you use pleated patterns at edges, be sure to use enough stitches for a full effect.

The easiest way to create a ruffled edge is to pick up at least twice the number of stitches as you would for a flat edge and use a flat pattern like stockinette or garter stitch to work the edging. Alternatively, you can begin with the same number of stitches, gradually increasing as you knit to flare the edge. Welted patterns, worked in narrow strips, can be gathered along one side and sewn along an edge. Ribbed patterns can be made to flare by working increases in the purl ribs. (See also p. 233 for bias bands, picot-point edgings and other dressmaker trims for edges.)

Joining *Edges* from a designer's point of view

There are various ways to join trims and edgings to a garment, and each creates a different visual effect. Trim can be knitted in as the garment is worked. Stitches can be picked up on a completed garment section and the trim knitted outwards to form an edge. Or trim can be worked separately and sewn in place after the garment body is finished.

I don't want to concern myself here with the how-to's of knitting and joining edges because there are many knitting texts that can provide you with this information (see the Bibliography on pp. 258-260). Instead, I want to point out the visual effect and physical characteristics of

Knit/purl edgings can be knitted in, picked up or sewn on; each method has a different effect. Clockwise, from upper left: a knitted-in invisible hem produces a firm, untrimmed look; a sewn-on ribbed edging creates a horizontal line; a knitted-in ribbing allows for elements of the ribbing to be continued, uninterrupted, into the main fabric; two swatches show the same edging worked in different ways — picking up stitches produce a furrow between the edging and main fabric (lower swatch), and knitting in the edging creates a flat, unbroken line from one pattern to the other.

each method of joining a trim or edging (see the photo above). Once you're familiar with the various effects possible, you can select a method of joining an edging based on the look you hope to achieve. Whatever method you choose, always experiment with joining the edging on your swatch.

When you knit in a trim, you create a smooth transition between the edging and main fabric and produce an edging that's very elastic. Depending upon the number of stitches used for the edging, it can be made to skim the body or cling to it, as it does with ribbing patterns. For an invisible or innocuous edging that will add only firmness to the garment's boundaries, try a knitted-in, folded-back stockinette hem (see p. 93).

When you pick up stitches to work an edging on a completed garment section rather than knitting the edging in, you create a stronger visual break between the edging and main fabric, and also slightly reduce the edging's elasticity. This method produces a small "dent," or channel, between the edging and garment body, especially when worked along a horizontal knitted edge. This small detail can add a tailored touch to a garment.

A sewn-on edge makes the firmest of the three joins and also forms a channel where the two fabrics meet. Sewn-on edges are best for flimsy knits, especially for attaching buttonbands, because the seam lends structure and support to the garment. Sewing is also useful when you want to orient the stitches in an edging in the opposite direction from those in the main fabric — for instance, for a horizontally aligned ribbing placed at the lower edge of a garment. Knit/purl pleated or flared edgings are best sewn on because you can more carefully arrange the gathers than you'd be able to do if you knitted them in.

Varying the width and thickness of edgings is another way to alter their appearance. At times you'll want trim that's small and discreet. (Be sure, however, that this small trim doesn't look skimpy. A very narrow, ½-in.-wide ribbing sewn along an edge should be worked with a generous number of stitches to give it bulk, or it will stretch out and virtually disappear.) At other times, you'll find that a bold, wider-than-average trim is just what's called for on a bold, bulky garment. If you find that a flat trim or ribbing looks flimsy or insignificant, add another layer by doubling the edging's length, folding it at the midpoint and sewing the bound-off edge to the inside.

Trim need not be an afterthought. You can base an entire design on the trim or edging, keeping the main body fabric very simple and the trim the focus.

Edge stitches for seaming and structure

I always add an extra stitch to my garment pieces to make seaming easier. I use a garter-stitch edge for a thick seam that will provide structure. For most garments, I work my edge stitches in plain stockinette, which is easy to see and seam into. A stockinette seam stitch adds just a bit of firmness to the seam. For a drapey, flowing garment, I may seam with only a half a stitch (see the drawing on p. 227), creating the most flexible seam. This works well only if your edge stitches are neat looking.

I also take selvage stitches a step further to outline my seams. I often keep two stitches in stockinette at each edge, then sew or pick up between these two easy-to-see stitches. The resulting edge or seam is outlined on the right side in smooth stockinette.

Decorative increasing and decreasing

If you're an experienced knitter, you're no doubt familiar with the characteristic appearance of various increases and decreases. If you're not, it's a good idea to get acquainted with them and make use of them for design details. For instance, the knit-two-together decrease (k2tog), leans to the right, and its mirror image slip-slip-knit decrease (SSK or sl1-k1-psso) leans to the left. Similarly, double decreases can lean either to the right or left, or be worked so that the center stitch stands straight up and down. Each of the common increases likewise has a distinctive look. The simple "knit into the front and back of the same stitch" creates a dot or bump of texture. The familiar "make-one" (M1), worked by lifting the connecting strand between two stitches and knitting into the back of it, forms a nearly invisible increase. For more information on these shaping elements and detailed drawings of them, look at Mary Thomas's *Book of Knitting Patterns* (see the Bibliography on pp. 258-260).

Wherever I need to use shaping elements, I ask myself which one will contribute the most visually to the design or best merge with the patterns. In a garment with interesting structure or one with a very plain fabric, the more obvious shaping elements will draw attention to the seam itself and add detail. In either case, I work my increases or decreases two to three stitches away from the edge, keeping a band of stitches in plain stockinette at that edge. This type of shaping, called full-fashioned, creates a visible line of increases or decreases that can serve as a design detail, which is often seen on

Edge stitches make seaming easier and can serve as decorative outlines. Increases and decreases can also be decorative accents. From top to bottom, these swatches show different shaping elements worked next to edge stitches: the textured p2tog-decrease and the knit-into-front-and-back-of-stitch increase resemble each other; increases and decreases worked into the pattern create a smooth line along the edge stitches; the k2tog decrease and M1 increase form subtle, decorative lines at the edges of stockinette; stockinette edge stitches on a reverse-stockinette fabric make seaming easier.

An interesting corner treatment can lend a great detail to a knitted garment. Clockwise, from upper left: a mitered V-neck worked with eyelet ribbing; two different ribbings separated by a crisp miter; a mitered ridge edging; and a double-thickness edging with a generous number of stitches picked up around the corner.

both hand-knitted and machine-knitted stockinette sweaters. For a smooth outline, I choose a decrease that leans in the same direction as the edge. For a more textured line, I slant the decreases away from the edge.

With a busy fabric, it's best to keep the shaping elements invisible. In this case, I work them at the very edge so they're hidden in my seam.

Corner treaments

Corners are a wonderful place to add detail, whether they're on an inside edge (as on a square or V-neckline) or outside edge (as on cardigan fronts, side slits, pocket flaps and the pointed edges of many collars). There are several ways of handling corners, from simply butting edges together where they meet, to overlapping edges, to mitering.

The most visually interesting treatment for a corner is to miter it, which gives it a crisp, tailored look. The diagonal line at the center of the miter can be variously handled. To help me decide what shaping elements to use in a mitered corner, I often refer to the main fabric. If the pattern has broad lines, I might create a bold two-stitch or three-stitch center line in the miter, working the increase or decrease shaping elements to either side of the line. To match a pattern with finer lines, like a twist-stitch pat-

tern, I might use a single-stitch line centrally placed in the miter. And to coordinate a miter with lace patterns, I try to use eyelets as shaping elements.

By eliminating a central stitch or stitches at the miter and working the increases or decreases right next to each other, you can make a small dent at the center of the miter instead of a raised line. Although only one kind of trim is generally used around an edge, I sometimes divide the area in half and use two contrasting patterns along the same edge. For instance, on one side I might work seed stitch and on the other side, moss stitch. Or I might work two different ribbings. For additional design detail, I often plan these patterns to meet where a miter is to be worked.

I am fond of double-thickness edgings with mitered corners, which always look special and are fun to knit. To work a double-thickness miter, knit the first half of the miter as usual. Then work the miter in reverse, starting from this halfway mark. This mirror edging is turned to the inside and produces a perfectly pointed corner.

To produce a sportier, less tailored look, you can overlap two edges where they meet at a corner. This treatment works best at inner corners where the extra thickness of double layers is confined and held in place. At outer corners, this treatment tends to be rather bulky and may cause the edge to bulge outward. If you want to use an overlapped corner, consider overlapping trims of different colors.

The most common and least distinctive way of handling a corner is to butt two edges together where they meet. This approach is good if a miter would be troublesome to work or if you want to avoid the extra thickness of an overlapped edge. A butted corner can be made more interesting by having the edges that meet be worked in different patterns.

Swatch project & *designer* notebook

Only swatching will tell you if you've made the right yarn and needle choice, and if patterns you want to combine will form a harmonious whole. When I think my garment might have a pocket, I work my swatch at least 6 in. square so that it can eventually be used for this purpose. Making a swatch at least this size is necessary anyway when you're combining several patterns in order to see clearly each pattern being tested. This is how I began to design the sweaters for the Designer Notebook in this chapter (see the photo on p. 101).

While swatching in basic knit and purl, I wanted to concentrate on designing just the pockets themselves, saving my thoughts about possible garments until I was happy with the fabric. Focusing on creating an interesting small piece of fabric often enables me to come up with details that would otherwise elude me if I were thinking about the whole garment.

When I began testing yarns and needle size, I challenged myself to both design new patterns and combine some familiar ones. I also wanted to work out some interesting edgings. Much to my surprise, I even found myself incorporating some shaping methods in the swatches. In all of them, I included a selvage stitch, worked in stockinette so that it wouldn't add bulk when seamed and would allow the pocket to lie flat.

My first small pocket combined simple vertical panels, worked in a smooth, greyish taupe, worsted-weight wool/cotton blend. I flanked the larger textured chevron panels with ladders of crisply twisted lines and garter ridges. I continued the ladders into the twisted 1x1 ribbing that edged the swatch. Since this yarn nicely highlighted the knit/purl texture, I decided to work another swatch with it in a rose color.

I sensed that seed stitch, my favorite, would work well for the second swatch. But rather than use it as an allover fabric, I charted it in a zigzag formation that had the same stitch multiple as the pattern in my first swatch. I repeated the zigzag until the pocket seemed about the right size, then edged it in reverse-stockinette ridges.

I wanted a ribbed fabric for my third pocket. To keep weight to a minimum with a rather heavy pumpkin-colored cotton, I wanted a flat ribbed pattern rather than a 3-D one. I worked a 2x4 rib (two-stitch knit ribs alternating with four-stitch purl ribs), hoping that the larger

Each of these Swatch Projects can serve double duty — first, as a test of gauge, pattern and edging, and, second, as a pocket for a garment it inspires. The taupe and rose swatches, worked in flat knit/purl patterns, prompted the design of the sweaters in the photo on p. 101. The aqua and pumpkin swatches may one day inspire other sweaters.

purl ribs would flatten the fabric. I broke the ribbing with two horizontal bands of diagonal lines, which further flattened it. In keeping with these diagonal lines, I bound off the top of the pocket gradually to create an angle. The pocket's edges seems a bit flimsy, so I picked up and worked a narrow mitered edging on three sides. Finally, I knitted a separate, skinny band of ribbing and then sewed it along the shaped upper edge.

Next, I wanted to try a 3-D pattern to make a pouch-like pocket that would flare at the lower edge and be gathered at the top. After working a knit/purl pleated pattern in a fine-gauge aqua wool/rayon blend to a depth that looked right for a pocket, I decreased about 10% of the stitches along a final knit row to draw in the fabric evenly. I bound off, then added a flat

The guernsey's most obvious characteristic is its deep yoke decorated with knit/purl patterns. Often the balance of the garment was worked in plain stockinette with tightly ribbed edges. Knitted circularly, the classic guernsey is close-fitting, with a dropped-shoulder sleeve and often a knitted-in underarm gusset to provide extra ease of movement. It usually has a little stand-up collar, too short to be a full turtleneck but tall enough to be close-fitting and provide some warmth for the neck.

For my sweaters, I decided to exaggerate the guernsey silhouette to slightly oversized proportion to accentuate the drape of my soft fabric. I kept the simple dropped shoulder because I could envision my zigzag border fitting in well at the top of the sleeves. I designed the short version first, choosing to interrupt the zigzag-patterned yoke with buttoned edges. For detail, I ribbed one front band and worked the other in seed stitch. Below the yoke and at the sides of the sleeves, my chevron and ladder pattern didn't fit evenly into my desired width, so I added a flat ribbed pattern at either side formed of single twisted stitches on reverse stockinette. The ribbing, like that on the pocket, incorporates the little ladder pattern for detail.

For a smock version of the sweater, I exaggerated the length, eliminated the close-fitting ribbed edges and added slits at the lower sides. To finish the edges, I used a roll of reverse stockinette for stability, knitted in on the sleeves and picked up at the lower body edge and side slits. To fill in the extra space at the sides of the chevron and ladder pattern, I used flat seed stitch—and I got to use my medium-sized pocket.

The guernsey provides a beginning designer with a simple and interesting format within which to work. (After swatching, you can use your schematic drawing as a kind of sketch, as I did, drawing in your pattern and details to create your own original guernsey.) In fact, no matter how many I make, I never tire of designing guernseys. There is really no end to the way you can combine patterns in the traditional yoke. Once in a while I like to stray from the classic silhouette and try something new, as I did in the smock sweater. A cotton/wool blend might not suit a fisherman's needs, but it will serve me well through every season of the year.

My schematic served to record measurements in my Designer Notebook and doubled as a sketch for this smock, inspired by traditional fisherman's guernsey sweaters. (Inset photo, courtesy of the Scottish Fisheries Museum Trust Ltd.)

garter-stitch edging for firmness at the upper edge. The sides of this pocket would have to be sewn at an angle to keep the pouch shape.

After working this group of pockets, I thought about how each could inspire a garment based on the elements within it, and I did some rough sketches. The first group of pockets reminded me of the classic knit/purl garment, the guernsey, and I decided to combine the patterns from both swatches to design two different guernsey-inspired sweaters.

Fisherman's guernseys (or gansies) from the British Isles are functional and good-looking. Designed for utility, the original guernsey was shaped simply for ease of movement and was tightly knit in warm, fine-gauge wool.

Instructions for guernsey variations

This placket-front pullover and hip-length smock have a slightly oversized fit. For the intermediate knitter.

SIZE
To fit 32 (34-36, 38-40, 42-44, 46-48, 50-52)-in. bust/chest.

FINISHED MEASUREMENTS (AFTER SEAMING)
Finished bust/chest at underarm, both: 36½ (40½, 42, 46, 50, 55½) in.
Pullover length: 24½ (24½, 25½, 25½, 26, 26) in.
Smock length: 27 (27, 28, 28, 29, 29) in.
Sleeve width at upper arm, both: 18 (19, 20, 21, 22, 22½) in.

MATERIALS
Both guernseys are knit with "Cambridge" from Classic Elite, a blend of 70% cotton and 30% wool; 1¾ oz = approx 85 yd. If you substitute another yarn, choose one with a similar yardage that will obtain same gauge.

Pullover
- 17 (18, 20, 22, 23, 25) skeins "Cambridge" in Pebble #3945.
- Knitting needles sizes 5 and 7, or size to obtain gauge.
- 6 buttons, ¾ in. wide.

Smock
- 18 (19, 21, 23, 24, 26) skeins "Cambridge" in Dark Rose #3962.
- Knitting needles sizes 5 and 7 or size to obtain gauge.
- Two circular knitting needles size 5, 16 in. and 24 in. long.
- 1 button, ¾ in. wide.

GAUGE
- 20 sts and 31 rows equal 4 in. with size 7 needles over chevron and zigzag pats.
- To save time later, knit a swatch pocket and check your gauge.

PATTERNS
Read all charts from right to left on RS rows, and from left to right on WS rows. Arrows indicate beg and end for each section and size.

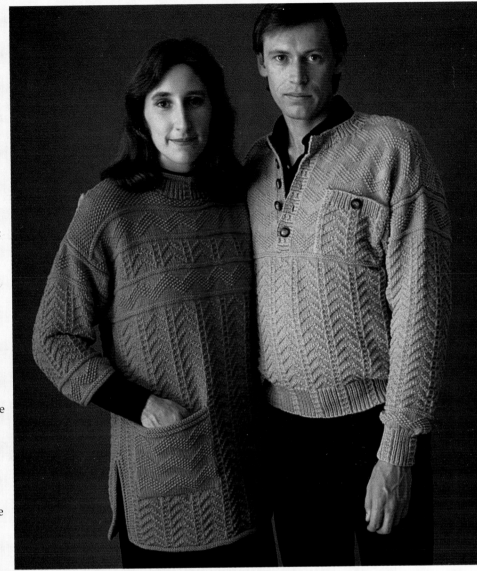

SWATCH POCKETS
Pullover
With larger needle, cast on 32 sts. Keep 1 st each end in St st, work rows 1-6 of chevron pat 5 times. Change to smaller needle.
Next row (RS): k1, {work as est over 4 sts, work 1x1 rib over 9 sts} twice, work as est over 4 sts, end k1. Work even for ¾ in. Bind off.

Smock
With larger needle, cast on 35 sts. P 1 row, k 1 row, p 1 row. Keep 1 st each end in St st, work 3 reps of zigzag pat. Work rows 3-8 of ridge pat. Bind off.

PLACKET-FRONT PULLOVER

BACK
With smaller needle, cast on 87 (95, 99, 107, 115, 127) sts.
Next row (WS): Work 1x1 rib over 9 (13, 15, 19, 23, 29) sts, {work ladder over 4 sts, work 1x1 rib over 9 sts} 5 times, work ladder over 4 sts, work 1x1 rib over rem 9 (13, 15, 19, 23, 29) sts. When rib measures 3 in., end with a RS row. P next row, inc 3 (4, 4, 5, 6, 7) sts evenly spaced BEFORE first ladder, then inc 3 (4, 4, 5, 6, 7) sts evenly spaced AFTER last ladder—93 (103, 107, 117, 127, 141) sts. Change to larger needle.

GUERNSEY VARIATIONS

Smock schematic

7 (7½, 7½, 7¾, 8¼, 8½) in.

2 in.

1 square = 1 in.

9½ in.

17½ (17½, 18½, 18½, 19½, 19½) in.

8 in.

27 (27, 28, 28, 29, 29) in.

18¼ (20¼, 21, 23, 25, 27¾) in.

Smock sleeve

18 (19, 20, 21, 22, 22½) in.

3 in.

10½ (10½, 11, 11, 12, 12) in.

13½ (13½, 14, 14, 15, 15) in.

10½ (11, 11½, 11½, 11¾, 12) in.

Pullover schematic

7 (7½, 7½, 7¾, 8¼, 8½) in.

3 in.

8½ in.

10, (10, 11, 11, 11½, 11½) in.

3 in.

24¼ (24¼, 25½, 25½, 26, 26) in.

18¼ (20¼, 21, 23, 25, 27¾) in.

Pullover sleeve

18 (19, 20, 21, 22, 22½) in.

3 in.

14¾ (14¾, 15½, 15½, 16½, 16½) in.

20¾ (20¾, 21½, 21½, 22½, 22½) in.

3 in.

10½ (11, 11½, 11½, 11¾, 12) in.

Next row (RS): k2 (edge); then, to set up twisted rib, p 5 (5, 2, 4, 4, 3) sts, {k1-b, p4} 1 (2, 3, 1, 2, 1) times; work chevron pat over center 69 (69, 69, 95, 95, 121) sts; then, to set up twisted rib, {p4, k1-b} 1 (2, 3, 1, 2, 1) times, p 5 (5, 2, 4, 4, 3) sts; end k2 (edge). Keep edge sts in St st, work in pats until 12 (12, 13, 13, 14, 14) reps of chevron pat are complete. Work rows 3-8 of ridged pat. Piece should measure approx 13 (13, 14, 14, 14½, 14½) in. Lengthen or shorten piece here if desired, not in yoke section.

YOKE

Next row (RS): k2, work zigzag pat over center 89 (99, 103, 113, 123, 137) sts, end k2. Work even until yoke measures 11½ in., end with a WS row. Piece should measure 24½ (24½, 25½, 25½, 26, 26) in.

SHOULDER AND BACK-NECK SHAPING

Mark center 15 (17, 17, 19, 21, 23) sts.
Next row: Bind off 9 (11, 11, 13, 15, 17) sts, work to center sts, join a 2nd ball of yarn and bind off center sts, work to end. Working both sides at same time with separate balls of yarn, bind off 9 (11, 11,

13, 15, 17) sts from next shoulder edge, then 10 (11, 12, 13, 14, 16) sts at beg of next 4 shoulder edges; AND, AT SAME TIME, bind off 5 sts from each neck edge twice.

FRONT

Work same as for back to beg of yoke, end with a WS row.

PLACKET OPENING

Mark center 7 sts.
Next row (RS): k2 (edge), beg as for back yoke, work zigzag pat over 39 (44, 46, 51, 56, 63) sts, k2 (edge), join a 2nd ball of yarn and bind off center 7 sts, k2 (edge), cont zigzag pat over 39 (44, 46, 51, 56, 63) sts, end k2 (edge). (Note: beg and end pat as for back.) Working both sides at same time with separate balls of yarn, keep edge sts in St st, work until placket opening measures 8½ in., end with WS row.

NECKLINE SHAPING

Bind off from each neck edge 3 (4, 4, 5, 6, 7) sts once, 2 sts three times, then dec 1 st every RS row 5 times— 29 (33, 35, 39, 43, 49) sts. When front measures same as back to shoulder, end with WS row.

SHOULDER SHAPING

Bind off from each shoulder 9 (11, 11, 13, 15, 17) sts once, then 10 (11, 12, 13, 14, 16) sts twice.

SLEEVE

With smaller needle, cast on 43 (43, 47, 47, 51, 51) sts.
Next row (WS): Work 1x1 rib over 13 (13, 15, 15, 17, 17) sts, work ladder over 4 sts, work 1x1 rib over 9 sts, work ladder over 4 sts, work 1x1 rib over 13 (13, 15, 15, 17, 17) sts. When rib measures 3 in., end with a RS row. P next row, inc 12 (14, 12, 12, 10, 12) sts evenly—55 (57, 59, 59, 61, 63) sts. Change to larger needle.
Next row (RS): k2 (edge), work zigzag pat over 51 (53, 55, 55, 57, 59) sts, end k2 (edge). Keep edge sts in St st, work in pat for 1 more row.

Next row, inc row (RS): k2, M1, work to last 2 sts, M1, end k2. Rep inc row after 5 more rows, then every 6th row after for a total of 19 (20, 22, 24, 18, 18) incs each side, then every 4th row after 0 (0, 0, 0, 8, 8) more times—93 (97, 103, 107, 113, 115) sts; AND, AT SAME TIME, cont until 14 rows of zigzag are complete. Work rows 1-4 of ridged pat (3 incs have been worked at each side)—61 (63, 65, 65, 67, 69) sts.

Next row (RS): k2; then, to set up twisted rib, p2 (3, 4, 4, 0, 1), {k1-b, p4} 1 (1, 1, 1, 2, 2) times; work chevron pat over 43 sts; then, to set up twisted rib, {p4, k1-b} 1 (1, 1, 1, 2, 2) times, p 2 (3, 4, 4, 0, 1), end k2. Cont as est, work incs into twisted rib, until 16 (16, 17, 17, 18, 18) reps of chevron pat are complete. Piece should measure approx 17¾ (17¾, 18½, 18½, 19½, 19½) in. Lengthen or shorten here if desired: rem pats will add approx 3 in. Work rows 3-8 of ridge pat.

Next row (RS): k2, work in zigzag pat to last 2 sts, centering pat if desired, end k2. (Note: if you are not centering, beg pat at any point on chart before 12-st rep.) Cont until 14 rows of pat are complete. Work rows 1-4 of ridged pat. Bind off.

FINISHING

Center and sew pocket on left front, above yoke ridge. Sew button on pocket edge if desired. Sew front to back at shoulders.

Neckline rib

With RS facing and smaller needle, pick up 88 (92, 92, 96, 100, 104) sts around entire neck edge.

Next row (WS): Work 1x1 rib over 3 (5, 5, 7, 9, 11) sts, {work ladder over 4 sts, work 1x1 rib over 9 sts} 6 times, work ladder over 4 sts, work 1x1 rib over 3 (5, 5, 7, 9, 11) sts. When rib measures 1½ in., bind off.

Right-front button band (work at left for woman)

With RS facing and smaller needle, pick up 54 sts along edge. Work in seed st for 1¾ in. Bind off. Sew 5 buttons evenly spaced.

Left-front buttonhole band (work at right for woman)

With RS facing and smaller needle, pick up 71 sts along edge.

GUERNSEY PATTERN CHARTS

Chevron pat

Twisted-rib pat

1x1 rib (worked over an odd number of sts)

Ridge pat (worked over any number of sts)

Seed st (worked over an odd or even number of sts)

Ladder pat

Zigzag pat

Note: Read odd-numbered RS rows from right to left, and even-numbered WS rows from left to right; beg and end each section with st indicated by arrow.

Key to sizes
To fit: 32 (34-36, 38-40, 42-44, 46-48, 50-52)-in. bust/chest
Size #: ①(②, ③, ④, ⑤, ⑥)

Symbols

☐ = k RS, p WS
⊟ = p RS, k WS
Ⅴ = knit into back of st on RS rows; purl into back of st on WS rows

Next row (WS): p2, work 1x1 rib over 3 sts, {work ladder over 4 sts, work 1x1 rib over 9 sts} 5 times, end p1. Work 4 rows, then on next row work 4-st buttonhole opposite each button. When band measures 1¾ in., bind off.

Place markers 10½ (11, 11½, 11½, 11¾, 12) in. down from each shoulder seam on front and back. Pin sleeve tops between markers, centering at shoulder. Sew in place. Sew sleeve and side seams.

SMOCK

BACK

With larger needle, cast on 91 (101, 105, 115, 125, 139) sts. P 1 row.

Next row (RS): Work seed st over 11 (16, 5, 10, 15, 9) sts, work chevron pat over 69 (69, 95, 95, 95, 121) sts, work seed st over 11 (16, 5, 10, 15, 9) sts. Work until piece measures 8 in., end with WS row.

Next row, inc row (RS): k1, M1, work to last st, M1, end k1 — 93 (103, 107, 117, 127, 141) sts. Mark each end of row.

Next row: p2, work to last 2 sts, work incs into seed st, end p2. Work even until 24 (24, 25, 25, 26, 26) reps of chevron pat are complete. Piece should measure approx 17½ (17½, 18½, 19½, 19½) in. Lengthen or shorten here if desired, not in yoke section.

YOKE

Work rows 3-8 of ridge pat.

Next row (RS): k2, work in zigzag pat over 89 (99, 103, 113, 123, 137) sts, end k2. Work until 14 rows of pat are complete. Work rows 1-4 of ridged pat.

Next row (RS): k2, p 10 (15, 4, 9, 14, 8) sts in rev St st, work chevron pat over 69 (69, 95, 95, 95, 121) sts, p 10 (15, 4, 9, 14, 8) sts in rev St st, end k2. Work until 2 reps of chevron pat are completed. Work rows 3-8 of ridge pat.

Next row (RS): k2, work in zigzag pat to last 2 sts, end k2. Work until 14 rows of pat are complete. Work rows 1-4 of ridge pat.

Next row (RS): k2, work seed to last 2 sts, end k2. When yoke measures 9½ in., end with WS row. Piece should measure 27 (27, 28, 28, 29, 29) in., unless lower portion was lengthened or shortened.

SHOULDER AND BACK-NECK SHAPING

Work same as for back of pullover.

FRONT

Work same as for smock back until yoke measures 7½ in., end with WS.

NECKLINE SHAPING

Mark center 15 (17, 17, 19, 15, 17) sts.

Next row (RS): Work to center sts, join a 2nd ball of yarn and bind off center sts, work to end. Working both sides at same time with separate balls of yarn, bind off from each neck edge 3 sts 1 (1, 1, 1, 2, 2) times, 2 sts once, then dec 1 st every RS row 5 times. When front measures same as back to shoulder, end with a WS row.

SHOULDER SHAPING

Work same as for front of pullover.

SLEEVE

With smaller needle, cast on 49 (51, 53, 53, 55, 57) sts. Work rows 1-8 of ridge pat, inc 6 sts evenly spaced on last WS row — 55 (57, 59, 59, 61, 63) sts. Change to larger needle.

Next row (RS): k2 (edge), work zigzag pat over 51 (53, 55, 55, 57, 59) sts, k2 (edge). Keep edge sts in St st, work WS row.

Next row, inc row (RS): k2, M1, work in pat to last 2 sts, M1, end k2. Rep inc row after 3 more rows, then every 4th row after for a total of 19 (20, 22, 24, 26, 26) incs each side — 93 (97, 103, 107, 113, 115) sts AND, AT SAME TIME, cont until 14 rows of pat are complete. Work rows 1-4 of ridge pat (4 incs each side have been worked) — 63 (65, 67, 67, 69, 71) sts.

Next row (RS): k2, M1; then, to set up twisted-rib pat, p 3 (4, 0, 0, 1, 2) sts, {k1-b, p4} 1 (1, 2, 2, 2, 2) times; work in chevron pat over center 43 sts; then, to set up twisted-rib pat, {p4, k1-b} 1 (1, 2, 2, 2, 2) times, p 3 (4, 0, 0, 1, 2) sts; M1, k2 — 65 (67, 69, 69, 71, 73) sts.

Cont as est, work incs into twisted-rib pat until 9 (9, 10, 10, 11, 11) reps of chevron pat are complete. Piece should measure approx 10½ (10½, 11, 11, 12, 12) in. Lengthen or shorten here: rem pats will add approx 3 in. Work rows 3-8 of ridge pat — 93 (97, 103, 107, 113, 115) sts.

Next row (RS): k2, work in zigzag pat over to last sts centering pat if desired, end k2. (Note: if you are not centering, beg pat at any point on chart before 12-st rep.) Cont until 14 rows of pat are complete. Work rows 1-4 of ridged pat. Bind off.

FINISHING

Sew pocket on lower right front.

Front lower edge trim

With RS facing and shorter circular needle, beg at side marker, pick up 31 sts to corner, pick up 1 st in corner, pick up 1 st for every cast on st along lower edge, pick up 1 st in corner, pick up 31 sts to marker. K 1 row, p 1 row, bind off in k on last row, and, AT SAME TIME, inc 1 before and after corner sts on WS rows. Rep on back. Sew front to back at shoulders.

Neckline rib

With RS facing and shorter circular needle, beg at center back neck, pick up 92 (96, 96, 100, 104, 108) sts around entire neck edge to beg, then cast on 7 sts.

Next row (WS): Work 7 sts in seed st, place marker, work 1x1 rib over 5 (7, 7, 9, 11, 13) sts, {work ladder over 4 sts, work 1x1 rib over 9 sts} 6 times, work ladder over 4 sts, work 1x1 rib over 5 (7, 7, 9, 11, 13) sts. When rib measures 1 in., end with a WS row.

Next row (RS): Rib 3, make 4-st buttonhole, work to end. When edge measures 2 in., end with a WS row.

Next row (RS): Attach short length of yarn at center back, pick up 11 sts along side of rib, pick up 1 st in corner, then, with rib yarn k to end, AND, AT SAME TIME, dec 10 sts evenly spaced along ribbed edge, pick up 1 st in corner, pick up 11 sts along side of seed st section. K 1 row, p 1 row, bind off in k on last row, AND, AT SAME TIME, inc 1 st before and after corner sts on WS rows. Sew button opposite buttonhole. Place markers 10½ (11, 11½, 11½, 11¾, 12) in. down from each shoulder seam on front and back. Pin sleeve tops between markers, centering at shoulder. Sew in place. Sew sleeve seams. Sew side seams above trim.

5 Color & Graphics

Color is perhaps the most exciting design element of all. When I see a wonderful color or combination of colors, I respond strongly to it. Bright, vibrant colors make me exuberant. Unusual mixtures excite me. And muted or softly blended shades soothe and relax me. As a designer, I use color to express all these moods and lend character to a garment.

But although color is exciting, it's also difficult to work with, and the mystique it has acquired makes many would-be designers shy away from it. Unfortunately, first attempts at working with color are often discouraging. Combinations frequently don't work the way you intend them to. Sometimes they'll simply not please your eye. One color may prove too strong and overpower the others. Or a color with lots of punch in the skein will mysteriously fade when knitted with others.

Some people—myself included—work intuitively with color. Others proceed more intellectually, relying on the color wheel and theories about color harmony (see the sidebar on

p. 108). Both approaches have merit, but in either case the only way to really learn about color is to practice and experiment with it.

In the simplest terms, working with color means making choices about which colors are compatible and which enhance or detract from one another and the overall design. There are no right or wrong choices about color combinations because color harmony is very subjective. What delights my eye may strike you as hideous. As with any other area of design, you must test your ideas by swatching and then assess the results.

Start learning about color in general by keeping your eyes open for intriguing combinations in magazines, books and movies; in clothes you see on the street; and even in your own wardrobe. As an exercise, go to your clothes closet and take out all the printed textiles. Note the color combinations they contain, the accent colors and so on. What makes these combinations effective—or ineffective? In each print, which color predominates, which one recedes? Once you've really studied these fabrics, sit

Facing page:
Detail of pullover
seen in full on
p. 137.

down with a few magazines. Don't look at the subject matter, only the use of color. Clip out several small paper "swatches" of color combinations and look carefully at them. Look for groupings of colors that contrast and others that blend together. Look for various color schemes—soft pastel shades, bright groupings and dark combinations. The idea is to sharpen your eye and to get into the habit of actually or mentally clipping swatches you like, wherever you find them, for future reference.

Color wheel

The color wheel is a graphic device used to show how different colors are related to one another. The wheel is based on the three primary colors (which are the broadest bands of colors the eye can see in the visible spectrum): red, blue and yellow. Mixing these colors in pairs results in the three secondary colors: purple (red + blue), green (blue + yellow), and orange (red + yellow). Together, these six colors complete the traditional color wheel.

I've never used the color wheel to help me design because I've preferred my own meandering, emotional, experimental approach. Recently, however, because of an interest in color drawing, I've read more about color theory and hope to explore it in the future to see how it relates to mixing yarns in knitting.

From my reading, however, I realize that several points in color theory have proven true in my own design work. First, the colors opposite each other on the traditional color wheel—red and green, yellow and purple, and blue and orange—which are known as complements, can be relied upon to produce a successful combination that pleases the eye. Thus, if you're at a loss for a palette, try one of these basic pairs to help you begin to set up a color scheme.

Alternatively, try starting with any three adjacent colors on the wheel, which, because they're related, tend to form pleasing a combination. For example, try red, orange and yellow; or yellow, green and blue; or blue, purple and red; and so on.

In color theory, white is the combination of all three primary colors, and black is the absence of color. Black and white form the ultimate in contrast and are therefore very striking when used together. To carry this a bit further, when you add white to a color, you lighten it. When you add black, you darken it. I've found that using two lightened colors together, or two darkened colors, creates a neutral combination, provided the colors have a similar visual weight to start with and are lightened or darkened to the same degree. For example, a pale pastel blue next to a pale yellow is very neutral. These two shades alone might be too bland for a whole garment, but they might create a successful background for another bright or dark color, or, conversely, work nicely as blended pattern colors set against a dark background. (For more information about the color wheel and traditional color theory, see the Bibliography on pp. 258-260.)

COLOR WHEEL

This color wheel shows the three primary colors (red, blue and yellow) at center, the three secondary colors (purple, green and orange) produced when two primaries are combined, and all the colors lightened, and, at the outer rim of the wheel, darkened.

As you start experimenting, you'll find that color behaves differently in a knitted fabric than when printed on the flat surface of a paint chip or magazine page. Because yarn is three-dimensional and has texture, it has a depth of color that's absent in the same color printed on a flat surface. Yarn knitted into a fabric produces small recesses between stitches that cast shadows and cause the yarn's overall color to appear deeper than it is in the skein. If the yarn is worked in dimensional patterns, stitches raised above the surface of the fabric are likely to appear lighter in color than those that recede into the "background" fabric. And if the yarn has a shiny surface, like that of mercerized cotton, it will reflect light and cause the overall color of the knitted fabric to appear lighter than it is in the skein. Remember, too, that dark colors may totally obscure a textured pattern. When combining different colors and yarns, all these elements combine to create often unforeseeable results.

As a knitwear designer, one of my biggest frustrations has been the limited range of yarn colors available in certain weights of yarn. Although it may seem that there's a huge yarn palette to choose from, in fact, the range of color within a single kind or weight of yarn is often quite limited. In order to experiment, you must build a large palette of yarns in different weights so that you really have some choice about color, rather than being dependent on what the local yarn store has available at a given moment. I suggest developing a network of color sources, both local and mail-order. Also learn to adapt tapestry and embroidery yarns for knitting to enlarge your range of colors. And when a knitting friend finishes a project using a wonderful color, ask for a leftover ball.

In addition to buying commercially dyed yarns, you might also consider dyeing your own yarns. When I first began to knit, I explored natural dyes and devised a wonderful palette. The first leaves of sumac in the spring gave a yellowy green, and summer leaves a more greyish gold. I mailed away for tiny, dried cochineal bugs, which yielded a rich madder red. The restaurant where I worked saved onion skins for me, which offered up several skeins of rich orange-gold. These natural shades always seemed to work well together, but often they were not colorfast and would fade. Chemical dyes produce more reliable colors, but using them can be difficult and dangerous if you don't know the safety rules. Re-search this area thoroughly before you begin working with commercial dyes (see the Bibliography on pp. 258-260).

Another way to get unusual colors is to knit with strands of different colors held together. For an equal mixture, use strands of equal weight. For a minute touch of color, like a fleck in the knitting, hold a strand or two of colored sewing thread or a fine knitting yarn together with your main color (you can also use a fine yarn called a "mixer" to add a fleck of color or texture, which adds only negligible weight to the main yarn and does not affect your gauge). For a soft, blended effect, choose colors that are similar. For a bolder, variegated look, combine colors that contrast or are similarly bright.

My approach to Color

For me, learning about color has been a long, slow process, which I expect to continue indefinitely. My early involvement with color was based on intuitive decisions and personal likes and dislikes. I began by designing with a single solid color or with the stark contrast of black and white. I went on to design with colors that shared obvious similarities—that is, shades of the same color or neutral, natural tones. With these experiments under my belt, I finally explored more complex combinations. I tried a somber shade with a bright, balanced a bright with another bright and tried mixing pairs of odd, sophisticated shades. After working with two colors, I moved on to larger groups. I used a solid color with several shades of the same color for a varied background—or sometimes used a solid background and blended various shades for the pattern.

From this lengthy process, I've learned some guidelines for working with color in knitted fabrics. First, it's useful to become familiar with some of the general properties of color (see the photo on p. 110). To begin with, colors can be pure, that is, vivid and clear, neither lightened by the addition of white nor darkened by the addition of grey or black. A pure color that's lightened, or whitened, generally softens and pales. A pure color that's greyed or darkened takes on a more somber, reserved quality.

Color also has what's referred to as temperature. It can be cool, that is, contain some blue in its makeup, or it can be warm and contain some red or even yellow. Usually cool colors in yarns work well with other cools, and warms

When using color, be aware of several basic principles. A color can be a pure shade or lightened, greyed or darkened (blue swatches, upper left). Colors have temperature, that is, they can be a cool or warm hue (blue swatches, lower left). Colors contrast when used in large areas and tend to blur in small patterns (red and purple swatches, upper right). And a color is affected by the other color or colors surrounding it (swatches, lower right).

mix nicely with other warms. Generally speaking, when cool and warm colors are used together in a pattern, the cools visually recede and warm colors advance and predominate. I rely heavily on touches of warm color to enliven many combinations, even those that are primarily cool.

It's important to keep in mind that colors used in combination influence one another significantly. That is to say, placing one color alongside another can change the way the eye perceives the first color. For example, a sky blue takes on a lavender hue when placed next to red and will likely appear greenish-blue when seated alongside yellow. If other colors are introduced into these combinations, they, too, will have an influence on the original colors (see the sidebar on the facing page).

Colors can have very different effects, depending on how they are used. If you juxtapose large areas of color, each color tends to retain its individuality. However, if the same colors are combined in a small allover pattern, they are likely to blur into a single color.

In most color combinations there is a pattern color and a background color (see the photo on p. 112). You can achieve a range of different effects with your choice of colors for these two areas. You can strive for strong contrast between pattern and background, or you can cre-

ate a subtle blending of the two by choosing closely related colors. After familiarizing yourself with these two basic approaches to pattern and background, you can try combining both contrast and blending in the same fabric.

Using contrasting colors for pattern and background usually produces crisp, bold patterning. The simplest way to set up contrast is to mix a dark color with a light one, which is an outgrowth of the relationship between black and white. Also, a dark and a light shade of the same color, like deep maroon and pink, will almost always create a successful contrast. You can also use a dark of one color and a light of another color, like a deep pine green with a pale yellow. And colors that are opposite each other on the color wheel—blue and orange, for example—will often create a strong, if not startling, contrast.

For greater visual interest, you can use multiple pattern colors, making sure that each one contrasts with the background. For example, traditional Scandinavian sweaters derive their success from strong contrast, often featuring several bold colors—like red, blue and black—on a background of white or ivory. Likewise, you can use more than one light worked over a single dark background.

Using pattern and background colors that do not contrast with one another will create a more blended effect, with the distinction between colors muted and perhaps blurred. If you want this effect, choose close shades of the same color, colors of the same visual weight or temperature or those that are close to each other on the color wheel.

You can also blend a group of shades to serve as a contrasting background for a solid pattern color. Alternatively, you could blend both pattern and background colors. Traditional Fair Isle knitting often both contrasts and simultaneously blends color in both background and pattern.

Avoiding a tangle

Swatching for colorwork

The basic fact of colorwork is that color and pattern each have their own identities. Each must be effective alone and yet also work well with the other. For this reason, until you've gained some experience, I suggest starting to explore colorwork by first isolating the issue of color. Later you can add pattern to the exploration.

I always begin color experiments by gathering more colors than I think I'll need, based on how the colors look in the skein. Then I start knitting with only two colors, working stripes, at least four rows each, in a small swatch about 4 in. square. I often aim for contrast rather than similarity when choosing the first two colors. By doing this, I'm immediately setting up a background color and a pattern color. If I find I don't like the first combined pair of colors, I begin again with two new colors and continue the process until I arrive at a pair that pleases me.

If I want to focus on pattern, two colors alone often suffice. Colors that contrast strongly (light versus dark or two complementary colors) will allow the pattern to emerge.

If my accent is on color, rather than pattern — or if I want color and pattern to be given equal play — I'll probably want to add one or more colors to the basic pair. After establishing this pair by swatching, I work a second swatch, setting up another pair of colors that will work with the first. In the second swatch, I often use one color from the first pair. I continue in this way, creating a group of swatches that are all related by shared colors. Then by trying out various combinations of the swatches, I can choose the best colors for my palette.

Another way to experiment with colors for a combination is to work a swatch of simple stripes in as many colors as you want to test. Choose the most neutral color of your palette to act as a divider or background color between stripes — usually the color closest to white or black. When you've worked all the colors, cover up the stripes, one at a time, to check the resulting combination until you find one that pleases you. The uncooperative colors can then be eliminated from your project, and you can check the new combination by swatching in your pattern.

When you've decided upon the colors you want to use, it's a good idea to swatch again, just to be sure, using all of the colors in one swatch. (If you love a particular color but can't seem to get it to work in combination with others, or if it loses something in a group, then put it aside. Plan to use it alone or in combination with white or black for a later project.)

Even after I've assembled a group of colors I like, they may not produce the pattern swatch I'm looking for — the pattern may look good in those colors but still lack spark. In this case I don't discard the colors and start again, but rather try introducing a new color to add punch to the group. This perky addition might be a plain stripe between repeats, or a few stitches embroidered for accent or simply one pattern row. When I'm working with darks, I like to add a spark of white or a touch of warm yellow or gold. With lights, I try a bright shade of one of the colors, or dramatic black.

Color can be used for pattern and background in several basic ways, the simplest being dark versus light (black and white swatch). More sophisticated high contrast occurs with brights used on a dark color or vice versa (two swatches, lower left). Also successful are a dark and light of the same color (pink swatch), and a dark of one color and light of another (purple and yellow swatch). Background can be shaded for a muted effect while contrasting with a strong pattern color (swatch, upper right), or both pattern and background colors can change and contrast for an electric effect (swatch, lower right).

When blending more than two shades of the same color for the background, arranging them from dark to light, or vice-versa, will produce the most subtle blend. However, if you arrange them in an ungraduated way, with the lightest shade next to a darker one and the other colors arranged around them, the mixture will look choppier. The result is not as classically pleasing, but often creates an offbeat look that is more visually interesting or that may suit a particular design.

Mixing different colors of equal weight can be trickier than blending similar shades or balancing darks against lights because colors of equal weight can compete with one another. For good results, try combining colors that are equally light or equally dark — or, for that matter, equally bright, like lemon yellow, fruity orange and cherry red. You can also work with this approach by choosing colors all greyed to the same degree, which produces sophisticated combinations like mauve, sage green and dusty blue. Whenever you have trouble combining colors of equal weight, it may be necessary to create a bit of contrast by adding a neutral color, a light or dark, or a paler or deeper shade of one or more of the colors.

My *Color groups*

After years of experimentation — during which I didn't always know exactly where I was headed — I've identified manageable groups of colors that work well together for me. I now consider these combinations safe and easy to work with.

To gain confidence about working with color, I suggest starting to experiment with these fairly predictable groups. Then, when you're ready, you can move beyond them to create your own personal palette. As you experiment, you'll find ways of upsetting the safety of these groups and creating some excitement by introducing an unexpected, unrelated color into their midst.

Black and white

Black and white are perhaps the easiest colors to combine (see the photo on the facing page). As opposites, they provide the ultimate in contrast and produce crisp, strong patterns. In fact, I find it very useful to work with black and white because the combination eliminates the struggle for color harmony and enables me to see the patterns themselves more clearly.

Black and white are a perfect combination for either sophisticated or sporty looks. To soften the strong contrast between these two colors or to blur the sharp line between dark and light in a pattern, choose yarns with hair or texture or use shades close to black or white. Black and white yarns, like other yarns, can have a shiny, luminous surface or a dull matte finish. To add another layer of interest to a knitwear design, try combining black and white yarns with different finishes.

Black and white can also help tie other colors together. You can successfully mix black and white with almost any number of other colors, especially the brights. If the other colors are very dark (like a deep maroon, navy and dark purple) or very light (like pale yellow, mint green and lavender), however, you'll lose the contrast that makes a successful mixture.

Of course, black and white don't always need to be used together. White can be mixed with almost any other color, though it may strongly brighten the resulting combination, depending on the proportion and way in which it's used. Whites range in hue from a bold, bleached shade to soft eggshell to warm ivory. The brighter the white, the more electric the resulting combination, especially if the white area is to be large. For colors to be successfully combined with a bleach white, they, too, need to be bright. In contrast to bleach white, soft ivory creates deeper shadows in a textured pattern and a subtler appearance. Yellowed shades of white, like those in natural yarns with lanolin, cast an almost antique look to a fabric, whereas a greyer white lends a more sophisticated, subdued look. Warm whites (those with a yellow cast) work best with warm shades or with browns or warm greys. Cool whites work well with cool shades with a blue or grey cast.

Blacks can range from the strong, dense color I call velvet black to a softer charcoal black, which has just a bit of white added, to greys. Velvet black nicely complements bright colors. Charcoal black is a better foil for softer, more muted colors. And greys are best paired with colors of the same temperature; that is, cool grey tinged with blue works best with cool colors, and warm grey tinged with yellow works best with warm shades.

Natural shades

Designing in what I call "sheepy shades" is easy. These natural, undyed colors come straight from the fleece and range from deep, rich browns to warm shades of ivory to warm and cool greys. All of these shades usually work well together and provide softer contrast with other colors than do black and white. Heathery naturals, which combine the natural shades themselves for heathered effects, are richer in color than their unheathered counterparts and produce a softer effect in the knitted fabric than do the solid naturals.

When you use natural shades, you don't always have to create contrast. Mixing shades of dark browns and greys can create subtle, rich combinations that are perfect for menswear.

If neutrality seems too tame, add a jolt of color. I love how South American knitters work bright, often hot colors alongside the warm shades of their native alpaca yarn. Natural brown shades almost always work with strong blues and greens, and they're an important part of my autumn color group (see p. 116).

A crisp black and white swatch (at top) is worked in a smooth wool. At left, black and white lines are softened by a curly yarn. The sleeve-cuff swatch features 'sheepy' shades of Icelandic wool, spiked with pumpkin. The swatch at lower right was inspired by wood grain.

Light shades of blue pattern contrast with darker background blues (top right). Primary colors make the 'wagon wheel' and 'lobster' swatches pop.

Shades of the same color

When you are mixing shades of the same color, harmony depends on matching color temperature. You can reliably use cool shades with cool shades, and warm with warm. But this can be boring if the colors are too similar. For more zip, add a bright shade of the same color; to tame a combination, add a dark shade.

For less predictable mixtures of the same color, try mixing cool and warm shades within the same fabric. As a test of your experimental skills, for example, try combining a cool cobalt blue with a warm turquoise. Since these two colors tend to clash, you might additionally need a neutral color, like a black or white, to serve as a bridge between them. You could also divide them from one another with a pale color

like a light, warm green. Or you might choose a lighter shade of the cobalt blue and the turquoise to act as dividers.

One of my favorite groups of similar colors is the berry family—the range between red and blue that includes wine reds and purples. This group is a wide and useful one for clothing. Often the addition of a bright fuchsia or even hot pink as an accent will make a fabric worked in these shades "pop." Warm berry shades frequently work well with a warm blue, like turquoise, while cool berries blend well with cool royal blue.

Another reliable grouping, the indigo blues, include bright blues and blue greys in what reminds me of Indonesian batiks, denim and Delft dinnerware. These colors can produce bright or subdued effects—or a mixture of both. Choose ivory white or grey to set up a contrast with the blues. Warm, bright blues near turquoise create a soft effect when mixed with ivory. Cool blues mixed with bright white tend to be very energetic and crisp. And grey will make a bit more somber and sophisticated grouping when mixed with cool blues (see the Ashanti-inspired fabric on pp. 246-247).

To expand on the indigo group, you might substitute a pale yellow or a warm brown, like caramel, for a grey or white. Or you might choose shades of blue and grey that are slightly purple, often referred to as periwinkle, which mix nicely with the indigo blues as well as with white, cool grey or greyish pink.

Primary colors

The primary colors—clear red, blue and yellow—plus clear green, the secondary blend of blue and yellow, are familiar as the colors of kids' toys. These colors work well together, but their effect is often electric. So using these colors in pairs instead of all together produces "perky" rather than overwhelming effects. When used with bright white, these colors look sporty or nautical. Take inspiration from the crisp energy of semaphore flags.

Sometimes garments in primary colors lack subtlety. For more sophisticated results with this color group, I prefer to use darker shades of the primaries and secondary green, which remind me of classic collegiate shades. Hunter green mixes well with cranberry, as does royal blue with mustard or pale yellow.

American Indian rugs and blankets frequently offer interesting primary-color inspiration. These colors, with white, also work well for traditional Scandinavian sweaters.

Neon shades or hot colors are primaries to which a jolt of bright yellow or yellow-green has been added. Lime green, hot pink, electric blue and chartreuse are youthful and connote funky vitality—they remind me of Hawaiian textiles, skateboarders and neon lights. They have limited appeal, as they're a bit hard on the eyes, but they're very potent. These shades work well with each other if they're of the same intensity. Bleach white will make them even more electric, while black tames them slightly. Use these colors as accents occasionally—and sparingly—to lend a bit of energy to an otherwise predictable mixture of colors. Since neon shades are rare to come by in knitting yarns, I buy them whenever I see them.

Pastel shades

Snowy pastel shades are really white tinted with color. Pastels are easy to use together, especially if they're of the same density of color. To create a punchy look with a pastel combination, separate the colors by white. To produce a softer, more delicate effect, try using ivory instead of white.

Be careful when purchasing pastel yarns not to select shades that are too light for some contrast. If your pattern is composed of small, dot-like units, the subtle differences in shades may be lost. To use very pale shades together, they must occupy large enough areas for the eye to distinguish among them. To set up a stronger contrast in a pastel grouping, add a brighter or deeper shade of one of the colors.

Groups of greyed pastels may look striking on black or on a dark shade of one of the colors. However, if they're too pale in contrast to the dark shade, they're likely to be overpowered and will all tend to look white.

Youthful clears

Perhaps no group of colors is as rewarding to work with as the brights—that is, the nonprimary colors that range from soft, clear Easter-egg colors (a step beyond pastel) to deep, rich fruit colors, like berry, orange, apple green and periwinkle blue. This past summer I was struck by flower colors in this group: clear orange daylilies, bright yellow coreopsis, clear blue balloon flowers and bright fuchsia loosestrife. Along the shore, other flowers offered colors in

this range that were just a bit washed out but still bright: buttery yellows, denim blues, slightly greyed greens and powdery pinks. In the vegetable garden I found straw and squash yellows, tomato and beet reds, and spinach and lettuce greens. I'm always inspired by colors like these that jump out in nature—and in the yarn skein before I knit with them.

When mixing bright colors, there are several approaches: For an evenly bright balance, choose colors of the same degree of brightness. To check this, line the colors up and squint your eyes. Do any of the colors recede and darken or fade and wash out? Those that do will not contribute much to your combination and should be culled out.

To highlight bright shades, pair each color with a lighter shade. To get a stained-glass effect, mix brights with black, which will also intensify them.

At top, mohair and ribbon yarns combine in soft pastels. At left, the summer vegetable colors pick up highlights with a shiny cotton. At bottom, flower brights are deepened by a matte cotton.

At far left, two swatches feature autumn colors: one a bold mix, the other subtle. At center, chartreuse and shades of purple form a sophisticated combination. At far right are three color specialties: tweedy diamonds, metallic stripes and space-dyed texture.

Autumn colors

Autumn colors are a wonderful source of inspiration. They can be subtle and soft, like pale shades of gold and brown in a field of wheat, or full of punchy contrast, like the grey-green foliage of bright orange and yellow pumpkins. As a New Englander, I know first-hand that fall foliage offers an endless array of colors and shades, ranging from pale yellow green to warm, deep browns to fiery reds and orange. I've found that many purples—from eggplant to mauvey greys—work well with the orange shades. Almost all of these autumn colors are warm, but for some reason they work well with cool blue, perhaps because it's the color of the sky.

Sophisticated combinations

There are some color groupings that I find very sophisticated and fashion-oriented. These rich, moody combinations are always interesting.

The deep, yet bright jewel tones—red ruby, purple amethyst, ambery topaz—can be fascinating when contrasted with rich darks, like deep mahogany or deep olive green. Dusty or smoky colors can be wonderful to work with. Greyed shades of blue and purple, for example,

reminiscent of lilacs and violets, are heavy and, I think, a bit morose. I particularly like this color grouping for menswear or for sedate womenswear classics, occasionally enlivening them with a touch of deep red. The whole range of greyed "herbal" greens is coolly sophisticated. These colors work well with pale violet, soft mauve and greyed periwinkle blue.

Olive, chartreuse and greenish yellows form a group I turn to often for accent colors. Adding green and/or black to yellow lifts the usually cheery color to a sophisticated moodiness. These complex shades are usually worn only by the most adventurous, but they are fun to play with. Rarely seen in knitting yarns, these colors should be purchased when you come across them to expand your yarn collection.

Color specialties in yarns

There are several kinds of specialty yarns, and these often can help decide your color combination. Variegated yarns have color schemes already dyed or printed onto the strand. By choosing a skein of one of these yarns, a lot of color decisions are already made. You need only match a solid color with one of the colors along the strand.

Often the colors in variegated yarn are introduced sequentially at regular intervals. If you swatch over a small number of stitches in one of these yarns, you may or may not see the real effect you'll get when working the yarn over a much greater number of stitches. Also, you can work from two different balls at the same time, alternating them every few rows to get a different mixture. With variegated yarns, don't expect your finished sweater to look exactly as your swatch does. A pocket made from a swatch would provide an interesting contrast.

Jaspe yarns are made by plying together two different colors to form a single strand. The effect of jaspe yarns in the knitted fabric is tweed-like and strongly two-color. If your yarns each share a color in one of their plies, it will be easy to make even the oddest combination of colors work together — the common ply acts as the mediator.

Tweed yarns are flecked with contrasting pieces of fiber that add color and texture in the fabric. When using tweed yarns in a multicolor scheme, base your choices on the main color in the yarns and let the flecks simply add another layer of interest. If you want to combine a tweed yarn with a matching solid color, choose a color of one of the flecks for your solid.

Heathered yarns are the mixture of two or more colors in a soft blend. The effect of heathers in the knitted fabric is rather like oatmeal — a soft blend of several shades of one color. Heathers tend to blend more successfully with each other than with solids. If you want to combine a heather with a solid, look closely at the heathered strand and choose one of the shades to match in a solid yarn.

Specialty yarns also include the metallics, which I enjoy using from time to time. I divide the metallics into warm and cool shades and try to match them in terms of their temperature with other yarns. Gold and brass are tinged with yellow and green and tend to be warm, whereas silver has blue overtones and is cool. However, since light reacts differently with metallics, often reflecting off the surface, you may be able to cross the temperature "lines" and mix them in whatever way may strike your fancy.

USING COLOR IN DIFFERENT WAYS

Solid-color design

Isolated graphic motifs and accents

Repeating colorwork patterns

*d*esigning with solid color & isolated graphics

There are several ways to use color in knitwear design. You can plan a solid-color garment to enhance a textured pattern or a complex silhouette. Or you can use two or more colors to create isolated graphics or to work overall repeating colorwork patterns (see pp. 128-132 for a discussion of repeating patterns). Isolated graphics can be as simple as using color as a contrasting accent, for example, at the edges of a garment. Graphics can also be used for abstract or pictorial motifs, and they can be combined with colorwork patterns.

Color and graphics go hand in hand, and working with them should always be an adventure. With every new design, try to expand on your experience. Use new color combinations, or perhaps simply add a new color to a grouping that's worked in the past. Occasionally go beyond what you find flattering or acceptable. With graphics, test your skills by trying the unfamiliar. If you favor conservative, small patterns, attempt something bolder, perhaps a pictorial project. If you prefer bold designs, simplify and try your hand at a more subdued approach to pattern. If you design with what you feel are odd, even objectionable colors and with patterns that you might not ordinarily try, you'll learn something that will help you design with the colors and patterns you love.

Designing with a solid color

In choosing a single color for a design, you must choose one that you like and that also highlights the knitted fabric. Light or bright colors emphasize textured patterns, whereas dark yarns absorb the contrasting highlights between different stitches that help show off texture. I find that all yarns tend to darken a bit when knitted in a solid area of color because of the shadows cast by the stitches themselves. So always choose a color a bit lighter than you like in the skein to compensate for the darkened effect in the knitted fabric.

There are several ways to add depth and intensity to a solid color. I find it very effective to use two or more yarns in the fabric, each a slightly different shade of the same color. If the yarns are similar in weight, you can work stripes and produce a slightly striated fabric. For a subtler result that gives the most depth of color, alternate the two shades in miniature checkerboard fashion, changing color every one or two stitches (as I did for the Hiroshige sweater discussed in the sidebar on p. 123 and shown in the top photo on p. 133). With yarns of different weights, try knitting with two or more strands held together as one.

Another way to add depth to a color is to use a yarn or fiber with texture or sheen. Hairy yarns, like mohair and alpaca, often have a frosted look, created by the layer of hairs that rise from the surface of the strand. Many shiny synthetics in pale shades look almost icy and iridescent. The characteristic glint of shiny yarns, like mercerized cotton or rayons, tends to intensify deep, rich colors and lighten pale shades. For the dusty look of soft flannel or suede, choose a rough cotton with a matte finish. (See the photographs of swatches of various yarns on pp. 16-22.)

Working with isolated graphics

Graphics can be bold or subtle. A graphic can be as simple as working pieces of a garment in different colors. Entire sleeves, for example, might contrast with the body, or each section of the garment might be worked in a different color to produce a new knitted version of Joseph's coat of many colors. Alternatively, you might contrast only the ribbing or other details, like the pockets, collar and cuffs. To heighten the graphic effect of this design, use bright, bold colors. For a subtler effect, choose subdued contrasts or shades of the same color as the body of the garment.

For a still subtler effect, work only a small line of color as an accent. I'm always tempted to add contrasting touches of color to a solid-color garment, usually at the edges. I cast on for all pieces in a contrasting color, then change to the main color to work the remainder of the piece. At the neck edge, I either pick up or bind off stitches—or both—in a contrasting color to tip the edges. If you like, you could edge each piece with a different color. Several different brights add a whimsical touch—good for kids—and shades of the same color create a subtler, more sophisticated detail.

A single row or stripe of color within the body of a garment makes more of a graphic statement than a contrasting line of color at its edges. The eye is drawn to the stripe, which divides the garment into separate sections. Be aware that wherever a line or stripe is placed, you create a focal point.

You can work a simple geometric shape as an isolated graphic within a section of the garment or repeat it several times to create a larger pattern. You could also work this graphic repeatedly across the fabric to produce an allover pattern (see pp. 128-132 for a discussion of allover patterns).

If the isolated graphic is complicated and involves several colors, it will require a separate strand of yarn for each color. This type of knitting is referred to as intarsia knitting. Intarsia graphics are most easily worked in smooth stockinette stitch. However, you can get extra texture and add visual interest to the design by working either the motif or background in reverse stockinette or in simple knit/purl patterns. (See the Bibliography on pp. 258-260 for basic knitting books, which will discuss how to do both intarsia techniques and the stranded-knitting techniques used for the allover color-work patterns discussed beginning on pp. 128.)

Some graphics are more suitable for knitting than others. The most effective graphics are bold. Those requiring great detail or many colors in small sections may be too demanding to knit successfully. If a lot of colors are used in a small area, the finished fabric in this area may become stiff because of all the separate yarn ends that must be woven in. If you want to work small details of a graphic in a variety of colors, think about adding them in duplicate stitch after the knitting is completed. Also with regard to shape, linear graphics translate better in the knitted fabric than curved images, which will have slightly jagged edges (for a detailed discussion of charting and plotting graphics, see pp. 124-128).

Color choice must be considered at the same time as planning graphics. For wonderful inspiration for both, look to Turkish kilim and other oriental rugs as well as to American Indian crafts. Generally speaking, the larger the areas of color, the more they retain their individual identity, even if similar shades sit next to one another. Conversely, the smaller the areas of color, the more they influence each other and the more similar shades blur into one another. If you want to use small accents of color with large areas of other colors, work the accents in stronger or brighter shades to keep them from being visually swallowed up.

Working with geometric graphics

Simple stripes are easy enough for a child to knit, and they offer an excellent place to test how colors mix. Wide stripes are easy for the eye to read and can be knitted in similar or contrasting colors. When working with narrow stripes, you can achieve a soft, blurred effect if you use similar colors. If you want a crisper look, choose colors of greater contrast.

There are endless possibilities for designing striped fabrics. The most obvious option is to alternate stripes of equal size. You might also try one of the following suggestions to help you develop your own variations: First, alternate wide stripes with bands of narrow stripes. Second, create gradations of color by working stripes in shades of the same color. Third, introduce texture as an added element in the stripes. Try some knit/purl patterns (see Chapter 4), changing color every few rows. When you experiment with stripes in these patterns, note how the two colors blend when they meet in purl sections and how the division is crisp in knit sections (see the photos on p. 27 for information on how to make crisp the line for purl sections).

Although stripes are most commonly aligned horizontally in knitting, you can use them in other ways. Vertically aligned stripes are less conventional and also tend to make a garment look longer and the wearer slimmer. For the easiest vertical stripes, knit your garment from side to side. And for a very bold graphic effect, try combining blocks of vertical stripes alongside blocks of horizontal stripes.

Color in ribbing

Since ribbing is such an important fabric in knitwear design, it's useful to know several ways to treat it with color. Ribbing that's horizontally striped is the most elastic, but vertically striped ribbing is perhaps visually more interesting.

Any ribbing can be striped horizontally by simply changing colors wherever desired at the beginning of a row and keeping in the ribbed pattern throughout. The break between colors will be clean in the knit ribs but softly blurred in the purl ribs where the interlacement of the old and new colors shows.

For a crisp line of color between horizontal stripes, I change to a smaller needle and work a plain stockinette row in the new color before resuming the ribbed pattern with the larger needle. This lessens the elasticity of the ribbing only slightly and gives a cleaner-edged stripe.

(continued on p. 120)

Color creates various effects in ribbing. Clockwise, from upper left: in horizontal stripes, a blurry line forms where the colors meet; working a firm stockinette row between colors before resuming the rib produces a crisper break between colors; to mix texture and color, work a reverse-stockinette row in the new color before resuming the rib; Shetland corrugated ribbing creates vertical stripes, which can be further enhanced by changing the colors of the background stripes.

(continued from page 119)

Horizontal stripes can be worked in any ribbed pattern but are most effective in simple knit/purl rib like a 1x1 or 2x2. A striped slip-stitch rib will create a slight zigzag line where the slip stitch pulls the color up from the row below. I avoid stripes in lace or cabled ribs because color often detracts from the pattern.

Ribbing can be worked with vertical stripes by working the knit ribs in one color and the purl ribs in a contrasting color. This technique is associated with the Fair Isle knitting of the Shetland Islands and is often called corrugated ribbing. Frequently traditional Fair Isle knitters use graduated color in this type of ribbing, as I did with my Hiroshige sweater (see the sidebar on p. 123 and the top photo on p. 133).

Made by knitting with two strands of color at the same time, corrugated rib is most effectively worked in a 1x1 or 2x2 pattern. Using a greater number of stitches tends to make the individual ribs bubble rather than lie flat.

Corrugated rib is not very elastic because the stranded back of the fabric restricts its stretch and hence will not cling or provide shaping as will regular knit/purl ribbing. Before deciding upon the width necessary for the edges, work a swatch to obtain an accurate gauge for the ribbed pattern.

To work a 2x2 corrugated rib, with the knit ribs in a light color and the purl ribs in a dark:

Cast on a multiple of 4 sts plus 2, with the light color.

Row 1 (RS): k2 light; * bring the dark yarn to the front of the work and p2, then return the dark yarn to the back, k2 light; rep from *, carrying the strand not in use loosely across the WS.

Row 2 (WS): p2 light; * bring the dark yarn to the back of the work and k2, then return the dark yarn to the front, p2 light; rep from *, carrying the strand not in use loosely across the WS.

Rep these 2 rows. (For a clean break between the cast-on row and the ribbing, k2 in each color across the first RS row.)

The same procedure can be followed for 1x1 corrugated rib. You can also work an uneven rib, the most effective being two knit stitches with one purl stitch.

You can also work a striped purl border as a variation on the corrugated rib. Instead of alternating knit and purl in the rib, work each separate stripe in reverse stockinette (knit the wrong side, purl the right side). For a checkered purl pattern, like my rainbow coat (see pp. 137-142), work a plain stockinette row before changing the position of the colors. This creates a clean break between blocks.

Like stripes, blocks and checks can be varied in numerous ways and offer wonderful terrain for experimenting with color. You can work a checkerboard, alternating different-colored squares of the same size, or you can break the regularity by mixing squares with rectangles. Blocks can be combined and/or overlapped to form a single motif, which can be isolated or used as a repeating graphic. Blocks can also appear as a grid on a solid background, with just one or a few stitches outlining the shapes.

Of all the geometric shapes, I think diamonds offer the most design possibilities in terms of shape and arrangement. The basic diamond shape can be altered to be short and squat, or tall and elongated. Diamonds can be used as isolated motifs or interlocked to produce a harlequin effect. You can form a lattice of diamonds on a solid background, working the outlines in single stitches and filling the open diamonds with smaller motifs. And to soften the hard lines of a diamond, you can simply curve its sides.

Rounded shapes are challenging to create in knitted fabric. Curved lines will always have somewhat jagged edges because of the V-shape of the individual stitches. Using a fine yarn and small stitches will create a softer curve than knitting with a heavier yarn. Because circles and ovals are hard to execute well in a knitted fabric, they can lend a fresh, intriguing look to knitted graphics.

In my mind, circles and ovals are always colorful and lighthearted. They make me think of Easter eggs, balloons, colored beads, buttons, marbles, polka dots, dominoes, dice and hubcaps—not to mention, since I'm writing this at lunchtime, fried eggs, apples and oranges.

Of course, graphics need not always be regular geometric shapes. They can just as easily be abstract, asymmetrical shapes, whether angular

From graphic inspiration to sketch

The elegant print below, *Plum Tree in Front of Moon* by the 19th-century Japanese artist Hiroshige, has always been a favorite of mine. When I saw it again in a museum show, I was intrigued by the print's simple shapes and soft shading, and I wanted to incorporate it into a knitwear design (print: Museum of Art, Rhode Island School of Design; gift of Mrs. John D. Rockefeller, Jr.).

To attempt a design based on this print, I needed to interpret and simplify it as much as possible. I was intrigued by the elongated shape of the print and hoped to use this as a basic element of the design. I isolated the most dramatic elements: the full, yet truncated moon; the graceful branches; and the softly shaded sky, ranging from pale ivory to grey to indigo.

I began by sketching with colored pencils. I tried plotting a panel-like graphic section into the garment structure I had in mind, keeping the basic proportion of the original print. It occurred to me that an asymmetrical placement of the graphic on the front would be the most dramatic, with the image taking up only a portion of the front. But the narrow panel just didn't seem to carry enough weight, so I extended the coloration of the sky outward along the sleeve. I drew in the moon and simple branches, omitting the tree trunk that appeared in the print to simplify the design. I decided to add the coral flowers later with duplicate stitch.

I felt that the color of the solid areas of the sweater was as important as the graphic itself. I considered using a dark blue for the nongraphic areas but decided this would weaken the effect of the sky. Black would be dramatic, but it would be too somber for my liking, especially against the coolness of the blues. I decided that a rich, deep red would brighten the garment and work well with the blue sky and the coral blossoms. To break up the solidity of the red sections and add an unexpected touch, I drew in a corrugated ribbing in shades of blue on one sleeve and part of the bottom edge (see pp. 119-120 for information on corrugated ribbing, p. 133 for a discussion of the swatching I did for this sweater and pp. 250-252 for the full instructions).

Small floral graphics accentuate the lines of these knitted day dresses from the 1920s. Duplicate-stitch roses and leaves trace the openings and seamlines of the maroon overblouse, while the embroidery on the blue overblouse mimics pockets, frames the lower edge and creates a strong center-front line. (Metropolitan Museum of Art. Maroon dress: gift of Eleanora Eaton Brooks, 1975; blue dress: gift of Emily Louise Jones Figuers, 1974.)

PLACEMENT OF GRAPHICS ON SCHEMATIC

Dead center

As border and accents   As spot decoration

The best way to visualize your graphic treatment is to sketch the graphics on a schematic in their approximate location, or sketch the graphic separately and lay it on the schematic. With swatches or charts of the graphics that you've done by this point, you should have some sense of the graphic's size. This will enable you to render the graphics proportionately on your schematic with colored pencils. If you don't like the arrangement, erase it and start over. Try different placements until you find the one that works best.

Charting isolated graphics

Charting graphics on graph paper is the most effective way to plan your design before you begin to knit. There are a few things to consider when preparing to chart graphics. Use proportioned knitter's graph paper to capture the image as it will appear in the knitted fabric. If possible, know the gauge of the yarn you'll be using, and establish the size and shape of the garment in schematic form if you're concerned about fitting the graphic onto a particular garment section.

I have devised two approaches to planning graphics. The first approach is a step-by-step method I use when I'm unsure of the direction I want to take with the graphic but know that it will be relatively small. In this approach, I swatch and chart small elements of the overall graphic I'm after and cumulatively arrive at the final motif. I use a second approach when I have a more concrete idea for the graphic or when I'm planning a large graphic that cannot easily be worked out in small swatches and charts. In this approach, I draw directly on graph paper, using it like a canvas to work out the image. Often I combine both approaches, working small charts and swatches, plotting the results on a large chart and then repeating the process until the large chart is complete.

In the step-by-step approach, I usually begin by thinking about one or two shapes that will eventually become part of the final garment. I experiment with these shapes in both swatches and charts. Sometimes the chart comes first; other times the swatch inspires the chart. I often experiment with different yarns and colors, testing my yarn choices to see how they translate into knitted fabric. Usually when I swatch, one swatch will lead to another. This is a very organic approach in which I let my mind explore ideas slowly.

After success with isolated pieces of the graphic, I consider how to merge my ideas into the larger whole of a garment. This may require setting up a pattern repeat. Or I may decide to enlarge the basic image. At this point, I often sketch an arrangement of the graphic elements on a schematic or garment drawing. After reworking the arrangement of elements, if need be, I transfer this information to a large piece of knitter's graph paper, which will become the final pattern.

In the canvas approach to graphics, I draw directly onto the knitter's graph paper, eliminating the step-by-step swatching. I use this for large pictorial images, like those that will span an entire garment section, which are simply too big for small swatches. Since large graphics must usually be planned to fit within a certain space, it's necessary to know the yarn and gauge I'll be working in. So I work a small swatch first, usually in stockinette, if that's my fabric. I also need a rough schematic too, so that I'll have an idea of space limitations. To help me envision the graphics before I draw on the graph paper, I make a rough sketch of the graphic, then draw it to the approximate size I want it to be on my schematic. This initial planning helps me get a sense of the graphic's size and shape within the confines of the garment.

Although I could simply draw my graphic—and I often do—I also find it useful to begin by outlining the shape of my garment pieces on knitter's graph paper. You can use knitter's graph paper with any size grid, provided the stitch-to-row proportion is correct. However, if you use graph paper that matches your knitted gauge—that is, if your gauge is 6 stitches to the inch, your graph paper would have 6 grid squares to the inch—your graphics will be life-size, which makes it easier to see what the final graphics will look like.

To begin the graphic, I first draw rough lines onto the graph paper, referring to my rough sketch. The first lines are very loose and don't necessarily follow the grid of the graph paper. I erase and redraw often, looking for the most pleasing arrangement. Finally I refine the "charted" lines by outlining the grid as close as possible along the rough lines of my drawing. I then often fill in the graphic sections with colored pencil to serve as a guide for the knitting.

Learning to draw on graph paper

If you want to design with graphics, you'll need to learn to chart or "draw" on graph paper. Sometimes you'll have a specific image in mind that you want to capture on paper, and at other times you'll just want to just fool around with shapes and lines to come up with an interesting arrangement. Getting smooth lines on a grid is more challenging than drawing on plain paper, where your pencil can move fluidly without concern for charting. Drawing horizontal and vertical lines on a grid, of course,

presents no problem. On the other hand, it's often difficult to draw curved lines and angles and to find a way to translate pictorial images.

In the section that follows I've tried to give you a few examples of how I might capture different kinds of graphics in a grid format. As you'll see, I tried groupings of geometric shapes and practiced drawing curves. Beginning with some inspiration to help get my efforts off the ground, I arranged some abstract shapes as well, and I tried my hand at a pictorial graphic. In each case, the problems of capturing the graphic are slightly different.

If you've never done this kind of charting before, I suggest you try to work out some small graphics just as I have, to become familiar with drawing on graph paper. Gather together some pencils and some knitter's graph paper. Since this is for drawing practice, it isn't important to match the paper to a specific gauge. From the graph paper, cut a square or rectangle, about 35 to 45 grid squares wide.

Give yourself time to play with graphics in the small-grid format, letting the process of charting be an end in itself. Practice drawing as well, creating a pleasing arrangement within the confines of the grid. Although it's not necessary, I encourage you to make a swatch from your best efforts so that you can see how they translate into the more textured knitted fabric. (Later you may find a use for your successful swatches, or they may inspire a larger project).

Plotting geometric shapes and curves

I began the exercises by charting geometric shapes because they are the easiest to draw. Square-edged shapes like rectangles are very simple. But to chart triangles, diamonds and other angular shapes, you need to practice.

I charted diagonal lines of several different angles on my first grid. I began at the lower edge, making an angle that moved one square over every "row." Then above this, I drew lines that moved over one square every two rows, and so on. In order to draw a curved line, I had to move over the squares in a more irregular fashion. I set up my lines in a symmetrical way to form a simple design and to fill the space on the grid. A design of this kind could be further enhanced by using color to fill in the different areas.

Inspired by Turkish kilim rugs and charted before being knitted, these swatches display graphics formed from geometric shapes. For the swatch at far left, I borrowed the four-diamond motif from a postcard of a rug and filled the corners with geometric motifs of my own invention. For the other swatch, I charted a motif and borders inspired by a small rug I own. I used traditional kilim colors in a grainy wool yarn that lent a rug-like texture.

MOTIF FROM KILIM RUG TRANSLATED TO KNITTER'S GRAPH PAPER

Practice drawing lines of all different angles and curves—try to see how many you can incorporate into your grid. For experience drawing curves, I suggest tracing your hand onto knitter's graph paper, then drawing the curves, following the lines of the grid. Refine the line as much as possible to capture the curves in the smoothest way.

To continue my exercise with geometric shapes, I turned to a postcard of a Turkish kilim rug and roughly sketched a motif from it onto ungridded paper (see the drawing above). It was a grouping of four diamonds, wider than they were high, each with a cross in its center. With my previous exercises fresh in my mind, I turned to my grid and tried to draw a squat diamond at the center. This required much erasing and trying different angles to

create a slightly curved diamond. Once I was pleased with the diamond, I repeated this shape again above the first. To complete the arrangement, I drew two more diamonds, one to either side of the central pair. For visual interest, I made them slightly different from the first two. I filled in the remaining space with other simpler geometric shapes. I liked this chart so much that I worked it into a swatch, shown at left in the photo above.

You can turn to other sources of inspiration for geometric motifs, such as American Indian textiles and pottery, quilts and the paintings of Paul Klee. You might try arranging numbers and letters in a graffiti-inspired way.

The sequined glove at left is decorated with bold abstract graphic shapes. The color scheme is startlingly effective, with warm red and hot pink contrasting with aqua and orchid, all highlighted by areas of bright white. (Metropolitan Museum of Art; gift of Kayser-Roth Glove Co., Inc., 1975.)

Plotting impressionistic images

Sometimes I use a more impressionistic approach to capturing a graphic on a grid. I sketch roughly on the grid itself, using smudges of color. Then I refine the individual shapes, following the grid lines along the smudged areas. I use this approach for both abstract and pictorial images.

I was inspired to create a graphic based on the glove in the photo above, from the Metropolitan Museum of Art's Costume Institute collection. The glove's boldly patterned, but delicately overlapping sequins look like shiny snakeskin from a fantasy world.

I liked the glove's abstractly patterned surface so much that I decided to sketch it impressionistically on graph paper. Using colored pencils in the same colors as the glove, I drew

rough arrangements of smudgy shapes, inspired by but not necessarily following the configurations on the glove itself. For the swatch that I later made from the chart, I selected a yarn that captured both the colors and sheen of the glove, with details added later in gold metallic yarn.

For other abstract inspiration where you might need to use this impressionistic approach, look to real snakeskin, or good pictures of snakes and other reptiles that might inspire interesting shapes. I keep a photocopy of an actual snakeskin in my inspiration file. Animal skins, like zebra, leopard, giraffe and even the patterned fur of my calico cat, could be captured this way.

To capture a complex pictorial image, I try to aim for a simplified version that's more a cartoon than a realistic depiction. To demonstrate this, I chose to work with a Russian shawl that I like (see the photo on p. 135). Borrowing the colors of the shawl, I made a rough sketch on grid paper to simplify the flowers and arrange a small bouquet. Then, as seen in the chart above, I interpreted the rose as a group of interlocking semicircular shapes. I simplified the lily by breaking it down into three pointed petals. I used the royal blue to make impressionistic smudges of color that became small flowers. For help in seeing how images can be simplified, look to American hooked rugs, pictorial quilts, dinnerware and hand-painted plates, to name a few sources.

When I complete swatches from exercises like these, I try to think about how each might inspire a larger project. I think my kilim-inspired swatch could be repeated as an allover fabric or as a border. For a more complex graphic with interlocking shapes, like the one based on the glove, I might take the basic arrangement and enlarge its proportion. Or I could plot a pictorial graphic like my small bouquet on a garment as a spot decoration, as a large corsage or inserted into a garment, as in the Designer Notebook project on pp. 134-142.

*d*esigning repeating patterns

After isolated graphics, repeating graphics are the second major category of colorwork patterns. (Although slip-stitch patterns represent yet another major category of color patterns, I haven't mentioned them here because there are so many different types of them. They are discussed at length on pp. 180-183. Nonetheless, the general color issues that are addressed on pp. 109-112 apply to slip-stitch color patterns as well.) Like many traditional repeating patterns from around the world, repeating graphic patterns are sometimes bold, but they usually tend to be smaller in scale and more delicate in line than most isolated graphics. These patterns are generally composed of a single unit that repeats across the fabric.

Most knitters find that repeating patterns are easier to knit than bold, isolated graphics. Unlike the intarsia knitting required for isolated graphics (see pp. 118-119), repeating patterns are worked by carrying, or stranding, the various pattern yarns across the back of the fabric. These stranded patterns, as repeating patterns are often called, are usually worked with two colors of yarn, a background and a pattern color, held at the same time (see the Bibliography on pp. 258-260 for some basic knitting texts that discuss stranded-knitting techniques).

Like the knit/purl family of patterns (see Chapter 4), these repeating patterns can be used as self-contained borders or allover fabric repeats. However, repeating colorwork patterns are less often used as panels.

These Persian slippers, dating from the 1830s, are finely knitted at a gauge of 18 stitches to the inch. They feature colorwork patterns with both rounded and angular motifs, which follow the contour of the slippers. (Museum of Art, Rhode Island School of Design; gift of Martin Birnbaum.)

Pattern characteristics

Repeating patterns have characteristics that must be considered when designing fabrics with them: line weight, size, shape and orientation. Each of these characteristics can be reinforced or downplayed with color.

What I call the line weight of a pattern refers to whether the major lines making up the pattern are bold or delicate. You can quickly discern this when looking at a pattern chart. If the major lines are three or more stitches wide, they will be heavy and produce a bold pattern. If the lines are only one or two stitches wide, they will be delicate and produce an almost filigreed pattern.

I use line weight to help me group patterns and arrive at various design effects. If I want a classic, even look, I combine patterns with similar line weights. For a more eclectic, visually interesting brew, I mix patterns with heavy and light line weights. Usually I aim to balance the mixture, or the odd pattern will sit awkwardly among the others. However, when I want to focus on a single bold pattern, I surround it with more delicate patterns that will fill space but not draw attention.

For a more traditional effect, work allover repeating patterns in fine yarns. In heavy, bulky or textured yarns, the same patterns will take on a graphic, bolder and more contemporary look. In these heavier yarns, small patterns will also, of course, be enlarged.

Repeating patterns come in many sizes. Small patterns make less of a visual impression than large ones and are good as fillers for areas between larger patterns. Small patterns worked in soft colors may almost disappear, but they'll appear much stronger in a bright color or one

The swatch at upper left shows bold pattern lines, while the swatch at upper right features panel patterns composed of fine, curving lines. At center are two swatches with horizontally aligned patterns: at left, a balanced combination with both heavy and fine lines; at right, angular patterns are combined in an eclectic way. The two swatches at bottom show the same pattern worked in two different yarn weights.

that contrasts greatly with the colors of the surrounding patterns or background. Large patterns can have a wide or a deep repeat—or both. Use these patterns where you want a strong focus, like at the lower edge of a garment or in the yoke area. To downplay large patterns, work them in subtle colors.

Patterns can be used allover and oriented horizontally or vertically. Either way, the patterns have a definite beginning and end. To align patterns neatly at side seams, linking up multiples so that there are full repeats, you will need to consider your garment size and your gauge. If you cannot fit full repeats into your space, you will need to center the patterns and leave the incomplete repeats equally divided to either side (see the sidebar on charting on pp. 86-88). Traditional Fair Isle sweaters, which are worked in horizontal bands, offer a wealth of allover patterns (see the Bibliography on pp. 258-260). These patterns can be stacked in Fair Isle fashion or can be used alone for borders at the lower edges of a garment.

In contrast to horizontal patterns, vertical patterns are confined to a certain width. They can be used as a single panel or lined up in side-by-side panels to form an allover pattern. These patterns occur less frequently in traditional knitting patterns, though they can be found among Turkish designs. I have always wanted to work a garment entirely in vertical color patterns, making a colorwork version of an Aran (for more on Aran sweaters, see p. 146).

With regard to shape, the edges of repeating patterns can be soft and curved or hard and jagged. Curvy patterns tend to look more feminine than hard-edged patterns, but there aren't a lot of them, probably due to the square, grid-like nature of knitted fabric. You'll find a few curved Fair Isle patterns and some in Scandinavian sources. Hard-edged, angular repeating patterns abound in traditional knitting. Perhaps the most striking are the Turkish patterns. The Shetland diamond patterns look a little softer because they often incorporate smaller motifs and dots of colors.

Adding color to a repeating pattern often changes the look of it, and color can thus be used to emphasize or downplay certain aspects of the pattern. Using soft colors tends to minimize all patterns and downplay hard edges. To emphasize hard edges and large, bold patterning, use strong contrast or bright colors. For subtle or delicate patterns, you may need to incorporate a bit of contrast in order to make them show up. Contrast is even more important with smaller patterns to keep one color from swallowing another and causing the pattern to be lost.

When patterns are combined, the effect can be harmonious or jarring, and subtle or dramatic. If the patterns share characteristics—for example, curved or angular edges—they'll usually combine harmoniously and produce a "classic," balanced look. Balancing the patterns in pleasing proportions—for example, alternating narrow horizontal bands with wide ones—contributes to a harmonious mix. Conversely, mixing patterns with opposite characteristics or combining them in unexpected ways produces more jarring effects.

Such mixtures are not necessarily bad, however, only more unusual, and they can often be more visually dynamic than their traditionally harmonious counterparts. Bright colors or colors that contrast strongly highlight odd mixtures; soft, more closely related colors help to unify disparate patterns. The subtlety or drama of a pattern combination depends on both the relative size of the patterns used and the elements that divide them, as well as on their colors. Several small "dotty" patterns worked together in similar colors would yield subtle results; combining two very bold patterns, perhaps divided by a strong solid stripe, would achieve dramatic results.

Charting repeating patterns

Just as with isolated graphics, you'll want to chart repeating patterns before beginning any project. Charting will also help you enlarge, alter and combine repeating patterns, design new patterns and record color information to make the actual knitting easier. As with other charting, however, you'll want to test your charted pattern by swatching, which will also enable you to analyze and refine—or make final—your choices about color.

After working with many knitters, I've found that stranded patterns usually yield a square gauge (that is, the number of stitches per inch usually matches or is very close to the number of rows per inch). This means that you can almost always use square-gridded graph paper when planning stranded patterns.

Most stranded patterns worked in the same yarn and needle size will share the same gauge. This means you can easily combine these patterns without increasing or decreasing stitches between them.

As when working with isolated graphics, it's useful to decide very early on upon the size and shape of your knitted pieces so that you have a canvas on which to place your patterns. This is not so important when working an allover pattern that can end at any point, but it's crucial when working with borders or planning groups of repeating patterns whose placement you want to control.

When designing a new repeating pattern or rearranging existing patterns, keep in mind that the best-looking knitted fabrics usually have no more than five or six stitches in one color before changing to another color. Occasionally I break this rule, but I always check by swatching to see if the results will adversely affect my fabric. If you work long runs in one color, try to vary their placement in the pattern, or plan to twist the yarns every few stitches to catch them in the knitting and eliminate lengthy floats.

When I want to combine a number of existing patterns, I first chart each of them separately. Then I arrange the charts in various ways, looking for a configuration I like. When I find one, I tape the charts together to serve as part of my knitting instruction.

When I want to alter an existing pattern, I sometimes chart part of the pattern and leave some areas blank, so that I can fill in with something new. If I want to make a delicate pattern bolder, I might simply alter the pattern by adding extra pattern stitches to increase the weight of the major lines. Then sometimes I smooth out the edges of an angular pattern to make it curvier and softer. Or I take a traditional motif and repeat it across the chart, orienting the pattern across the horizontal band, as I did in the wide border at the lower edge of the black and white sweater on p. 137.

You can also adapt knit/purl patterns to color very successfully. Use one color for the purl symbols, and another color for the background knit stitches.

Creating original repeating patterns

Designing your own knitting patterns from scratch is fun and rewarding. Remember that the strength or delicacy of your pattern depends on how dense you make the major lines. For example, a simple zigzag border may have a strong graphic appeal if the lines are four stitches wide but will be far subtler if formed of a single-stitch line. And remember that the pattern tends to be visually stronger charted on paper than it is in the knitted fabric because the V-shaped stitches carry less visual weight than filled-in or darkened squares.

Sometimes I begin charting with nothing in mind. Faced with an empty grid, I'll start X'ing in squares, and follow along like tic-tac-toe until something interesting happens. I often erase and re-X quite a bit. Sometimes I roughly sketch lines or shapes onto the paper, then I make the X marks follow the lines or shapes.

You may find this process difficult at first and want to start with a small area no larger than 10 to 15 stitches square. When you have

**DESIGNING
A REPEATING
PATTERN**

Step 1
'X' in a few lines or shapes on a small grid.

Step 2
Repeat grid four times to see how pattern works as a whole.

Step 3
Refine chart if desired for final pattern. Mark repeat lines.

Using the photocopier as a design tool

The photocopier is a valuable tool for designing charted patterns. Copying the design by machine is obviously much faster and easier than copying by hand. Because photocopying is so quick, rearranging patterns is easy and fun.

You'll often find a copier at the library, post office or local college. Look for one that will reduce and enlarge. Since some machines will not pick up blue-lined graph paper, I use paper with black or grey lines. To allow for rearranging the charts, I join the copied patterns with clear, easy-to-remove tapes.

There are several ways to use a copy machine. You can make multiple copies of several repeats and try combining them in different groupings. You can tape patterns together along both their width and length. To make a large chart less cumbersome, you can reduce it on the copier so that it fits on one piece of paper. (The techniques discussed on p. 89 can be applied to photocopying colorwork patterns.)

I usually make several copies of a blank piece of graph paper before I begin to chart. After charting a pattern, I copy it too. I can then keep my original chart intact, cutting up the copied version instead and rearranging pieces of it on a clean piece of graph paper. Sometimes I'm pleased with my alterations of the pattern and sometimes not, in which case I can return to the original and make new copies to start over.

I love to use the copier to make what I call a puzzle pattern. I photocopy a traditional pattern or small geometric shapes many times, then cut the patterns into pieces. I rearrange the pieces, even turning some upside down or sideways, until I'm pleased with the results, which are often delightful.

My brother, a cartographer, taught me to copy blank graphs onto clear plastic, 8½x11 overlay film, the material used for overhead projectors, which is available at stationery or art-supply stores. Photocopy a grid onto it at a copy shop by sending the overlay film through the copier like a sheet of paper. You can then overlay this clear grid over images to help you convert and adjust them, if need be, for charting.

an effective grouping of X marks in the small area, you can then repeat it across the chart. You can arrange the grouping differently too, making it into a checkerboard or a half-drop setup (see the drawings on p. 89).

Borders and panels are somewhat easier to design than allover repeats because they will be worked within a more limited space. To design a border or panel, first draw some lines on your chart to establish the length or width of the pattern. Then start charting your pattern within this area just as you would begin for a regular repeating pattern. You can also break up a larger existing pattern to form a border or panel. You may, however, need to add some additional patterning at the edges to give the border or panel a more enclosed, finished look. (For additional information on charting pattern repeats, see pp. 86-88.)

Combining graphics & allover patterns

As you gain confidence in working with color, you may want to try combining isolated graphics with repeating patterns. The first and easiest way is do this is to alternate horizontal areas of intarsia graphics and stranded repeating patterns, keeping the different knitting techniques separate. Alternatively, you can superimpose isolated graphics on a background of a smaller repeating pattern. Finally, you can make areas of a smaller repeating pattern become part of a larger graphic treatment.

The challenge in this kind of work is not setting up the patterns, but actually knitting them. This knitting can become fairly tedious when stranded areas intersect areas of intarsia with its bobbins or loose yarn ends. Design what you will enjoy knitting. If you like stranded knitting, be restrained in how much intarsia you add to it. The results should definitely be worth the extra effort, so let your level of patience and skill dictate your plan.

If both the intarsia and stranded patterns share a color, your knitting will be simpler. If they don't, try to limit your colors to keep the knitting more manageable.

Swatching for the Hiroshige sweater: combining graphics and allover patterns

Having sketched a version of the Hiroshige print that I was pleased with (see the sidebar on p. 123), I was ready to begin swatching. I spent much more time than usual swatching for this design, trying to blend the colors of the sky. I tried a variegated yarn, but it could not give me the gradual blending that I was after. I tried alternating stripes of different shades of blue and grey, but the shading just wasn't subtle enough.

In desperation, I tried a stranded allover pattern. This upset my game plan slightly because I had not expected to use stranded patterns in an intarsia piece. I was pleased to find that the simplest checkered pattern (one stitch equals one check) gave me the most even shading thus far. And the strands carried across the back gave the fabric a nice heft, which was absent in my previous swatches.

The pullover at right, inspired by the Hiroshige print on p. 123, combines both stranded colorwork and intarsia graphics. Numerous swatches, some of them shown below, were needed to work out the design. The sky and moon were knitted in, with the branches and flowers worked afterwards in duplicate stitch.

I proceeded to knit what seemed like hundreds of small swatches in the checkered pattern to test the combination of several shades of blue and grey for the sky. To settle on the background, I worked a long skinny swatch, about the same length of the final sweater, based on the most effective of the smaller swatches and shading from light to dark as smoothly as possible. I then tested ivory and beige for the moon, working them in stranded checkerboard fashion too, and also tested corals for the flowers. The stranded pattern helped me in the solid red areas, too, where I combined three different reds to come up with a deep, complex shade. I worked another swatch to test how the stranded patterns in the moon and sky would join where they met in the knitting.

To simplify the knitting in the graphic sections, I decided to knit in only the sky and moon. The branches and blossoms would be duplicate stitched or embroidered later.

With the fabric decided, I drew out the schematic to the proportions of my original sketch. The schematic helped me to decide the size and placement of the moon, the most crucial graphic element. I plugged in all of my stitch counts, based on gauge and measurements.

The final step before knitting was to make a large chart that would capture the shape of the knitted piece and graphics, and record the colors. My pattern had the same stitch and row gauge, so I used square graph paper. I found a small dinner plate the same size as the moon and, referring to the schematic, I laid it down at the proper place and traced around it, then translated the curves to the grid as smoothly as possible. Referring to my large swatch, I noted the background colors at the beginning of each row. For the sleeve, I decided to use the same background as the front, omitting the moon (see pp. 250-252 for the final charts and instructions for this sweater).

Swatch project & *designer* notebook

One way to gain experience with color patterns is to work them first in black and white and then adapt them to color. I used this process to design the two garments described in this Designer Notebook.

The inspiration for my first project came from a photo of little Dutch girls (inset on the facing page), dressed in a patchwork blend of fabrics. I was excited by the pattern mixture of the fabrics that combined rounded florals with the hard lines of simple plaids. The photo would inspire both pattern and the initial black and white color combination.

Before starting to chart patterns and swatch for the project, I gathered some thoughts and questions to get the design process off the ground. Even though I may drop or add some items from the list as I proceed through the design process, this initial assessment helps me to survey the design possibilities:

1. I wanted an eclectic mix of patterns inspired by the photo. Should I use traditional color patterns or design my own?

2. I wanted to use an edging that would also incorporate pattern. A striped ribbing? A checkered edging?

3. Could I find a way to incorporate one of my colored graphics swatches, either the kilim (see p. 126) or the bouquet swatch (see p. 128) as part of the design?

4. My aim was to adapt the final black and white design to color. What would be the color scheme?

5. A garment knitted in the round would make the color knitting easier for both versions. A simple garment shape would keep the focus on the patterns. Perhaps a cap sleeve would give a better fit?

To begin the project, I had to develop several patterns that would work well together, even though they might be very different in appearance. I wanted at least three patterns, perhaps more, to give a strong patchwork effect: an angular plaid, a softly rounded pattern and another that might combine both angular and rounded shapes to act as a visual bridge between the first two.

My Designer Notebook shows several items that influenced my colorwork garments: the photograph of the little Dutch girls, which inspired the eclectic mix of patterns; the Russian shawl, which was translated into my floral swatch and eventual sweater yoke; and the Peruvian hat, whose colors inspired the palette for my lively colorwork coat version of this design. (Inset photo, The Bettmann Archive.)

From experience, I knew that my swatching for this project would be in two phases. First, I would work small individual swatches on straight needles, looking for a group of patterns that would work well together. Second, in preparation for the larger project, I would work a circular swatch in order to test my gauge in the round.

I designed a plaid pattern by swatching. I first worked a sequence of horizontal stripes, then embroidered the vertical lines, spacing them fairly close so I could knit them later as a stranded pattern. I translated my plaid to graph paper.

Next I wanted to design a contrasting pattern with curving lines. I designed this first on paper. From my books of traditional color patterns, I chose a handful of rounded motifs, X'ed the patterns onto graph paper and photocopied them many times. I had fun arranging and taping the little motifs on graph paper in interesting formations. I came up with my version of a *mille fleur* pattern — a field of many flowers of various sizes.

I found a bold Turkish panel that worked well with my other patterns to use as a border at the lower edge of the body. I softened the hard lines by adding some small, rounded motifs. I also added patterning at the sides so that the multiple repeats would link together gracefully.

Finally, I thought about using a narrow border I had charted from a 16th-century knitted garment I had seen at the Metropolitan Museum of Art (see the top left photo on p. 5). I swatched the pattern and found that it worked well with the others.

Swatch project

I needed to establish whether black or white would be the background color and what my circular gauge would be. To choose the background color, I worked a rectangular swatch in the round. On each half of the swatch, I worked two repeats of the large border, one with black as the background and the other side with white. I worked two small swatches for each of the plaid and narrow border patterns. I decided that the black background would be more dramatic.

I knitted these hats in the round for this chapter's Swatch Project to help me establish gauge for the two Designer Notebook garments. The black and white hat is edged with a red hem worked in a finer yarn. The brightly colored hat has a welted edging.

Working a circular hat swatch is not something I invented. It has probably been done in other countries as well as in the United States, where Elizabeth Zimmermann first put together guidelines for her *Knitter's Almanac* (see the Bibliography on pp. 258-260). There's no better way to test circular gauge, and, what's more, hat swatches are great fun to make. You can, of course, vary your hat in many ways. I used 120 stitches for a loose-fitting hat. For a snugger fit, cast on 100 stitches. After you work it to desired length, you can bind off all at once, as I did, or decrease gradually to a form a point, or work a long tube and gather the stitches into a pouf. Add any lower edging you like. I used an invisible hem and a folded-up welting. Don't forget to decorate the top with a pompom, tassel, loops, bell or button. If you have made smaller swatches to test other patterns, as I did, you can use two of them for ear flaps.

After working my hat, I still had more design decisions to make. A sketch and schematic allowed me to test the pattern's placement and think about the shape of the garment. I decided to break the garment up into rather large sections, to mimic the look of the fabrics in the photo. I chose a garter-stitch edging I had seen in a Swedish hand-knitting book, which was worked in stripes of black and white. I wanted to insert some color into the sweater to provide some startling contrast. I considered designing something special at the yoke but saw no reason not to use a swatch I had already made. I decided that my graphic bouquet swatch, inspired by the Russian shawl and seen in the Designer Notebook photo on p. 135, would make an interesting yoke insertion, contributing to the patchwork nature of the garment.

Because the black and white pullover was designed with pattern in mind, the idea of next translating it into color was challenging, to say the least. While thinking about possible color combinations, I found a hand-knitted Peruvian hat that I had bought the early 1970s (see the photo on p. 135). The warm beige background was embroidered with every color of the spectrum in bright, hot shades. I had never designed with such bright colors before, and the prospect intrigued me.

Finding all of these colors in a traditional knitting yarn was difficult. I turned instead to a needlepoint yarn, which offered me a wide range of colors and would work to the same gauge as my black and white yarns.

As with the black and white sweater, a circular hat swatch helped me decide background. I made half of it beige like the background and used the pattern on the other side. I worked the colors in a rainbow progression. Other smaller swatches helped me to decide how I might use the colors in other ways.

I planned the final layout of the color patterns in a rough sketch. I took the original pullover a step further by splitting it up the front to form a coat. And, in keeping with my inspiration, I used a textured checked edging, similar to one I had seen on another Peruvian hat.

Instructions for black and white pullover & rainbow coat

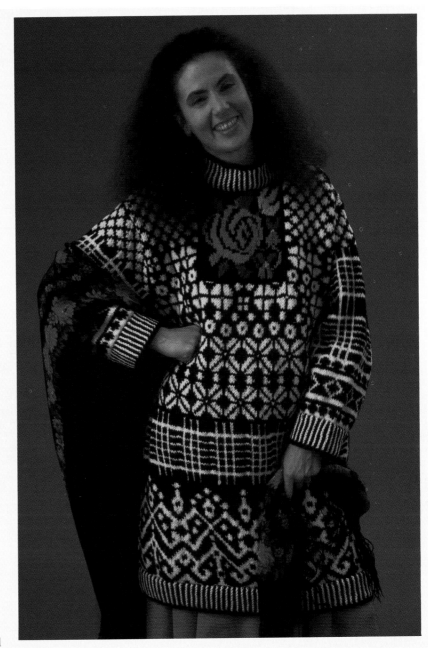

These two circularly knitted, oversized garments use the same stranded colorwork patterns in different colorways. For the intermediate knitter.

SIZE
To fit 32-34 (36-38, 40-42)-in. bust.

FINISHED MEASUREMENTS
Bust at underarm:
    Pullover: 42½ (48¾, 52¾) in.
    Coat (buttoned): 43¾ (49¾, 53¾) in.
Length: 34 (34½, 35) in.

MATERIALS
For pullover, I used my favorite worsted-weight yarn: soft, long-wearing Brunswick "Germantown." For coat, I used brilliant Paternayan "Persian" tapestry yarn. You may substitute another yarn that will give you same gauge.

Black and white pullover
• 4 (5, 6) skeins "Germantown Knitting Worsted" from Brunswick (100% wool; 3½ oz = 220 yd) in color white #400 (W).
• 6 (7, 8) skeins "Germantown" in color black #460 (B).
• Scraps of worsted-weight yarn in following colors: red, deep rose, lime green, kelly green, yellow, gold, royal blue and purple.

Rainbow coat
• 6 (7, 8) skeins Paternayan "Persian" from Reynolds Yarns (100% wool; 4 oz = approx 172 yd) in color beige #475 (B).
• 1 (1, 2) skeins in following colors: #541 royal blue (RB); #592 aqua (A); #591 turquoise (T); #331 purple (P); #352 fuschia (F); #941 red (R); #811 orange (O); #770 yellow (Y); #670 lime (L); #631 green (G).
• 1 pair size 6 knitting needles.
• 1 crochet hook, size F.
• 5 buttons, 1½ in. wide.

For both
• Circular knitting needles sizes 7, 8 and 9, both 16 in. and 24 in. long, or size to obtain gauge.
• 1 set dpn size 7, 8 and 9.
• Sewing machine and sewing thread.

GAUGE
• 20 sts and 22 rnds equal 4 in. with size 9 circular needle over color patterns.
• 20 sts and 24 rows equal 4 in. with size 7 needles for yoke insert.
• To save time later, take time to swatch and check your gauge.

NOTES ON PATTERN CHARTS FOR BOTH GARMENTS
• Unless indicated, k every rnd, read charts from right to left, beg each rnd as indicated.
• Carry color not in use loosely across WS, twist when necessary to avoid long floats. On solid-color rnds, change to needle one size smaller.

BLACK AND WHITE PULLOVER AND RAINBOW COAT

Pullover schematic

← 15 (18¼, 20¼) in. →
6½ (7, 7½) in.

9 in.

8 in.

1½ (2, 2½) in.

10½ (11, 11½) in.

21 in.

42½ (48¼, 52¾) in.

2½ in.

▮ = cut areas

‡ = seamless fold

Coat schematic

← 15 (18¼, 20¼) in. →
6½ (7, 7½) in.

2½ in.

8 (8½, 9) in.

34 (34½ 35) in.

16½ (16½, 17) in.

42¼ (48¼, 52¼) in.

(All measurements are after cuts have been made.)

Key to sizes
To fit: 32-34 (36-38, 40-42)-in. bust/chest
Size #: ① (②, ③)

Key to colors:
See "Materials" on p. 137.

1 square = 1 in.

Sleeve schematic

← 21¼ (22½, 23½) in. →

4 in.

14 (14, 14½) in.

2½ in.

12 (13¼, 14½) in.

Rainbow coat starts here.

Black and white pullover starts here.

BLACK AND WHITE PULLOVER

BODY

With size 9 circular needle and B, cast on 210 (242, 262) sts. Do not twist cast-on row, place marker and join.

Notes: All rnds begin at left side. Below armhole, both left and right sides are marked with a single "seam" st, which separates front from back.

Next rnd: sl marker, k1 W (left seam st), work Row 1 of wide border over front 104 (120, 130) sts, k1 W (right seam st), work row 1 of wide border over back 104 (120, 130) sts to end. Keep seam sts in W, except on solid B rnds, work even until 48 rnds are complete, inc 1 st at both center front and center back on last rnd—212 (244, 264) sts.

Next rnd: * k1, work Row 1 of black and white plaid pat over 105 (121, 131) sts; rep from * to end. Work even in black and white plaid pat for 25 more rows.

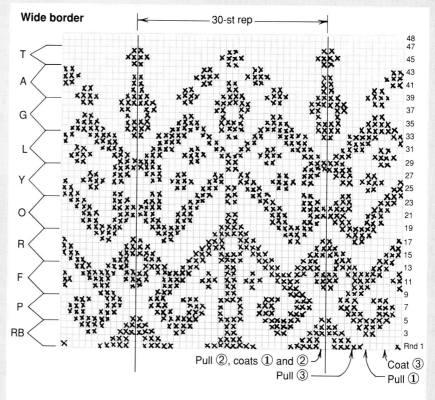

Wide border

← 30-st rep →

T
A
G
L
Y
O
R
F
P
RB

48
47
45
43
41
39
37
35
33
31
29
27
25
23
21
19
17
15
13
11
9
7
5
3
Rnd 1

Pull ②, coats ① and ②
Pull ③
Coat ③
Pull ①

Black-and-white plaid pattern

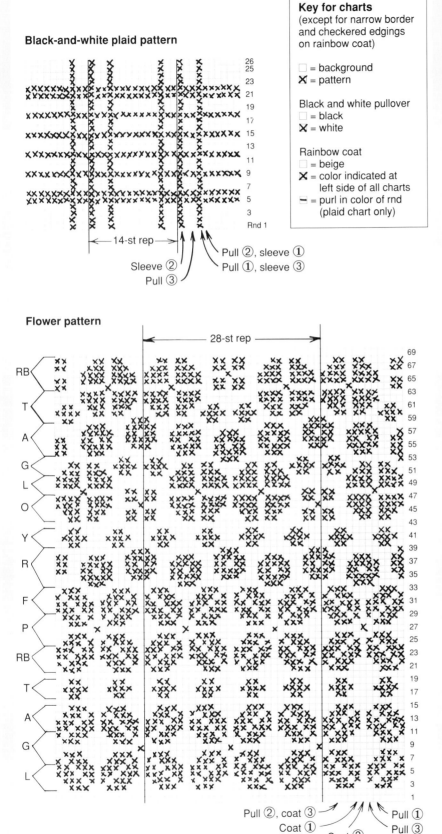

Key for charts
(except for narrow border and checkered edgings on rainbow coat)

☐ = background
✕ = pattern

Black and white pullover
☐ = black
✕ = white

Rainbow coat
☐ = beige
✕ = color indicated at left side of all charts
⊟ = purl in color of rnd (plaid chart only)

Next rnd: * k1, work Row 1 of flower pat over 105 (121, 131) sts; rep from *. Work even until piece measures approx 21 in., or to desired length.

ARMHOLE SHAPING
Next rnd: Bind off 5 sts (includes seam), work to 4 sts before next side seam st, bind off 9 sts (includes seam), work to last 4 sts of rnd and bind them off. Pull yarn through last st and cut—97 (113, 123) sts each at front and back.
Next rnd: With RS facing, cast on 5 sts, work to next bound-off section, cast on 5 sts, work to end of rnd, place marker and join.
Next rnd: * Work in divider pat over 5 cast-on sts, ssk, work in pat to 2 sts before next 5 cast-on sts, k2tog; rep from *. Rep this last rnd 10 more times—75 (91, 101) sts each at front and back, not including divider sts; AND AT SAME TIME, cont until armhole depth measures 1½ (2, 2½) in.

FRONT OPENING
Mark center front 33 (35, 37) sts.
Next rnd: Work 5 sts, work to center sts, bind off center 33 (35, 37) sts, work to end.
Next rnd: Work to bound-off sts, cast on 5 sts (keep in divider pat), work to end. Cont until 69 rnds of flower pat are complete. Keep divider sts, beg dot pat on fronts and back on next rnd. Work even until armhole depth measures 10½ (11, 11½) in.
Next rnd: Work in pat, bind off 5 sts of each divider section—21 (28, 32) sts each side of front, 75 (91, 101) sts at back.

Divider pat
(for sections to be cut)

Dot pat

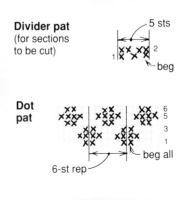

Shoulder Shaping

Left-front shoulder shaping: Work back and forth over left-front section only, bind off 7 (10, 10) sts at beg of 1st RS row, then 7 (9, 11) sts at beg of next 2 RS rows.

Right-front shoulder shaping: With RS facing, join strands at beg of front opening. Work back and forth over right-front section only, work RS row. Turn. Bind off 7 (10, 10) sts at beg of WS row, then 7 (9, 11) sts at beg of next 2 WS rows.

Back shoulder shaping: Mark center back 13 (15, 17) sts. With RS facing, join strands at beg of front opening. Work back and forth on back sts, bind off 7 (10, 10) sts on 1st row, then work to center 13 (15, 17) sts, join a 2nd set of balls, bind off center sts, work to end. Work back and forth with 2 sets of balls, bind off 7 (10, 10) sts at beg of next row, then 7 (9, 11) sts at beg of next 4 rows; AND AT SAME TIME, bind off 5 sts from each neck edge twice.

Sleeve

• With size 9 dpn and W, cast on 60 (66, 72) sts. Do not twist cast-on row, place marker and join. {When sleeve is large enough, change to 16-in. circular needle.}

• Each rnd begins with a seam st: keep seam st in B, except on solid-color W rnds.

Next rnd: sl marker, k seam st, work Row 1 of narrow border to end. Work 2 more rnds.

Next rnd, inc rnd: k1, M1, work to end of rnd, M1. Rep last rnd every 3 rnds 22 more times, working incs into pat; AND AT SAME TIME, cont until narrow border is complete (note: 10 incs have been worked each side)—80 (86, 92) sts.

Next rnd: k1, work Row 1 of plaid pat to end. Work 2 complete reps of plaid pat, AND AT SAME TIME, cont until sleeve measures 14 (14, 14½) in. or to desired length—106 (112, 118) sts.

Cap Shaping

Next rnd: Bind off 5 sts, work to last 4 sts and bind them off. Pull yarn through last st and cut.

Next rnd: With RS facing and B, cast on 5 sts, work in pat to end, place marker and join.

Next rnd: Work 5 sts in divider pat, ssk, work in pat to last 2 sts, k2tog. Cont to dec at beg and end of every rnd as described 19 more times; AND AT SAME TIME, cont until 2 reps of plaid pat are complete, then work 1 rnd with B.

Next rnd: Work 5 sts, ssk, work dot pat over to last 2 sts of rnd, end k2tog.

Cont until all decs have been worked—57 (63, 69) sts.

Next rnd: Bind off 9 sts, work to end; turn. Working back and forth, bind off 4 sts at beg of next 3 rows. Bind off rem 36 (42, 48) sts on next row.

Finishing

Steam pieces, flatten fabric with your palms.

Sewing and Cutting Openings

With RS facing, sew a line of very small sewing machine sts down center st in divider pat sections. Sew down each of rem 4 sts. Cut along center, from cast-on edge to bind-off edge. Sew fronts to back at shoulders. Sew sleeves in armholes next to divider st section.

Floral Insert

With size 7 needles and B, cast on 35 (37, 39) sts. P WS row. Working back and forth, work rows 1-48 of chart, beg and end where indicated, using scraps of yarn to match colors in chart below.

Shape neck edge

Next row (RS): k10, join a 2nd ball B and bind off center 13 (15, 17) sts, k to end. Work both sides at same time with separate balls of yarn, bind off 2 sts from each neck edge 5 times. Steam. Sew insert into front opening.

Narrow border

Key
(Note that color key differs from key for other charts.)

FLORAL INSERT

35 (37, 39) sts

beg ① ② ③

BANDS

Striped band for sleeves (make 2):
With B and size 7 needles, cast on
12 sts. * K 2 rows B, k 2 rows W; rep
from * until piece measures 9½ (10½,
11½) in., end with W ridge. Bind off.
Trim band: With RS facing, size 7
needles and B, pick up 1 st for every
ridge along edge. K 1 row. Bind off.
Sew ends of band tog. Pin untrimmed
edge to lower sleeve. Sew, easing in
any fullness in sleeve.
Striped band for lower body: Work as
for sleeve until piece measures 38 (45,
49) in. Trim band. Join. Pin to lower
edge of body, then sew.
Neckline band: Work as for sleeve
bands until piece measures 16 (17,
18) in. Trim band. Join. Pin to neckline
edge, then sew.

RAINBOW COAT

BODY

With size 7 circular needle and O, cast
on 200 (230, 248) sts. Do not twist cast-
on row, place marker and join. All
rnds begin at front of coat.
Rnds 1 and 2: With O, k5, p to end.
Change to B and k 1 rnd, inc 13 (15,
17) sts evenly (do not inc in first
5 sts)—213 (245, 265) sts. From this
point on, work first 5 sts of every rnd
in divider pat, except on solid-color
rows, k these 5 sts.

Beg checkered edging

Rnd 1: Work 5 sts in divider pat, work
rnd 1 of lower edge pat to end. When
13 rnds of chart are complete, change
to B and k 1 rnd, inc 2 (0, 0) sts evenly
(do not inc in first 5 sts)—215 (245,
265) sts. Change to size 9 circular
needle.
Next rnd: Work 5 sts as est, work
Row 1 of wide border to end. Work
even until 48 rnds are complete, inc
1 st at center back on last rnd—216
(246, 266) sts.
Next rnd: Work 5 sts, work Rnd 1 of
rainbow-coat plaid pat to end. Work
even until 26 rnds of chart are
complete.
Next rnd: Work 5 sts in divider pat,
work Row 1 of flower pat to end.
Work even until piece measures
23½ in., or to desired length.

ARMHOLE SHAPING

Next rnd: Work 5 sts, work 49 (56, 61)
sts, bind off 8 sts, work 97 (113, 123)
sts, bind off 8 sts, work to 49 (56, 61)
sts to end.
Next rnd: Work in pat, cast on 5 sts
over each bound-off section.
Next rnd: * Work to 2 sts before cast-
on sts, k2tog, then work divider pat
over 5 cast-on sts, ssk; rep from *
once, work to end. Rep this last rnd 10
more times—38 (45, 50) sts each front
section and 75 (91, 101) sts in back
section, not counting divider sts.

Work even until 69 rows of flower pat
are complete. Keep divider pat sts,
beg dot pat in all other sections on
next rnd. Keep background in B, and
work 3 rnds each: * P, F, R, O, Y, L, G,
A, T, R; rep from * if necessary. Work
even until armhole depth measures
8 (8½, 9) in.

FRONT NECKLINE

Next rnd: Bind off 5 divider pat sts,
then bind off 7 (7, 8) sts, work to last
7 (7, 8) sts, then bind them off. Pull
yarn through last st and cut.

Rainbow coat plaid pattern

Color sequence:

Rainbow coat checkered edgings
Note: Squares with (–) symbol = p RS, kWS in color of previous row or rnd.

Next rnd: Place marker, cast on 5 sts, join, and work to end.
Next rnd, dec rnd: Work 5 sts in divider pat, ssk, work to last 2 sts of rnd, end k2tog. Rep dec rnd 9 more times—21 (28, 32) sts each front, not including divider-pat sts. Work even until armhole depth is 10½ (11, 11½) in.
Next rnd: Work in pat, bind off each 5 sts divider pat st section—21 (28, 32) sts each side of front, 75 (91, 101) sts at back.

SHOULDER SHAPING
Work same shoulder shaping as for black and white pullover.

SLEEVE
With size 7 dpn and O, cast on 52 (56, 62) sts. Do not twist cast-on row, place marker and join. {When sleeve is large enough, change to 16-in. circular needle.} P 2 rnds. Change to B and k 1 rnd, inc 4 sts evenly—56 (60, 66) sts. Work rnds 1-13 of checkered lower-edge pat. With B, k 1 rnd, inc 6 sts evenly spaced—60 (66, 72) sts. At this point, each rnd begins with a single seam st: keep seam st in lightest color, except on solid-color rnds. (Photo on p. 141 shows alternative underarm seam using several seam sts rather than one.)
Next rnd: k1, work row 1 of narrow border to end. From this point on, work as for pullover sleeve, except work rainbow-coat plaid pat twice, in 2 different color sequences as indicated. K 1 rnd in B. Beg dot pat, keeping background in B, and work 3 rnds each in L, G, A, T and RB.

FINISHING
Plaid lines
•With crochet hook and color indicated on chart, chain vertical lines into p ribs as follows: hold yarn beneath piece on WS, and insert hook from RS to WS, beneath lowest p "bar." Pull through a loop to RS.
* With loop on hook, insert needle 2 p bars above last, and pull through another loop, then pull this loop through original. Rep from *. Chain loosely to keep tension even. On last st, cut yarn, pull to RS and through last loop. Rep on all p ribs.

•In body and sleeve's lower plaid section, chain lines with B. In upper plaid section, chain lines as in chart.
•Steam pieces, flatten fabric with your palms. Machine stitch and cut openings as for pullover. Sew fronts to back at shoulders.
Neckline trim
With RS facing, size 7 needle and B, pick up 92 (96, 100) sts evenly around entire neckline edge. Work rows 1-13 of neckline edge pat. With B, k 1 row, dec 9 sts evenly. With O, k 2 rows, p 1 row, bind off in p.
Left-front buttonband
•With RS facing, size 6 needle and B, pick up 12 sts along neckline trim, then approx 1 st for every row in body, then 12 sts along lower edge trim to yield a multiple of 4 sts. Work rows 1-9 of front edge chart. With B, k 1 row, dec 10 sts evenly. With O, p 1 row, bind off in p.
•Sew 5 buttons along band. Work right-front band same as for left, working a buttonhole opposite each button. Sew sleeves in armholes next to divider-st pat sections.

WHAT IF...?

What if I combined my black and white pullover with the rainbow coat?

New garment shape — raglan

Millefleur dots along raglan line

Plaid body and sleeves

Shorter jacket style

2 rose bouquet patch pockets

Millefleur dots inserted into striped edgings

Deeper edgings

the Comfortable Classics

Certain garments retain their appeal generation after generation and influence each new succession of designers in novel ways. The popularity of many of these classics can be attributed to the simple fact that they're comfortable—witness the appeal of American-born blue jeans. Sold first by Levi Strauss in California in 1853 and once worn only by cowboys and farmers, blue jeans have been varied endlessly in color, shape and detail over decades and have moved from pure function to high fashion. Not all classics achieve such widespread appeal, but many make their way into popular clothing designs. Whatever the breadth of their appeal, classics usually have one or more unique details that set them apart from other garments of their kind. Some classics recall the flavor of a certain historical period. Others remind us of a famous celebrity, profession, costume, particular national dress or uniform.

I don't limit my notion of "classic" to favorite designs from the current decade or century. Nor, as a knitwear designer, do I look only to knitted classics for inspiration (if I did that, my range of inspiration would be sorely limited). I have always found it useful to be acquainted with all kinds and periods of classic clothing, which I find in books, paintings and museum collections, since these garments offer innumerable familiar, yet interesting details that can be varied endlessly for new designs. The classics themselves can be recreated almost exactly, or they can be altered so extensively that the original source is no longer recognizable. What's important is that the classics or their details hold the seeds of ideas that can inspire any one of many designs.

Sweater classics

There are many classics among knitted garments, and their appeal usually stems from either the garment's unique pattern stitches or its distinctive shape. In some cases, for example, the guernseys in the inset photo on p. 100, the knitted classic is characterized by both distinc-

Facing page: My classic Aran pullover, designed from photos of many traditional Aran sweaters. Instructions for this sweater are found on pp. 252-254.

tive patterns and shape. Some sweater classics are also associated with a particular region of the world or a specific historical period.

Perhaps the most popular sweater classic of all is the cabled Aran pullover (see the photo on p. 144). Worn by fisherman in the Aran islands off the western coast of Ireland, this garment was worked in natural ivory wool. This sweater's most striking characteristic is its heavily textured fabric with patterns arranged in vertical panels. Most Aran patterns are cabled and include knots or bobbles, but often they contain knit/purl patterns mixed with twist-stitch or simple lace panels. Also interesting is the fact that the Aran is often knitted from the top down and incorporates a shoulder strap that extends from the upper sleeve. This strap allows the patterns to be carried over the shoulder to the neck edge.

The Aran sweater has been varied in every way possible by hand- and machine-knitters alike. My first published design, in fact, was a variation on an Aran sweater—though my interpretation was not very traditional. It was worked in a plum color, and the textured vertical bands were interrupted at chest level by a strong vertical line, in a distinctly non-Aran pattern (see the sweater at left in the photo on p. 7).

Although it looks complex, the Aran is really one of the easiest sweaters to design. Cable patterns can be swatched separately or together to determine the width of the panels, and these cable widths can be plotted onto a schematic to plan the appropriate width for the sweater pieces (as done for the guernsey on pp. 101-103). Also, an Aran need not be made up of a multitude of patterns. A single, centrally placed cable can be flanked on both sides by a simple allover pattern. (For more pattern inspiration, see the discussion of twist stitches and cable patterns on pp. 183-189.)

The tennis sweater was born in the early part of this century and continues to be a favorite classic. I suppose there's no single definitive tennis sweater, but no one could fail to recognize one of its several variations. The classic version almost always has a bold striped pattern that frames a V-neck and often the edge above the ribbing. Frequently the stripes are worked in plain stockinette stitch. In contrast, the body of the sweater is often cabled or widely ribbed. The sweaters in the photo above left have a classic silhouette that eliminates bulk and allows for ease of movement.

There are many ways to alter the basic personality of a tennis sweater. The simplest variation is to switch the traditional contrast between the dark stripes and the light body. You can also vary the stripes, perhaps working them into the cable pattern of the body. The

1920s tennis great Bill Tilden and a young friend wear excellent examples of the classic tennis sweater. Look closely and you'll see that the boy's sweater has an interesting round neck set into the striped section. Look also at the folded-up lower edges—how might you use this detail as a design feature? (Photo, Smithsonian Institution.)

VARIATIONS ON THREE SWEATER CLASSICS

Tennis sweater: coat variation

Twin set: cardigan over cardigan

Letter sweater: Fair Isle-type pattern made from letters

(knitted fabric decorated with grosgrain ribbon in basketweave pattern) depth of the V-neck can also be raised or lowered, and the silhouette can be varied for nonsports use.

The classic two-piece twin set usually combines a cardigan with a sleeveless or short-sleeved pullover (sometimes the under sweater is also long-sleeved, and occasionally both sweaters are short-sleeved). Created in the 1940s and popular throughout the 1950s, the set's cardigan often had a matching grosgrain-ribbon band sewn along the front edges, onto which buttons were sewn and the buttonholes reinforced. The twin-sweater concept makes use of the notion that if one sweater is good, two are even better. I agree because this twosome offers so much room to play with details.

There are many ways to alter the basic shape and proportions of this classic duo. You can match the patterns in both sweaters or work each in unrelated fabrics. And, as with any cardigan, borders and buttons are important details. For instance, a plain cardigan can be jazzed up by using an unusual edging, either flat or ribbed, very textured or wider than normal. Buttons that exactly match the cardigan's color can unify the set. Alternatively, large or contrasting buttons can lend the set a sporty feel, and dressy rhinestone or pearl buttons can transform it into an evening suit.

The letter sweater is one of the true indigenous American sweater classics. Emblazoned with the symbol of a favorite sports team, this sweater is simple, yet striking. The letter can be knitted in, but more often it is a sewn-on felt appliqué. I wasn't much of a sports fan in high school, but I did admire the thick cheerleader pullovers and long, comfortable letterman cardigans with big pockets.

Although space prevents me from including photos here, when you're looking to sweater classics for inspiration, don't forget the Argyle golfing sweaters with matching socks, Icelandic circular-yoke sweaters, Shetland Fair Isle jumpers, Poor Boy ribbed sweaters of the 1960s and classic knitted bathing suits of the 1930s and 1940s (see the photo on p. 6).

Although most of my designing results in a hand-knitted product, probably half of my inspiration for shaping, silhouette and detail comes from nonknitted garments. I don't actually need a garment in hand to be inspired by shape, edging, collar and other details, although it can be helpful to refer to a specific garment. Instead, I always have an eye open for interesting wearables and always have a

A classic cheerleader's pullover can have a bold sewn-on or knitted-in monogram letter. To update this sweater, consider altering the letter's placement or using several letters as a monogram. Instead of a solid-color background, why not try stripes or another colorwork pattern? (Photo, The Bettmann Archive.)

magazine in hand, whether current or vintage, and I also collect books about clothing and textiles. I'm intrigued by family photographs, which always turn up interesting clothing — look through your own family album to see what inspiration you may find there.

Rarely do I turn away from any garment and say that it offers nothing by way of design ideas. Sometimes a garment will translate easily into knitted fabric, either because it has a simple shape or its fabric is one I can easily simulate in knitting. At other times, I'll be able to adapt only details from the garment for my design. When you analyze any garment for possible translation into knitwear, consider two main issues: what it is about this particular garment that interests you, and what problems you'll encounter in translating it into a knitted garment. To help you see how successful or problematic your design will be, you'll need swatches and a schematic drawing.

In the Gallery of Classics that follows, I've begun the process of exploring a design inspired by an existing garment, in each of these cases, by a classic garment. Included in this gallery — which could have expanded endlessly — are various types of classic clothing I find exciting: some fashion favorites, a classic uniform, some traditional folkwear and some classics associated with famous people.

Gallery of Classics

Cowboy shirt

Gene Autry's classic cowboy shirt intrigues me because it combines a distinctive button-front detail with a showy all-American flag graphic (photo, The Bettmann Archive). The simple lines of the garment made me confident that I could use this image as the basis for a design.

I wanted a flat, simple fabric but something more interesting and a bit denser than stockinette. I chose some knit/purl patterns that all shared moss-stitch details. In my swatch, I used the boldest pattern for the body and sleeve sections, and a less complicated pattern for the button-on front flap. For the test collar, picked up along the edge of the swatch, I used simple moss stitch. I translated the contrasting piping of the cowboy shirt with a reverse-stockinette roll at the edges, and my buttons borrow the horsey theme of the photo. I chose a classic-fitting silhouette and altered the proportion of the button-front detail, as shown in my schematic. (See pp. 77-98 for more about knit/purl patterns and edgings.)

Seeing this shirt, you can't help but also think about the more familiar yoked cowboy shirt, decorated with pearl snap buttons and embroidered curlicues. How would you translate that classic into a knitted fabric? And how about knitted riding chaps?

Surely no designer can avoid the challenge of using the American flag at one time or another. I think the plain-stockinette pocket swatch on the facing page is the perfect beginning for a kid's Fourth-of-July cotton pullover.

Gibson Girl blouse

With its leg-o'-mutton sleeves, high collar and full blouson front ending in a narrow, fitted waist, the turn-of-the-century Gibson Girl blouse is distinctive in shape (photo, The Bettmann Archive). My version of this classic would end at the waist, with a narrow ribbing to hold in the body's fullness. To retain the broad-shouldered effect, I would shape the sides from above the rib to the shoulder to allow for fullness at the bust without bulk at the waist. The sleeve would be narrow at the wrists and full at the upper arm, with the extra fullness gathered into the shoulder seam.

I wanted my version to be lacy like the original but far less fussy and more contemporary. Using a lightweight wool, I experimented with edgings and settled on a scalloped, garter-stitch lace border. I matched this border with Barbara Walker's garter-based pattern with a diamond-shaped motif for the body and inserted eyelets in the ribbing to extend the notion of lace. (See pp. 190-192 for more about lace and pp. 41-42 for a discussion of silhouette.)

Sailor suit

The most obvious detail of the classic American sailor's uniform is the square-edged collar with its softly knotted tie (photo courtesy of Claire Phillips). I've used this type of collar on many designs, and one of the most successful was worked in unlikely mohair. It is an easy collar to knit, and my schematics below offer two approaches to shaping. Remember that, for the best fit, the collar must follow the shape of the neckline itself. (See pp. 220-224 for more information about collars and neckline details.)

Flapper fashions

The fashions of the 1920s ushered in a new era of comfort for women. Shorter skirts, loose kimono coats and a boyish silhouette all characterize this period. My favorite fashion illustrations come from this period, especially the ones that depict women in head-hugging cloche hats and narrow dresses (photo on facing page, The Bettmann Archive; illustrations top and center, courtesy Dover Publications, Inc.).

Perhaps the most striking aspect of 1920s dresses is the focus on the hip line. Usually the dress's skirt began and fell from the hip, often gathered or softly flounced. Invariably this lowered waistline was belted or sashed in an interesting way.

The few dresses I've knitted were planned to be as lightweight as possible since the bulk of even a medium-weight yarn would cause the garment to stretch out of shape. The narrow 1920s silhouette is the perfect inspiration for knitted dresses because it eliminates bulk.

My flapper-inspired "scarf dress" is really a bit of a cheat. It has a long, knitted body ending at the hip line, a knitted belt and a pleated skirt formed from a lightweight silk shawl (several matching scarves would also work) attached to the body's lower edge. For this design, I chose a shiny, fine-gauge cotton, worked firmly in an allover lace pattern. For more support, I might line the body of the dress with a lightweight, light-colored silk that would show the lace off well.

Two other fashion items from the 1920s intrigue me. I've always been simultaneously attracted and repelled by the small fur wraps that include the head of the animal. These must have been enduring classics because, four decades later, I remember my grandmother wearing what my sister and I, as kids, called her Skelenski. I also love the 1920s coats, which enclose the wearer like a cocoon, with a voluminous body and short narrow sleeves.

I merged these two favorites into a fanciful coat. I swatched a drapey rayon/wool fabric for the coat's body and a fox-colored bouclé, complete with beady Skelenski "eyes."

Chanel suit

In the 1930s, French designer Gabrielle (Coco) Chanel created a suit that has inspired countless variations up to the present day. Like many classic garments, this suit—a version of which Chanel wears in the photo on the facing page—is very simple looking (Cecil Beaton photograph courtesy of Sotheby's London). What makes it special is its combination of details: its close-fitting silhouette; the jacket's lower edge falling at the high-hip line; the distinctive, often nubby-textured fabric, always made of a luxury fiber or blend; the signature trim on the jacket's edges; and the fancy buttons, often with the trademark linked double C of the couture House of Chanel.

I worked three very different swatches: one with a ribbed border, one with a trim that I hand-braided from matching yarn and sewed on, and one with a mosaic-patterned edge. It is easy to see how literally thousands of suits could have been derived from the basic Chanel formula: two-piece, close-fitting silhouette + distinctive fabric + trim and buttons = classic Chanel suit. (See pp. 232-234 for more on trims.)

Matador's costume

The bullfighter's short bolero jacket, traditionally encrusted with ornate trim, is ideally suited to layer over a garment with waist interest (photo, The Bettmann Archive). The jacket works best when it conforms to the body, and its lower edge can fall somewhere between the waist and just below the bustline. However, I also like small trapeze-shaped bolero jackets that swing out from the shoulder.

You couldn't draw inspiration from the matador's jacket without thinking about decoration. Why not add a ready-made trim at the front edge, as I did? In addition to undulating twist-stitch patterns decorated with popcorns planned for the body of the jacket, I knitted some fancy epaulets and planned to use buttons and tassels for decoration. The effect: a little jacket that's big on trim. (For more about dressmaker trims, see pp. 232-234.)

Chinese robe

This woman's robe from 18th-century China intrigues me because of its bell shape and distinctively curved neckline border, typical of many traditional Chinese garments (photo, Isabella Stewart Gardner Museum, Boston). The ornate fabric is decorated with stylized chrysanthemums and butterflies. The closure edge and cuffs contrast strongly in color with the fabric of the body.

This Chinese robe inspired a brightly colored coat design. I played with traditional snowflake patterns, softening them into rounded forms to avoid a pointed "star" look. And, using colored pencils, graph paper and photocopy techniques to combine patterns, I came up with a busy floral-like design. I worked a large swatch in bright, bulky wools, curving the edge to test a contrasting border. This coat, with its special opening, seemed to warrant some special buttons.

To understand the unusual bell shape of the original Chinese robe, I experimented with measurements in schematic form, trying to simulate the look of the robe in the photo. Before knitting the full garment, I would carefully chart the lower edges of my coat to see how the shaping would affect the charted pattern. (For more information about designing knitted coats, see p. 67; for more on planning curved lower edges, see pp. 215-216.)

Tuxedo

The traditional tuxedo with tails in the photo at left (photo, Springer/Bettmann Film Archive) is worn by the quintessentially elegant Fred Astaire. I have included this garment because, although it may seem a difficult design to translate to hand-knitting, its characteristic elements are endlessly intriguing—the basic contrast of black and white; the short, cropped front and sweeping tails behind; and the traditional bow tie.

For my knitted tuxedo jacket, I wanted to retain the tails and shawl collar but modify the shape to produce a softer, less fitted garment. For elegance, I chose to work with winter white —almost as formal as black—in a soft, cabled wool, which would be firm enough to lend just a bit of structure without stiffness.

My swatch shows how I tested the curved front edge of the coat. I also worked a miniature ribbed shawl collar and trimmed both edges with discrete I-cord. For detail, covered buttons seemed perfect. The matching skirt in my sketch, which splits at the lower back to mimic the tails of the jacket, is also trimmed in the same way. (See pp. 224-227 for information on lapels.)

Fortuny dress

In the 1920s, the Italian designer Fortuny was inspired by garment shapes from Greek antiquity and developed many distinctive dresses and two-piece ensembles. In direct contrast to the tuxedo, Fortuny's column-like garments were soft and drapey, and made of a silk fabric folded into tiny allover pleats. When the garment was worn, the minuscule pleats opened up to cling softly to the body underneath. Off the body, the pleated garment could be "wrung" into a skein-like tube for storage. The dresses laced up in interesting ways, and the edges were decorated and weighted with beads. The Delphos tea gown (c. 1910-1930) in the photo below right is one such dress (photo, Jud Haggard; The Museum of Fine Arts, Houston; gift of Janie C. Lee).

I wanted to make as close a translation as possible of these wonderful dresses. I knew that any knitted fabric would be much heavier than the lightweight, crinkly silk Fortuny used, so, in order to eliminate bulk, I opted for a shorter design whose asymmetrical lower edge would fall between the waist and hip. To simulate a pleated effect, I tried several knitted fabrics, decorating each with beads—a lace rib, a garter-ridge fabric, a pebbly knit/purl pattern and a slip-stitch pattern. (See pp. 180-183 for information about slip-stitch pleat patterns.)

Finding inspiration in your own *Comfortable classic*

In addition to finding inspiration from classic garments, look to your own wardrobe for a personal classic that fits and flatters and which can serve as the basis for a new design. A favorite knitted sweater can help you with measurements for a new design, and many other nonknitted garments, from blouses to sweatshirts, can provide details and shaping ideas.

If you are planning to borrow actual measurements from another garment, follow these simple guidelines:

1. Analyze the weight of the fabric. To translate the measurements successfully to knitted fabric, you'll need to pick a yarn that will yield a similar weight.

2. Decide what characteristic of the garment you want to borrow. Is it its size and shape, length or width? Or a detail, like a sleeve or collar type?

MEASURING AN ANGLE

Ruler, set parallel to centerline of garment, measures height of angle.

Length

Raglan seamline

Base

Second ruler, set perpendicular to first, measures base of angle.

Centerline

MEASURING A CURVE

Half of body

Length

Ruler, set parallel to centerline of garment, measures height of curved armhole.

Second ruler, set perpendicular to first, measures width of curved armhole.

Width

Curved shirttail edge

Length of curve

Width

Angle plotted on graph paper

Raglan line

Length of raglan

Width of raglan

Centerline

1 square = 1 in.

Garment width

Curves plotted on graph paper

Half of garment width

Armhole

1 square = 1 in.

Length of curve on shirttail edge

Width of curve

3. Measure the garment pieces or details and record their dimensions on graph paper to create a schematic drawing. When it's time to convert these measurements to stitches, multiply your widths by your gauge to calculate stitch counts; then adjust these general stitch counts to accommodate a pattern repeat. You can also use this schematic drawing to help you plot isolated patterns.

Measuring your classic

Simple garments with very little shaping and boxy, geometric lines are easy to measure, but plotting curved areas in a garment can be challenging. Most difficult to capture are tailored garments or those with darts or shaping within the body of the pieces (for more information about this, see pp. 211-218).

Whatever the garment shape, here are some guidelines that can help you record measurements on graph paper. Starting with the body section of the garment, first draw a simple rectangle based on lengths and widths. After completing this basic outline, you can measure the individual parts of the garment (armhole, neckline and so on) and refine the dimensions within the rectangle. If the back and front of a garment are different, draw both. Follow the same procedure for the sleeves, beginning first with a rectangle based on the full length and width of the sleeve. Then refine the rectangle to shape the lower sleeve and any cap shaping above the underarm.

Consider the following important widths, and note any special characteristics: widest part of the body (at the bust or the hip?); neck width (is the back neck curved?); and cross-shoulder width (does it vary at different points, depending on the armhole shaping?).

You will also need to consider the following lengths: from the back neck to the lower edge of the garment; side lengths, from the underarm to the garment's lower edge; armhole depth (is there shaping in this area?); and neckline depth (does this vary from front to back?).

After you have the basic rectangular outline of your pieces, you'll need to plot the more refined lines. Straight edges are easy to measure and record. More difficult to plot are curves or angles, like those at the armhole edge or along a neckline. In the drawings on the facing page, I've plotted some details from two very different garments: a comfortable raglan sweatshirt and a favorite blouse with a curved armhole and shirttail lower edge.

The simplest way to recreate an angle is by using basic geometry. For instance, to measure the angle of a raglan armhole (or any other uncurved, slanted line), follow this procedure:

1. Lay a ruler or tape measure from the top point of the angle straight downward and parallel to the centerline of the garment.

2. Lay a second ruler or tape measure perpendicular to the first and parallel to the lower edge of the garment, at the bottom point of the curve. These two rulers together will show you the base of the angle and its height.

3. Plot three points on your graph: first, where the angle begins at the lower edge; second, where the rulers intersect; and, third, where the angle ends at the uppermost point. Connect the first and third points to recreate the angle of the raglan line.

Curved edges at necklines, armholes and sleeve caps can be measured in a similar way:

1. Set up your two rulers perpendicular to each other along the top and bottom points of the curve.

2. Measure the height and width of the curve at regular intervals and connect these points.

One-size-fits-all garments

One-size-fits-all garments are usually large enough to cover a big frame, yet proportioned so that they still drape attractively over a smaller body. Many one-size-fits-all garments simply fall from the shoulder, and, if they have sleeves, these sleeves are often planned to fold over or turn up.

A number of traditional ethnic garments come to mind when considering one-size-fits-all, like the South American serape, African caftan, Japanese kimono and eastern European felted mantle. Capes of all sorts are usually one-size-fits-all. They can be rectangular in shape, falling from the shoulders, or made up of triangular, pie-shaped wedges that allow the cape to flare out from the shoulders.

In addition to shirts, coats and shaped capes, there are some classic one-size-fits-all pants. The pair of early 20th-century, embroidered Nupe pants from Nigeria (see the photo on p. 164) has excess fabric that drapes between the legs, and narrow openings for the feet at the outer corners. I'm sure the waist must be pleated, wrapped or gathered with a drawstring. Just recently I saw this traditional African design adapted for a lightweight pair of

These embroidered Nupe pants from Nigeria — which are drawn in at the waist when worn — have a very oversized fit that might offer inspiration for an unusual one-size-fits-all pair of knitted pants. (Photo, Fowler Museum of Cultural History, UCLA.)

DRAPEY PANTS

1 square = 1 in.

pants imported from Morocco. I've drawn my knitted version below left, which I'm sure would be extremely comfortable. It would be best worked in a lightweight yarn. I might also choose to shape the pants slightly to eliminate extra bulk.

When designing one-size-fits-all garments, you need to use an exaggerated silhouette. Generally, a boxy rectangular shape with deep armholes is best. Sleeves should be on the short side, unless they're to be folded up. Shaping at the shoulders and neckline is important if the fabric is at all thick or stiff, so that the garment will follow the line of the body. If the fabric is soft, then unshaped shoulders will drape. I think garments in this category look best when they're a bit longer than they are wide, which lends the illusion of less bulk.

Capturing the design: Learning to sketch

Like most designers, I find it useful to capture designs in sketch form to test both a garment's proportions and the arrangement of its details. While I always draw schematics to work out the particulars of a design, I also like to express my ideas in a more life-like sketched rendering.

I almost abandoned sketching at first because I found it so intimidating. Sweaty-handed, I would hold the pencil with a vise-like grip and produce stiff, awkward lines. But by sketching just 15 minutes every day, I soon began to relax. Gradually I developed a cartoon-like style that serves my needs.

When you, too, learn to loosen your hand, you'll find that sketching can become an enjoyable end in itself. You really need only patience, which, as a knitter, you already possess. When you begin, just concentrate on making lines on the paper. Try hard not to dislike your own drawings or compare them to drawings by other people. Gradually, almost imperceptibly, your drawing skills will strengthen. You might also find books that introduce basic drawing techniques helpful (see the Bibliography on pp. 258-260).

My one-size-fits-all classic

The traditional Japanese kimono is one of the most elegant garments in the one-size-fits-all family. It is T-shaped, formed of rectangles that are pieced together to create a very simply constructed robe with overlapping fronts.

A kimono is a showplace for wonderful woven fabrics dyed in unusual ways, embroidered or printed. Silk is the fiber traditionally associated with kimonos, but they are also made from wool, cotton, linen, and, now in the 20th century, a variety of synthetics. Often the lining is a totally different fabric from the main fabric, creating a startling contrast from inside to outside.

I own a kimono-type garment called a *haori*. It is simpler in construction and shorter in body and sleeve length than the kimono, with front edges that meet and tie together, rather than overlap. I enjoy wearing this garment in a very Western way as a comfortable jacket and find pleasing both the movement it allows and the drape of the silk. Although the full sleeves seem unwieldy to wear at first, the ease of the movement and the fabric's drape make up for this minor inconvenience.

When I decided to make a knitted version of my *haori*, I considered the following design issues:

Dimensions: I decided simply to measure my *haori* and plot its shape on graph paper.

Fabric weight: My *haori* was made of a lightweight outer fabric and lining, which together felt similar to a medium-weight knitted fabric.

A traditional Japanese *haori* (behind) inspired my knitted silk version, which hangs in front.

Fiber: I chose a lustrous, multi-plied 100% silk. This fiber was the obvious choice of material both because it is traditionally associated with kimonos and also because, given the fact that knitted silk fabric tends to stretch and grow, there are so few garments in which pure silk would be suitable. And if the fiber did stretch or grow, it would prove less problematic in a loose garment than in a more fitted one. (See p. 20 for more about knitting with silk).

Color and pattern: Since I was using silk, I wanted patterns that would be firm. I fell in love with a mocha shade in a piece of woven silk, enlivened by small stripes of bright colors. With this in mind, I chose a cobalt blue silk to accent the mocha. I decided to combine two slip-stitch patterns: a diagonal herringbone and an energetic two-color pattern that was faintly reminiscent of my original *haori* fabric. (For more about slip-stitch patterns, see pp. 180-182.)

Construction: The body of a kimono or *haori* is usually cut in one piece, with the back extending over the shoulders and the center front separated from the neckline. I decided instead to work the front sections and back separately, with shoulder seams to provide stability to the fabric. I also decided to work my patterns in contrasting panels, which I would seam together and which would provide more structure to the garment. To reduce bulk, I eliminated some of the sleeve material.

My own personal touches: In order to personalize my *haori*, I planned to add ribbed borders on the sleeves and around the fronts, which, when folded in half, would provide a thick, luxurious edging that would accent the front edges and give them some body. A hem was unnecessary because the cast-on edges were firm and flat. (On pp. 254-256 you'll find charts and a full set of written instructions for making this kimono.)

Drawing tools and materials

Before talking about the specifics of sketching, I want to mention some useful drawing materials. I recommend visiting an art-supply store so that you'll have a wide range of choices.

There are many kinds of pencils, some brittle and hard, others soft and some waxy. To start, I suggest using a somewhat soft pencil, like an everyday No. 2, which can be erased easily. As you gain experience, you may prefer pencils like the Staedtler brand, which are designed especially for drawing and range from soft to hard leads. For very fine lines and/or a consistently reliable point, try a mechanical pencil. Until you have a little experience under your belt, avoid very soft pencils, like pastel or charcoal pencils, which smear.

I recommend colored pencils to beginners because they're easier to use than markers. With a light hand, they can produce subtle effects, or, if pressed hard, a dense area of color. I've amassed a collection to match every possible color of yarn. Good colored pencils can be bought individually or in sets. Avoid children's colored pencils, which lack vibrancy and are too hard. I prefer a softer, slightly waxy pencil, like the Berol Prismacolor, which is available in dozens of colors. There are also pencils that, when wetted, will produce watercolor effects, like Supracolor pencils by Caran d'Ache. These are fun but more difficult to handle.

Pens and markers come in a wide range of colors and tip widths. I usually sketch with a fine point. Since new markers move too quickly for me, I use them for writing until they get "drier." For a final refined sketch, I rough first in pencil, then work my final, cartoony outline in marker. Calligraphy markers, those with a slanted tip, are often useful for drawing textured stitches.

As with pencils, there are many kinds of drawing papers available in notebook form or pads, or sold singly by the large sheet. To find a favorite, you really need to buy several kinds and experiment. For rough sketching, I use a slick, smooth paper that allows me to sketch faster and more loosely. For more detailed sketches, I prefer a heavy paper with a bit of texture or "tooth" to keep my pencil or marker from moving too fast.

White paper gives the best contrast to colored pencils or markers. When drawing a white or pastel garment in colored pencil, I often use buff or neutral grey paper, so that pale colored lines won't disappear. I have also used brown grocery bags. And I find that tracing paper or lightweight typewriter bond is very useful for lifting outlines from photographs or other sketches.

The sketching process

Like most designers, I use sketching in two different ways. First I sketch to open my mind and explore ideas in a loose and relaxed way. Rough sketching, as it's called, is a private, enjoyable playtime, when I don't care about making a fine drawing. The whole point is to let my mind wander and to capture my thoughts in a series of small thumbnail sketches.

The second kind of sketch is made after settling on a swatch and design. This is a more refined sketch that helps me capture the final look of the garment.

I suggest that you begin by acquainting yourself with rough sketching. Put away all notions of refined drawing. Limit your sketching sessions to five to ten minutes at first. Try different kinds of papers, pencils, pens and markers, and draw all kinds of lines on your paper. Draw fine lines, fat lines, squiggles and zigzags. Try drawing geometric shapes as well as soft swirls and curved lines. Don't attempt to depict anything in particular. This process will help you loosen your hand and become more comfortable with the kinds of lines your tools can produce.

After a while, you'll find a favorite pencil, one that feels good in your hand. Use this to begin roughly sketching small, schematic-like shapes without the aid of graph paper. You need not erase. When you're dissatisfied with a line or a shape, work over it. It's better if the outlines are sketchy and rough to help you relax. Later, you will learn to refine these sketchy lines or incorporate them as part of your style. When you are comfortable with this kind of sketching, you're ready to move on to some of the exercises on pp. 167-168.

Freehand figures

Working with a pencil, try lightly drawing a rough body shape on paper. Work at seeing the body as a combination of different geometric shapes. Begin by drawing the head as an oval and the upper body as a large triangle, with the base at the top. For the lower body, use a smaller triangle, joining its point to that of the upper-body triangle to make the waist. Use long, narrow ovals for the upper and lower arms. For hands, I always draw graceful "paws." Over this basic body shape, you can outline a garment.

Tracing and photocopying

Once you've made a successful sketch of your own, you can trace it and reuse or modify it. Or you can trace another illustration or magazine photograph and use its basic outlines as a beginning for your own sketch.

To do this, attach tracing paper to a drawing or photograph. Using a soft black pencil, trace the outlines of the picture beneath with heavy lines. Remove the tracing paper. Attach it, face down, to a piece of drawing paper. Then, with the side of a pencil point, firmly rub back and forth over all traced lines. When the tracing paper is removed, your traced lines will be transferred to the drawing paper. You can re-use the tracing by placing the rubbed side, face down, on a drawing sheet. Firmly redraw all of the traced lines. The image will be transferred, unreversed, to the paper.

Don't forget what a useful a tool the photocopier can be (see the sidebar on p. 132). You can draw a rough body outline and then photocopy it many times to use this outline again and again for working out new designs.

Collage and fix-it techniques

You can draw a garment separately, cut it out and glue it over a body outline. Or you can work with colored papers, cutting out shapes and gluing them in place to depict your design. And rather than discard a drawing because of a small mistake, glue a small piece of paper over the mistake and redraw.

FREEHAND LINES, SHAPES AND BODY FIGURES

Rough lines to loosen your hand

Rough, sketchy lines can be refined later.

Body drawn with geometric shapes

Garment drawn over body sketch—body lines can be erased.

Drawing knitted patterns

There are several ways to depict knitted patterns and motifs. It's important to note that you need not strive to draw each pattern with detailed accuracy. Instead, reduce each pattern to a basic shape or outline.

On a larger garment outline, it's easier and often more effective to suggest a pattern rather than try to fill in a whole area. For instance, if you have an allover textured pattern, you can draw in a small section of it, implying that the rest of the area is filled with the same pattern.

Here are some suggestions for ways to depict common patterns:

Ribbing: quick vertical, parallel lines.

Seed stitch or other small check patterns: dots, little squares or cross-hatching.

Cables: S-shaped lines or squiggles, or interlocking diamonds and oval shapes.

Twist stitches: lines with little teeth to indicate texture.

Lace: lines and dots or tiny circles.

Colorwork: Matching colored pencils to your yarns, draw in the boldest lines or motifs roughly in light pencil, then fill in with color. Small motifs can be just dabs or dots of color to give a soft, impressionistic effect.

Tweed, heathered and variegated fabrics: Layer or blend colors with your colored pencils, then add bright marker dots or squiggles on top.

DRAWING KNITTED PATTERNS

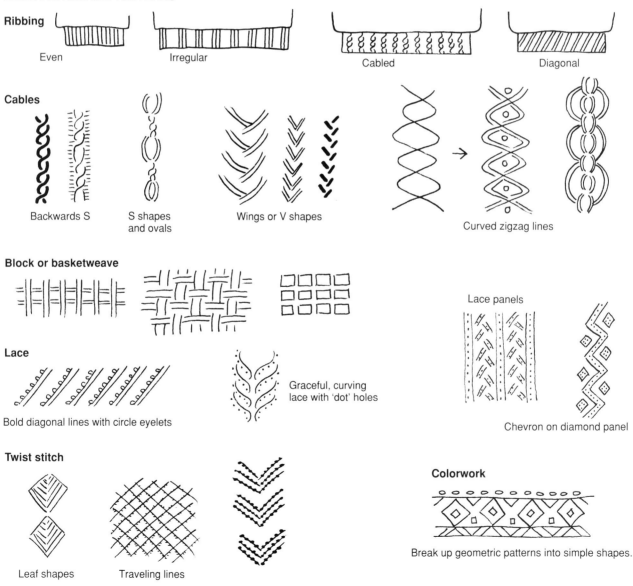

Ribbing
Even   Irregular   Cabled   Diagonal

Cables
Backwards S   S shapes and ovals   Wings or V shapes   Curved zigzag lines

Block or basketweave

Lace
Bold diagonal lines with circle eyelets   Graceful, curving lace with 'dot' holes

Lace panels   Chevron on diamond panel

Twist stitch
Leaf shapes   Traveling lines

Colorwork
Break up geometric patterns into simple shapes.

designer notebook: The classic Aran meets the motorcycle jacket

To end this chapter, I wanted to explore some variations on the classic Aran sweater—first, a fairly traditional Aran-style garment with details I had not tried before and, second, a recreation of a nonknitted comfortable classic rendered in Aran-style cabled fabric. For the traditional garment, I chose a man's vest and decided to work out its design before settling on the second garment.

The obvious way to design an Aran is to choose a new combination of cabled patterns to make up the fabric. In terms of the less obvious Aran design details I wanted to play with for the vest, I settled first on handling the traditional saddle-shoulder construction in a new way. I had never added a shoulder strap to a sleeveless garment before and decided that it would nicely accentuate the shoulder line. I also decided to alter the traditional vertical placement of patterns on the vest by moving some of the cable panels diagonally across the fabric.

With all this in mind, I began the swatching process. I chose a lofty, three-ply wool yarn that was slightly heavier than worsted weight. I swatched several patterns, hoping one of them could serve as my "swatch project" and become the shoulder strap of the vest, which it did. As always with a multi-patterned design, I swatched extensively with more patterns than I actually needed until I found a grouping that pleased me. I arranged the swatches in different combinations to help me visualize the finished fabric. Then I measured the widths of the individual cables and took a gauge over the noncabled textured patterns.

I drew the outline of the vest on graph paper, based on the necessary ease. The shoulder strap would add half of its width to the armhole depth on both front and back.

I aligned my main body cables in three major groups on the schematic. One group would remain stationary at the center. The two other major panels to each side of the center group would move diagonally toward the shoulder. I chose to flank these "traveling" panels with the simplest of textured patterns, in which stitches could be easily increased and decreased. By decreasing a stitch in the section before a cable

This classic Aran-inspired vest became the point of departure for my Aran motorcycle jacket (shown on p. 171). You can choose from a range of sizes to make this vest for a man or woman. I encourage you to alter the pattern to personalize it for yourself by choosing another color, type of yarn or length.

and increasing a stitch in the section after it, the cable would slant to the right. To move the panel to the left, I reversed the process.

As with other Aran-inspired garments I've designed, I planned to extend the smaller cables in the body into the ribbing. This dresses up the ribbing and creates a flowing line from the lower edge of the garment to the shoulder. Later, in the finishing stages of the vest, I also wanted to use the smaller cables to decorate the ribbing at the neck and armholes. Instead of making the ribbing continuous around the neckline, I would open it at center front, to add a last discreet detail to this Aran design.

The vest allowed me to experiment with familiar details of the classic Aran, but I was anxious to try something much more challenging

My Designer Notebook shows the considerable swatching required to plan my Aran-inspired garments. In the end one of my swatches became a shoulder strap for the vest. To plan my knitted motorcycle jacket, I studied photos of the real thing. The studs, zippers and buckle all contributed detail and visual weight to what I wanted to be a very bulky garment.

with the second garment. I looked at a lot of nonknitted garments for inspiration. A friend suggested the traditional leather motorcycle jacket, translated into a cabled Aran-style fabric. At first, I cringed at the difficulty of this prospect, but the more I considered it, the more the idea appealed to me. A cabled fabric could capture the bulky look of this classic, and the details—the glint of metal zippers, buckles and studs—were, in the end, irresistible.

My first task was to understand the basic structure of the jacket. Referring to photos of motorcycle jackets, I was able to see the way the wedge-shaped flaps at the fronts overlapped and closed with diagonally placed zippers. I also borrowed a real leather jacket from a friend, which, although much too large to provide measurements, gave me a sense of the classic shape and proportion.

I wanted to use the same fabric and patterns as in my vest. If you look at my schematic, you'll see that I used the same back, minus the ribbing. On the front, I planned the overlapping flaps to fall within the central triangular section formed by the moving cable panels. The flaps themselves needed to be reversible because both sides would show when the jacket was unzipped. Luckily, one of the patterns I used in the vest looked good on both sides. The flaps would need to be worked separately and

more firmly than the body to accommodate the weight of the zippers. I planned openings for pockets and sleeve zippers. Because of the complexity of this design, only one size is presented in the instructions that follow.

Once the shape had been established, the success of the garment depended on the details. I bought long, heavy metal zippers (with black zipper tape, since I could not duplicate my color yarn) and a large silver buckle to match. For a belt, I planned on using a length of stiff dressmaker belting material, covered with a long strip of knitted cable and edged in stockinette, which would curl nicely to cover the edges. In the end, the belt proved firm enough without the backing. To complete the look, I applied lightweight metal studs, backed with teeth, which grabbed into the knitted fabric to hold in place. I also used studs to decorate the zipper tape, which would show when the front was unzipped. Finally, I needed to equip the jacket with shoulder pads to help support the garment's weight and give structure at the shoulder line.

It's not often that I pursue such a complex garment in knitted fabric. The experience was a lesson to me that almost any garment can be translated into knitwear.

Instructions for Aran vest and motorcycle jacket

Variations on the classic Aran sweater, the vest has moving cable panels and a classic to slightly oversized fit, and the cabled motorcycle jacket has decorative metal studs and zipper, and an oversized fit. For the experienced knitter.

SIZE
Vest (5 sizes): To fit 32-34 (36, 38-40, 42-44, 46-48)-in. bust/chest.
Jacket (1 size): To fit 36-38-in. bust/chest.

FINISHED MEASUREMENTS (AFTER SEAMING)
Vest
Finished bust/chest at underarm: 39 (42½, 46, 49½, 53) in.
Length, from center of shoulder strap: 25 (26, 27, 27, 27½) in.

To suggest the bulk of a true motorcycle jacket, I chose an oversized silhouette and deeply textured patterns that would produce a heavy fabric. Using metallic details to add visual weight, I planned to cover the zipper tape on the folded-back front flap until I read about British designer Zandra Rhodes, who often prefers to decorate a zipper rather than hide it.

ARAN VEST

← 15½ (17¼, 19, 20¾, 22½) in. →

7 (7, 7½, 7½, 8) in.

1 in.

10 (10½, 11, 11, 11½) in.

23½ (24½, 25½, 25½, 26) in.

9½ (10, 10½, 10½, 10½) in.

Vest front and back

4 in.

← 19½ (21¼, 23, 24¾, 26½) in. →

1 square = 1 in.

Jacket
Finished bust/chest at underarm: 46 in.
Length from center of shoulder strap: 23 in.
Sleeve width at upper arm: 22 in.

MATERIALS
Vest
•7 (7, 8, 9, 10) skeins "Fleur de Laine" from Pingouin (100% wool; 3½ oz = 182 yd) in color grey #20.
•Knitting needles sizes 5 and 7 (or size to obtain gauge).
•1 circular knitting needle, size 5, 16 in. long.
Jacket
•14 skeins of Pingouin's "Fleur de Laine" from Laninter (100% wool; 3½ oz = 182 yd) in color purple #15.
•Knitting needles sizes 6 and 7 (or size to obtain gauge).
•5 heavy metal separating zippers (one at least 22 in., others at least 8 in. — all can be cut to required lengths).

•Belt buckle, 2 in. wide.
•Metal studs with prong backs (optional).
•Shoulder pads (optional).
•Needlenose pliers to remove extra zipper teeth.

GAUGE
•20 sts and 26 rows equal 4 in. with size 7 needles over shadow rib.
•18 sts and 26 rows equal 4 in. with size 7 needles over garter rib.
•Also for jacket only: 23 sts and 30 rows equal 4 in. with size 6 needles over shadow rib (for front flaps).
•To save time later, take time to swatch and check your gauge.

BACK, VEST AND JACKET
Note: The jacket does not have a ribbed lower edge. To beg jacket back, move to section following vest ribbing.

Vest ribbing
With smaller needle, cast on 109 (117, 125, 133, 141) sts. Set up rib pats as follows:
Next row (WS): p2 (St st); 1x1 rib over 9 (13, 17, 21, 25) sts; FC cable over 6 sts; k1, (p2, k2) 4 times, p2, k1; wave of honey cable over 6 sts; 1x1 rib over center 23 sts; wave of honey cable over 6 sts; k1, (p2, k2) 4 times, p2, k1; FC cable over 6 sts; 1x1 rib over 9 (13, 17, 21, 25) sts; end p2 (St st).
Next row (RS): k2; 1x1 rib over 9 (13, 17, 21, 25) sts; BC cable over 6 sts; p1, (k2, p2, RT, p2) 2 times, k2, p1; wave of honey cable over 6 sts; 1x1 rib over center 23 sts; cont wave of honey cable over 6 sts; p1, (k2, p2, LT, p2) 2 times, k2, p1; FC cable over 6 sts; 1x1 rib over 9 (13, 17, 21, 25) sts; end k2.
Rep last 2 rows until rib measures 4 in., end with a WS row.
Next row, inc row (RS): K 11 (15, 19, 23, 27) sts, and at same time inc 7 sts BEFORE BC cable; then work BC cable; k next 20 sts, and at same time inc 6 sts before wave of honey cable; then work wave of honey cable; k next 23 sts, and at same time inc 6 sts before next wave of honey cable, then work wave of honey cable; k next 20 sts, and at same time inc 6 sts BEFORE FC cable, then work FC cable; k last 11 (15, 19, 23, 27) sts, and at same time inc 7 sts — 141 (149, 157, 165, 173) sts. Change to larger needle.

SET UP BODY PATS FOR VEST AND BEGIN JACKET BACK
For jacket: With larger needle, cast on 157 sts.
For both, next row (WS): p2 (keep in St st), trinity st over 8 sts;
For vest: Garter rib over next 7 (11, 15, 19, 23) sts;
For jacket: 1x1 rib over next 15 sts;
For both: k1 (rev St st); FC cable over 6 sts; LT cable over 4 sts; bold cable over 22 sts; wave of honey cable over 6 sts; shadow rib over 3 sts; large-twist cable over 6 sts; open cable over center 11 sts; large-twist cable over 6 sts; shadow rib over 3 sts, wave of honey cable over 6 sts; bold cable over 22 sts; RT cable over 4 sts; BC cable over 6 sts, k1 (rev St st);

PATTERN CHARTS

Key for all charts:

⊟ = p RS, k WS   □ = k RS, p WS

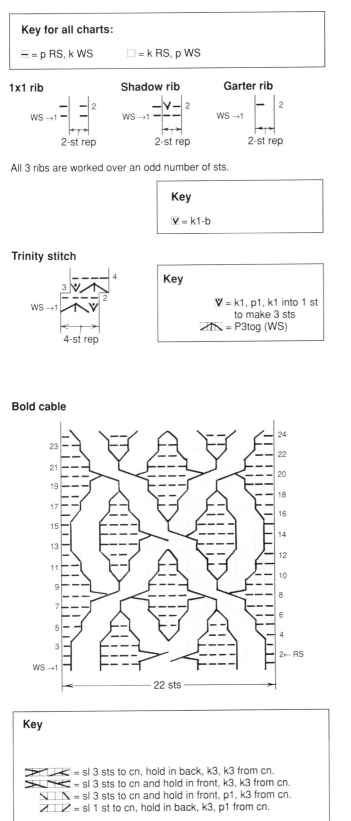

1x1 rib

WS →1   2

2-st rep

Shadow rib

WS →1   2

2-st rep

Garter rib

WS →1   2

2-st rep

All 3 ribs are worked over an odd number of sts.

Key

Ⓥ = k1-b

Trinity stitch

WS →1

4-st rep

Key

Ⓥ = k1, p1, k1 into 1 st to make 3 sts

⟋⟍ = P3tog (WS)

Bold cable

22 sts

Key

⟍⟋ = sl 3 sts to cn, hold in back, k3, k3 from cn.
⟍⟋ = sl 3 sts to cn and hold in front, k3, k3 from cn.
⟍⟋ = sl 3 sts to cn and hold in front, p1, k3 from cn.
⟋⟍ = sl 1 st to cn, hold in back, k3, p1 from cn.

Front-cross (FC) cable

WS →1   2← RS

6 sts

Back-cross (BC) cable

WS →1   2← RS

6 sts

Wave of honey cable

WS →1   4 / 2← RS

6 sts

Left-twist (LT) cable

WS →1   2← RS

4 sts

Right-twist (RT) cable

WS →1   2← RS

4 sts

Large-twist cable

WS →1   2← RS

6 sts

Key

⟍⟋ = sl 2 sts to cn and hold in front, k2, k2 from cn.

⟍⟋ = sl 2 sts to cn and hold in back, k2, k2 from cn.

⟍⟋ = sl 1 st to cn and hold in back, k1, k1 from cn.

⟍⟋ = sl 1 st to cn and hold in front, k1, k1 from cn.

Key

⟍ = LT   ⟋ = RT

Open cable

11 sts

Note:
Omit bobble on jacket pieces.

Key

⟍⟋ = sl next 3 sts to cn and hold in back, k2, sl the p st back to LH needle and purl it, k2 from cn.

⟋⟋ = sl next p st to cn and hold in back, k2, p1 from cn.

⟍⟍ = sl next 2 sts to cn and hold in front, p1, k2 from cn.

Ō = make bobble as follows: knit into front, back and front of st [turn and k these 3 sts] 3 times, then turn and sl 1-k2tog-psso.

For vest: Garter rib over 7 (11, 15, 19, 23) sts;

For jacket: 1x1 rib over 15 sts;

For both: Trinity st over 8 sts; p2 (St st). Work even for 8 more rows, so end with a WS row.

TO MOVE PANELS

Next row, moving row (RS)

For vest: Work to last 2 sts in 1st garter rib section;

For jacket: Work to last 2 sts in 1st 1x1 rib section;

For both: k2tog, work to shadow rib section, M1, then work as est to END of 2nd shadow rib section, M1.

For vest: Work to 2nd garter rib section;

For jacket: Work to 2nd 1x1 rib section;

For both: SSK, work to end. Rep this row after 11 (11, 9, 9, 9) more rows, then every 12 (12, 10, 10, 10)th row after for a total of 8 (11, 14, 14, 14) times, working made sts into shadow rib; AND AT SAME TIME, cont until vest measures 9½ (10, 10½, 10½, 10½) in. above rib; and jacket measures 12 in., end with a WS row.

ARMHOLE SHAPING

• Bind off 3 sts at beg of next 2 rows, then bind off 2 sts at beg of next 6 rows—123 (131, 139, 147, 155) sts.

• Keep 1 st each end in St st, cont until armhole depth measures for vest 10 (10½, 11, 11, 11½) in.; for jacket 9½ in., end with a WS row.

SHOULDER AND BACK-NECK SHAPING

For vest: Bind off 14 (14, 15, 17, 18) sts at beg of next 2 rows, then 13 (15, 16, 17, 18) sts at beg of next 4 rows. Bind off 43 (43, 45, 45, 47) sts.

For jacket: Bind off 16 sts at beg of next 6 rows. Work even on rem 43 sts for 1½ in. Bind off.

VEST FRONT

Work same as for back until armhole depth measures 9 (9½, 10, 10, 10½) in., end with a WS row.

ARAN MOTORCYCLE JACKET

19 in.

7 in.

1½ in.

1 in.

9½ in.

21½ in.

Pocket opening (for front only)

8 in.

12 in.

Back, 23 in.

Right front, 9½ in. — 4 in. — Left front, 9½ in.

1 square = 1 in.

NECKLINE SHAPING

Mark center 21 (21, 23, 23, 25) sts.

Next row (RS): Work to center sts, join 2nd ball of yarn and bind off center sts, work as est to end. Working both sides at same time with separate balls, bind off from each neck edge 3 sts once, 2 sts 4 times—40 (44, 47, 51, 54) sts. When vest front measures same as back to shoulder, work same shoulder shaping as for back.

VEST SHOULDER STRAPS (MAKE 2)

With larger needle, cast on 25 sts.

Next row (WS): p1 (St st), work large-twist cable over 6 sts; work open cable over center 11 sts; work large-twist cable over 6 sts; end p1 (St st). Work even until strap, slightly stretched, measures same as width of 1 shoulder. Bind off.

VEST FINISHING

Sew shoulder strap sides to front and back shoulders.

Neckline rib

With RS facing and smaller circular needle, beg at center front, pick up 113 (113, 117, 117, 121) sts evenly around entire neckline edge. Turn.

Next row (WS): k2 (k every row); work LEFT SIDE PATS over next 30 sts as follows: {work wave of honey cable over 6 sts, 1x1 rib over 7 sts, RT cable over 4 sts, 1x1 rib over 7 sts, BC cable over 6 sts}; work 1x1 rib over center 49 (49, 53, 53, 57) sts; work RIGHT SIDE PATS over next 30 sts as follows: {work FC cable over 6 sts, 1x1 rib over 7 sts, LT cable over 4 sts, 1x1 rib over 7 sts, wave of honey cable over 6 sts}; end k2 (k every row). Turn. Work even for 11 more rows. Bind off.

Left armhole rib

With RS facing and smaller needle, beg at front lower armhole, pick up 125 (131, 137, 137, 145) sts around entire armhole.

Right sleeve

Right-front flap

Collar

1 square = 1 in.

Next row (WS): Work 1x1 rib over 13 (16, 19, 19, 23) sts; LEFT SIDE PATS (see "Vest Finishing" section on facing page) over 30 sts; 1x1 rib over 39 sts; RIGHT SIDE PATS (see "Vest Finishing" section on facing page) over 30 sts; 1x1 rib over 13 (16, 19, 19, 23) sts to end. Turn. Work even for 11 more rows. Bind off. Rep on right side. Sew front to back at sides, including armhole rib.

JACKET FRONTS
Jacket's 2 overlapping fronts zip together to close. Each front is made of 2 pieces: a side piece and a center flap.

SIDE PIECE FOR RIGHT FRONT
With larger needle, cast on 66 sts.
Next row (WS): p2 (St st), work wave of honey cable over 6 sts; bold cable over 22 sts; RT cable over 4 sts; BC cable over 6 sts; k1 (rev St st); 1x1 rib over 15 sts; trinity st over 8 sts; end p2 (St st). Work even in pats for 8 more rows, so end with a WS Row.

Shape front edge
Next row, dec row (RS): Work to last 2 sts in 1x1 rib section; k2tog, work to end—65 sts. Rep dec row after 9 more rows, then every 10th row after 12 more times—43 sts; AND AT SAME TIME, cont as est until piece measures 8 in., so end with a WS row.
Vertical pocket opening
Next row (RS): Work to 4 sts of RT cable; then k1, join a 2nd ball of yarn and bind off center 2 sts of RT cable, work to end. Work both sides at same time with separate balls of yarn, keep 1 st at each side of opening in St st, until opening measures 7½ in., end with a WS row.
Next row (RS): Work across row to opening, cast on 2 sts, work to end. Cut extra ball of yarn. Resume RT cable panel as est before opening; AND AT SAME TIME, when piece measures same as back to underarm, end with WS row.

ARMHOLE SHAPING
Bind off 3 sts at beg of next RS row, then bind off 2 sts at beg of next 3 RS rows. Work even until armhole depth measures same as back to shoulder, end with a WS row.

SHOULDER SHAPING
Keeping in pat, bind off 15 sts at beg of next 2 RS rows, then 13 sts at beg of last RS row.

SIDE PIECE FOR LEFT FRONT
Work same as right-side front, reversing placement of pats and all shaping, working FC and LT cables instead of BC and RT cables, omit vertical pocket opening. AND AT SAME TIME, when piece measures 8 in., end with a WS row.
Horizontal pocket opening
Next row (RS): Work to 1st st of large cable, then, bind off next 30 sts in pat, work to end.
Next row: Work to bound-off sts, cast on 30 sts, work to end. Cont in pats as est before opening.

CENTER FLAP FOR RIGHT FRONT

With smaller needle, cast on 25 sts. Keeping first 2 and last 2 sts in st st, work in shadow rib for 10 rows.

Next row, inc row (RS): k2, M1, work to last 2 sts, M1, k1 —27 sts sts. Rep inc row after 9 more rows, then every 10th row after for a total of 15 incs each side, working incs into pat —55 sts. When piece measures 21½ in., end with a WS row.

NECKLINE SHAPING

Bind off 43 sts at the beg of the next RS row, then 3 sts at beg of next 2 RS rows —6 sts. Bind off on next RS row.

CENTER FLAP FOR LEFT FRONT

Work same as for right flap, reversing neck shaping.

RIGHT SLEEVE

To make a zipper opening, lower sleeve is worked in 2 sections at same time with a separate balls of yarn. With larger needle, cast on 50 sts; then with a 2nd ball of yarn, cast on 22 sts.

Next row (WS): In small section, p2 (St st); garter rib over 3 sts; trinity st over 8 sts; k1 (rev St st), wave of honey cable over 6 sts; p2 (St st); then, with 2nd ball of yarn, in large section, p2 (St st); large-twist cable over 6 sts; open cable over 11 sts; large-twist cable over 6 sts; shadow rib over 5 sts; wave of honey cable over 6 sts; k1 (rev St st), trinity st over 8 sts; garter rib over 3 sts, p2 (St st). Work even for 10 more rows, so end with a WS row.

Next row, inc row (RS): k2, M1, work large section, then work small section to last 2 sts, M1, end k2. Rep inc row after 3 more rows, then every 4th row after for a total of 22 incs each side — 117 sts; AND AT SAME TIME cont until 11 incs have been worked each side, so end with a RS row — 33 sts in small section, 61 sts in large section.

JOIN SECTIONS

Next row (WS): Work to end of small section, cast on 1 st, then with same ball of yarn work to end of large section —95 sts. Cut extra yarn.

Next row (RS): Work to last 2 sts of former large section, work shadow rib over next 5 sts, work as est to end. Work WS row.

MOVE PANELS

Next row, moving row (RS): Work to last 2 sts in 1st garter-rib section, k2tog, work to shadow-rib section, M1, work to END of 2nd shadow-rib section, M1, work to 2nd garter-rib section, then SSK, work to end. Rep this row after 5 more rows, then every 6th row after 9 times, working made sts into shadow rib, keep in rib pats as est. Cont until sleeve measures 16½ in., or to desired length, end with a WS row.

CAP SHAPING

•Bind off 2 sts at beg of next 8 rows, 3 sts at beg of next 6 rows, 4 sts at beg of next 10 rows, then 9 sts at beg of next 2 rows —25 sts.

•Keep edge sts in St st, work even until strap, slightly stretched, measures same as 1 back-shoulder section. Bind off.

LEFT SLEEVE

Work same as for right sleeve, reversing placement of zipper opening.

COLLAR

With smaller needle, cast on 119 sts.

Next row (WS): p2 (St st), work in trinity st over 12 sts, garter rib over center 91 sts, trinity st over 12 sts, end p2 (St st). Work even for 3 more rows, so end with WS row.

Next row, dec row (RS): Work 14 sts, ssk work to last 16 sts, k2tog, work to end —117 sts. Rep dec row every 4th row after 6 more times —105 sts. When collar measures 5 in., bind off 4 sts at beg of next 20 rows, then bind off rem 25 sts.

JACKET FINISHING

Sew right flap to right side front.

Trim for left side front, each side of sleeve openings, each side of vertical pocket opening

With RS facing and smaller needle, pick up 3 sts for every 4 rows.

Work trim: k WS row, bind off in k on RS.

Trim for left flap: With RS facing and smaller needle, pick up 1 st every other row. Work trim.

Sleeve zippers

With zipper pull at lower edge, pin closed zipper along opening, leave any extra length unattached at back. Sew in place, sewing in ridge between main fabric and trim. If zipper needs to be cut, sew thread at top of zipper teeth to act as a stop. Cut zipper leaving 1 in. at top. Remove extra zipper teeth with pliers if necessary. Rep on vertical pocket opening.

Front edge zipper

•Sew right front to right flap for 1 in. at upper edges. Separate zipper. Pin right side of zipper to open edge of right side front. Sew in place. Pin right flap to underside of zipper tape, then sew.

•Zip left and right zipper halves together. Pin left side of zipper to left flap edge. Unzip and sew in place. If zipper needs to be cut, sew thread at top of zipper teeth to act as a stop. Cut zipper, if necessary, leaving 1 in. at top. Tuck excess to inside and tack, remove extra zipper teeth if necessary.

•Sew zipper to vertical pocket opening. Sew collar around neck edge, centering at front flaps.

Pocket flap

With larger needle, cast on 27 sts. Keep 1st and last sts in St st, work in trinity st over center 25 sts. Work even for 1 in., then dec 1 st each end every RS row until 1 st rem. Bind off. Work trim along sides. Sew to upper right pocket opening. Make 2 inner pockets, using swatches if desired.

Belt

With larger needle, cast on 19 sts.

Next row (WS): p4 (St st), work open cable over center 11 sts, end p4 (St st). Work even, omit bobbles, until piece measures 44 in. Attach metal studs along belt fabric. Attach buckle.

Finishing touches

Decorate jacket with metal studs, if desired. Attach shoulder pads, if desired.

What if I combined Aran patterns with another Comfortable Classic?

Belted or buttoned shoulder straps

Aran-inspired farmer's overalls (or motorcycle pants to go with my jacket?)

Moving cables go down leg to lower edge

Wide cable

Themes
7 & Samplers

My most interesting designs have been those that combine a multitude of stitch patterns in interesting ways. But before I was able to mix these patterns successfully, I had to discover the basic characteristics of the different pattern families. Next I had to learn to look at these groups of patterns with a designer's eye, to see what each offered visually. Some patterns were better suited to one garment than another, while others seemed to work well on any piece at all.

I first learned to design successful combinations of patterns by staying within a single family of patterns. I found it easy to mix cables with cables and lace with lace, for example, because these patterns shared similarities in weight and gauge. I found that such related patterns always work well together visually and produce what I call "theme knitting."

More challenging for me was learning to combine unlike patterns from different families. Almost as an extension of theme knitting, I began looking for similarities among different pattern families. For instance, I would find a lace pattern that incorporated a cable detail and combine it with a larger cable pattern. And sometimes I would deliberately set up contrasting patterns to create an eclectic blend. Whatever the combination, I always swatched to see if the patterns were compatible and, by doing this, learned to avoid mixing certain patterns that were too dissimilar to marry well.

Along the way, I also became intrigued with knitted graphic motifs that looked like everyday objects. For instance, I was inspired by my collection of bow pins—which you can see in the photo on the facing page—to play with the knitted bow motif. I hunted for traditional bow patterns, designed large graphic ribbons that tied and tried my hand at three-dimensional knitted bows. And, in time, I learned to combine my favorite motifs with various different families of patterns to produce what I call "sampler knitting."

This chapter is all about individual families of stitch patterns and intriguing graphic motifs, and how to merge the two in successful theme and sampler fabrics. At heart, the chapter is

Slip-stitch patterns offer a range of different-looking fabrics, whose dissimilarities are enhanced by working them in unusual yarns. Clockwise, from upper left: ribbon yarn draws attention to the slipped strands of a solid-color pattern; an elongated colorwork pattern in a nubby yarn forms a web over a variegated background; two smooth yarns of the same weight produce a smaller, refined colorwork web pattern; a garter-stitch mosaic pattern, worked in chenille and metallic yarns, is luxuriously ornate; a smooth, geometric colorwork pattern with changing background colors resembles stranded colorwork.

really about creating fabrics with as much interesting detail as possible, the basis for this being the mixture of stitch and graphic patterns.

One look at any knitting dictionary will tell you that there are numerous families of knitting patterns. Unfortunately, space doesn't permit discussing them all here, so I have chosen four major pattern families to acquaint you with the basic issues of "familial" knitting: slip-stitch, twisted-stitch, cable, and eyelet and lace patterns. Unlike the basic knit/purl patterns discussed in Chapter 4, each of these pattern families requires some special manipulation of the stitches. I present both a few representative patterns and a few specialties in the discussion of these families, and I end each section with some counsel on designing your own patterns. Do take a look in a pattern dictionary for a broader overview of each of these families and to see what other families you might enjoy exploring (see the Bibliography on pp. 258-260).

Slip-stitch patterns

The slip-stitch family of patterns is so wide-ranging that it defies simple description. This family is composed of three basic groupings: solid-color patterns; colorwork patterns; and mosaic patterns, which are the most distinctive of the three and were invented by master knitter Barbara Walker. (See also pp. 212-213 for a discussion of slip-stitch pleats.)

Within each of these three categories, there is a vast range of different types of patterns. The one thing that binds this spectrum of patterns together is their simple technique. All of the patterns, whether monochromatic or intricately colored, require handling only one yarn at a time on any given row. They are created by simply slipping some stitches from one needle to the other on certain rows without working these stitches on those rows. This slipping of stitches causes the fabric to shorten and become dense, resulting in a tighter-than-average row gauge, which makes them incompatible, when worked side by side, with most patterns from other families. They are thus best combined with other slip-stitch patterns or patterns with an unusually dense row gauge, like those with a garter-stitch base.

Solid-color slip-stitch patterns

The solid-color group of slip-stitch patterns is visually the quietest of the family. The patterns in this group often resemble knit/purl patterns, since the elongated slip stitch lends texture to an otherwise smooth stockinette fabric. Some patterns can look like woven fabric (see the kimono-like garment on p. 165), and others have puffy, almost quilted-looking surfaces. Some are narrow panels that are cable look-alikes, with a slipped stitch stretched diagonally to simulate a cable cross. And many are small slip-stitch motifs that can be used in allover fabrics or as accents.

Since these patterns are classic in appearance and form dense fabrics, they are well suited for designs demanding warmth and weight. I love these patterns for tailored coats and jackets. And I've made a heavy fake-Aran pullover, mixing the narrow slip-stitch panels with allover, honeycomb-like patterns.

I avoid heavy yarns for these patterns because they're so dense. However, if a heavy yarn would suit a particular design, I use a rather large needle to open up the fabric. I love using ribbon yarns with these patterns because the strand itself is highlighted. To get the most dramatic effect with flat ribbons or tapes, look for a pattern with a very elongated stitch or with surface strands. As with the silk "kimono" (see p. 165), these patterns can help stabilize fibers that tend to stretch.

You may need to knit a couple of swatches to settle on the best feel for your slip-stitch fabric. And remember to check your row gauge carefully since it can be much tighter than you would imagine. Slip-stitch swatches may not need any blocking because many of them are very flat.

Colorwork slip-stitch patterns

There is a huge range of possibilities with slip-stitch colorwork patterns. Unlike traditional stranded colorwork knitted in continuous stockinette stitch, slip-stitch colorwork patterns combine color and texture, and frequently include garter-stitch elements. At the same time, many have a bulky crocheted look because the slipped stitches squeeze the rows together.

Because there are so many members in the colorwork branch of the family, I was forced to choose three representative groups. I hope my examples will lead you to think about others. Note that these patterns tend to be allover repeats, with virtually none used as panels.

First, there are the smooth stockinette-based patterns that look like stranded stockinette-stitch knitting. The slipped stitches make these a bit denser than most stranded patterns, but because only one strand is worked every row, they are definitely quicker and easier to knit than regular stranded colorwork. Sometimes these patterns look far more complex when they are worked in three or four colors as opposed to the usual two. I use these patterns wherever I would use stranded colorwork patterns, and with similar results, especially if the needle is larger than generally used for the given yarn weight.

Second, there are some delicate patterns that appear to have a spidery web of yarn laid over a smooth contrasting surface. In some cases this web is formed by very elongated contrasting stitches paired with the yarn-over maneuver that is the basis of knitted lace. Using soft, lightweight yarns supports the delicate look of these patterns.

Third, there are the brick and honeycomb types, as well as the more geometric tile-like patterns, all of which have more texture than their smooth, delicate counterparts in the first and second groups. These textured patterns tend to be bulkier and resemble crochet. Use them for their boldness and in designs where you don't mind extra weight. Recently I successfully used them as bold edgings. And on my list of future projects, I want to knit a heavy rug in stained-glass colors with rug wool. For garments, I find these patterns more appealing with subtle colors.

Needle size can make a big difference in the kind of fabric you produce with colorwork slip-stitch patterns. Small needles will produce a tight, dense fabrics, while large needles will create a looser fabric with more drape.

Mixing yarn weights and types is entirely feasible with these slip-stitch colorwork patterns, although it could be disastrous with regular stranded colorwork. Try a heavy yarn with a lightweight one, a smooth yarn with a hairy one, or a soft angora with a heathery wool. To me, these patterns cry out for novelty yarns to emphasize their unusual looks. But, if your classic pattern sensibility finds them too odd or bold to wear, try choosing soft, related colors and yarns that emphasize texture rather than pattern.

Think as a designer when working these patterns and occasionally try them in a solid color. Because you thereby eliminate the contrast of color, the focus of the fabric becomes its texture. Similarly consider introducing color or using it as an accent in the solid-color slip-stitch patterns. Although they're usually most successful when worked in a single color, you can produce different effects with several colors, which you might find interesting.

Mosaic slip-stitch patterns

Mosaics are the third major type of slip-stitch pattern. These patterns were invented and fully explored by Barbara Walker in her inspiring manual, *Mosaic Knitting* (see the Bibliography on pp. 258-260). Here, I only want to present these patterns as fabrics and look at them from a design point of view.

Boldly geometric and often maze-like in appearance, these patterns always make me think of the drawings of M.C. Escher. Some resemble Arabic tile formations, and others look as if they've been derived from mathematical formulas—though I don't mean to scare off the uninitiated because they're much easier to knit than they appear to be. Mosaic patterns come in all types—allover patterns, panels and borders—and all can be worked either in the regular stockinette-stitch version of the given pattern or a garter-stitch variation of it.

In the garter-stitch method of working these patterns, the stitches that are not slipped are knitted on both right-side and wrong-side rows. These patterns share all of the characteristics of plain garter stitch, producing a thick fabric and very square motifs. As a garter-stitch fan, I find these garter patterns infinitely intriguing from a pattern point of view, but they are more challenging to use in garments because of their weight and boldness. I have used them most successfully as accents or to fill small areas. With their almost beaded surfaces, the garter-stitch versions make especially beautiful borders and edgings (I used a fretwork border on one of my Chanel swatches on p. 155). I think of them when I want drama, for example, for large garments like coats or jackets.

The stockinette-stitch versions of mosaic patterns, in which the unslipped stitches are purled on the wrong-side rows, yield smoother fabrics with more drape than their garter-stitch counterparts. All the geometrics tend to elongate, and this can ruin the effect of square motifs, which look better worked in garter-stitch mosaics. I find that the smooth stockinette-stitch mosaics are more sophisticated and less overwhelming when used in large areas. In my

"kimono" (see p. 165), the narrow stockinette-stitch mosaic strips add color and pattern without overpowering the design.

Mosaics depend greatly on color contrast for their effectiveness and must therefore be worked in at least two colors. For an almost electric effect, contrast black or a hot, bright color with white. I like to soften the boldness of the patterns by using two close shades of the same color, making sure at the same time that they're different enough to produce some necessary contrast. To lessen the visual power of a large area of pattern, I change the background color subtly every few rows or every couple of inches. One of my best past efforts in this vein used tweedy autumnal shades for the blended background of the mosaic with a warm chocolate for the patterning.

With mosaic patterns, you can use a wide range of yarns. To maintain a crisp pattern, choose a yarn with a smooth surface. For a softer effect, choose a hairy yarn like mohair, still picking colors that contrast. As with all bulky slip-stitch patterns, avoid overly heavy yarns, which would make the fabric unmanageable.

Designing your own slip-stitch patterns

For clarity's sake, I've presented here only one of the many kinds of slip-stitch colorwork patterns, which is slightly different from any of the colorwork patterns described above. This type of pattern is worked on a garter-stitch background, with groups of slip stitches forming raised lines and giving the fabric an embossed look. Once you learn the rules for making these patterns, you can invent a multitude of them. These patterns can also be made to resemble cables by crossing the raised lines, but they're made without an extra cable needle.

To learn the basic rules for this type of slip-stitch colorwork, cast on 20 stitches with a yarn of your choice (A).

To form the basic embossed vertical band:
Row 1: Knit.
Row 2: k9, p2, k9.
Row 3: k9, sl 2 with yarn in back, k9.
Row 4: k9, sl 2 with yarn in front, k9.
Rep these 4 rows a few times, and you will create an embossed line at center of swatch.

The slip-stitch technique described on pp. 182-183 can be used to form a wide variety of patterns. At lower left, the slip-stitch lines form a subtle vertical pattern on a plain garter-stitch background. At right, contrasting slip-stitch lines move across a striped background. At upper left, the liveliest version of the three combines color in a basketweave-like arrangement.

For another variation, you can stripe the garter-stitch background:

Attach a new color (B).

Rep rows 1-4, but work rows 3-4 with new color B, and cont to work rows 1-2 with A.

Rep these rows a few times. The embossed strand stays same color, but background alternates striped ridges of A and B.

To move the strand across the surface of the fabric:

With B, work rows 3 and 4.

Row 1: With A, work to 2 embossed sts, sl them off needle and let them sit at front (they will not ravel), k1, then k the 2 sts at front, k to end.

Row 2: k the k sts, p the 2 embossed sts. Note that embossed sts have moved to left. Now work 2 rows, slipping embossed sts as est.

Keep in mind:
• In addition to the directions above for moving the embossed strand to the left, you can also move this strand to the right by doing the following: work to one stitch before the embossed strand, slip the stitch off the needle and let it sit to the back; then knit the embossed two stitches, and finally knit the stitch at the back.

Some design possibilities:
• You can change colors in the embossed stitches or background stitches.
• You can work many groups of embossed stitches on a large piece of knitting.
• The embossed stitches can move in regular cable-like patterns, crossing where they meet.
• The embossed stitches can move in odd directions, crisscrossing in irregular patterns.
• You can slip a larger groups of stitches than called for in the above directions to produce a bolder embossed line.

*t*wist-stitch patterns

Twist-stitch patterns are perhaps my very favorite. They can take on a variety of looks, but they're always crisp and elegant. For some reason, these subtle patterns remind me of the abstract shapes and textures that I see in nature—fat grains of wheat, riverine curves and gently corrugated bark.

Twist-stitch patterns are formed from a basic twist-stitch unit: two stitches that cross one another—which really amounts to the simplest form of cabling, without the need for an additional cable needle. Individual twist stitches form dots of texture and, worked in patterns, generally link up to form smooth diagonal

Twist-stitch patterns produce crisp, refined fabrics. Clockwise, from upper left: a Bavarian panel worked at center, with different twist-stitch ribbings picked up at each side; a very angular pattern that looks woven when worked in a tweedy yarn; two twist-stitch patterns incorporating elements from other pattern families (at top, large eyelets nestle in the twist-stitch lattice; at bottom, seed and slip stitches are added in the twist-stitch chevron); and one of my favorite twist-stitch patterns, featuring simple columns of graceful curves.

lines or curves, which move nicely across a smooth stockinette or a more textured reverse-stockinette (or other flat knit/purl) background. These patterns mingle well with one another and with cable patterns, and produce firm but drapey fabrics, which can be used for all kinds of garments, from the sportiest to the most elegant of tailored sweaters.

Just two simple techniques are needed to work most twist-stitch patterns: right twist and left twist (see the directions in the next section). These twists usually occur on right-side rows, but they can also be worked on the wrong side of the fabric.

I think the allover patterns with twist-stitch lines moving over stockinette are the most beautiful, though many interesting panels can be made by working just one or two repeats of an allover pattern. Also within this family are some intriguing ribbings and delicate cable-like panels. And perhaps most impressive of all are the twist-stitch patterns used by Bavarian knitters to decorate their traditional knee-high stockings. They used single, tightly twisted accent stitches along with intricate twist-stitch patterns to form marvelous panels and motifs.

These patterns follow the shaped contour of the stockings from calf to ankle to form almost sculpted effects. My swatches (see the photo above) present some nice examples of the range of twist-stitch patterns, and you'll find other sources of them in pattern dictionaries listed in the Bibliography on pp. 258-260.

Be sure when working these patterns not to use yarns that will obscure their subtle texture. Almost any color works well with these patterns, except perhaps the darkest of shades.

Designing your own twist-stitch pattern

All you need to design a twist-stitch pattern is graph paper and a knowledge of the basic twists. These twists, whose charted symbols are shown in the drawing on the facing page, are worked as follows:

Right twist (RT): k2tog, leaving sts on LH needle; insert RH needle between 2 sts just knitted tog, and k 1st st again; sl both sts from needle tog.

Left twist (LT): with RH needle behind LH needle, skip 1 st and k 2nd st in back loop; then insert RH neeedle into front of 1st st and k it; sl both sts from needle tog.

In the photo below right are two swatched examples of patterns that I developed first in charted form. The pattern of zigzagging lines, reminiscent of many traditional twist-stitch patterns, was easier to plan. I began by plotting three diagonal lines toward the right using twist-stitch symbols, as shown in the chart at right. Then I repeated the grouping once more to set up the pattern repeat you see in the swatch. Note that I changed the direction of the lines at various points to create the zigzag.

The other pattern was more challenging because I wanted to form a more complex lattice-like design. I also had the idea of inserting a motif within the lattice openings. I ended up forming a lattice, working some openings with different patterns, such as stockinette stitch, reverse stockinette and seed stitch. I placed a variety of twist-stitch textures in the openings.

Keep in mind:

• When two stitches are twisted, one stitch is embossed, and the other becomes part of the background. With a traveling twist-stitch line, the embossed line is always worked as a knit stitch, while the background stitch could be worked either as a knit or a purl, depending on the surrounding stitches. If you want the background to be stockinette, work the right and left twists as described above. If you want the background stitch to be textured, that is, a purl stitch, work the right and left twists as follows:

Right purl twist: skip 1st st, then k 2nd st in front loop, bring yarn to front between needles, purl 1st st, then sl both sts from needle tog.

Left purl twist: with yarn in front, bring RH needle to back of work and insert into 2nd st on LH needle from left to right (turn WS of work slightly towards you to make this easier), then p this st from this position, then bring yarn to back between needles and k 1st st, then sl both sts from needle tog.

Some design possibilities:

• Design a narrow panel of twist-stitch diagonal lines, then form an allover pattern by repeating the panel across a fabric.

• Embellish a plain stockinette fabric with small motifs formed of twist stitches.

• As a visually compatible companion pattern, combine twisted knit stitches (see p. 80) with twist-stitch patterns.

• For a less bulky texture than that in a traditional Aran-inspired sweater, use the more delicate twist-stitch patterns arranged in panels.

TWIST-STITCH SYMBOLS AND THEIR USE

Right twist (RT)

Left twist (LT)

The symbol for a right- or left-twist stitch spans two blocks, because one stitch crosses over another.

Left-twist line   Right-twist line

To simulate the embossed line that will appear in the knitted fabric, draw two vertical lines to link each twist-stitch symbol with the square below or above it.

These two twist-stitch lines may look as if they are separated by a single stitch, but they're not—the twists fall right next to each other, with each occupying two squares. Shading the lines on the grid prevents confusion.

This small arrangement of diagonal twist-stitch lines became the basis for the swatch at left in the photo below.

Twist-stitch patterns are fun to design on paper. For the swatch at left, I simply drew two groups of closely spaced lines zigzagging across the paper. For the swatch at right, I drew a lattice design on paper and then filled in the diamond-shaped areas, sampler-style, while knitting.

Cable patterns

Highly embossed cables are formed when groups of stitches are crossed and knitted out of order. The resulting fabric strains to produce graceful waves or rope-like strands, depending on the number of stitches crossed and the frequency and direction of the crossings. These variables produce a range of cables, from delicate to bold. Delicate cables resemble twist-stitch patterns, while their more distinctive, beefy cousins are perhaps the boldest of all knitting patterns.

Cable crossings can be worked on an even number of stitches (for example, four stitches crossing over another group of four) or on an uneven group (for example, a large group of stitches can move over a single stitch). A cable can be worked on as few as two stitches—one stitch crossing over another—or as many as eight to ten stitches. Working cables on more stitches is possible, though not very practical since the resulting fabric would prove very bulky. When the first set of stitches is held to the front of the knitting for the crossing, the front cable strand will angle to the left. Conversely, when this set of stitches is held to the back of the work for the crossing, the front cable strand angles to the right. Cable crossings can occur frequently, producing a stiff, thick fabric, or infrequently, producing a soft drape in the fabric.

Cables are most often worked as vertical panels, with the crosses contained within a certain width. They can, however, be worked as allover repeats. Cables offer great design flexibility because they always combine nicely with one another. Panels can be lined up next to each other to form wide allover patterns, and allover cables can be broken up into units to form beautiful panels divided by either knit/purl patterns or other textured patterns that have the same row gauge.

Usually the strands of a cable are worked in smooth stockinette. I'm fond, however, of the rare cable with a grainy strand that's worked in garter or seed stitch. The cable at upper left in the photo below looks like bamboo, with the texture provided by a yarn-over that gets pulled over a smooth stockinette strand.

The background fabric of a cable pattern also affects the cable's look. Most common cables are worked on a reverse-stockinette ground, which elevates the smooth cabled strands above the background more than any other stitch. For a change, try working plain stockinette cables on another background, for example, garter stitch, which provides more texture but less height than stockinette and causes

Cables offer a wide range of design possibilities, which are further expanded by the choice of yarn. Clockwise, from upper left: the unusual texture of the barred braid cable enhanced by the use of a soft, rayon ribbon yarn; a bold, deeply corrugated cable worked in a heavy yarn; wavy allover cables worked in a hairy yarn for a soft, feminine effect; and a flat filigree cable with crisp outlines knitted in a smooth wool.

the cable to flatten and spread. Working allover cable patterns on an uninterrupted stockinette background results in a fabric that has a soft, wavy look.

In addition to being highlighted by the background stitch, a cable can also be enlivened by a stitch from another family of patterns. For instance, you might make a simple two-strand cable more textured by working one of the strands in seed or garter stitch. Sometimes a cable will have ribbed or other knit/purl texture, or it could have a lace detail that falls in a flat stockinette section. I like to combine these special cabled patterns with patterns from the family whose characteristic stitches they use as accents.

You can find a cable pattern suited to almost any kind of garment or project. Most cable patterns are chosen for their texture, but their heavier-than-average fabrics can offer warmth too, depending on the yarn in which they're worked. There is nothing more dramatic or luxurious than an oversized pullover sweater covered with enormous bulky cables. If you want a close-fitting, flexible garment, use a lightweight yarn.

Cables can be worked in any kind of yarn, with various effects. In springy yarns like wool, cables will be pronounced and showy. In slinky yarns like rayon, the patterns will flatten and produce more subtle textures. In heavy summer yarns like cotton, the fabric will usually be weighty and flatten out the cables.

I read gauge very carefully when working with cabled patterns because cables compress the fabric into a unexpectedly narrow space. When cable panels are grouped together, separated by reverse stockinette, the result can be a rib-like fabric that will draw in considerably. If you don't measure gauge carefully, your garment may be much smaller than you want, especially if worked in a springy yarn like wool.

Although I may swatch cables individually in the early stages of a design, I prefer to check groups of cables in one large swatch to be sure of how they'll behave and look together. I then measure their combined width. If you plan to isolate a cable panel on a plain fabric, swatch the cable with some of the plain fabric to either side. This way you'll know how the cable will sit in the fabric.

Cables should never be blocked or stretched flat. Steam your swatch but do not flatten it. With wool, you can then pinch the steamed

Bobbles

Bobbles have traditionally gone hand and hand with cabled patterns. These touches of texture are easy to work and come in all shapes and sizes, ranging from sophisticated dots of yarn that nestle in the fabric and which I usually refer to as knots, to funny blobs of stitches that hang loosely. Bobbled effects are created by working new stitches into a base stitch (or stitches) for a given number of rows to produce extra fabric that protrudes from the surface. I like bobbles to be neat and trim, even if they're large, so I work them tightly.

Bobbles can be incorporated into almost any pattern for added texture. They can be used singly or grouped to form motifs, or horizontal or vertical lines. If you're creating motifs, it's useful to work them out by plotting the bobbles on graph paper. Use one square to represent one bobble. Swatching, in turn, will show you how the units sit next to each other. For a dense effect, plot groups of bobbles adjacent to one another or slightly separated by one or two stitches, depending on their size.

When designing a bobbled fabric, try mixing different kinds of bobbles for varied texture. Plan on extra yarn for a heavily bobbled fabric. To keep the weight of the fabric to a minimum, work with smaller knots.

Below I've described a few of my favorite techniques for making these dots of texture. Each has its own look and is therefore suited to a different use.

Knotting
Knotting is my favorite form of bobble-making because the knot produced is small and firm, and sits close to the surface of the fabric. These subtle knots are well suited to more reserved, classic garments or to close-fitting sweaters. Knots are a good choice for inelastic yarns, which, if worked into a larger bobble, might sag. Knots can be made smaller or larger by varying the number of stitches worked into the base stitch.

To make a very small knot:
On a RS row, (p1, k1, p1) into front and back of a single st, then p3tog into these sts on WS row.

(continued on p. 188)

(continued from p. 187)

For a larger knot:
(k1, p1, k1, p1, k1, p1, k1) into same st to make 7 sts from one. Then, with LH needle, pull sts, one by one over last st made.

Short rowing

Short rowing is the most common bobble technique, and it forms a larger unit than the knots described above. I think large bobbles can be almost comical, especially if they overpower other patterns.

For a medium-sized bobble:
Knit into front and back of a single st to form 5 sts, or you can (k1, yo) into same st until you have 5 sts. Turn, and p these sts. Turn, ssk, k2, k2tog. Turn and p3. Turn and sl 2 tog k-wise, k1, psso—1 st rem. On return row, you may want to work into back of bobble st, to twist and anchor it more firmly.

For a bolder bobble:
Make 7 sts as described immediately above, then work an additional 2 short rows to return to 1 st. For a huge bobble, increase into 2 adjacent sts, instead of 1. Follow same short-rowing process above.

For more texture in any bobble, knit the wrong-side rows. For a squatter, wider bobble, decrease every row, rather than only on right-side rows.

Chaining

Chaining creates bobble-like loops or little chains that dangle from the surface of the fabric. These units are less bulky than knots or bobbles and can form an interesting allover pattern if grouped together. When repeating these units, separate them from each other by a stitch. The drawback of these loops is that they tend to leave a little opening below them in the fabric.

Work into one st as follows:
k1, (sl this st back to LH needle and k into back of st again) 3 times or more. Purl this st on next row.

Knots and bobbles can be used as details or to form allover fabrics. Clockwise, from left: a bulky cable with large bobbles, made even more comical-looking by their contrasting color; a traditional pattern, featuring smaller knots and with a more delicate, feminine look; an allover fabric, one of my favorites, featuring little raised loops; and subtle patterning formed with an arrangement of simple knots.

cable strands to "set" them and make them stand up from the surface of the fabric. Measure any panels from side to side after blocking, including any background stitches that may flank the panel on either side. If these background stitches naturally curl and recede into the fabric, don't stretch them out—you must measure your gauge over the fabric as it wants to lie. With allover patterns, measure the gauge over at least 4 in., as you would with any textured fabric, and be sure not to flatten the fabric.

An interesting way to design a cable pattern is to alter an existing cable. Starting with a cable used in my Designer Notebook projects in Chapter 6 (pp. 169-176), I made four new cable swatches (from left to right), changing the background, adding stitches to the cable strands, elongating the cable and introducing color.

Designing your own cable patterns

In the photo above are four variations I worked on the traditional cable used in the Designer Notebook projects in Chapter 6 (see pp. 169-176). The suggestions below for altering cables can be applied to many cable patterns:

Changing the background fabric: I altered the background of the original cable in two ways. First, I expanded the background from two purl stitches to six purl stitches on either side of the cable. This change enabled me to switch from plain reverse-stockinette stitch for the background pattern to reverse stockinette-stitch ridges.

Adding stitches to the cable strand: The original cable had three stitches in each strand. For the second swatch from the left in the photo above, I increased each strand to five stitches, which produced a much bulkier effect.

Elongating the cable: The original cable was crossed every sixth row, with the strands at the center of the crossing angling roughly at 45°. To make the angle of the crossing steeper and elongate the cable, I worked the crosses in the third swatch from the left every 12 rows.

Introducing color: In the cable at right in the photo above, I achieved a multicolor effect by working background and strands with bobbins of different colors.

Keep in mind:
• Swatching is the only way to see how alterations will affect a traditional pattern. Start simply with a two-strand cable, then move on to more complicated, multi-strand cables.
• Try not to duplicate a feature that a cable already has. For instance, if a cable already has an elongated look, with crosses occurring at widely spaced intervals, adding extra rows may only distort it.

Some design possibilities:
• You can combine the approaches mentioned above. For instance, you can add stitches to the strands as well as elongate them. Or you can add color to the cable and also change the color of the background.
• In addition to widening the cable strands, you can separate them more by increasing the number of background stitches between them.
• You can add seed and moss-stitch texture to the central background of large cable patterns, like cable diamonds and open-lattice cables. Ribbing and small block patterns, like 2x2 checks, will nicely fill these open spaces too.
• With multi-strand cables, try altering the crosses to upset the way the strands interweave. It will not look like a mistake if you do it consistently over a length of cable, and this technique can yield interesting results.

Eyelet and lace patterns can be paired with a wide range of yarns for different effects. Clockwise, from top right: widely spaced eyelets are well suited to a heavy cotton yarn; a wavy-edged pattern is emphasized by crisp lines of shiny yarn contrasting with soft kid mohair; worked in shiny ribbon, the undulating lace pattern has a modern graphic quality; a slightly hairy alpaca enhances a dense fern lace; at center, a lightweight wool captures the delicate grace of traditional Shetland bead diamond motifs without adding bulk.

*E*yelet & lace patterns

Eyelet and lace patterns offer the designer a wide range of openwork effects, all based on creating openings or holes in the fabric with yarn-overs. Eyelet fabrics are worked with fewer holes than lace and are hence denser and less net-like than lace fabrics.

Eyelets can decorate an otherwise smooth stockinette or garter-stitch fabric with subtle indentations or large Swiss-cheese holes, depending on the yarn weight and number of yarn-overs used for each eyelet. Lace patterns can be plain and geometric, or frilly and ornate. Depending on your yarn choice and tension, lace can be dense and rustic or as airy as a cobweb. The same applies to the wide variety of lace-patterned edgings. In addition, there are many wonderful lace panels and motifs that can make the simplest sweater seem elegant.

The yarn-over at the heart of eyelets and laces is usually worked in one stitch, with the yarn wrapped once around the needle. Some very open laces, however, are worked with two yarn-overs, wrapping the yarn twice around the needle. Each yarn-over must be paired with a decrease to bring the stitch count back to the original number.

Although it's the yarn-over that gives lace its holes, it's the type and placement of the decrease with which the yarn-over is paired that determines the kind of lace produced. There are two single decreases that can be paired with a yarn-over: knit-two-together (k2tog), which leans to the right; and slip, slip, knit (ssk), which leans to the left. Since lace tends to bias, or slant, in the direction of its decreases, you can produce a right-slanting lace by consistently using k2tog as the decrease or, conversely, a left-leaning lace with ssk decreases. Similarly, by alternating bands of right-bias lace with left-bias lace, you'll produce a vertical zigzag effect with scalloped side edges. When panels of left-bias and right-bias lace are juxtaposed, a point will be formed at the lower edge where they meet.

In addition to single decreases, of course, there are also decreases to eliminate two or more stitches. Double decreases, which are the most commonly used multiple decreases, can be worked to slant to the right or left or to stand straight up vertically (for information on how to work these decreases, see the basic knitting books in the Bibliography on pp. 258-260). Double decreases are almost always flanked on either side by a yarn-over.

When the decreases and yarn-overs are separated by several stitches, the fabric tends to undulate and often forms scalloped lower and upper edges, which can become a design detail. Some of the most famous of these scalloped motifs are the Shetland shell patterns.

Many laces are smooth surfaced, with a stockinette-stitch base and the wrong-side rows purled. Some allover lace patterns and many lace edgings have a garter-stitch base, with both right-side and wrong-side rows knitted. The garter-stitch base makes these laces heavier, but they have the advantage of being reversible. The most open, net-like laces have yarn-overs worked on every row. Over time, lace and eyelets units have found their way into the other families of patterns and serve to open up more heavily textured fabrics. The denser eyelet patterns mix better with more solid fabrics, while very open lace should be matched with lighter fabrics, except when it's used in very small doses.

Yarn and needle size are crucial to the look and effectiveness of lace patterns. Lace can be knitted in almost any fiber, but wool is best for keeping its shape. For firm garment fabrics, I prefer small to average needles and springy lightweight to medium-weight yarns. For delicate openwork, suitable for shawls, use fine yarns with needles that are at least three to four sizes larger than you would normally use with these yarns. Cobweb-weight wools on rather large needles (from size 5 to size 7) make the most lightweight laces of all.

Often you'll need to block lace patterns to open up the holes. I usually steam the swatch, then stretch it slightly with my fingers. All lace should be allowed to dry completely and, if possible, to sit from a few hours to a day before being measured for gauge. You'll usually find that the lace will compress a bit in this time, especially if worked in wool.

When blocking very open patterns, like lace shawls, wet the fabric completely and blot the excess moisture with a towel. Then lay the fabric on a clean flat surface, stretch it severely and pin it in place. Allow it to dry completely. No matter how stretched the fabric looks while it is wet, it will still shrink and fluff up slightly after being unpinned.

Designing your own lace

To begin the process of designing lace, you might try altering an existing pattern or simply try designing while you're swatching. You can also chart a pattern and then swatch to see what happens in the knitted fabric. However, no matter what your approach, you need to understand how yarn-overs pair with different decreases and the effects of these pairings in the knitted fabric.

When I began to design lace, I studied pictures of these different yarn-over/decrease combinations in technical knitting books. Pictures are helpful, but nothing can substitute for actually knitting different combinations.

To help you get involved with the pairing of yarn-overs and decreases, let me describe a process that I've found helpful. I begin by charting a simple shape using only a yarn-over symbol. At the bottom of the top drawing on p. 192 you'll see my initial motif, a simple V-shaped arrangement, in which I didn't bother to indicate the wrong-side purl rows. I then pair each yarn-over with a decrease, either to its right or left. If two yarn-overs are separated by a single graph square, I plot a double decrease between them, or a single decrease to either side of each. I draw several variations of the initial motif, placing the decreases in different places to give me a range of possibilities for swatching. After knitting a small swatch of each charted motif, I study the results. Then I decide upon one of my motifs and work out an arrangement of it to design my new pattern.

At top left on p. 192 is the swatch with the four variations on my initial V-shaped motif. The variations were knitted in the same sequence as their charts, shown in the accompanying drawing. (The V-shaped motif could, of course, have been a small diamond or a box shape or anything you like.) In the first motif, the diagonal lines formed by the decreases are crisp and outline the yarn-overs clearly. Even inexperienced knitters will recognize that this type of yarn-over/decrease pairing occurs in many successful traditional lace patterns.

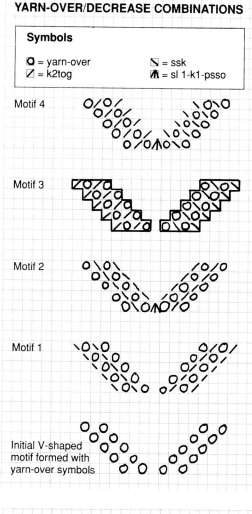

YARN-OVER/DECREASE COMBINATIONS

Symbols

O = yarn-over   **N** = ssk
Z = k2tog   **M** = sl 1-k1-psso

Motif 4

Motif 3

Motif 2

Motif 1

Initial V-shaped motif formed with yarn-over symbols

If you want to design lace patterns, it's important to know what the different yarn-over/decrease pairings look like. The bottom drawing at right shows my initial motif, from which I derived four more motifs (shown charted and knitted). The first motif is crisp, with lines moving clearly outward; the second is less distinct, with short diagonal lines pointing inward; the third resembles the first but has a grainier texture; and the last has short, grainy lines pointing inward.

CHARTED PATTERN BASED ON MOTIF 3

I designed this lace panel, inspired by the third motif in the photo and drawing at the top of this page, which reminded me of a wheat stalk. With this in mind I separated the halves of the motif and repeated them in staggered fashion.

The second motif looks like indented Swiss-cheese fabric, without much distinction. The decreases seem to be pointing toward the center of the V, but the effect is muddy. I would use this only if I wanted a very soft, innocuous patterning to add openness but not crisp detail.

In the third motif, the diagonal lines formed by the decreases have a nice texture, like ears of wheat. They also have softer lines than those in the first swatch, but the lines are still well defined.

The fourth motif has short, textured decrease lines pointing toward the center of the V. This variation resembles the second one but is slightly more interesting because it's a little crisper.

I chose to use the elements of the third motif to design a larger pattern, shown in the bottom photo and chart on the facing page. I staggered the halves of the V-shaped motif on top of each other so that the panel would seem to grow from the center outward. You may find, as I did here, that your pattern resembles one you've seen before. This process leads to a greater appreciation of how laces are constructed and will help you to design your own lace patterns more successfully.

Keep in mind:
• You can use any kind of arrangement of yarn-overs to form your small initial motif. Vertical or horizontal lines forming a small square are enough to start with. Try a small diamond or a triangle or an upside-down V.
• You can place your decreases in any configuration you like. With my small initial charts, I placed all of my decreases to one side of the V. You might try mixing up the placement to see what results you get.

When you have finished testing your motifs, there are a few ways to form a larger pattern.

Some design possibilities:
• Repeat the motif.
• Keep the shape of the motif, but enlarge it.
• Divide the motif in half (as I did) and place the half in an interesting arrangement.
• Omit wrong-side purl rows and see what your motifs (or finished pattern) looks like when the yarn-overs and decreases are worked every row, instead of on right-side rows alone.

Families of knitted *M*otifs

In addition to families of stitch patterns, there are also families of knitted motifs, both color-work and embossed, that are often worked into garments. Knitted motifs generally depict an object, plant or animal impressionistically. While recognizable, knitted motifs are, of course, never entirely realistic in their depiction, which contributes to the primitive charm of these knitted fabrics.

When working with motifs, you will need to think about how to chart them, how to create new variations and how to combine them with other patterns. Some objects, such as a key, are very graphic in nature or can be easily rendered in simplified form. These motifs translate fairly easily into embossed-stitch and colorwork patterns. Other motifs, such as a spring bouquet, are far more complex and detailed, and therefore are more difficult—and often impossible—to render in embossed and colorwork patterns. If you want to use such complex motifs, you will need to find a way of visually simplifying them (see p. 125 for a discussion of learning to draw on graph paper and pp. 127-128 for a discussion of charting).

At right and on p. 194 you will find a small gallery of some of my favorite motifs. Some of these motifs are from very old sources, some are from contemporary sources, and some are of my own invention (or adaptation).

My favorite knitting motif, as you might guess from the photo on p. 178, is the bow, which can be worked in numerous embossed and colorwork variations. Leaves, which can also be rendered both in colorwork and as embossed patterns, are my next favorite motif. At right and on p. 194 are swatches for the embossed variety—smooth stockinette leaves on a background of reverse stockinette.

The graceful, embossed leaf patterns are built up gradually by first increasing over several rows with a yarn-over to either side of a single stitch. These extra stitches are next worked over several rows and then gradually decreased alongside the central stitch or at the

In the green swatch, horizontally staggered embossed leaves form an allover pattern. The coral swatch features leaves on a graceful twining vine.

Letters, plants and animals can inspire countless knitting motifs. At top, letters of different sizes and shapes spell out my nephew's name. Below, bands of leaves with rose-shaped buttons accent a few roses. At right are three charted reindeer designs (top chart, courtesy Dover Publications, Inc.).

outer edges, until only the original stitch remains. This produces a leaf-like puff of fabric with a central vein, rising above the background fabric.

Because the beauty of these patterns lies in their raised surface, be sure not to block them severely. I use the steam-and-pinch technique that I suggested on pp. 187-188 for cable patterns. For other variations on leaves, see the Designer Notebook project on pp. 199-204.

Monograms are indispensable for personalizing hand-knitted garments. You can work either isolated letters or full names or words, or plot one or several letters to form allover graphic patterns. Colorwork, either knitted in or worked with duplicate stitch, is the most obvious way to render letters (see my swatch pocket in the photo on p. 201). But knit/purl dots of texture, or groups of knots or eyelets can also be used, as can embroidered or beaded letters (see the photo on p. 197). For inspiration for monograms, look to embroidery books as well as alphabet books that show examples of different typefaces.

Reindeer motifs come in all shapes and sizes. To demonstrate the variety, you'll find three charts of reindeer on the facing page. The top chart is very old, harking back to the Renaissance, and was planned for square netting lace (called "lacis") or embroidery, though it can be used for a knitted graphic image. I find it especially beautiful because of the way it's confined within a border. In the bottom chart, I plotted a large, less delicate reindeer, which, if worked in a heavy yarn, would cover a large area. In the middle chart, I rendered three small reindeer, which could easily be adapted to an allover repeat or dropped into a sampler of traditional winter motifs—perhaps skiers and snowflakes. A reindeer might also serve in a pinch as a horse, provided you substituted a mane for its antlers!

Many knitwear designers, myself included, have used roses almost ad nauseum, but they're so much fun to work with that they're hard to resist. Just like the real ones in my garden catalogs, there are many varieties that can be knitted, ranging from huge, graphic American Beauties to small Sweethearts and even small knotted buds. I have long planned to work a sampler sweater commemorating the climbing Blaze Rose that covers the bus-stop sign outside my apartment.

A rose is easy to chart because it's just a swirl of color. For larger roses, you may want to interlock swirls, as I did in my impressionistic rose drawing and chart on p. 128. I often try to use more than one shade of a color to give the petals depth. You can add bright spots and shadows with duplicate-stitch details. Leaves and stems are also details you should consider adding, perhaps in colorwork or embroidery.

The list of motifs is endless. Some other motifs that intrigue me and which you might want to consider working into a design are human figures, standing or skiing (look to Scandinavian patterns for inspiration), snowflakes (see my Chinese coat on pp. 158-159), trees, houses, hearts, coffee cups (look to quilting books), fruit, vegetables, stars, keys, and watches and clocks. Don't forget about other distinctive flowers like tulips, irises or waterlilies, or insects like dragonflies and butterflies. And don't overlook the rich terrain of maps for motifs.

Combining like patterns

When combining patterns from the same family, you can be reasonably sure that they'll produce fabrics of about the same weight, but you can't be sure that they'll share the same gauge or work well together visually. For these reasons, extensive swatching is crucial when planning a garment with several diverse patterns in the main fabric. The five-step swatching procedure I use is outlined below:

1. I choose different patterns, either from my files or a dictionary, aiming for an interesting mix. At this point, I don't always know how the patterns will be used in the garment. I may look for pattern similarities or conversely try to set up contrasts. I like to vary the visual weights of patterns for balance, sometimes choosing a large, bold pattern to predominate in a combination with several smaller patterns, and at other times mixing several patterns of the same visual weight for a more even effect.

2. I swatch each of the patterns in the yarn I plan to use. Sometimes, to get a more accurate idea of how two patterns will meld, I test them together in the same swatch.

3. I juggle all the swatches on a flat surface, moving them around in different groupings. I eliminate any that don't seem to work—one

may be too similar to another, or it may be the wrong visual weight. I might try simplifying matters by scaling down to only two patterns. If my choices look weak, however, I might swatch some additional patterns to see if they add the needed spark.

4. After assembling an appealing group of swatches, I sketch out a few rough design ideas to decide the final pattern groupings within the confines of a garment. I then determine the ease and dimensions of the sweater pieces.

Beaded and embroidered embellishments

Of all embellishment techniques, beading and embroidery are my favorites. They can add detail and elegance to an otherwise plain fabric. Beads add shine and texture and can be used randomly or grouped to form motifs. Embroidery adds yet another textural dimension to the knitted surface and offers an easy alternative to knitting in color details on a design.

As a designer, I use beading in several valuable ways. First and foremost, it's the easiest way to glamorize a simple garment. You need only add a line of beading at the edges or along seamlines to accent a garment's shape. An already dressy design, worked in an ornate lace or wonderful novelty yarn, can be elevated to spectacular by adding beads.

Beads can also serve to highlight a pattern stitch or colorwork motif. For example, you can outline the shape of a lace pattern with beads, nestle beads in the recessed areas of stranded cables, or let them sit high on the surface of an embossed pattern. You can use beads to form a pattern of their own on a smooth stockinette surface. You can align them in columns to create "ribbing," or work a knit/purl

These swatches show some of my favorite ways to embellish knitted fabric — using beads within a knitted pattern, knitting beads in close rows to form a densely beaded surface, knitting in paillettes to form a dramatic allover fabric or edging (blue swatch), and embroidering details to add texture and color.

FRENCH KNOTS

You can wrap yarn around needle more times than shown here to make larger knots.

A

B

SATIN STITCH

Take care not to make stitches too long or they will pull out of place and pucker fabric beneath.

5. Finally, I measure each swatch and plot each pattern on a schematic. Measuring and plotting all the patterns to scale on a schematic lets you test different arrangements and see how much space they'll take up on the surface of the garment. It doesn't matter if the gauges of the several patterns are different. Later you can figure out the stitch counts for each pattern and make any adjustments necessary (for information on charting, see pp. 200-201).

pattern on stockinette fabric ground, substituting beads for the purl stitches.

There are many kinds of beads in all colors and shapes to choose from. Beads can contrast with your fabric, or add a pearly or shiny glint in the same color. Beads made of wood and clay can be a interesting accent for ethnic-inspired garments or chunkier rustic yarns. Small beads lend themselves to accessories or fine-gauge yarn projects; large beads need a heavier fabric base on which to sit. (For information on the various techniques for knitting beads into your fabric, consult *Mary Thomas's Knitting Book* and *Vogue Knitting*, which are listed in the Bibliography on pp. 258-260.)

With regard to embroidery, I find duplicate stitch and a few other techniques—French knots, satin stitch and my woven stitch (explained below)—useful for adding more color and texture in sampler-style sweaters. I embroider sparingly in order to avoid stiffening the supple knitted fabric. (For a discussion of duplicate stitch, consult the basic knitting references in the Bibliography on pp. 258-260.)

I often use French knots in place of colored bobbles simply because they're easier to make. They are fun to make (see the top drawing on the facing page), and they can be placed anywhere (see also my Hiroshige sweater in the top photo on p. 133).

Satin stitch is useful in small touches. As my swatch at bottom left in the photo on the facing page shows, this stitch offers many decorative possibilities. I like to use it for leaves and other flat color accents.

By fooling around with a swatch, I invented a woven stitch that threads a strand of yarn through stitches on a flat fabric. In the swatch at bottom left in the photo on the facing page, I planted a diamond of duplicate stitches, four rows apart, around a central motif. Then I threaded a contrasting color on a tapestry needle and wove the strand in and out of the duplicate stitches to form an embossed wavy line. As you can see, many multicolor variations are possible.

Several other kinds of embroidery will also work well for knitters. Check the embroidery sources in the Bibliography (pp. 258-260) for other favorites of mine: cross-stitch (which can be worked over individual stitches to produce a grainier substitute for duplicate stitch), outline stitch (good for outlining graphics in contrasting colors) and blanket stitch (for adding color along the outer edges of garments and trims).

Beading embellishes these 19th-century knitted accessories. Each fingerless glove features the wearer's initials and a sampler of lace and beaded motifs. A leaf-like pattern sampler adorns the bag, which also include a knitted-in name at the lower edge. (Metropolitan Museum of Art. Gloves: gift of Mr. Lee Simonson, 1938; purse: gift of Stella Jolles Reichman, 1980.)

To combine various lace patterns, my starting point for swatching was a lovely old photo of a woman in a wrapped scarf. To design a similar scarf, I tried two lace panels and a scalloped edging in a crisp wool (at right), and a chevron border in silk (upper left). Both would have worked for my sketched scarf design, but, when I fell in love with a gossamer mohair in a bias-lace pattern, my project grew from a scarf into a shawl, shown in the photo at right. (Inset photo, The Bettmann Archive.)

For my knitted spiderweb shawl, I combined very angular lace patterns, using the naturally slanting bias patterns to create the shape. The shawl is made from a very lightweight mohair yarn, which has a springy feel and a slightly hairy surface. (For knitting instructions, see pp. 256-257.)

I often begin a design with one idea in mind, then change plans after swatching, only to end up with a totally different result. This project proved to be an example of just that. I was inspired by the lovely fashion picture in the inset photo above left from the 1930s of a woman wearing a wrapped scarf. I could imagine making a lace version, with long sashes or cords at the corners to wrap around the body. The back view might be squared off like a sailor collar or pointed like a traditional scarf. After swatching in a fine wool and a silk, as you can see in the photo above left, I ran across a wonderful fine mohair, which yielded a spiderweb effect. I was unable to resist this yarn, but I knew it would make a better shawl than a scarf. My swatches made the decision for me—some day I'll return to make the scarf version.

Lace shawls are great fun to knit because you don't have to be careful about gauge since fit isn't a real issue. These lace pieces work up fast, with fine yarns on large needles, and blocking evens out irregularities in the fabric.

My design is a simple plan for combining every kind of lace pattern: panel-type patterns, isolated motifs, a border, an allover bias-lace

pattern and a lace edging. I used two simple bias-lace patterns, one that slants to the left and one that slants to the right. I took advantage of the natural shape of the bias patterns to give the shawl a chevron shape (see the schematic and full instructions for this shawl on pp. 256-257).

You can endlessly alter this "wing-shaped" format to design other shawls or small scarves. The size and shape of the piece are determined by the widths and lengths of the different sections. For the largest of shawls, a very long center panel of at least 36 in. is needed. For a small neck scarf, about a 12-in. long panel is sufficient. This center panel can be wide or narrow. Borders might be bold or just a discreet divider between the panel and the larger allover pattern. If you use a non-biasing pattern at the sides, you'll form a rectangular shape.

The yarn and needle size will determine the look of the finished fabric. Fine yarns on large needles yield the most dramatic openwork. For my gossamer spiderweb of a shawl, I used a fine 100% mohair on a size 6 needle. The hairiness fills in the very large lace holes—the fabric floats rather than drapes. My swatch in a fine cabled wool is a heavier, crisper alternative, well suited to a shawl or scarf. My third choice, a smooth 100% silk, is soft and luxuriously limp, best used for a smaller scarf. I would also recommend lace-weight Shetland wools and crochet cotton for these projects.

Other decorative details can add interest. Beads can be worked into the shawl to outline patterns. And each section could be knitted in a different color or shade of yarn to accentuate the separate sections.

The patterns I chose to combine all had sharp geometric lines. For an alternative "theme," you might choose to combine soft, undulating patterns, perhaps those that form scalloped edges. Or hunt through your dictionaries for other bias-lace patterns, which could be another theme to explore.

If you decide to design your own shawl or scarf, here are some guidelines to help you:

1. Swatch and block to find the best-looking fabric for your project. Your swatch will yield a rough gauge for any of the lace patterns you'll use. Since the shawl does not need to fit the body like a garment, slight discrepancies in gauge matter little. The row gauge should help you plan the number of stitches that need to be picked up at any edge—usually two stitches for every three rows.

2. To avoid tight edges, which may make blocking difficult, always cast on and bind off loosely. Or use a "looped" edge as I did (see p. 257 for a description of how it's done).

3. Lace edgings are often worked side to side, that is, differently oriented from the way the main fabric is knitted. An edging can be worked separately and sewn on after the main fabric is completed, or it can be worked first and then stitches can be picked up along the edging and worked to produce the main fabric. As a last alternative, you can work the main fabric and then begin working the edging and, as you knit, join it to the live stitches on the main fabric. This is the way I worked my shawl, since it allows for maximum stretch.

4. Wet the piece and blot away excess water. Stretching the fabric severely, pin it to a large, flat surface, either a large bed covered with a sheet, your carpet or a cardboard blocking board. Allow the garment to dry thoroughly before removing it from the blocking surface.

Combining unlike patterns

When combining unlike patterns, I work from swatching to plotting the patterns on graph paper, just as I do for combining similar patterns. However, since there are likely to be more dissimilarities among patterns in this type of combination, I compare the swatches carefully to see if their weights are compatible. For example, I probably would not combine a very open, flimsy lace pattern with a dense, bulky cable pattern because they are so unlike in weight that they would create a very unbalanced fabric.

With unlike patterns, I try to create a grouping that looks good. To do so, I try to articulate my intentions for the design. I ask myself, for example, if I'm aiming for patterns that share the same visual weight and will produce a balanced mixture, or if I want one pattern to predominate. Limiting your colors helps unify dissimilar patterns; using a separate color for each pattern highlights the individuality of each. Keep in mind that you need not always strive for balance when mixing patterns. You may find that a particular design benefits from a choppier, patchwork effect.

designer notebook

To explore mixing unlike patterns, I chose leaf motifs, with an idea of combining them in a sampler sweater. To help merge the wide variety of patterns, I chose a fine yarn because it would yield more stitches to the inch than a heavier yarn and would give me more room to play around with pattern placement. Also, a fine fabric and a conservative garment shape would offset what I feared could be an almost wild blend of motifs. I began by swatching the patterns in smooth wool/rayon blend yarns for a trans-seasonal garment, choosing ivory and periwinkle for strong contrast and a limited palette that would help unify the many different types of patterns.

Successful theme and sampler combinations

Here are a few rules for avoiding bad combinations:

• Do not combine flimsy patterns with dense, firm ones. Disparate weights will not usually mix well.

• Look for shared visual elements among motifs that you want to combine: bold lines, similar texture or shared backgrounds.

• Do not place patterns with different row gauges next to one another in panels because the sections with tighter gauges will shorten and draw up (if you're attached to an arrangement like this, short-row in the tighter sections to balance out the differing row gauges). Instead, try mixing these patterns in a horizontal arrangement.

• Use color to unify patterns that are not as compatible as you might like. And to add zest to patterns that might be a bit too similar and otherwise boring, add various colors to different areas.

My Designer Notebook shows the several leaf-inspired swatches I knitted to work out my design for a sampler cardigan of leaf patterns, shown in the photo on p. 202. Also included are my sketch and a large chart for the sleeve.

In the photo at left you'll see the swatches for several leaf patterns—some colorwork, some lace, others embossed. You'll also see a few discarded swatches that I thought would work, but just didn't.

After swatching, I sketch the patterns in several different ways, then I often draw them onto a schematic, taking garment shape and fabric weight into account. At this point, I try to use all of my patterns, but I'm prepared to discard some if the garment proves too busy.

Charting a garment stitch by stitch

As a supplement to my schematic, I always chart a challenging project on a large sheet of graph paper. I've had great success with this method because it allows me to "knit" the garment on paper first. I can check pattern placement more carefully, see how my garment shaping will affect my patterns and center motifs, and plan what row each pattern will begin and end on. Making the charts forces me to scrutinize every part of the design.

Here are some guidelines for setting up a large chart:

1. For each garment piece, use a large (17-in. by 22-in.) sheet of graph paper, with approximately eight or ten squares to the inch.

2. For convenience, number your rows along the right side, every eighth to tenth row, or according to where the heavy lines fall.

3. Referring to your schematic and your pattern row gauges, mark the length of the garment piece, with one square representing one knitted row. Indicate where the armhole and

shoulder will fall. Draw lines out to the side of the chart to indicate lengths at various points, usually where patterns begin or end.

4. Referring to your schematic and to your pattern-stitch gauges, start at the bottom of the chart and draw in the width, with one square representing one stitch.

5. Outline the different pattern areas. Plot any vertical or horizontal patterns. If you need to increase or decrease between sections to maintain an even width in your garment piece, indicate this on the chart. Outline the shape of the neckline and shoulders.

Some erasing or lengthening or shortening may be necessary to plot the patterns exactly as you want them.

6. On the chart, record pertinent information about yarn and gauge for future reference.

The planning for my leaf-patterned cardigan proceeded well because I had swatched thoroughly. I enjoyed sketching to find an interesting arrangement of patterns for a raglan-sleeve cardigan. I placed the large colorwork border at the lower body, with the other colorwork (the small border and slip-stitch leaf patterns) at the edges of both sleeve and neckline. I chose 1x1 ribbing for the lower edge of the body because it was so compatible with the ribbed leaf pattern I wanted to insert at intervals. This ribbed leaf pattern also became a panel that decorated the center of the sleeve. As filler for the remaining areas, I decided to use the allover twist-stitch leaf pattern.

Among my swatches was a small stockinette one that I used to test needle size with my yarn. This swatch (see the photo at right) was lightweight enough and just the right size to become a small inner pocket for the sweater, so I duplicate-stitched it with the letters that spell out the sweater's theme. At the top of the swatch I worked a row of slip-stitch leaves for detail; along the sides I tested a narrow edging.

While I was plotting patterns on my schematic, the raglan garment shape made me think about an idea I had never tried before: Could I add the small color border along the raglan line to enhance my sampler effect? I measured the height of the border, then carved out a section from the front to accommodate it. To my delight, this design worked out well.

PLOTTING A GARMENT PIECE ON GRAPH PAPER

I always chart knitted pieces on graph paper before beginning to knit, using one grid square to represent one stitch. Above I've charted a sample cap sleeve with various patterns and shaping. For easy reference, I note row numbers at right. Sleeve begins at lower edge with garter ridges and colorwork pattern. Directly above, I indicated an increase row before charting central cable panel and adjoining garter-stripe patterns. Desired length is indicated at underarm, where row gauge is checked. Bind-offs are shown as horizontal lines, with number of stitches to be bound off written above.

After deciding that one of the stockinette swatches used to test yarn for my leaf sweater was just the right size for an inner pocket for this garment, I duplicate-stitched the sweater's theme on the pocket.

Instructions for leaf-sampler cardigan

This raglan cardigan sampler of colorwork and embossed leaf patterns has a classic, loose-fitting silhouette. For the intermediate knitter.

SIZE
To fit 32-33 (34-35, 36-37)-in. bust.

FINISHED MEASUREMENTS (AFTER SEAMING):
Finished bust at underarm (fronts meet): 39 (41¾, 44½) in.
Length (from back neck to lower edge, not including neckline trim): 22 (22¾, 23¼) in.
Sleeve width at upper arm: 15½ (16½, 17¾) in.

MATERIALS
•10 (12, 14) skeins "Paisley Light" from Classic Elite (50% wool, 50% rayon; 1¾ oz = 135 yd) in color Thistle blue #1607: main color (MC).
•3 (3,3) skeins Natural #1616: contrasting color (CC).
•1 circular knitting needle each, size 6 and 7, 24 in. long, or size to obtain gauge.
•1 pair each, knitting needles size 5, 6 and 7.

GAUGE
•25 sts and 26 rows equal 4 in., with size 7 needles over large color-border pat.
•29 sts and 32 rows equal 4 in., with size 6 needles over twist-st leaf pat.
•Ribbed leaf panel, worked over 19 sts, with size 6 needles should measure 2½ in. wide.
•To save time later, take time to swatch and check your gauge.

BODY
•Note that body is worked in 1 piece, back and forth on a circular needle below underarms.
•With size 6 circular needle and MC, cast on 283 (303, 323) sts.
Next row (WS): p1 (edge: keep in St st), work in 1x1 rib over 5 (15, 25) sts, * work ribbed-leaf panel pat over 19 sts, work in 1x1 rib over 23 sts; rep from *, end by working ribbed leaf panel over 19 sts, then work 5 (15, 25)

sts in 1x1 rib, p1 (edge: keep in St st). Work even in pats as est until all 32 rows of ribbed-leaf panel pat are completed, so end with a RS row. Piece should measure approx 4 in.
Next row (WS): With MC, p across, dec 42 (42, 44) sts evenly spaced by p2tog—241 (261, 279) sts. Change to size 7 circular needle.
Next row (RS): Work Row 1 of large color border, beg and end where indicated on chart. Work even in pat until all 36 rows of border are complete, so end with a WS row.
Next row (RS): With MC, k across row, inc 42 (42, 44) sts evenly spaced— 283 (303, 323) sts. Change to size 6 circular needle.
Next row (WS): p1 (edge: keep in St st), work in twist-st leaf pat over center 281 (301, 321) sts, end p1 (edge: keep in St st). Work even in pat until piece measures 13 in., end with a RS row.
Next row (WS): Work 53 (59, 65) sts, bind off 25 sts, work back 127 (135, 143) sts, bind off 25 sts, work 53 (59, 65) sts to end. Note: At this point, each front and back section will be worked separately. Leave right-front sts on needle, sl back and left front sts to holders.

RIGHT FRONT
Next row (RS): Keeping in pat, work to last 3 sts, k2tog, k1.
Next row: p2, work to end. Rep last 2 rows 30 (32, 34) more times. Bind off rem 22 (26, 30) sts on next RS row.

LEFT FRONT
With RS facing, sl left front sts on holder to needle. Join yarn at armhole edge at beg of RS row.
Next row (RS): k1, ssk, work to end.
Next row: Work to last 2 sts, end p2. Rep last 2 rows 30 (32, 34) more times. Bind off rem 22 (26, 30) sts on next RS row.

BACK
With RS facing, sl back 127 (135, 143) sts to needle. Join yarn at armhole edge at beg of RS row. Keeping in pat, bind off 2 sts at beg of next 6 (4, 4) rows.

Next row (RS): k1, ssk, work to last 3 sts, k2tog, k1.
Next row: p2, work to last 2 sts, end p2. Rep last 2 rows 31(35, 39) more times. Bind off rem 51 (55, 55) sts on next RS row.

RIGHT SLEEVE
With size 6 needle and CC, cast on 49 (49, 53) sts. K WS row. Change to MC. K 2 rows. Work rows 1-20 of sl-st leaf pat. With MC, k 2 rows. With MC, k next RS row, inc 18 sts evenly—

PATTERN CHARTS FOR LEAF-SAMPLER CARDIGAN

Large color border

End body small
End body medium and large

18-st rep

Beg body small
Beg body medium and large

Stitch key

☐ = k RS rows, p WS rows
⊟ = p RS rows, k WS rows
╱ = k2tog
╲ = ssk
Ⅴ = k1-b RS rows, p1-b WS rows
5 = k1, yo, k1, yo, k1 into 1 st to make 5 sts out of 1 st
⌁ = p1, wrapping twice; drop extra wrap when st is worked on next row
Ⅰ = sl 1 wyib RS rows; sl 1 wyif WS rows
■ = no stitch, placeholder in chart
╱╱ = RT
╲╲ = LT
╲╱ = k3tog, before slipping sts off, k 1st st, then k 2nd st, then sl all off

Color key

☒ = CC (white)
☐ = MC (blue)

Small color border

6-st rep

Beg right armhole trim for all on Row 2

End all sleeves

Beg sleeve large
End medium armhole trim Row 2
End large armhole trim Row 2
Beg sleeve small and medium
End small armhole trim Row 2

Left small color border
(use for left armhole trim only)

6-st rep

End all left-armhole trims on Row 2

Beg small Row 2
Beg large Row 2
Beg medium Row 2

1x1 rib

2-st rep

WS →1

end   beg

Slip-stitch leaf pattern
(multiple of 4 sts plus 1)

Blue MC
White CC
Blue MC
White CC

end all   beg all

Twist-stitch leaf pattern
(multiple of 10 sts plus 1)

WS →1

end all   10-st rep   beg all

Ribbed-leaf panel pattern

Note: On sleeve, work rows 1-30 of ribbed-leaf panel pat only.

19 sts

WS →1

end all   beg all

Schematic for leaf-pattern sampler sweater

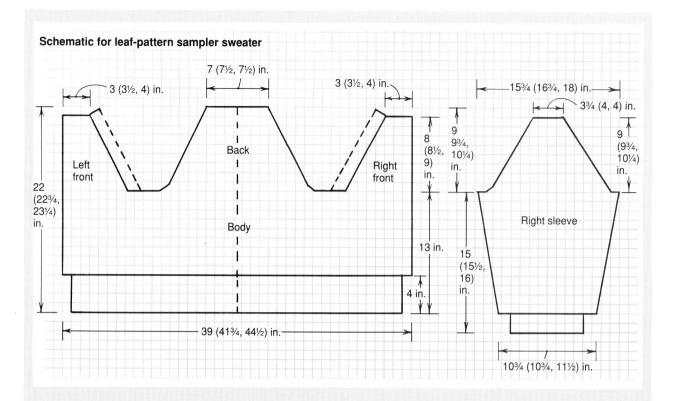

67 (67, 71) sts. Change to size 7. With CC, p 1 row. Work rows 1-9 of small color border, so end with a RS row. With CC, p 1 row. Change to size 6. With MC, k 2 rows. With MC, k RS row, inc 18 (18, 34) sts evenly — 85 (85, 105) sts.

Next row (WS): p2 (edge sts: keep in St st), work row 1 of twist-st leaf pat over 31 (31, 41) sts, work Row 1 of ribbed-leaf panel pat over center 19 sts, work Row 1 of twist-st leaf pat over 31 (31, 41) sts, end p2 (edge sts: keep in St st). Work even for 2 more rows.

Next row, inc row (RS): k2, M1, work to last 2 sts, M1, end k2. Rep last row after 5 (3, 1) more rows, then every 6 (4, 6)th row after, for a total of 15 (19, 13) incs each side, working incs into pat — 115 (123, 131) sts. Note: rep ribbed-leaf panel pat rows 1-30 only for rem of sleeve. Work even until sleeve measures 15 (15½, 16) in. or to desired length, end with a WS row.

CAP SHAPING

Bind off 7 sts at beg of next 2 rows — 101 (109, 117) sts.

Row 1 (RS, front edge of sleeve): k1, ssk, work to end.

Row 2 (back edge of sleeve): Bind off 2 sts, work to last 2 sts, end p2. Rep the last 2 rows 2 more times — 92 (100, 108) sts.

Row 1 (RS): k1, ssk, work to last 3 sts, k2tog, k1 — 90 (98, 106) sts.

Row 2: p2, work to last 2 sts, end p2. Rep last 2 rows 31 (34, 36) more times. Bind off rem 28 (30, 34) sts on last RS row.

LEFT SLEEVE

Work same as for right sleeve, reversing shaping of sleeve cap.

RIGHT-FRONT ARMHOLE TRIM

With RS facing, size 6 needle and CC, beg at neckline edge, pick up 52 (56, 60) sts evenly along raglan edge to bound-off section at underarm.

Next row (WS): Work Row 2 of small color border, beg and end where indicated. Cont until 9 rows of pat are complete, AND AT SAME TIME, cast on 2 sts at beg of next 4 WS rows, working these sts into pat — 60 (64, 68) sts. With CC, p WS row, then bind off. Rep on left-front armhole, following left small color-border pat.

FINISHING

Sew lower edge of armhole trim to bound-off edge at armhole, over an 11-st section closest to front. Sew front edge of sleeve cap to armhole trim at front. Sew back edge of sleeve cap to back armhole edge.

NECKLINE TRIM

With RS facing, size 6 needle and CC, pick up 89 (101, 113) sts evenly around entire neck edge. K 1 row. Change to MC and k 2 rows. Work rows 1-10 of sl-st leaf pat, so end with a WS row. With CC, k 2 rows, then bind off in p on RS row.

RIGHT-FRONT EDGE TRIM

With RS facing, size 5 needle and CC, beg at lower edge, pick up 122 (126, 130) sts evenly spaced along front edge to corner of neckline trim. K 1 row, then bind off. Rep on left-front edge.

WHAT IF...?

What if I worked my leaf-patterned sweater using roses instead?

ROSE
Alternate swatch pocket

Same layout of patterns

Panel of "brocade" roses ↗

Round ↗ knit/purl motifs

Wide colorwork ← border

"Brocade" roses in rib

Another design combining roses and embossed leaf patterns with an allover cable pattern

Embossed leaves in ribbing

Trellis background formed of cabled strands

8
Dressmaker details & finishing

*d*ressmaker shapes and details long ago won my heart and have since influenced many of my designs. I have always been attracted to the beautifully shaped blouses and dresses of the 1930s and 1940s. I am equally intrigued by the mixed silhouette of the 1950s — a tight-fitting bodice with a wide, flared skirt. And the zip-front, bell-shaped tent dress of the 1960s will, in my mind, forever be worn by Twiggy, the pencil-thin model of the day.

I am also a great fan of menswear. I love broad-shouldered, double-breasted jackets with big lapels. Similarly, I am intrigued by garments with oddly shaped edges and small details, like the multipocketed waistcoat worn by the White Rabbit in Alice in Wonderland. I love inner pockets, the shaped lower edges of men's vests and the luxurious shawl collars of men's traditional dressing gowns.

My best designs have been those inspired by dressmaker and tailoring details. I may be a traitor to my craft, but I love a knitted garment that doesn't look like one. I prefer complex sil-houettes, with more attention given to shaping the garment's body than is usually found in traditional knitwear. And I love to experiment with garment details and occasionally simulate the drape and flow of supple woven fabrics with lightweight yarns.

The adjective *dressmaker* traditionally refers to women's sewn garments, and *tailored* to men's custom-made suits. In an age of almost complete freedom with regard to acceptable dress, these terms may be a bit dated. Yet they nonetheless recall the techniques and details that we associate with traditionally sewn, as opposed to knitted, garments, and which are still a vital part of today's clothing.

Whatever the dressmaker's or tailor's prod-uct, whether a blouse, dress, suit, jacket or coat, it differs from a knitted garment, first and fore-most, in its fabric, which is usually woven. And because knitted and woven fabrics are struc-turally different from one another, they require different construction methods and produce garments that are distinctly different.

Woven fabric comes in a wide variety of weaves, textures and weights but, generally speaking, stretches much less than knitted fabric. Woven fabric produces garments that can, on the one hand, be stiffer and more structured than knitwear and, on the other hand, can be far more fluid and lighter in weight (for example, a silk dress). Because of the characteristics of woven fabric, dressmaker and tailored garments are usually shaped with more detail than knitwear. Since any shape can be easily cut from a length of woven fabric, these sewn garments often incorporate curved or irregular edges and are frequently embellished with separately made and sewn-on edges like collars and cuffs. And because woven fabrics ravel and fray when cut, sewn garments require seam allowances, hems, and often linings and facings to stabilize their edges and give them structure.

Because of the construction methods that are required for knitwear, I can't actually put to use authentic dressmaker or tailoring techniques in my designs. Instead, I draw inspiration from these techniques and adapt dressmaker and tailored shapes, structure and details whenever possible for my knitwear. Since I came to knitting after many years of sewing, borrowing from these sources seemed natural to me. But even if you can't sew, you can still use dressmaker and tailoring techniques and details in your knitting.

*d*ressmaker silhouettes

On the facing page are a few of my favorite dressmaker silhouettes, which fit or drape in ways not generally associated with knitted garments but which can be adapted for knitwear. There are, of course, many more dressmaker silhouettes than space permits mentioning here. For a look at some of these other shapes, consult sewing books in your local library, and, of course, go through books about famous couturiers for inspiration from their garment shapes. Remember that for any of these silhouettes, you could start with the basic skeleton chart (see p. 60), add ease and then expand on this adjusted chart to create a schematic for a dressmaker shape.

Princess style

A princess-style garment—usually a dress or blouse—is made up of separate, hourglass-shaped panels. The simplest version has three panels each on the front and back—a center panel flanked by two mirror-image side panels. The assembled garment conforms closely to the body's curves and can be very slimming.

Princess panels can be shaped in one of two ways: The seams can begin at mid-shoulder and extend over the bust point and down to the garment's lower edge (the fabric covering on a professional dress form is constructed this way). Alternatively, the seams can begin within the lower half of the armhole, curve diagonally out from the armhole and over the upper chest to the bust point and then fall straight to the garment's lower edge.

The primary features of the princess line—its fitted shape and seamlines—adapt nicely to knitting. For a very simple princess style, you can plan to work the front (and back) in a single, relatively unshaped piece, with the only shaping occurring at the center and side waistline. Simple cables or other textured lines can be inserted within the body of the front and back to simulate the seams (see the photo on p. 239 for an example of false seams).

For a more challenging approach to the princess style, experienced knitters may want to look at a dressmaker pattern to see how the individual pieces are shaped. You can duplicate the shaped pieces individually and sew them together, or you can knit the body in one piece with increases and decreases plotted to simulate the shaping and thereby eliminate the seams. The shaping for this more authentic princess style would occur not only in the waistline but also in the hip and either the mid-shoulder or lower armhole area, depending on the type of princess style chosen. The style with a "seam" from shoulder to lower edge is the easier of the two to make.

There are many possible variations on this silhouette. For contrast, each separate panel can be worked in a different stitch or colorwork pattern. The princess style can also flare below the waist to create a peplum effect (see pp. 210-211), or it can be adapted for a trapeze-shaped garment (see the facing page).

DRESSMAKER SILHOUETTES

Princess (two style lines shown)   **Trapeze**   **Surplice**   **Peplum**

Close-fitting   Drapey

Fronts criss-cross, held
in place by button or ties.

Flared lower edges held
in place by ribbed waist

1 square = 1 in.

←Center→
←Side→   ←Side→

Should be close
to waist in length

Tuck or gather shoulder,
back neck and lower
edge to fit.

½ back-neck
width

Peplum
section

Decrease at four to six points
to taper peplum gradually.

Lower edge of peplum
should measure 8 in. or more
beyond hip measurement.

Trapeze

A trapeze, or tent-shaped, garment usually fits closely in the shoulder area, flares below the bust point and has an oversized, curved lower edge. A sewn trapeze can be constructed in two basic ways, both of which can be adapted to knitwear. Both front and back can be made in a single piece, with angled sides (see the schematic example of this on p. 158), or, for a sturdier garment, a princess-style structure with seams from the shoulder to the lower edge, can be adapted to support the weight.

The trapeze is a dramatic shape, well suited to firmly knitted coats and jackets. Worked in a lightweight yarn with drape, it would make a nice soft, short blouse.

Surplice

Surplice garments have separate right- and left-front sections that overlap, wrap around the body and button or tie at the back or side. Depending on the cut of the front sections, they can drape in soft folds or stretch taut across the body like a leotard. In either case, they usually form a V-neckline. The surplice is a rather close-fitting garment, often ending at the waistline. The back of this garment can be shaped to conform to the body or hang loosely until gathered in by wrapping and tying the ties of the front sections.

The simplest surplice, when wrapped, lies flat across the body, with the edges of the two front sections crisscrossing one another at an angle. A surplice that has some drape needs extra fabric on the front sections in order to fall in folds. This drapey surplice can also have a collar, which is knitted as an extension of the two front sections, and then joined and sewn to the back neck. If the collar extensions are wide, they will form a deep collar that falls gently in folds.

Since the surplice style needs to cling or drape, I've found that it works best when it is knitted in lightweight yarn in a smooth fabric like stockinette. The heavier the fabric, the clos-er the surplice should fit to eliminate a bulky look. I've had success with sewing the body sections into a waistband or belt, which buttons or ties at the side.

Peplum

A peplum is a short, flared extension below the waistline of a fitted blouse or jacket. The peplum can be either an extension of the garment's body or a separate section attached below the

Knitting dressmaker and tailoring fabrics

I've taken inspiration for knitted fabrics from various dressmaker and tailoring materials. The photo below shows some of my favorites. **Plaids** are formed by combining horizontal and vertical stripes in the same fabric. Most famous are the Scottish tartans, which provide endless inspiration for knits.

A **houndstooth** fabric is composed of tiny, interlocking pinwheel motifs. There are many houndstooth knitting patterns (for one example, see p. 154); to add an extra touch to these patterns, work them in nubby or textured yarns.

Pinstripes, the classic menswear suiting fabric, can be copied in colorwork by using an individual bobbin of color—and possibly different colors—for each stripe. You can also recreate the feel of this fabric by chain-stitching or duplicate-stitching the stripes on the plain stockinette fabric. **Twills** have characteristic slanted lines in the weave, worked either solid or in two colors. You can simulate a solid-color twill with diagonal lines of purl stitches on a stockinette background. **Herringbone** is a two-color twill, often worked in charcoal and white for tailored garments.

Nubby textured fabrics like those often used for classic womenswear suits can be simulated by knitting with many novelty yarns, used singly or in combination. For the look of real **velvet,** only chenille yarns will do, worked in the smoothest stockinette stitch.

When I see checked **gingham,** I always think of Judy Garland's dress in *The Wizard of Oz*. Inspired by this, my ideal gingham look-alike would be knitted in lightweight cotton yarns, in a slip-stitch checkerboard pattern. And when I think of gingham, **polka dots** are not far behind (see the rounded motifs in the chart on p. 139). You might also explore the swirling **paisley** motif, working it in deep shades inspired by traditional Scottish shawls or in the bright colors of American bandannas.

These knitted swatches were all inspired by dressmaker fabrics, among them, velvet (worked in chenille yarn), polka dots, pinstripe, herringbone, plaid, houndstooth check and solid twill weave. My favorite is the red and white 'gingham,' worked with a slip-stitch pattern from Barbara Walker's *A Second Treasury of Knitting Patterns* (see the Bibliography on pp. 258-260).

waist. Peplums usually have an oversized fit at the hip, but they can also be styled to follow the lines of the body.

To adapt the peplum to knitwear, you can plan a wide lower edge for your garment, then decrease gradually as you work toward the waist. This keeps bulk to a minimum at the waist but allows for extra fabric to flare over the hip. If, instead, you work the decreases all at once when you get to the waist, you'll have a more bell-shaped peplum, with a less graceful line. A ribbed waistline also works well for a peplum.

If tight enough, ribbing can be used instead of decreases to draw in the waist, and it will also create a bell-shaped peplum. Worked above a flared and shaped peplum, ribbing helps maintain a close fit at the waist and is stretchier and more comfortable than flat fabric alone. A lovely peplum can be made from a ribbed fabric with large purl ribs at the hip, which gradually decrease in width as they near the waist.

Shaping techniques

The complex silhouettes of dressmaker garments involve more shaping and fitting than is generally used with knitted garments. This shaping can occur both at the garment's edges and within its body, and is produced in sewn garments by either working with carefully contoured pattern parts or by strategically positioning darts, tucks or pleats to take up fullness. In knitwear, this shaping can be produced by various methods: contouring garment sections (see the drawing below), working vertical or horizontal darts within the fabric, ribbing and welting the fabric, and working pleats or tucks. Each of these methods helps transform flat pieces of fabric into 3-D shapes that conform to the curves of the body.

Ribbing is the easiest way to shape a garment to make it conform to the body. Ribbing can be worked as a band around the waistline or in panels along the sides of the garment to make the silhouette narrower (see the discussion of ribbing used for shaping on pp. 81-83).

ADAPTING SCHEMATICS
Adding fabric to expand the silhouette
Drop lines from bust point and sides to desired length.

Right-front side panel
Center panel
Left-front side panel
Right-front side panel
Desired length
Right center front
Left center front
Left-front side panel
Right-front side panel
2 in.

Eliminating fabric to make a fitted garment

Trapeze front (and back) worked in one piece
13 in.
13 in.
13 in.

Princess line from shoulder
Bust point
3½ in.
7 in.
18 in.

Princess line from lower armhole
1 square = 1 in.
3½ in.

USING RIBBING TO SHAPE GARMENT AREAS

Body

For slight shaping at sides

For close fit at hips and to widen gradually toward bust

To create close fit below bust

Sleeves

To create very narrow sleeve below puffed cap

To widen sleeve gradually from lower edge

To draw in fabric in cap area

Alternatively, ribbing can be worked in a triangular or diamond-shaped area at the waistline, which will more severely draw in the garment than will a simple ribbed band. Knitting triangular or diamond-shaped ribbing requires gradually working into the main pattern above the ribbing, knitting a few stitches of the pattern at each side every row until, finally, the entire row is worked in the pattern. Another ribbing variation involves working isolated areas of ribbing at the sides or in the center sections of the garment.

Welting can also be used to shape the garment that is worked side to side. Since welting is less elastic than ribbing, it will cling less firmly. The smaller the welts, the more effectively they will shape the garment. Welting, like ribbing, can be worked in isolated areas within the body of a garment to shape it.

As an alternative to ribbing and welting, a drawstring can be used to gather and hold fabric at the waist or wrist close to the body. I like drawstrings for very feminine garments, in which gathers do not seem out of place.

The cord for a drawstring can be woven in and out of eyelet or buttonhole openings worked into either a flat pattern or ribbing. Plan an even number of openings so that both ends of the cord fall on the outside of the garment. I prefer small eyelets, but buttonholes work better for wide cords or belts (for information on buttonholes, see the basic knitting books in the Bibliography on pp. 258-260). For a bloused effect with a corded waist, add an extra inch or two to the length of the body or sleeve, which will enable the fabric to drape softly over the cord.

Pleats and tucks

Pleats and tucks also serve to draw in excess fabric and are more tailored than gathers. Pleats can be made with repeating geometric knit/purl patterns (see pp. 84-85) or with strategically placed slip stitches in a plain fabric like stockinette. Slip-stitch pleats are crisper than knit/purl pleats, but because they add some extra weight to a garment, I reserve them for shaping and dressmaker details, and use knit/purl pleats for allover fabrics.

Slip-stitch pleats involve slipping a given stitch on every right-side row and purling this stitch on wrong-side rows, which produces a permanent crease and natural fold in the fabric. For tailored garments on which I want to create a facing at the edges, I use a single slip stitch to create a crisp folded edge between the facing and the main fabric. This type of slip-stitch fold can also be used to make a facing from which to hang a knitted or fabric pocket.

To a make a pocket with a slip-stitch fold, knit an extension at the same place on the side edges of both front and back, working a slip stitch where the extension meets the body. When the front and back pieces are seamed together, the pocket will fold neatly along the slip-stitch line to the inside.

A single fold requires only a single column of slipped stitches. A pleat requires at least two folds: an outer fold produced by the slip stitch on the right side of the fabric, and an inner fold in the opposite direction, produced by a second slip stitch on the wrong side of the fabric. (To slip a stitch on the purl side of stockinette, hold the yarn to the back as you slip the stitch and then, of course, be sure to purl this slipped stitch on the right-side rows.) Creating a series of these opposing slip-stitch folds results in permanent pleats. I like to experiment with folded paper before incorporating pleats into a design in order to understand the nature of the pleat I'm planning and to decide both the dimensions of the pleats and how I want them to fold. Then I can plan where the slip stitches for these pleats must fall.

The swatches in the photo below right show three kinds of slip-stitch pleats: two-layer knife pleats that all fold in the same direction; three-layer box pleats, formed by a pair of folds in opposite directions; and shaped, three-layer box pleats with decreases worked that gradually make the pleats narrower and eliminate some of the bulk of a regular box pleat.

A pleated fabric is knitted in a wide section, with slip stitches worked where the folds will occur. When you reach the desired pleat length, you can join the layers at the top to hold them in place. To join the pleats at the top, slip the stitches for each layer—whether two or three layers—to a separate double-pointed needle for each layer, and allow the pleat to fold into place. Then, with another needle, knit each stitch from the two or three stacked layers together as one.

My favorite dressmaker use for these pleats is to create a peplum effect. They can also be used to add ease to a garment, for example, like a box pleat on the back of a shirt or a kick pleat on a straight skirt. These pleats work well in fabrics that are not too bulky. The crease will form with any yarn, but with heavier yarns the pleats may sag or bulge. Remember that with box pleats—or any pleats for that matter—you'll use about twice as much yarn as you would for the same width of unpleated fabric.

A tuck is a simple fold of fabric that, like a pleat, serves to draw in excess material. A tuck, however, lacks the crisp fold of a pleat and is, in effect, a single "gather" held in place at its top edge. In dressmaking, tucks are often topstitched either along their top width to hold the layers together or partially along their length to flatten them for this distance. I avoid vertically topstitching to tack tucks along their length because it's too bulky for most knitted fabrics. Instead, I tack a tuck along its top edge only and let it fan out softly into the main fabric.

I use tucks to gather excess material when I plan to add a close-fitting cuff or belt to the lower edge of the sleeve or body. I usually tack the fold in place, then pick up stitches along the edge through the folded layers to join them and work a cuff or edging (alternatively I could sew through the layers to join them). I also use tucks at the shoulder line and at the center back to allow fabric to fall gracefully and softly drape at these points.

USING PLEATS AND TUCKS

Soft tucks at shoulder and cuff

Pleated peplum

Box-pleated coat

A useful, crisp fold can be made in knitted fabric by carefully positioning a column of slip stitches. Clockwise, from upper left: an extension worked along a slip-stitch fold line at the edge of the fabric would neatly accommodate an added inner pocket; crisp knife pleats, made with two folds, all face the same direction; a pair of box-pleated swatches, the one at right shaped with decreases on the inner sections to eliminate bulk.

Darts

A dart is one of a dressmaker's principal shaping tools. It's formed by removing an area of material from a garment section to eliminate fullness and shape the section to conform to the body. In dressmaking, there are two basic types of darts: triangular and diamond shaped. Triangular darts are usually positioned horizontally at the edge of the fabric and used mainly at the elbow, bustline and shoulder; diamond-shaped darts are positioned vertically within the body of the garment and used generally to draw the fabric in at the waist.

GUIDELINES FOR DARTS AND THEIR PLACEMENT

Horizontal darts should be even with bust points and stop ½ in. to 1 in. short of them.

Vertical darts for waist shaping should fall below bust points and extend 4 in. to 6 in. above and below waist to desired length, usually 3 in. to 5 in.

Bust points

Waist

1 square = 1 in.

These machine-knitted mesh cocktail sweaters, labeled Kargere, were made in France in the late 1940s. Their close-fitting silhouette is shaped at the sides and nipped in at the waist with darts that are sewn rather than knitted in. (Metropolitan Museum of Art; gifts of Mrs. Miles Harrison, 1978.)

The most common horizontal darts fall at the bustline, extending from the side seam to ½ in. to 1 in. short of the bust point. These darts effectively remove a small triangle of fabric at the side of the bust and usually need be no more than 1 in. to 2 in. deep at the side seam, narrowing to nothing near the bust point.

Because most knitted fabric stretches to conform to the body, I generally find bust darts unnecessary in knitwear. They're useful, however, in a close-fitting garment for a very full-busted woman. I would also use them if I wanted an exact copy of a sewing pattern with bust darts.

Vertical darts draw the fabric in, side to side. They're used primarily in the waistline area, below the bust point, whenever a great deal of shaping is needed. Were this shaping worked entirely at the sides of the garment, rather than distributed evenly around the waist with vertical darts, it would produce very steep, unnatural lines along the sides of the garment. Vertical darts also serve to eliminate fullness in the last 4 in. to 6 in. of skirts that are worked from the lower edge.

In contrast to dressmaking and tailoring, where darts are cut or folded into the fabric and then sewn in place, in knitting most darts are worked by short-rowing or by increasing and decreasing stitches to eliminate fabric. These knitted darts therefore have no seams and produce shaped, yet relatively uninterrupted fabric. In the case of an extremely lightweight knitted fabric, however, you could fold the fabric and sew genuine dressmaker darts to shape the garment, cutting away the excess material after the darts were completed (see the cocktail sweaters in the photo at left).

A regular, knitted horizontal dart at the edge of a garment section is worked as follows: first, short-rowing in steps gradually eliminates the dart's width, then gradually starting to work the stitches left behind increases back to the original number of stitches (see the sidebar on short-rowing on the facing page). A vertical, wedge-shaped dart is worked as follows: first, gradually decreasing makes the fabric narrower at the dart's mid-point, then gradually increasing back to the original number of stitches completes the dart.

There are several methods of increasing and decreasing stitches, which alternatively slant to the left or right or remain unslanted. Some of these methods produce invisible increases and decreases; others produce decorative increases

Short rowing and its uses

Short rowing is a simple knitting technique that involves working only a portion of the stitches on a row, then turning and working back over these stitches one or more times, leaving some of the stitches on the original row unworked throughout. The effect of this maneuver is to elongate the fabric in the section of additional stitches, while shortening the fabric in the section of unworked stitches. Short rowing can be worked at the edge of the fabric or anywhere within it, and can be put to various uses. Short rows can serve to create horizontal darts and shape a garment, form ruffles, even out lengths when combining patterns of different row gauges and raise up the strands of a cable. After you learn this technique, you'll think up other uses for it too. But no matter how you plan to use short rowing, always test it in swatch form first before integrating the technique into your design.

Short rowing is best worked in simple fabrics so as not to interrupt patterning. To avoid a noticeable break or small hole between the short row and its neighboring unworked stitches, you must "wrap" the turning stitch on the first row, then work this wrapped strand together with the stitch that it surrounds when you work across the full row again.

The best way to learn about short rowing is to experiment with a stockinette swatch. Work straight for 1 in. or so, ending with a purl row. On the next row, knit only a portion of the stitches. Before you turn to work back in the opposite direction, bring the yarn to the front, slip the next stitch to the right-hand needle, move the yarn to the back again and slip the last stitch back to left-hand needle, completing the wrap around the slipped stitch. Then turn the swatch and purl back to the end. Knit the next row, and when you reach the wrapped stitch, knit it together with the strand that wraps it. If you short row on a purl row, repeat the same actions, purling the stitch rather than knitting it, together with its wrap.

For the smoothest shaping when working multiple short rows, stagger the wrapped stitches so they do not fall in the same place every row. You can gradually shorten your rows to form a dart-like triangular section, then work back over the entire row at one time. Alternatively, you can work back over the short rows in several steps, gradually lengthening the rows until you're working with the full number of stitches again.

and decreases. If you are unfamiliar with these various increase and decrease methods, consult the basic knitting books in the Bibliography on pp. 258-260. When you want to incorporate these shaping methods into your design, swatch to determine which one will look best for your needs. And when working a vertical dart, be sure that you keep the increases and decreases aligned in the fabric.

Whether you're working horizontal or vertical darts, you'll need to mark the dart's shape and position on your schematic. To find out how many stitches make up the dart at its widest point, measure its width at this point and multiply this width times the stitch gauge. To find out how many rows deep or long the dart is, measure the dart's depth or length and multiply this by the row gauge.

Shaping lower edges

In addition to interior shaping, a garment may also require complexly shaped edges. Curved edges like those on a rounded neckline or a shaped sleeve cap—that is, those worked at the cast-off edge—are relatively easy to plan. However, curves worked at the lower, cast-on edge (for example, on a trapeze coat) or those that feature a point (like on the lower edge of a tailored vest or patch pocket) are more difficult to plan and execute.

There are two ways to shape the lower edge of a garment to form a curve or point: by short rowing or by casting on gradually at the lower edge until the full number of stitches has been established. Short rowing is the better choice when knitting in an edging at the beginning of a garment section. A generous ribbed edge works well because it is flexible enough to spread and accommodate the curve. A flat trim, however, may tend to flip forward, especially if the curve is more than 3 in. to 4 in.

PLOTTING A SHAPED LOWER EDGE

1 square = 1 st

Approx 6 in.   Approx 3 in.

3 in.

6 in.

3 in.

1 square = 1 in.

deep. Casting on gradually is best worked when it can be hidden by a picked-up trim since this method, though it is easier than short rowing, creates a slightly jagged edge.

A pointed edge can be symmetrical or asymmetrical, that is, each side of the point can be angled the same or differently. With a pointed lower edge that is to have an additional edging, it's easiest to work the main section first, then later pick up the edging, which will have to be mitered to accommodate the point.

Whether the edge is curved or pointed, you'll need to plot it in schematic form to establish the look you want and to calculate the stitches and rows needed to produce it. For a curved edge, try to get as smooth a line as possible, using a curved ruler if you like. I allot one-quarter to one-third of the stitches at the center of the curve and then work the remainder of the stitches evenly on either side. For a symmetrically pointed edge, I mark the point at the center of the piece. For an asymmetrical point, I play around on graph paper until I find a depth and point placement I like.

*d*ressmaker methods of deriving a pattern

Dressmakers derive patterns in three basic ways: They draft flat patterns on paper; they drape and pin fabric on a 3-D dress form, or mannequin, then cut the draped fabric to produce a pattern; or they modify a commercial pattern that's close to the design they're after.

Drawing, or drafting, flat patterns on paper is based upon altering and expanding upon what's known as a "sloper." The sloper is itself a flat pattern, a two-dimensional recreation of the body and its curves, based on body measurements. As a flat pattern, the sloper bears little resemblance to the body. But assembled, seamed and darted, it fits the body like a glove.

To derive patterns from a sloper, the patternmaker works with the individual pattern parts making up the sloper, adding ease and any shaping required for different garment designs. Each new pattern piece is thus a variation on the original sloper part.

Creating a sloper is a fairly complex process, which will be of little practical use to most knitters since knitwear designs rarely require the intricate shaping incorporated into a sloper. Nonetheless, I think it's useful to be aware of this method of patternmaking. I also find that pattern-drafting books occasionally help me envision the shapes of pieces making up a garment silhouette I'm unfamiliar with.

Draping is a very free-form, creative method of patternmaking used by the great couturiers and fashion designers like Vionnet and Balenciaga. Draping involves making a fabric pattern on a dressmaker's mannequin, using large pieces of muslin that are pinned to the dress form, then manipulated and "sculpted" into the desired shape. The fabric is then marked, adjusted as needed and cut into pattern pieces for the design.

Working with commercial sewing patterns to derive a pattern is the easiest patternmaking method of all—someone else has done the tough work of creating the basic pattern. Even if you have little or no sewing experience, don't be intimidated at the prospect of working with a commercial sewing pattern. You'll find it easy once you get started.

Many commercial patterns can be adapted for knitwear, though some are easier to work with than others. The best patterns are those with a minimum of shaping. Avoid those with many darts since they may be too complex to knit easily and are better reserved for sewn fabric. I especially like to use sewing patterns to understand any shape or construction detail, like an unfamiliar collar. Not only does the pattern help me understand the shape of a garment detail, it also guides me in the crucial planning of the surrounding areas into which the detail will fit, for example, the neckline area in the case of a collar.

I begin by analyzing a pattern to see if I can simplify it without losing details or shaping I want. For example, can I straighten out any slightly curved edges? If there are vertical darts, can I eliminate them by working shaping only at the sides, or are the darts so deep that eliminating them will produce awkward lines at the sides? After I've simplified the pattern as much as possible, I plot my schematic—that is, the outline of the garment pieces on graph paper.

To work with a commercial pattern, always begin measuring the pattern piece along the straight of the grain or along a fold line, both of which are usually indicated by arrows printed on the pattern. Set up this same measurement on graph paper along a vertical line. Then measure all of the pattern's lengths, for example, its side or sleeve length, and transfer these measurements to your schematic. Next measure all the pattern's widths. If a pattern piece is gently shaped, for example, with a curve of ½ in. or less along a side-seam edge, I often straighten the line out to make it easier to plot and knit, provided I'm sure that this adjustment will not affect the design or fit. However, with more crucial curves, like the armhole edge of a close-fitting garment, I try to recreate the exact curve on the schematic to get the same fit.

If you have any doubts at all about the pattern's fit, I suggest making a mock-up to ensure a good fit before you start knitting. In fact, whenever I'm trying out a new shape, I usually make a mock-up, and I also find it especially helpful to do so when planning a garment for a larger-than-average woman or anyone who has fitting problems (see the sidebar on p. 218). If you're working with a commercial pattern, you can use it to make your mock-up; if you're working with simple silhouette for your design, you can drape a mock-up on a mannequin without a pattern.

The process of draping a pattern for knitwear is essentially the same as for working with woven fabric. Instead of muslin, however, I prefer to use a machine-knit fabric that's similar in weight to the final hand-knitted fabric I've chosen for my design, which allows me to simulate the stretch and drape of the final garment, and also to estimate the correct ease. I also like to use a light-colored commercial knit for my "muslin" so that any marker notations I make on the pattern are easy to see.

Be sure the person you're draping—whether yourself or someone else—wears a leotard, a T-shirt and shorts or something that's not bulky and can easily be pinned. If you're trying to fit yourself, ask a friend to help. If you're un-

STEPS FOR ACTUAL DRAPING ON THE BODY

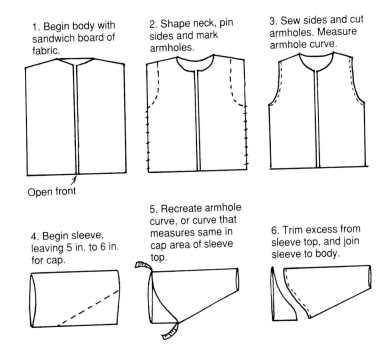

1. Begin body with sandwich board of fabric.
Open front

2. Shape neck, pin sides and mark armholes.

3. Sew sides and cut armholes. Measure armhole curve.

4. Begin sleeve, leaving 5 in. to 6 in. for cap.

5. Recreate armhole curve, or curve that measures same in cap area of sleeve top.

6. Trim excess from sleeve top, and join sleeve to body.

able to find a helper, work in front of a full-length mirror to see your progress—and be patient. You'll need the following materials:
• 2 to 3 yds. of machine-knit fabric about 54 in. to 60 in. wide, preferably in a light color;
• T-pins or long dressmaker pins (smaller pins tend to fall out easily);
• Tailor's chalk or a marker pen in contrasting color;
• Scissors;
• A sewing machine (optional), or needle and thread.

Draping a mock-up garment Draping a basic mock-up garment with a cap sleeve can give you a basic pattern that can be further varied for other designs. The drawing above outlines the actual draping steps.

Begin by ironing the fabric and making sure the fold or folds—some machine knits are tubular—are aligned along the straight grain, or length, of the knit. For the body pieces, cut the fabric into large rectangles, with the lengths positioned along the grain, so that they're wider and longer than you think the garment requires. It's important that fabric be cut along the straight grain so that it will hang properly when aligned with the imaginary centerline of the body—and produce a pattern that likewise hangs properly on the body.

Draping a mock-up on a full-figured woman

When designing for a large figure, I've found that making a mock-up garment enables me to check the fit before the garment is knitted. This may seem time-consuming, but the results are worth it since you can be absolutely sure of a good fit. Since the cap sleeve produces a good fit for a larger woman, I've used it to demonstrate the mock-up process. To make other styles, you can use the same steps, but the fitting process may be lengthier and more challenging. I used a dropped-shoulder garment that fit the model well as a starting point for draping my mock-up, then adapted it for a cap sleeve. You can also base your mock-up on a commercial sewing pattern, or, if you're working with a simple shape, you can drape without any pattern at all.

The cap-sleeve mock-up begins with unshaped pieces of fabric. These pieces are then fitted to the body, with the armhole and sleeve cap shaped in the process.

Begin by making a rough schematic of the garment's front and back, based on the bust measurement plus ease. Establish a simple neckline opening, which can be changed in the fitting process, and the shoulder shaping. Plot a rectangle for the sleeve, with the width based on the upper-arm measurement plus ease, with about 6 in. of extra length added for a cap.

Next, find a manufactured knitted fabric that simulates the weight of your hand-knitted fabric. Outline

the shapes of your pieces on the fabric in tailor's chalk, aligning the center of the pieces lengthwise with the grain of the fabric and adding a seam allowance everywhere, except at the neckline edge. Add extra length in both sleeve and body, about 2 in. to 4 in. beyond what you think you'll need. Cut out the body pieces and baste them together, allowing a 8-in. to 10-in. armhole. Do not attach the sleeve.

Try the body section on the wearer and take a good look at it. Measure the wearer from shoulder to shoulder and try to envision the best placement for the armhole seams. Pin or chalk a curve around the armhole, beginning at the side seam and reaching the cross-shoulder approximately halfway up the armhole. Is the armhole deep enough to clear the underarm sufficiently? Is the curve gradual enough and not too steeply shaped? The whole shaped area under the

arm should measure about 3 in. to 4 in. wide. When you're satisfied, add seam allowance, then cut out the armhole. The front and back should be the same.

Now you must figure out the measurements of the sleeve cap. Lay the mock-up body flat. Measure around the front armhole at the seamline. Lay the sleeve tube flat, folded along the seamline. Place a tape measure on its side to create a curve for the cap, making the curve measure the same as the armhole, plus 1 in. to 2 in. of ease. The resulting cap height should be from 3 in. to 5 in., and have a broad top (8 in. to 12 in.). Mark the line, add seam allowance and cut. Baste it into the armhole and adjust the fit again if necessary. At this point, you can also shape the sleeve sides and adjust the neckline. Transfer all these measurements to a schematic. You can then plot the patterns and figure your stitch counts.

I made this mock-up before designing a cap-sleeve, V-neck cardigan for my full-figured friend. The mock-up's original measurements were borrowed from a nonknitted dropped-shoulder garment that fit her well. The wrist is pinned to see how the sleeve will drape above ribbing. (Photo reprinted from *Threads* magazine, issue #18.)

For a pullover, cut two identical rectangles. For an open-front garment, each of the two front sections should measure at least a few inches more than half the back. This extra fabric ensures that you'll have enough room to carve out whatever shaping you want. For the sleeves, reserve two large rectangles, both longer than necessary and larger than you expect the sleeve to be at its widest point.

To save time, baste front to back at the shoulders before beginning to drape, sloping slightly to a depth of 1 in. Begin the actual draping with a sandwich board of fabric (see Step 1 in the drawing on p. 217). First shape the neckline at front and back by marking the curve with pins (Step 2), then cutting along the line. A seam allowance is necessary only if you plan to add a collar. To envision the shape of the armholes, mark the desired cross-front width a few inches below the shoulders, with pins at each end of the desired armhole edge. Then pin a curve around the armhole itself at both front and back, 2 in. to 3 in. deep, to meet the cross-shoulder measurement. Now remove the mock-up and cut out the extra material, leaving a seam allowance, and sew the sides (Step 3).

At this point the sleeve is an unshaped tube. Shape the sleeve from the top down (Step 4), first planning a cap or sleeve top to fit your armhole, then fitting the sleeve along its length. To plan the curve of the cap, measure around the armhole. Then place a tape measure, on edge, at the top of the sleeve to simulate a cap curve, to measure slightly larger (1 in. to 2 in.) than the armhole itself, so there will be some ease (Step 5). Add a seam allowance, and trim the sleeve (Step 6). Now pin the sleeve top or cap to the armhole. If the cross-front of the mock-up is too wide, pin the cap in further toward the body, trimming the armhole after the new position is settled.

After all the adjustments have been made on the mock-up, baste the pieces together. Now the mock-up can be shaped at the sides or with waist darts. You could also add a collar or form lapels at the front edges. With a marker, draw any details like pockets, colorwork or graphics onto the surface of the mock-up to check their placement (see the photo above right). Take the mock-up's pieces apart, measure them (omitting seam allowances), then transfer all the measurements and markings to a schematic.

To test the fit of a garment, I often sew a mock-up of lightweight knit fabric and fit it to my dressmaker mannequin. can test details on the mock-up, like my close-fitting split collar, and draw on patterns (or pockets) I've swatched to test their placement. I later transfer all mock-up measurements and placement of details to a schematic drawing.

Constructed edges and details

A garment can have one or several constructed edges or details that are either worked separately and added on (like a shaped collar) or which are knitted in as the garment is made and thus require special planning (like lapels). In addition to collars and lapels, cuffs, pockets, pleats and belts can all be constructed (see the drawing on p. 220). When using one of these edgings or details, you'll need to consider its special shape as well as how to attach or join it to the body of the garment.

In the case of collars and lapels, you'll also need to plan the two fronts of the garment and the neckline before you can plan or add these constructed edges. The two fronts can meet or close in different ways. They can fall straight from the neckline with no closure. Their edges can abut and close with a zipper or clasp. Or the edges can overlap and close with buttons or various other closures, like snaps or hooks and

CONSTRUCTED EDGES (SHOWN SHADED)

eyes. (For a woman's garment, the right buttonhole band traditionally crosses over the left band where the buttons are placed, and the reverse is true for a man's garment.) If the two fronts are to overlap, they can be symmetrical or of different widths. In the case of asymmetrical fronts, a closure is needed to keep the wider front from falling to the side.

Usually the combined widths of the two fronts equal the total width of the back. If the fronts are to overlap, their combined width will, of course, exceed the width of the back. And when each front, whether overlapping or not, has an additional edging or buttonhole band, you will again have a combined front width that differs from the back width. To calculate the width of front sections with an edging or button band, there are two possible approaches (remember that only one front edging or band contributes to the width of the body when the cardigan is buttoned): First, you can simply divide the back in half (or into unequal sections if you want asymmetrical fronts). This method works best if the front bands will not be wider than 1½ in. and will not drastically affect the fit of the garment. A small amount of extra width can actually be an advantage for the fuller-busted woman.

The second approach to figuring the width of the fronts works only if you want the back and buttoned fronts to have exactly the same measurement. To arrive at this figure, subtract the width of one band from the back width. The remaining figure can then be divided in half (or in unequal sections) to obtain the width of each front.

Collars

There's no better way to crown a garment than with an interesting collar. Over the years I've experimented with a steadily evolving line of collars, many of them dressmaker-inspired. Bored with the plain ribbed neckline, I started with the simplest of collars, the polo, then explored all its possible variations. I moved on to the shawl collar, then to the more challenging notched collar with lapels.

Before adding any collar, you must establish a good fit in the neckline of the garment, just as you would if you were adding a simple ribbed edging (see pp. 55-59). If you're working with a wider-than-average neckline, you may want to narrow it ½ in. to 1 in. before working a collar since a collar will add more weight than a narrow ribbed edging and hence can cause an overly wide neckline to sag.

A collar can stand up, fold over, drape from or wrap around the neckline. It can be worked as a continuation of the neckline by picking up stitches and knitting from there, or it can be worked separately and sewn on. Picked-up collars are usually fairly simple in design and produce the most flexible join with the body. Separately worked collars can be more varied and sophisticated in shape, but the sewn join naturally constricts the neckline a bit. This can be an advantage and offer stability, however, if the collar is fairly heavy or if the neckline is wider than normal.

When planning any collar, I like to consider what the join to the body will look like. Usually when picking up or sewing on a separately worked collar, a ridge forms to the inside where the two pieces meet. I don't like this ridge to show. To make a collar or lapel that opens enough to show the wrong side of the body fabric, match the right side of the collar with the wrong side of the body, then sew them together with these sides facing, which places the ridge of the join on the underside of the collar. When both sides of the join will show, as with a sewn-on collar that can both fold over and stand up, butt the edges of the collar and neckline together, with right sides facing, and weave the attaching strand in and out so that no ridge results.

For additional detail, a sewn-on collar can emerge from under another narrower edging picked up at the neckline. This treatment is useful when you don't want a collar to fill the entire neckline edge, but you also don't want the front neck to be entirely bare. If you add this extra trim, the neckline will need to be about ½ in. to 1 in. wider to accommodate the double-layer thickness of edging and collar. For a discreet picked-up edging, I often use a small roll of reverse stockinette around the neckline. I sew the collar to the inside ridge formed by the picked-up stitches.

Split collars There is a wide range of collars that split at some point along the front neckline edge. The edges can butt together or be separated by an inch or two, or they can overlap. These collars can stand up along the neck and roll over softly or lie flat across the shoulders. Their points can be small and discreet, long and sharp, or softly rounded. If you were inspired by sporty menswear, you could also make the collar points button down.

The simplest split collar, often called a polo collar, is easy to knit. It can be picked up, just like a simple neckline ribbing, and split at the center, or it can be worked separately and sewn on. If it's worked separately, the polo should measure the same as the neckline edge to which it will be attached. A short polo of 1 in. to 2 in. may have enough body to stand up straight. A longer version from 3 in. to 6 in. will stand up only slightly before rolling over.

A polo collar can be worked in any kind of stitch pattern—ribbed, flat, heavily textured or lacy. The ribbed polo is most successful when worked with a smaller needle over a generous number of stitches, at least 20% more stitches than for a regular ribbed edge. Fewer stitches will cause the points to strain apart. For flat patterns, measure the neckline edge and make the collar edge measure the same, or 1 in. to 2 in. larger. Ease in any excess width evenly around the edge of the neckline.

For all but the smallest of polos, I suggest shaping the collar's corners to form more pronounced points and allow the collar to sit better around the front neckline edge. I usually increase one stitch at each collar edge every two or four rows until I reach the collar depth

SPLIT COLLARS

1 square = 1 in.

Upper body

Neck edge, 16 in.

Rectangular polo collar

Neck edge, 16 in.

Polo collar with elongated points

Collar with stand (which is hidden but makes collar higher at back neck)

Stand shown shaded

Semicircular collar

4 in.   4 in.   4 in.   4 in.

25 in.

that I want. The more often you increase, the sharper the corners will be and the more they will point downward.

To round the corners of a collar, you'll need to shape both the sides and lower edge of the collar. Work increases at each end as described above, that is, one stitch at each edge every two or four rows. When approximately one half to two-thirds of the collar is completed, begin binding off from each corner of the collar, starting with a single stitch and gradually binding off successively larger increments of stitches until you've reached the collar depth you want.

For a more refined fit with a polo collar, you can add a collar stand, the dressmaker term for an additional wedge of fabric at the back neck. This stand raises the collar slightly at the back neck, allowing the points to lie smoothly at the front without straining or pulling to the sides. To make a collar stand, you need to form a curve along the base of the collar that meets the neckline edge. I like the stand to be at least ¾ in. to 2 in. in height. In heavy yarns or for exaggerated collars, I may even make it 2 in. to 4 in. high.

To plot a collar with a stand in schematic form, first draw a rectangle to represent the basic collar. Then add a curve at the lower inside edge to create the stand. This edge, not the outer edge that lies across the shoulders, should measure the same as the neckline.

The stand at the back neck can then be created either by gradually casting on for the collar or by short rowing after picking up the stitches along the entire neck edge. I mark the center section of the collar-stand curve, which is equal to the back neck of my garment. I then plan to cast on or pick up the center third of the stitches for the stand. Next, I multiply the depth of my collar curve by my row gauge to give me the total number of rows needed to create the curve. Then I plan to cast on or pick up the remaining stitches of the collar, on either side of the center stitches, equally over these rows. The remainder of the collar is worked over the total number of stitches. (Alternatively, you could begin working the collar from its outer edge and end it by binding off gradually to create the collar-stand curve.)

Circle collars   Round or semicircular collars lie flat across the shoulders and radiate outward so that the outside edge is much larger than the neckline edge. This type of collar can be split or completely encircle the neckline. It can be worked to any width, whether a small Peter-Pan collar 2 in. to 3 in. wide, or a capelet collar extending over the shoulders.

Imagine a circle collar as a simple expansion of the basic rectangular polo, split into sections, between which a triangular wedge is inserted. I find it useful to plot this collar in schematic form to help me envision where the increases, or wedges, need to fall. Its inner measurement should be the same as the neck edge. To help figure out the measurement for the outer edge of the collar, lay a tape measure around or over your shoulders at the desired point.

The easiest way to work the circle collar is to knit from the neckline to the outer edge. Plot increases at regular intervals to form the wedge-shaped sections that widen and curve the collar. This collar can be picked up or worked separately.

If your collar is knitted in plain stockinette, the increases can be decorative or invisible. With more complex patterns, it may be difficult or unsightly to work the increases into a pattern. Instead, work them in a plain pattern and use the wedges as a decorative feature, worked in another pattern.

When working the collar from side to side, you need to short-row to create the wedges that produce the collar's curve. It's best to plan the dimensions of the collar in schematic form to decide where the shaping should occur. Plan to work at least four short-row sections in the collar. The fewer the sections, the larger the wedges will need to be to curve the collar.

Draped necklines   The dressmaker term *cowl* refers to a drape of extra fabric in the neckline or upper chest area of a garment. A cowl effect can be created in several ways: by working an oversized turtleneck (which is easily done in any weight yarn), by knitting a cowl extension of the front itself or by inserting a shaped piece of fabric into the garment front. With the last two methods, a lightweight fabric creates the best drape. And, of course, inserted sections can be worked in a pattern or color that contrasts with the garment body.

To enlarge a turtleneck to cowl dimension, you can pick up the same number of stitches as you would for a regular turtleneck, then increase gradually until the opening is at least twice as large as the original neckline. Or you can immediately increase to the larger number of stitches and work straight. Increasing gradually creates a more graceful cowl, while working straight over a large number of stitches creates a bulkier effect, with fabric falling forward on the upper chest area.

For this type of neckline, you might try using a larger needle than you would for working a closer neckline. Loose ribbing or a soft, flat fabric produced by the large needle will emphasize the drape. Since both sides of the cowl may show, choose a pattern that's reversible.

DRAPED NECKLINES

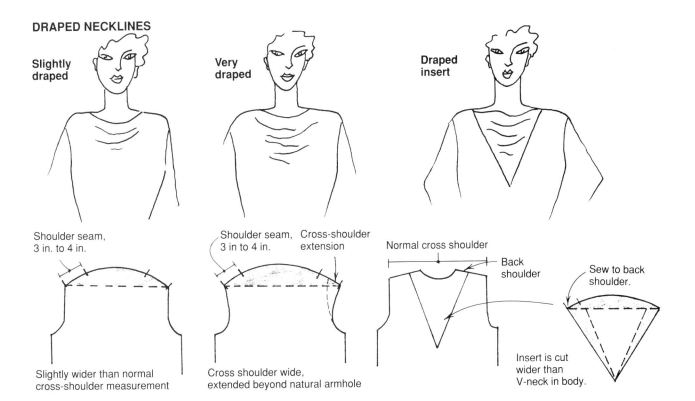

Slightly draped

Shoulder seam, 3 in. to 4 in.

Slightly wider than normal cross-shoulder measurement

Very draped

Shoulder seam, 3 in to 4 in.   Cross-shoulder extension

Cross shoulder wide, extended beyond natural armhole

Draped insert

Normal cross shoulder

Back shoulder

Sew to back shoulder.

Insert is cut wider than V-neck in body.

For a dressmaker-inspired draped neckline, you can expand upon the basic bateau neckline (see p. 57). This is best worked in a smooth fabric like stockinette. To create extra fabric at the neckline edge, work to the shoulder line, then bind off gradually from each edge to form a curve at the upper edge of the front of the garment, extending above the neckline and shoulder area. The higher the curve, the more fabric there will be to drape. The edges of the front curve are sewn to the back shoulders, allowing a wide neck opening of 8 in. to 9 in. The extra fabric will drape in soft folds, with the top of the curve falling to the inside so that the reverse of the fabric is not seen.

For an exaggerated drape, you can also gradually widen the cross-shoulder section of the garment after you've reached the armhole. When you reach the shoulder line, create a curve by binding off gradually at the top. This creates more fabric at the front and produces a more dramatically draped area.

A similar draped effect can also be made by inserting a wedge of fabric into a deep V-shaped neckline. The insert should be larger than the opening so that the excess fabric will drape, and the top edge of the insert should be gently curved. Plan a wide V-neck of at least 8 in. to 9 in. The insert should be the same depth as the V-neck, but wider.

Shawl collars A shawl collar is one continuous piece of fabric that rolls around the neck and extends downward into what are effectively unnotched lapels (see the drawing on p. 224). This collar can be worked on a pullover or a cardigan garment, whose fronts may or may not overlap.

You'll need to consider several measurements when planning a shawl collar. First, of course, the inner edge of the collar must fit properly around the edge of the neckline. Second and more important, the collar must be deep enough to roll over and produce the look you want.

A shawl collar starts at the base of the neck, stands up slightly, then rolls over. Depending on the fabric weight, a slightly rolled collar needs to be at least 3 in. to 5 in. deep. A deep, luxurious, rolled collar should be anywhere from 6 in. to 12 in. deep. Fine-gauge yarns are better suited to narrow shawl collars. If used on wider collars, these fine yarns will droop or collapse of their own weight unless you're careful to choose a springy or firm pattern stitch. Medium- to heavyweight yarns and fuzzy yarns in general tend to work nicely for deep shawl collars since they have enough body to hold the rolled edge in place.

SHAWL COLLARS

Square-neck pullover

← 6 in. →

8 in.

← 6 in. →

(Suggested measurements can vary with design.)

Rectangular collar

Deeper, rolled collar with curved edges

Curved edge is longer than straight.

← 8 in. →← 6 in. →← 8 in. →

Rectangle for collar

↕ 6 in.

Curved for deeper roll

← 7 in. →

Cardigan

9 in. 1 in. 9 in.

1 square = 1 in.

Straight-edged shawl

Shawl with two curved edges

9 in. on curve   9 in. on curve

← 7 in. →   ← 7 in. →

1 in. ← 9 in. →← 7 in. →← 9 in. → 1 in.

Straight-edged shawl (good for picking up)

Better fit, higher stand at back neck

A shawl collar is most effective in a ribbed fabric. The pattern's elasticity helps the collar conform to the neckline and lie flat along the garment's front. Many ribbed patterns (but not all) are reversible, which is nice since both sides of the fabric can show on shawl collars. You can also use other flat, reversible patterns for this collar if you're working with a narrow neck width, since the narrowness will hold the collar close to the neck and support its shape.

Very effective in a single thickness of fabric, a shawl collar is luxurious if knitted double thickness. However, if the edges of a double-thick collar overlap, you'll have four layers of fabric, which adds up to a lot of bulk. Working the collar double-thickness is thus best suited to lightweight yarns, and you may also need to add an extra inch to the neck width to accommodate the extra thickness.

Lapels

The lapel is probably the best-recognized detail in menswear and lends an air of crisp distinction to a garment. A knitted lapel will be softer and less structured than its sewn counterpart, but it can still capture the flavor of a tailored garment. The lapel is traditionally associated with open-front garments, but it can also be adapted for pullovers.

Lapels are generally formed by folding back at an angle the top edges of the two garment fronts to create triangular flaps that lie flat along the chest. A lapel can vary in width and length, and can be designed with or without a collar. When coupled with a collar, the lapel can be designed to abut and join the collar in continuous, shawl-collar-like fashion; it can abut but not join the collar, forming a slit; or it can be shaped to have a point and create a notch where it meets the collar. This notch can be a mere sliver of an angle or as wide as a right angle.

A lapel can be made in three ways, the easiest of which involves simply folding back the front section at an angle. This method works well works only if the body fabric is reversible or if the wrong side has an acceptable appearance. A lapel can also be made separately and then attached to a front section with V-neck shaping. Use this method if you don't like the wrong side of the body fabric, or if you want a lapel in a contrasting pattern. Finally, you can knit both body and lapel sections in different patterns at the same time, which eliminates the need to seam them together.

Neck width affects the look of a lapel. For a classic menswear look, the back-neck width must be close-fitting to ensure that the fold of the lapel lies close to the base of the neck. If the neckline is wide, the lapels should be widened from 1 in. to 3 in. along the front edges so there's enough fabric to fold back over the chest. To widen the lapels, space the increases evenly from the upper button to the point of the lapel.

I was drawn to this 1939 photo of the Duke and Duchess of Windsor, fashion trendsetters of their day, because of the lapels on their coats. Her coat has bold, wing-like lapels that seem to start at the waist. His classic, double-breasted suit has a perfect notch where lapel meets collar. Note the range of the fabrics —his polka-dotted tie and pinstripe suit, her houndstooth coat and pleated dress, adorned with frog-like closures. (Photo, UPI/Bettmann Newsphotos.)

Usually there is some neck shaping at the two garment fronts. The deeper the front neckline, the lower the top of the lapel, or the notch, will fall.

The fronts of a garment with lapels can overlap for from 1 in. to 8 in. When the overlap is more than 3 in. to 4 in., two rows of buttons are generally used to keep the under layer from shifting. The resulting buttoned garment is then termed *double-breasted*. If you don't want a double row of buttons, you can anchor the overlap with a belt or ties.

The placement of the top button(s) affects the width of the lapel. In a single-breasted garment with a high upper button at chest level, the lapel can be 3 in. to 4 in. wide. However, if the upper button is placed lower, the folded-over lapel will be only a narrow and skimpy 1 in. to 2 in. at the top. To widen a lapel, gradually enlarge the front edges above the top button by evenly spaced increases that add the desired

width. In a double-breasted garment, the extra fabric that crosses over at the front may create a broad lapel without additional shaping. If all of these issues seem confusing, take a look at my schematic method for planning lapels in the sidebar on p. 226.

To produce the simplest, folded-back lapel, you can eliminate all front-neck shaping and simply bind off at the shoulder. This will cause the point of the lapel to fall in the high-chest area (see the coral jacket in the photo on pp. 68-69). For the point of the lapel to sit lower in the chest area, round the front neckline slightly to a depth of 2 in. to 4 in. As a variation on traditional collarless lapels, think about using just a single lapel, which will lend an interesting asymmetrical look to your design. The other garment front can have an angled edge, shaped like half of a V-neck.

To produce a lapel with a collar, you will always need to shape the front neckline. You can round the neckline, as you would for a crewneck (see pp. 57-58), or you can angle the neckline from the point of the lapel to about 1 in. below the shoulder shaping.

LAPELS

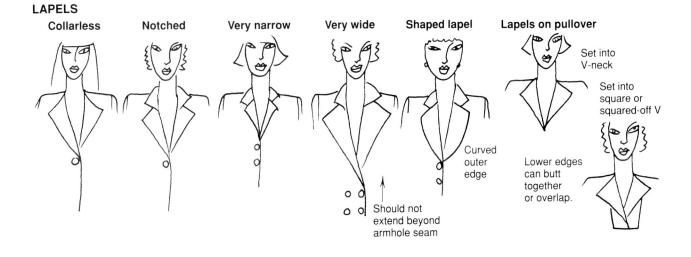

Envisioning collars and lapels in three dimensions

I was very disappointed with my first attempts at lapels. They were either too narrow, or the notch placement seemed too high or too low. And in both cases, I was unsure where to position the top button.

Searching for a way to understand lapels, I tried to draw them on the body portion of my schematic. This helped, but it wasn't until I learned how to work with the schematic in three dimensions, using what I call my paper-doll method, that I really began to see how to shape lapels.

To work with the paper-doll method (see the drawing below), use graph paper with four to five squares to the inch and first draw the back section of the garment to determine the body's length and width. Then establish the back-neck width. Next, based on the back, draw a front section, omitting any neck shaping. With small scissors or a mat knife, cut a vertical line along the front edge of the front section of the schematic. Then cut a horizontal line across the neck width, which will be half the back-neck width.

Fold the resulting triangle of paper at an angle to simulate the shape of the lapel and to decide where to place the top button. Outline in pencil the rough front-neck shaping on the top edge of the folded-over lapel. At this point, you can also consider the shape of the top of the lapel. After you're satisfied with the look of the neck and lapel shaping and the relationship of the two, cut out the shaping in the neck area.

If the cut-out lapel section turns out to be too narrow, tape a paper extension at the front edge. Then draw an angled line outwards above the top button to enlarge the lapel, and trim off any excess paper. Mark the placement of the top button just below the fold line at the lower lapel.

To help design the collar, I often cut a small "tape measure" out of a strip of the same graph paper. Standing it up on its side edge, I measure the front-neck edge to which the collar will attach. The combined measurement of the neck edge of the left and right fronts,

plus the back neck, gives me the measurement needed for the inner collar edge.

Next I draw the collar, which should be shaped to incorporate a collar stand (see pp. 221-222). I use the neckline measurement to help me draw the curve of the collar stand. Although it's more difficult, I also cut out the collar and hold it along the neck edge. This helps me see the shape of the notch and decide whether to shape the collar sides too. Once the paper-doll cut-outs meet with my approval, I draw a cleaned-up schematic version of the front section and collar.

PAPER-DOLL LAPEL METHOD

Back-neck width

Front-neck width

Back

Front

Waist

Folded-back lapel

Extension to enlarge lapel

Neckline depth, 1 in. to 3 in.

Upper buttonhole, ½ in. below beginning of lapel

Collar — Center back
Collar attaches here.

Notes
• Lapel width before enlarging depends on placement of upper button.
• Upper buttonhole should not fall much below waist.
• Lapel should be at least 2 in. wide and no more than 6 in wide.

For the best fit, a collar for the notched lapel should have a collar stand of between 1 in. to 2 in. for the average neck width of 6 in. to 8 in. (see the discussion of collar stands on pp. 221-222). You can also slightly curve the outer edge of the collar to a depth of about ½ in. for a more elegant look.

Lapels take on an added level of interest when worked in a fabric that contrasts with that of the body. As with other lapels, you can knit a contrasting lapel at the same time as the front, working it in another pattern (in which case, knit the right side of the lapel on what is the wrong side of the body fabric so that the right side shows when the lapel is folded back). You can also work a contrasting lapel either by picking up along a V-shaped front or by knitting it as separate piece and sewing it on (in which case, add a selvage stitch to both the lapel and front edges to make seaming easier). Additionally, you can use a facing, or extra layer of fabric, whether knitted or woven, to cover the face of the lapel and produce contrast with the body fabric.

If you've drawn your fronts on a schematic, you can easily figure out the size of the piece that will cover the lapel. It should be the size of the lapel itself, from the fold line to the outer front edge, plus a bit extra at the fold line. The drawing in the sidebar on the facing page shows how to create lapels in schematic form.

If you're covering the lapel with a facing, the inner edge of the facing should extend at least ½ in. beyond the lapel itself, so that this edge disappears on the inside of the garment. Since a facing adds extra bulk, I usually knit it in a lighter weight yarn.

The easiest way to attach a separately worked facing that covers the lapel is first to work a trim, like a flat knit/purl fabric or ribbing, at the edge of the lapel. (If there's a collar, work a trim around it too.) Then you can sew the facing in the groove formed between the edging and the main lapel fabric.

After the edging is complete, pin the facing in place, with wrong sides together, and sew along the trimmed edge first, using mattress stitch (see the drawing below left), or weaving the sewing thread in and out invisibly. Before sewing the facing along the inside edge, allow the lapel to fold over and settle into position. Then pin the facing's inner edge in place and sew it down as loosely as possible.

Pockets

Pockets are always useful, and they're one of my favorite ways to add decorative detail to a garment (see the drawing on p. 228). Pockets come in many styles, but there are two basic types: the patch pocket, which is sewn to the outside of a garment and is quite visible; and the invisible—or less visible—pocket, which falls to the inside of the garment and is announced only by its trim or covering top flap. Patch pockets can be square or shaped, buttoned in place or covered by a flap. Pockets that fall to the inside can slit the fabric and have bound edges or be positioned in a seam. Pocket openings can sit horizontally or vertically, or, for more visual interest, be placed at an angle. For function alone, make an invisible pocket that disappears into a slit at the side seam. But for decorative effect, use your imagination. Whenever I see a large expanse of unbroken fabric on my sketch, I ask myself if there should be a pocket. Usually my answer is yes!

To design the pocket I have in mind for a garment, I first check its placement on the schematic, and I often measure myself to see where a comfortable opening would fall. Unless the pocket is purely decorative, it should be positioned so that it's readily accessible to the hand. The opening of a hip-level pocket should fall in the high hip area, a few inches below the waist, and it should be at least 5 in. wide. A breast pocket should fall 2 in. 3 in. above the bust point and be about 3 in. wide.

I always use my schematic to plot the size of the pocket or opening, and to see how it looks relative to the proportions of the garment. I also draw on the schematic any edging that may occur along the pocket opening. I check to see that the opening or edging will not awkwardly intersect any crucial patterning.

MATTRESS STITCH

To join two edges inconspicuously, align side edges, right sides out, and sew between edge and second stitch. Bring needle under two bars and out on right-hand side, then under two bars and out on left-hand side. Needle always enters hole it previously exited. After every six stitches, tug yarn to bring edges together.

POCKETS

Patch types

Pleated   Asymmetrical   Pouch or rounded   Odd-shaped

Alignment of opening for invisible pocket

Horizontal   Vertical   Angled   Round opening

Within body of garment, slightly below waist for hip pocket or 2 in. above bust point for breast pocket   In side seams or in body of garment   Sporty looking   Must be backed with a knitted, sewn-in lining

Edgings for openings or pocket trim

Durable rib   Interesting button placement   Cable sewn side to side   Picot point

Flaps

Rounded, edged with discreet trim   With point, edged with mitered rib   Ribbed   Flat trim

A patch pocket is worked separately and sewn onto the garment with a mattress stitch, matching row for row, if possible, and seaming with a single or half-stitch to eliminate bulk (see the photo on p. 101). I also use patch pockets for inner breast pockets in tailored garments, but only if I can sew them in so that the stitching does not show on the outside. If the fabric is thickly textured or a colorwork pattern, I "hang" the stitching that attaches the inner pocket on the pattern's texture or floats on the wrong side of the fabric.

My favorite kind of pocket is one that hangs to the inside from an opening in the garment body. This free-hanging inner pocket can be knitted in or sewn from lining material. In either case, to create the pocket opening, you need to bind off a section of stitches on one row and cast these stitches back on on the next row. To create an angled opening, knit to the point where you want the opening to begin, then join a second ball of yarn and work to the end of

the row. Working both sides of the opening with separate balls of yarn, increase on one side of the opening and decrease on the other. Binding off and casting on one stitch on each side of the opening will produce the steepest angle for the opening. To establish the best angle for the pocket opening, test on a swatch.

If I'm adding trim on the front edge of the pocket opening, I start it by picking up stitches on the lower edge. The trim can match or contrast with the body trim. For extra detail, trim can be buttoned in place, with a buttonhole worked on the trim's center row.

Instead of a trim, I sometimes work a pocket flap along the upper pocket opening. I have experimented with many shapes for pocket flats, and my favorite is one that ends in a point. The flap can be plain, buttoned or edged with a neat trim.

Cuffs

It's true that a ribbed cuff is the most functional lower sleeve treatment of all. But I'm always intrigued by more decorative cuffs that are like small collars for the wrist and are often formed of flat or decorative fabrics.

There are many cuff variations. A cuff can have the same silhouette as the sleeve and lie smoothly on top of it. Or it can be narrower than the sleeve and serve to hold the extra fullness in place. It can be a simple, unshaped tube or flare slightly, like a cone. It can have a decorative slit or, at its most sophisticated, be attached to a placket opening in the lower sleeve and close with a button or cuff link like a man's dress shirt.

The simplest cuff extends from the lower edge of the sleeve and is folded up. This cuff is easy to knit in before the sleeve is begun, or you can pick up stitches for this cuff along the wrong side of the completed sleeve that has not yet been seamed. After the cuff is knitted, it can be seamed along with the sleeve. If worked in a flat fabric, this cuff must be just wide enough for the hand to pass through. Because it will not cling, the sleeve length must be perfect or the cuff will hang awkwardly over the hand.

For a folded-up cuff, be sure to work the fabric so the right side will be visible when the cuff is turned back. I make a reverse-stockinette fold line at the point where I want the cuff to turn so that it folds nicely to the outside and stays in place.

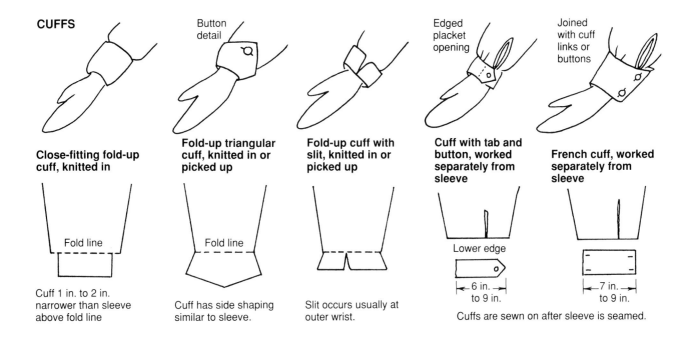

CUFFS

Close-fitting fold-up cuff, knitted in

Fold line

Cuff 1 in. to 2 in. narrower than sleeve above fold line

Button detail

Fold-up triangular cuff, knitted in or picked up

Fold line

Cuff has side shaping similar to sleeve.

Fold-up cuff with slit, knitted in or picked up

Slit occurs usually at outer wrist.

Edged placket opening

Cuff with tab and button, worked separately from sleeve

Lower edge

←6 in.→ to 9 in.

Joined with cuff links or buttons

French cuff, worked separately from sleeve

←7 in.→ to 9 in.

Cuffs are sewn on after sleeve is seamed.

A folded-up cuff can have an opening for detail. Place the opening at the outside of the wrist or at the center of the sleeve for the most visibility. Since I like to work this cuff after the sleeve is seamed, I use double-pointed needles to work it back and forth to make it in one piece and eliminate a seam.

For a tight, buttoned cuff inspired by a man's dress shirt, you'll first need to form an opening in the lower sleeve, then add the cuff. To create an outer wrist opening, work the lower sleeve in two sections, then join these sections at the top of the opening. This opening may be a mere slit, or wide enough to add trim later.

The sleeve opening should be edged for stability with three or four stitches knitted in a flat pattern at the same time as the sleeve. Alternatively, it can be edged by a one-row bind-off, a reverse-stockinette-stitch roll (see p. 92), or a bias band (see p. 233). To apply any of these edges in true dressmaker fashion, open the slit and pick up stitches along the entire length of the slit, rather than working the trim separately on each side.

The added cuff must have a tab of extra fabric about 1 in. wide for a button closure. Work one or more buttonholes on the cuff where you want them, centering them nicely. For a buttonless French cuff, make an extension about 1 in. at both sides of the cuff and form an eyelet where your cuff link is to be inserted.

*d*ressmaker finishing

Finishing can make or break a garment. It's a different process from knitting and requires different skills. If you are unfamiliar with basic finishing techniques, refer to one of the knitting manuals in the Bibliography on pp. 258-260. Here I want offer some hints about finishing techniques from a designer's point of view.

Because I make most of my garments in separate pieces, I have a four-stage finishing process. First I block, or prepare the pieces so they're flat and manageable when sewn. Next I seam and join the pieces, then pick up or sew on any edging or trim. Finally, after the garment is assembled, I lightly block the seams and edges if I decide this is necessary.

This order of events can change if need be. Sometimes it's easier to work small details, like pocket bands, before assembling the pieces. And blocking may not be necessary for some textured fabrics or yarns made of a particular fiber (see the blocking chart on p. 230).

Finishing should actually begin before you start a project. Consider your fiber content and test block your swatch if you think it needs it. As you work garment pieces that will need to be joined, prepare them for easy seaming by including appropriate edge, or selvage, stitches (see p. 97). Pick up stitches along your swatch to test any edgings you plan to use, then measure your gauge to help you plan how many stitches to pick up along the garment.

Blocking

Depending on your materials and the garment's construction, you can block pieces individually or wait until the whole garment is assembled. Usually I prefer to block the pieces first, then touch up the seams, if necessary, after the garment is completed. Always test any blocking method on your swatch first.

To block a dimensional fabric, first lay it on the blocking surface, letting it do what it wants to, without flattening it with your hands. Then, if the fabric is ribbed or pleated, tug it vertically or pat it to make it draw in as much as possible and allow the ribs or pleats to stand up. (If the fabric is welted, tug it horizontally.) Hold a hot steam iron at least 1 in. above the fabric for about 15 seconds, allowing the steam to permeate the fabric below. Then allow the fabric to air dry thoroughly.

When you wash a garment made of 3-D fabric, do so carefully, then blot it and block it into shape. For ribbed and pleated areas, tug vertically on the fabric to draw it in as much as possible and pat it into shape, squeezing the damp folds into place. Air-dry thoroughly.

If you decide that you want to flatten a 3-D fabric for a textured flat-fabric effect, steam the piece and pat it flat it with your hands, or immerse it entirely in water, then pull or flatten it with your hands allow it to dry flat on a towel.

METHOD	WHY AND WHEN	WHAT FIBERS	HOW	NOTES
No blocking	If surface is acceptable, without irregularity.			Even if pieces require no blocking, you may still need to steam seams lightly, provided the fiber permits (see below).
Light steaming	To even out slight surface irregularities. To flatten selvages slightly to prepare for seaming. To set textured patterns, by fulling the fibers ever so slightly. To fluff hairy nonsynthetic fibers. To flatten seams.	Most natural fibers. Take care with rayon or viscose. NO SYNTHETICS. Check yarn label if available.	Lay piece or seam flat. Hold warm/hot iron ½ in. to 1 in. above surface of material, and allow steam to permeate fabric. Flatten slightly with palms, and pinch up 3-D texture to set the pattern. Let dry slightly.	Lay curved seams over a rolled towel before steaming. To set and even out ribbing, lay it flat, allowing it to draw in as much as possible. Steam as above, applying no pressure. Tug in direction of ribs to make narrower—do not widen or flatten.
Heavy steaming	To even out major irregularities. To slightly enlarge pieces that were knitted too tightly. To open up lace patterns.	Wool, cotton, linen. NO SYNTHETICS.	Lay piece flat, or pin in place if it needs to be opened up or enlarged. Cover one area at a time with a damp cotton cloth. Touch hot iron lightly to cloth—APPLY NO PRESSURE. Allow steam to permeate fabric. Flatten slightly with palms, and pinch 3-D texture to set the pattern. Move on to another area, dampening cloth again when necessary.	Less time-consuming than wet blocking, but produces similar results, provided your fiber permits it. You can use this method to block smaller areas, like isolated lace panels.
Wet blocking	To even out major irregularities. For allover lace that needs to be severely opened up.	All fibers.	Immerse pieces in cool water. Squeeze gently without twisting, then blot with towel to remove excess water. Lay flat, patting flat areas and pinching texture into desired shape. To open up lace, stretch and pin to shape. Dry thoroughly before removing.	More time-consuming than heavy steaming.
Machine washing	To shrink and full the fabric.	Primarily loosely spun wools and wool/mohair blends.	Small pieces, like mittens or hats, can be hand scrubbed in warm, soft soapy water to full them to desired size and texture. Larger pieces are more manageable in washing machine. To warm water, add mild soap flakes and baking soda. Agitate to desired size and texture, checking frequently. Dry flat. For details on the process, see the sidebar on the facing page.	Test large 8-in. by 8-in. swatch first.

Fulling

Fulling is a finishing method that intentionally shrinks knitted fabric to resemble felt. Loosely spun wools knitted in a loose garter stitch yield the best results. Cottons and synthetics, as well as wools that have been treated to prevent shrinking, will not full at all. You can full different types of wool and wool-blend yarns to varying degrees, with results that range from soft and slightly stretchy to thick, hard and rug-like.

Fulling requires agitating the fabric for from five to 20 minutes (depending on the softness of the fiber) in warm water and soap, which causes the scaly surface of the wool fibers to swell and become entangled. This process is speeded up by adding a water-softening agent like baking soda. Although fulling can be done by hand, it is more quickly and easily done in the washing machine.

A deliberately fulled garment must be carefully planned to shrink to the desired size. For those new to this process, begin with an oversized coat-like garment to allow room for error. Once you have more experience, you can plan close-fitting garments, like my vests shown above, which were inspired by Bavarian fulled garments.

The following guidelines will help you through the fulling process. Remember that each yarn will full differently, so it's important to keep records of your experience.

1. Work a large swatch at least 8 in. by 8 in. Record the gauge of the swatch before fulling.

2. Set your washing machine for warm water at a low level with normal agitation. Add a small handful of baking soda to soften the water, a large handful of mild soap flakes (not liquid detergent), like Ivory Snow®, and add a small washcloth along with your swatch, which will provide abrasion while the machine is working. Turn on the machine and check the swatch every five minutes, to see if it's nearing the look you're after. Allow it to go through the rinse cycle. Record the approximate time in the machine this degree of fulling required. You may need more than one cycle.

3. Dry the swatch on a flat towel. Measure the gauge after fulling, and plan your garment based on this gauge. Comparing the gauges before and after fulling will give you a general idea of the rate of shrinkage for fulling this yarn.

4. Full the completed garment in a larger amount of water, proportionately increasing the amounts of baking soda and soap flakes. Add a large towel for abrasion. Check every few minutes. Remove when the fabric resembles the fulled swatch in feel and texture. Run the garment through the rinse and spin cycles, then dry it flat on a towel.

These garter-stitch vests were knitted of loosely plied Shetland-type wool and then fulled to a thick, dense texture for a traditional Bavarian look. Dressmaker/menswear details include lapels at the front, lapel-like extensions at the armholes, and a separately worked belt, fulled along with the vest and sewn on later at the back waist.

It's a good idea to keep a couple of other things in mind when fulling a garment. Test a buttonhole and any planned edgings on your swatch to see how they respond to fulling (you may discover that you need to work a wider buttonhole than you thought).

Complete the garment before fulling. Avoid seams if possible because they may stiffen up. Omit side seams by working back and forth on a circular needle, graft shoulders, and pick up stitches for sleeve and work them downwards.

The edges may stretch slightly during the fulling process. To return them to the proper length after fulling, sew an invisible running stitch with a strand of yarn through the edge before drying. (See also the fulled fabric on pp. 246-247.)

Seaming hints

I'll never understand why anyone would seam knits from the wrong side of the fabric. I always seam with the right side of the pieces facing me in order to be able to see what the seam looks like. I sew seams with what is known as a mattress stitch, joining row to row (see the drawing on p. 227). Even when an edging has a different row gauge from the main fabric, I still use this method, pinning the edges together, then joining one row for two rows when necessary to match them.

Appropriate tension in the seam itself enhances the look of the garment, though too much tension will cause the seam to bunch up. Vertical seams should have a bit of stretch to match the feel of the knitted fabric. Vertical sewn-on bands at front edges should be a little more firmly sewn than other vertical seams in order to provide a bit more structure to the body and help it stand up to wear. Shoulder seams should be firm, with little or no stretch, to help support the weight of the garment.

Perhaps the trickiest seams are those at the shoulders and those that join cap sleeves to the body. To join shoulders, I seam bound-off edges by weaving or grafting them together, with right sides butted together and facing me. This creates a firm seam, with a ridge forming to the inside, which provides both support and a good place to attach shoulder pads.

A designer garment will not make the grade if the cap sleeves are not perfectly joined (see pp. 50-52 for information on planning cap sleeves). With right sides facing, I first join the lower 2 in. to 3 in. of the cap to the armhole at front and back, leaving the upper cap free. I can then see if the upper cap will fit well. If the cap fit is not right, I make adjustments. To eliminate any extra fullness beyond ease, I rip the upper cap down a few rows and reshape it by binding off a few rows earlier than before. If the upper cap is too skimpy, I would again rip it out and reshape it by adding a few rows. With the lower sections of the cap seamed, the knitting and reworking may be a little awkward, but it's worth the effort.

Picking up stitches

Often a dressmaker garment will have a ribbed edge, which is picked up rather than knitted in (see pp. 93-95 for more information on these two approaches). If this ribbed edge is skimpy, the look of an otherwise nicely designed garment will suffer. To ensure thick, luxurious ribbing, I always pick up more stitches than normally prescribed in most knitting manuals—often one stitch for every row (knitting books usually say to pick up two stitches for every three rows, or three stitches for every four rows). To keep the edge from flaring, I bind off firmly or decrease approximately one stitch every inch as I bind off.

Dressmaker edgings

There are several knitted edgings with dressmaker origins—facings, bias bands, picot point and ruffles. All can trim any edge, but facings and bias bands are perhaps most useful for adding firmness to curved necklines and sleeveless armholes. To avoid bulk when working these edgings, switch to a finer yarn than that used for the body (plan on picking up a few more stitches to work an edging with the finer-gauge yarn).

A **facing** is a narrow strip of fabric, best worked in stockinette, which lines the inside of the knitted edge and supports it (see also the discussion of lapel facings on pp. 224-227). When added along a straight bottom edge of a garment or a sleeve, this facing becomes a hem, another dressmaker term that is infrequently used in knitting. I use a facing at places like the neckline or armhole edge where I want firmness without the obtrusive look of an edging.

A facing is best worked after the garment pieces are assembled and, for circular facings (as for an armhole) should be knitted in the round to avoid bulky seams. Pick up stitches with a smaller needle than used for the body along the entire edge to be faced to produce a very firm join. Along a horizontal edge, pick up one stitch for every bound-off stitch. Along curved edges, pick up stitches below or to the side of the little holes made by working increases or decreases. And along vertical edges, pick up about two stitches for every three rows.

After picking up your stitches, knit a wrong-side row or purl one round for flat facings to provide a fold line so the facing folds nicely to the inside. Work even in stockinette for about ½ in., then increase a few stitches around curved areas (one stitch for 1 in.) so that the facing will lie flat.

When the facing is wide enough to provide stability to the edge, you can sew each stitch down rather than binding off, for the most flexible join. You can take the live stitches off the needle, pin the facing in place and then sew it in, stitch by stitch. (If your fiber permits, a shot

Some dressmaker details can be easily adapted to knitting. Clockwise, from left: a swatch edged with a lightweight sewn-on ruffle, flared by gradual increases; a swatch edged with a knitted bias band; a picked-up facing forms an invisible edging when folded to the inside; and a swatch pocket with a picot-point edging.

of steam from your iron before sewing will help keep the facing in place.) Alternatively, you can bind off, then sew the facing down as loosely as possible and finally steam it lightly from the wrong side, flattening it with your fingers.

In dressmaking, a **bias band** is a strip of fabric cut diagonally across the grain. Unlike a piece of fabric cut on the straight of the grain (along its length) or cross-grain (across its width), a diagonal, or bias-cut, strip stretches slightly. Because of this stretch, a bias band will lie flat and smooth around a curved edge, while a band cut on the straight grain or cross-grain will buckle when applied to a curve.

You can knit a stockinette bias band whose rows fall on a diagonal. This kind of band will curl naturally in half and stretch to cover any straight or curved edge. Though the band itself is stretchy, when sewn into place, it makes a firm, finished edge. In fact, this band shouldn't be used for an edge that needs to remain elastic. To use a bias band along a close-fitting neckline, you may need a placket or buttoned opening so the wearer's head can pass through.

To make a knitted bias band:
Cast on 1 st, work in St st and inc 1 st at beg of every row until you have desired number of sts for twice width of folded band.
WS rows: P.
RS rows: Inc 1 st at beg of row, k to last 2 sts, k2tog. Rep these 2 rows to desired length, then dec 1 st at beg of every row until no sts rem. Pin bias bands along edge and sew 1 side at a time.

Picot point is a pretty, double-thickness, jagged stockinette edging that looks as if it were cut with pinking shears. Picot-point edges add detail to very feminine garments and baby things. You can use this edging in place of a facing or as a button band, working with a fine yarn that will not be too bulky.

To work picot-point edging:
Pick up same number of sts as you would for a facing. If working back and forth in rows, use an odd number of sts; if working in circular rounds, use an even number.
Work in St st for desired length. Then work a row of eyelets across fabric to create a fold.
On a RS row: Rep (k2tog, yo), then end k1.
On a WS row: Rep (p2tog, yo), then end p1.
On a RS round: Rep (k2tog, yo). Work to same length as before eyelet row, then bind off. Fold, then sew to inside along ridge formed by picked-up row.

To form the buttonholes on the picked-up row, pick up to the point where you want the buttonhole to fall. Then skip a small section equal to the size of the buttonhole in the body and cast on a few stitches on your needle before starting to pick up stitches again for the next section of the band. Repeat the process for each buttonhole.

When using fabric trims as decoration, test their application first on a swatch. Clockwise, from upper left: rickrack is threaded through floated strands on the face of the fabric; a wonderful patch from TFLK-brand trims would add a terrific touch to a simple garment; an embroidered gingham fabric trim would work nicely at the lower edge of a sleeve; an embossed silk trim decorating a mohair band would be a perfect cuff or front edge of a coat.

Ruffles can add a classic feminine frill to a garment. They can be used singly at an edge or layered for a tutu-like effect.

A common dressmaker ruffle is a simple rectangle, cut two to three times the length of the edge to which it will be attached, then gathered to fit. This is easy to simulate in knitted fabric, using a lightweight yarn to avoid bulk.

Another kind of dressmaker ruffle is cut on a curve. The inner, shorter edge of the ruffle is the same length as the edge to which it will be attached. The longer outer edge will fall in soft folds. To knit this kind of ruffle, you might pick up along an edge, then increase gradually. Or you could knit a side-to-side rectangle for the ruffle, short-rowing one side to curve it.

Dressmaker linings

A lightweight fabric lining can be used for jackets and for coats, dresses and skirts to help prevent the seat from stretching. I use linings very rarely, since I prefer to design garments that are firmly enough knitted not to need linings. But they are nonetheless occasionally useful, especially for garments that will receive hard wear.

A lining should be made from very lightweight material so as not to add unnecessary weight to the garment. Before sewing the garment sections together, use them as pattern pieces to cut out the lining, adding ½ in. or ⅝ in. beyond the pattern pieces for seam allowances and an extra 2 in. for hems. (I often add an extra 3 in. to 4 in. at the center back lining to form a pleat that provides the lining with a little give.) Then sew the pieces together.

A dress form is a big help when sewing in the lining. Place your garment inside out, over the form. Put the lining over the garment, with wrong sides facing. Pin the lining in place, turning up the hems on the sleeves and body. Turn the knitted garment right side out, and try it on to see if the lining pulls. Adjust the lining if necessary, and sew it loosely to the garment at the shoulders and along front and neckline edges. I prefer to leave the lining unattached at the lower edges of the sleeves and body, tacking it only at the seams.

Buttons and other closures

For me, one of the great thrills of designing is choosing buttons. When I visit New York, I prefer the button stores in the garment district to any store on Fifth Avenue. And I can't go home until I've visited my favorite spot in the city, Tender Buttons, on 63rd Street off Lexington Avenue.

A wonderful button can elevate the simplest garment to celebrity status, or it can do purely functional duty. I love buttons so much that they're often the starting point for a design. My favorite buttons are mother-of-pearl, with horn and wooden buttons a close second (the latter are best suited to rustic garments and blend well with autumn colors). I also like hefty plastic buttons because of the wide color range they come in, and antique buttons, which can help capture the flavor of another era. For an unusual touch, I mix different buttons on the same garment, and sometimes place buttons in interesting groupings, rather than equidistant from one another.

After many experiments, I have finally found a way to use fabric-covered button kits successfully to make buttons that perfectly match my knitted fabric. I split my yarn into plies, then knit a very lightweight piece of fabric. I fuse a small circle of featherweight interfacing on the

My three favorite knitted belt fabrics, from top to bottom: a simple 1x1 rib; a cable panel flanked by a few stockinette stitches that roll to the back; and a double-knit fabric.

The Pearly Kings and Queens of cockney England sport festive outfits for the annual harvest celebration. Their costumes are decorated exclusively with buttons — added cumulatively over a lifetime — which spell out words, outline seams and edges, create patterns or cover entire surfaces. Every button lover might take whimsical inspiration from the Pearlies for a design now and then. (Photo, UPI/Bettmann Newsphotos.)

Making shaped shoulder pads

Dressmaker shoulder pads are shaped to curve over the shoulder and are often thicker at the outer end to fill the top of a cap sleeve and provide structure for wide-shouldered garments. I've designed a shoulder pad with a shaped extension that provides for this extra thickness at the end of the pad (for easy swatch shoulder pads, see p. 66). To make the shoulder pad:
  With worsted-weight yarn and size 6 or 7 needles, cast on 3 sts. K 2 rows. Work in garter st (k every row), inc 1 st at each end of next row (RS), then on every RS row until there are 51 sts, end with a RS row. Mark center st.
  Dec row (WS): K until 1 st before center st, sl this st and center st knitwise tog; k1, p2sso, k to end of row. Cont to inc at each end of every RS row until there are 63 sts. Rep dec row — 61 sts. P 1 row on RS (for fold at center of shoulder pad).

Beg short rows as foll:
  Row 1 (WS): K to last 20 sts, leave these sts unworked, turn.
  Row 2: Sl 1, k to last 20 sts, leave these sts unworked, turn.
  Row 3: Sl 1, k to last 10 sts, leave these sts unworked, turn.
  Row 4: Rep Row 3.
  Row 5: K all sts.
  Row 6: P 61 sts.
  Inc row (WS): K to 1 st before center st, inc 1 st in next st, k to end. Rep inc row every 7th row twice more AND AT SAME TIME dec 1 st at each end of every row until 3 sts rem. K 2 rows. Bind off. Fold pad and pin in place to check fit before sewing along ridge formed by shoulder seam.

Puffed or very full sleeve caps tend to collapse under their own weight. To avoid this, I fill the cap with fine bridal tulle, or netting, which is available at fabric stores and is virtually weightless but has lots of body. I form a roll of tulle about the size of two fingers held together and sew it along the armhole seam to extend slightly into the cap.

For even more support, I layer two rectangles of tulle, each 4 in. to 6 in. wide and twice as long as the gathered section of the cap. I fold along the length, then gather along the stacked edges, thereby shortening the edge by half. I sew the gathered edge to the armhole seam. The frilly side expands to fill the cap.

wrong side of the knitted fabric to keep it from stretching and stop the sheen of the metal base from showing through.

Knitting books abound with directions for various buttonholes, and most knitters have their favorite. Mine is Barbara Walker's self-reinforcing, one-row buttonhole from her *A Second Treasury of Knitting Patterns* (see the Bibliography on pp. 258-260).

Plot the placement of your buttonholes on the schematic drawing for your garment. Draw a band the desired width along the button edge of your piece. Draw in any trim that will be at the neckline edge that may have a button. Arrange and rearrange the buttonholes on the schematic until you're pleased with the overall effect and spacing. Then measure and note on the schematic the distance from the garment's bottom edge to each buttonhole mark. Refer to these measurements as you knit to be sure you're correctly positioning the buttonholes.

There are many ways to close a garment without using buttons. Some of these specialty closures are more challenging to apply than buttons, but they can make a sweater look more like a fancy dressmaker garment. Test any new kind of closure on your swatch to be sure it will work with knitted fabric.

You can make some of these closures and purchase others from dressmaker suppliers. Design the opening in your garment with the actual closure in hand by testing it on a swatch. You'll often need to invent a special overlap, a way for the edges to butt neatly together or a reinforcement on the inside of the garment so that the knitted fabric will not stretch when the closure is attached.

Ties or belted closures can either be knitted or made from fabric or ribbon (for three of my favorite knitted belts, see the photo at left on p. 235). Rope-anchored toggles look nautical or sporty and might be just the closure needed for a "bench-warmer" jacket. Norwegian pewter clasps are perfect for traditional Scandinavian sweaters—try using them in the same garment with pewter buttons. And try making your own curlicue frog closures (see my matador design on pp. 156-157) or choose a ready-made frog that matches your yarn.

Zippers lend a very sporty look to a knitted garment. They're made of various materials, and each has a different weight and flexibility. Most common is the lightweight zipper with nylon coil rather than individual zipper teeth. Nylon zippers work well in woven fabric but tend to bubble and fail to lie perfectly flat in a hand-knitted fabric. I would use these zippers cautiously and only in short lengths, where they will not be a focal point of the design.

I prefer zippers with individual plastic or metal teeth because they're more flexible and a better weight for knitwear. Small, lightweight plastic or aluminum teeth are very good for light- to medium-weight garments. Those with heavier brass or stainless-steel teeth are nice for heavy jackets. Unfortunately, it seems to be increasingly difficult to find good metal zippers.

There are also other invisible closures to consider for your garment, though I find most dressmaker snaps, and hooks and eyes too light and flimsy for knitwear. Nonetheless, I do have a stock of heavy thread-covered hooks and eyes, the kind used for fur coats. These make wonderful closures for knitted coats on which you don't want to use buttons.

*d*esigner notebook

I had several goals when deciding upon a project to end this chapter on dressmaker details. I wanted to design a two-piece suit with a coordinated jacket and skirt. I wanted to base the design on a dressmaker style described in the chapter and use a commercial sewing pattern as the point of departure. And I wanted to create a design for a petite-figured person, something I had never done before.

I began by testing various stitch patterns before planning the suit. I wanted a firm, slightly textured fabric, perhaps with a woven look. I chose a soft, refined, silky, worsted-weight merino wool in a rather unusual blue-green color, inspired by buttons I had bought with this suit in mind.

I swatched several stitch patterns from Barbara Walker's books (see the Bibliography on pp. 258-260), which you can see in the photo on the facing page. I liked a twill-like slip-stitch pattern, especially its wrong side! A couple of twist-stitch patterns were also pretty and had a nice, subtle texture, but they weren't quite thick enough. The most distinctive swatch was a cabled rib pattern with graceful diagonal lines that could be worked to either the right or left.

To my delight, a petite friend was enthusiastic about serving as my model. I began by taking her measurements, then compared them to sizing charts for commercial sewing patterns. As is often the case, she was a size larger in the hip than in the upper body. Her cross-shoulder measurement was also very narrow. Since I was in new sizing territory, I wanted to make any fitting adjustments to a mock-up garment, before beginning to knit.

While browsing through commercial pattern books for inspiration, I kept my eye open for a simple, basic pattern that would be easy to adapt to knitting. I considered a suit fitted with darts but was concerned that these shaping elements would interrupt the cabled rib pattern in an unsightly way. I looked at surplice-style garments that draped and wrapped, but they seemed inappropriate for my rather flat, firm fabric. I finally settled on a princess style, and decided the characteristic seamlines would move from the jacket's lower edge over the body to the shoulder area.

The simplest princess-style pattern I could find was for a dress. I bought it in my friend's size and shortened to it hip length to make a mock-up garment of medium-weight machine-knitted fabric. I slightly extended the outer hip area of both front and back to accommodate my friend's measurement. I also omitted the front-neck shaping, keeping the front edges straight from lower edge to the top of the piece.

The mock-up was a good fit, except that the cross-shoulder area was wide, as I suspected would happen. I pinned the sleeve cap in toward the body to reduce width in the shoulder. I also folded and pinned the fronts to the inside to make a pleasing V-neck, to which I could later add a lapel or collar.

I traced my pattern pieces, with alterations, onto heavier paper that would hold up better than the original tissue-paper pieces. I then measured each pattern piece and made a rough schematic of the garment.

The most crucial consideration with the princess style was how to handle the vertical seams as a design detail. I continued swatching and liked the way a narrow twist-stitch panel paired with the cabled-rib pattern. I sensed that this little panel would make an interesting false seam, replacing the real princess-line seam.

I planned the twist-stitch panels as links between the pieces, redrew the schematic and plotted the stitch counts for each piece. The pieces would be shaped to either side of the narrow decorative "seam" panels to create the look of the princess style.

I plotted the straight knee-length skirt in schematic form as well, planning the twist-stitch panels to interrupt the cabled-rib pattern

Searching for a suit fabric with a woven look, I tried several patterns from Barbara Walker's pattern treasuries (see the Bibliography on pp. 258-260). After deciding on a cabled-rib pattern, I knitted it together with a small twist-stitch panel to see how it would look as a false seam in my princess-style jacket. My Designer Notebook sketch shows the three lapels I considered.

and mimic the jacket's princess lines. Since I wanted the skirt to have a great deal of stretch, it would be knitted on a circular needle to omit seams. To taper the skirt gradually toward the waistline, I planned decreases above the hip to fall next to the false-seam panels.

I waited until after the pieces were knitted and assembled to decide on a lapel treatment. I considered a narrow shawl collar, a collarless lapel, and a lapel with a notch and collar, shown in the sketch above. I used my schematic to help me plan this crucial area.

Much to my disappointment, the buttons that inspired the color scheme didn't work with the final garment—too shiny, too decorative. So I searched for a simpler, more refined button to add the final touch to the suit.

As I completed the garment, I realized that designing for a very small person was really not much different from designing for anyone else. It required analysis of measurements and a careful step-by-step movement through my usual design process. The commercial pattern helped me overcome my trepidation about moving into a new area and provided a reliable foundation for developing the design for a dressmaker-style garment.

Instructions for princess-line suit

A close-fitting princess-line suit with shawl-collar jacket and knee-length skirt. For the expert knitter.

NOTES ON READING PATTERN CHARTS
•For jacket pieces, which are worked back and forth, read odd-numbered WS rows from left to right, and even-numbered RS rows from right to left.
•For skirt, which is knitted circularly, read all chart rows from right to left.

PATTERN ABBREVIATIONS FOR CHARTED PATTERNS
Right cable: sl 3 sts to cn and hold in back, k1, then sl 2 p sts from cn back to LH needle and p them; then k1 from cn.
Left cable: sl 3 sts to cn and hold in front, k1, then sl 2 p sts from cn back to LH needle and p them; then k1 from cn.
Right twist (RT): k2tog but do not drop from LH needle; k 1st st again and sl both sts from needle tog.
Left twist (LT): With RH needle behind LH needle, skip 1 st and k 2nd st in back loop; then insert RH needle into front of 1st st and k it; slip both sts from needle tog.

SIZE
To fit 30-31 (33-34, 36-37)-in. bust.

MATERIALS
Jacket
•14 (16, 17) balls of "Maratona" from Lane Borgosesia (100% wool; 1¾ oz = approx 121 yd) in color #25777.
•1 pair size 6 and 8 knitting needles or size to obtain gauge.
•1 cable needle (cn).
•8 buttons, ¾ in. wide.
Skirt
•9 (10, 11) balls of "Maratona."
•24-in. circular knitting needles sizes 5, 7 and 8, or size to obtain gauge.
•1 cable needle (cn).
•approx ¾ yd. of flat elastic, 1 in. wide.

GAUGE
•30 sts and 32 rows or rnds equal 4 in. with size 8 needles over cable patterns.
•Twist panel of 10 sts should measure approx 1 in. wide, unstretched.
•To save time later, take time to swatch and check your gauge.

FINISHED MEASUREMENTS (AFTER SEAMING):
Jacket
Finished bust at underarm, buttoned: 35 (38¼, 41½) in.
Length: 24 (24½, 25) in.
Sleeve width at upper arm: 13¾ (14¾, 15¾) in.
Skirt
Hip (at widest point): 33½ (36½, 38) in.
Length, below ribbed waistband: 21 (21½, 22) in.

NOTE
The most difficult part of making this suit is keeping track of various incs and decs within body section of jacket pieces. Before you begin to k, carefully read through instructions. You may find it useful to chart these body pieces on a large sheet of graph paper, noting all incs and decs.

JACKET

LEFT FRONT
With larger needle, cast on 70 (76, 82) sts.
Next row (WS): p2 (edge sts: p WS, k RS), work Row 1 of right-cable pat over 22 (28, 34) sts, place marker B (note that on RS rows, markers will be in alphabetical order), work Row 1 of right-twist panel over 10 sts, place marker A, work Row 1 of right-cable pat over 34 sts, end p2 (edge sts: p WS, k RS). Work even for 8 more rows, so end with a WS row. Note: on following dec rows, it is necessary to remove marker before working dec, then replace after dec is made so it cont to act as divider between cable pat and 10 sts of twist panels.

Next row, dec row (RS): k2 (edge sts), p2tog, work to last st in cable pat before A marker, then p2tog this last st with 1st st of twist panel, work to last st of twist panel before B marker, then p2tog this st with 1st st of cable-rib pat, work to last 2 sts, end k2 (edge sts), for a total of 3 decs—67 (73, 79) sts. Keeping in pats, cont to dec, as described, at sides after 7 more rows, then every 8th row after for a total of 8 decs at side; AND AT SAME TIME, cont to dec, as described, at A and B markers after 15 more rows, then every 16th row after for a total of 5 decs at each point. Work even in pats as est until piece measures 10½ in., end with a WS row—52 (58, 64) sts.

INCREASE TOWARD BUSTLINE
Next row, inc row (RS): k2 (edge sts), M1 (lift strand and k into back of it), work to A marker then M1 before it, work to B marker and sl it, then M1, work to last 2 sts, end k2 (edge sts), for a total of 3 incs—55 (61, 67) sts. Working incs into cable pats, cont to inc, as described, at sides and A marker after 7 more rows, then every 8th row after for a total of 5 incs at each point; AND AT SAME TIME, cont to inc, as described, at B marker after 9 more rows, then every 10th row after for a total of 11 incs at this point. Cont until piece measures 14 (14½, 15) in., end with a WS row.

FRONT-NECK SHAPING
Next row (RS): Work as est to last 4 sts, p2tog, end k2 (edge sts).
For smallest size: Cont to dec at this edge after 3 more rows, then alternately every 6th and 4th rows after for a total of 18 decs at this edge.
For 2 larger sizes: Cont to dec at this edge after 3 more rows, then every 4th row after for a total of—(20, 22) decs at this edge; AND AT SAME TIME, cont until piece measures 15½ in., end with a WS row.

ARMHOLE SHAPING

Cont as est, bind off 3 sts at beg of next RS row, then 2 sts at beg of next RS row.

Next row (RS): k2 (edge sts: k RS, p WS), p2tog, work as est to end. Work WS row as est, then dec at armhole edge, as described, again on next row, then every RS row twice more, then every other RS row 3 times; AND AT SAME TIME, when 2nd single dec has been worked at armhole edge above bind-offs, end with a WS row. Dec 1 st at A marker as at lower front on next row (see note that follows) and every 4th row after for a total of 15 decs at this point (Note: to work dec, remove marker, p2tog in last st of cable pat and 1st st of twist panel, then replace marker to separate cable pat from 10 sts of twist panel.) Cont until armhole depth measures 4 (4½, 5) in., end with a WS row. Inc 1 st at armhole edge (by M1 after 2 edge sts) on next row and every 6th row after for a total of 6 incs at this point, working incs into cable pat.
Cont until armhole depth measures 8½ (9, 9½) in., end with a WS row.

SHOULDER SHAPING

Cont neck shaping if nec, AND AT SAME TIME, bind off 6 (7, 7) sts at beg of next 5 RS rows, then bind off rem 4 (3, 7) sts on last RS row.

RIGHT FRONT

Work same as for left front, reversing placement of patterns at lower edge, substituting left-cable pat and left-twist panel, and reversing shaping so that right front is a mirror image of left front.

BACK

With larger needle, cast on 162 (174, 186) sts.

Next row (WS): p2 (edge sts: p WS, k RS), work Row 1 of right-twist panel over 10 sts, p2 (keep in St st: p WS, k RS), work Row 1 of right-cable pat over 34 sts, place marker D, work Row 1 of left-twist panel over 10 sts, place marker C, work Row 1 of right-cable pat over center 46 (58, 70) sts, place marker B, work Row 1 of right-twist panel over 10 sts, place marker A, work Row 1 of right-cable pat over 34 sts, p2 (keep in St st: p WS, k RS), work Row 1 of right-twist panel over 10 sts, end p2 (edge sts: p WS, k RS). Work even for 8 more rows, so end with a WS row. Note: on following dec rows, it is necessary to remove marker before working dec, then replace after dec is made so that it cont to act as divider between cable pat and 10 sts of twist panels.

Next row, dec row (RS): Work 14 sts as est, p2tog in first 2 sts of cable pat (side dec), work to last st in cable pat before A marker, then p2tog this st with 1st st of twist panel, work to last st of twist panel before B marker, then p2tog this st with 1st st of cable pat, work to last st in cable rib pat before C marker, then p2tog this st with 1st st of twist panel, work to last st of twist panel before D marker, then p2tog this st with first st of cable pat, work to last 2 sts in cable pat and p2tog (side dec), work as est to end, for a total of 6 decs — 156 (168, 180) sts. Keeping in pats, cont to dec as described at sides and B and C markers after 7 more rows, then every 8th row after for a total of 8 decs at each point; AND AT SAME TIME, cont to dec as described at A and D markers after 9 more rows, then every 10th row after for a total of 6 decs at each point. Work even in pats as est until piece measures 10½ in., end with a WS row — 118 (130, 142) sts.

INCREASE TOWARD BUSTLINE

Next row, inc row (RS): Work 14 sts as est, M1 (lift strand and k into the back of it), work to A marker and M1 before it, work to B marker and sl it, then make 1, work to C marker and M1 before it, then work to D marker and sl it, then M1, work to last 14 sts, make 1, work as est to end, for a total of 6 incs — 124 (136, 148) sts. Working incs into cable pats, cont to inc as described at each side and A and D markers after 9 more rows, then every 10th row after for a total of 4 incs at each point; AND AT SAME TIME, cont to inc as described at B and C markers after 7 more rows, then every 8th row after for a total of 13 incs at each point. Cont until piece measures 15½ in., end with a WS row.

ARMHOLE SHAPING

Cont as est, bind off 15 sts at the beg of the next 2 rows, then 2 sts at beg of next 2 rows. Note: to help with sewing sleeve into armhole later, tie a yarn marker at center of each bound-off twist panel.

Next row (RS): k2 (edge sts: k RS, p WS), p2tog, work as est to last 4 sts of row, p2tog, end k2 (edge sts: k RS, p WS). Work WS row as est, then dec at each armhole edge, as described, again on next row, then every RS row twice more, then every other RS row 3 times; cont until armhole depth measures 4 (4½, 5) in., end with a WS row. Dec 1 st at A and D markers on this row and every 6th row after for a total of 6 decs at each point. Work even until armhole depth measures 8½ (9, 9½) in., end with a WS row — 100 (112, 124) sts.

SHOULDER AND BACK-NECK SHAPING

Bind off 6 (7, 7) sts at beg of next 4 rows. Mark center 12 (16, 20) sts.

Next row (RS): Bind off 6 (7, 7) sts, work in pat to center 12 sts, join a 2nd ball of yarn and bind off center 12 (16, 20) sts, work to end. Working both sides at same time with separate balls of yarn, bind off 6 (7, 7) sts at beg of next 5 shoulder edges, then 4 (3, 7) sts at last 2 shoulder edges; AND AT SAME TIME, bind off 5 sts from each neck edge twice.

LEFT SLEEVE

With larger needle, cast on 76 (76, 82) sts.

Next row (WS): p2 (edge sts: keep in St st), work in right-cable pat over next 40 (40, 46) sts, place marker, work right-twist panel over next 10 sts, place marker, work in right-cable pat over next 22 sts, end p2 (edge sts: keep in St st). Work even as est for 6 more rows, so end with a WS row.

Next row, inc row (RS): k2, M1 (lift strand and knit into back of it), work as est to last 2 sts, M1, end k2 — 78 (78, 84) sts. Working incs into cable pat, rep inc row again after 5 more rows, then every 6th row after for a total of 16 (20, 21) incs each side — 108 (116, 124) sts. Work even until sleeve measures 15 (15½, 16) in., or to desired length, end with a WS row.

CAP SHAPING

Bind off 11 sts at beg of next 2 rows, then bind off 2 sts at beg of next 4 rows — 78 (86, 94) sts.

Next row (RS): k2 (edge sts: keep in St st), p2tog, work as est to last 4 sts, p2tog, end k2 (edge sts: keep in St st).

Next row (WS): p2, k1, work as est to last 3 sts, k1, end p2. Rep last 2 rows 12 more times.

Next row (RS): k2, p2tog, work as est to last 4 sts, p2tog, end k2.

Next row (WS): p2, ssk, work as est to last 4 sts, k2tog, end p2. Rep last 2 rows 6 (8, 10) more times. Bind off rem 24 sts on next row.

RIGHT SLEEVE

Work same as for left sleeve, reversing placement of patterns at lower edge, also substituting left-cable rib pat and left-twist panel.

JACKET FINISHING

Sew fronts to back at shoulders. Sew sleeve seams. Sew 2 buttons at each lower sleeve, next to twist panel. Match sleeve seam to marker on bound-off edge of back armhole, then sew sleeve cap to armhole, centering cap at shoulder seam.

Left-front band

With RS facing, starting at beg of neck shaping, with smaller needle, pick up approx 1 st for every row to lower edge, to yield a multiple of 6 sts.

Next row (WS): p1, * p1, k2; rep from * to last 2 sts, end p2. Work rib as est until band measures 1 in., end with a WS row. Bind off on next row, AND AT SAME TIME, p2tog in p2 ribs so that rib does not flare. Rep on right front, working 4 three-st buttonholes evenly spaced on center row, with top buttonhole 3 sts from edge, and lower buttonhole approx 3 in. from lower edge. Sew buttons opposite buttonholes.

Back-neck panel

With larger needle, and WS facing, pick up 14 sts in a 2-in. section at center-back neck.

Next row (WS): p2 (edge sts: p WS, k RS), work twist panel over 10 sts, end p2 (edge sts: p WS, k RS). Work until piece measures 5 (5½, 6) in. Bind off.

SCHEMATIC FOR SUIT

Left front

1½ in.

8½ (9, 9½) in.

24 (24½, 25) in.

4 (4½, 5) in.

5 in.

14 in.

Lengthen or shorten here.

10½ in.

3 (3¾, 4½) in.　1 in.　4½ in.

Lower edge, 8½ (9¼, 10) in.

Back

Cross back at shoulder, 12¾ (14¼, 15¾) in.

1½ in.

Side marker to match sleeve seam

Lengthen or shorten here.

8½ (9, 9½) in.

24 (24½, 25) in.

4 (4½, 5) in.

5 in.

10½ in.

10½ in.

24 (24½, 25) in.

1¼ in.　4½ in.　1 in.　6 (7¾, 9½) in.　1 in.　4½ in.　1¼ in.

Lower edge, 19½ (21½, 23) in.

Left sleeve

14 (15, 16) in.

5½ (5½, 6½) in.

15 15½, 16) in.

9½ (9½, 10½) in.

5½ (6, 6½) in.　1 in.　3 in.

Skirt

2 seam sts

2 seam sts

3 (3, 3) in.

5 (5, 5) in.

Lengthen or shorten here.

16 (16½, 17) in.

Complete hip, 33½ (36½, 38) in.

1 square = 1 in.

PATTERN CHARTS

Right-twist panel
(worked over 10 sts)

|← 10 sts →|

Left-twist panel
(worked over 10 sts)

|← 10 sts →|

Right cable
(multiple of 6 sts plus 4)

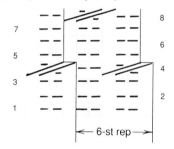

|← 6-st rep →|

Left cable
(multiple of 6 sts plus 4)

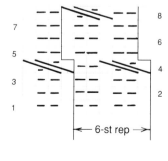

|← 6-st rep →|

Key

☑ = (RT) right-twist panel
☒ = (LT) left-twist panel
☑ = right cable
☒ = left cable

Left side of shawl collar

With larger needles, cast on 14 sts.
Next row (WS): p2 (edge sts: p WS, k RS), work Row 1 of right-cable pat over 10 sts, end p2 (edge sts: p WS, k RS). Work even in pat for a total of 13 rows, so end with a WS row.
Next row (RS): k2, M1, work to last 2 sts, M1, end k2. Working incs into pat, cont to inc 1 st at each end as described after 7 rows, then every 8th row after for a total of 11 (13, 15) incs each side—36 (40, 44) sts. Work even until collar is long enough to reach around left neck edge and meet twist panel at back neck. To be sure of length before binding off, sew cast-on edge to front trim, leaving sts on needle. Then sew collar side to body, matching row for row, then sew across back neck. Shorten or lengthen collar side if necessary, end with a RS row. Bind off 18 (20, 22) sts at beg of next 2 WS rows. Sew bound-off edge to side of center-back panel.
Right side of shawl collar: Work same as for left side, working left-cable pat.

SKIRT

With size 7 circular needle, cast on 260 (284, 296) sts. Place marker for right side "seam" and join.
Next rnd: sl right side marker, * k1 (edge, k every rnd), work Rnd 1 of right-cable pat over 28 sts, place marker, work Rnd 1 of twist panel over 10 sts, place marker, work Rnd 1 right-cable pat over 52 (64, 76) sts, place marker, work Rnd 1 of twist panel over 10 sts, place marker, work Rnd 1 of right-cable pat over 28 sts, k1 (edge), place marker for left side; rep from * across front to beg of rnd. Work even REPEATING ONLY RND 1 of right-cable pat to form a ribbed edge, and repeat rnds 1-4 of twist panel pattern. When piece measures 1¼ in., change to size 8 circular needle. Beg with Rnd 2, work full reps of cable pat. Work even until skirt measures 16 (16½, 17) in., end with Rnd 1 or Rnd 5. Note: If desired, you should shorten skirt before this point, or lengthen skirt at this point, not above, when shaping toward waist. Refer to schematic and measure yourself to decide best length.

SHAPING TOWARD WAIST

Note: On following dec rnds, it is necessary to remove markers that divide pats before working decrease, then replace after dec is made so that it cont to act as divider between cable pat and 10 sts of twist panels.
Next rnd, dec rnd: * k1 (edge), p2tog, work to last st in cable pat, then p2tog it and 1st st of twist panel tog, work to last st of twist panel, then p2tog it and 1st st of cable pat tog, work to last st in cable pat, then p2tog it and 1st st of twist panel tog, work to last st of twist panel, then p2tog it and 1st st of cable pat tog, work to last 2 sts in cable pat and p2tog, k1 (edge), sl marker; rep from * to end for a total of 12 decs— 248 (272, 284) sts. Work even in pats as est for 3 more rnds, always retaining full 10 sts in twist panel in pat, and reducing sts in cable pat, then rep dec rnd on next rnd and every 4th rnd after for a total of 7 dec rnds or 84 decs in all—176 (200, 212) sts. Work even if necessary until skirt measures 21 (21½, 22) in. Change to size 5 circular needle.

WAISTBAND

Rep row 1 of cable pat until ribbed band measures 3 in. Bind off very loosely with larger needle.

SKIRT FINISHING

Fold waistband in half to WS and sewn down loosely, leaving a 1½-in. opening. Measure elastic to fit waist snugly, then thread through ribbed band. Sew ends of elastic tog. Sew opening closed.

WHAT IF...?

What if the Designer Notebook Suit was unfitted, with a slightly oversized silhouette, and I added new details?

Larger Shawl collar

Heavier yarn for coat-like effect

Wide shoulders need shoulder pads

No fitted details at sides of cables

Longer skirt

A sophisticated color— maybe mauve or slate blue

Addendum:
Pushing the limits

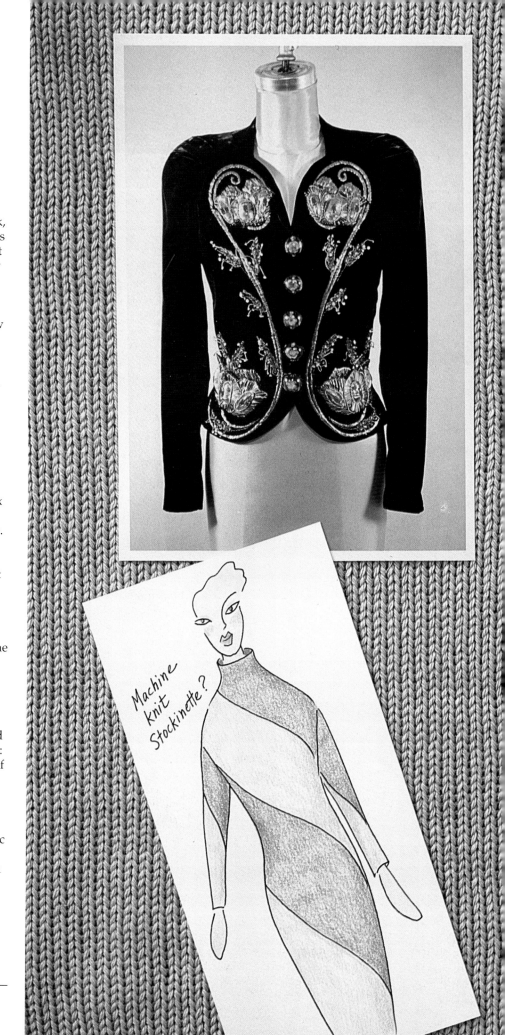

*a*s I said at the outset of this book, designing is an ongoing process that involves continually looking at and assimilating new things. Every designer builds upon experience.

After years of designing for myself and for publication and after completing this book, I'm now interested in pushing the limits of knitwear. I'm anxious to explore new territory and new ideas. Yet even so, I know that I'll still rely on my design process since it's now part of how I see the world.

What follows suggests where I hope to go.

Moving forward with the familiar...

After learning to deal with complex ideas and detailed designs, I'm interested in returning to the basics. I want to work with stockinette fabric and explore very simple garment shapes, which some might call minimalist.

I want to use familiar techniques in new ways, exploring accessories like my colorwork glove (at center) and small projects that will allow me to experiment with fine yarns. The fringed gloves (bottom photo, far right), which are knitted in silk and gold threads in lace patterns and were probably ecclesiastical, might inspire a fringed hat or even knitted and fringed jewelry (fringed gloves: Metropolitan Museum of Art; gift of Miss Irene Lewison, 1942).

New materials...

I'm intrigued by the idea of designing and knitting with metallic strands. The jacket in the photo at upper right (Metropolitan Museum of Art; gift of Julia B. Henry, 1978), which was designed by Elsa Schiaparelli in the late 1930s, inspires me with its lavish metallic embroidery and false gemstones.

Machine knit Stockinette?

KNITTED HAT

FAKE JEWELS

FRINGED & EMBROIDERED WITH METALLIC STRANDS

KNITTED & FRINGED PIN

USE THIN WIRE? SOLDERING WIRE?

BACK OF
KENTE CLOTH-INSPIRED
COAT

BIRD
PANEL AT
CENTER
BACK

BIRDS ON
COLLAR, CUFFS
& BELT

New tools...

After a few lessons on the knitting machine, I see great potential in this tool as a means of exploring new design ideas. I don't think it can replace hand-knitting for me, but it could allow me to take my knitwear in new directions—perhaps even beyond garments. For the moment it serves to provide the background fabric for pp. 244-247.

New techniques...

I've long felt limited by the colors available to me in the yarn market and have never been satisfied that I've explored color thoroughly enough. I look forward to learning to create my own colors with dyes and inks, coloring both yarns and finished knitted fabrics.

New fabrics...

While writing this book, I attended a lecture on West African Ashanti weaving (photo, early 20th-century Ashanti women from Ghana, Library of Congress). I was captivated by the colors and motifs of traditional kente cloth, which is woven in strips and then pieced together. I hope to design a knitted coat or perhaps a series of garments inspired by this wonderful fabric. Along the upper edge of these pages you'll see my first fabric inspired by a piece of kente cloth. I began by knitting strips, then sewed them together and finally fulled the fabric.

New images...

Many artists like to work again and again with the same image. For some, it's realistic imagery like flowers; for others, it's more abstract. Until recently I had not found an image that struck a chord in me. Then the remarkable, hand-knitted South American hat, at left, came my way. I find the birds that cover it a wonderful symbol, which I'd like to explore and make my own—my symbol of design freedom and flight.

New inspiration...

Who knows what my new inspiration will be? As long as my eyes are open, I'll continue to look for it.

For knitters outside the United States

*W*hen writing this book, I used measurements, needle sizes and yarn weights that are standard in the United States. If you're a reader from another country, your needles may sport a different numerical marking. And you'll need to convert my measurements to metric in order to read the schematic drawings and follow the instructions for my designs. The yarns available to you may be offered in grams rather than ounces, so you'll need to convert my quantities to their equivalent in grams. All of these conversions are easy to do. I know because I've been reading imported patterns for years, and I now do all the conversions in my head.

Remember that the design issues presented in the book remain the same no matter where you live — you need only change your needle size and adapt the figures to the system of weights and measures used in your area.

Measurement conversions

In this book I've used inches and yards as the units of measurement. The following equations will help you to convert these measurements to their metric equivalents:

1 inch = 2.5 centimeters
1 yard = .9 meters

To convert inches to centimeters, multiply the inches by 2.5. For instance, gauge is usually measured over 4 in. In metric terms, then, gauge should be measured over 4 in. x 2.5, or 10 cm.

To convert yards to meters, multiply the yards by .9. For instance, if a pattern uses a skein of yarn measuring 220 yd, the metric equivalent of this length is:

220 yd x .9, or 198 m.

Note too that all of the schematic drawings in this book are charted so that one grid square equals 1 in. To translate these schematics to metric measurements, keep in mind that one square equals 2.5 cm. Thus, if a schematic notes that a garment piece measures 20 in. wide, multiply this width by 2.5 to get the metric equivalent: 20 in. x 2.5 = 50 cm. To create a new schematic, assign each grid square a measurement of 2.5 cm.

Weight conversions

Most American and European yarns intended for hand-knitting are now labeled with their weight noted in both ounces and grams. If your yarn label does not state this dual information, know that the two most common skein/ball weights and their equivalents are:

1¾ oz = 50 g
3½ oz = 100 g

However, the skein's weight alone is not always enough information to make a successful yarn substitution. More important is getting an equivalent yardage in a yarn of the same weight. Thus, if a pattern calls for five 3½-oz skeins of yarn, each with a total length of 100 yd, you'll need to look for the equivalent of 5 skeins x 100 yd, or 500 total yd — that is, .9 m x 500 yd, or 450 m of yarn in the same weight.

If you're using a less conventional yarn for knitting, like a coned yarn, conversion by weight will be tricky and perhaps inaccurate. In this case, it's crucial to find an equivalent by comparing the length of the yarn called for in a pattern with the yarn you're considering substituting. In such cases it's always safest to buy more than you think you'll need. And as always, swatch in your chosen yarn to make sure that you obtain the gauge called for in the instructions.

Needle equivalents

This chart should be used only as a guideline for conversion. After choosing a needle size, you should still swatch to obtain the gauge given in any pattern.

US	Metric	UK
0	2 mm	14
1	2¼ mm	13
	2½ mm	
2	2¾ mm	12
	3 mm	11
3	3¼ mm	10
4	3½ mm	
5	3¾ mm	9
	4 mm	8
6		
7	4½ mm	7
8	5 mm	6
9	5½ mm	5
10	6 mm	4
10½	6½ mm	3
	7 mm	2
	7½ mm	1
11	8 mm	0
13	9 mm	00
15	10 mm	000

Knitting abbreviations used in this book

approx Approximately.

beg Begin(ning)(s).

bkgrnd Background.

CC Contrasting color.

cont Continue(ing)(s).

cn Cable needle.

dec(s) Decrease(ing)(s).

dpn Double-pointed needle.

est Establish(ed).

g Gram(s).

in. Inch(es).

inc(s) Increase(ing)(s).

k Knit.

k1-b Knit one stitch through the back loop.

k2tog Knit two stitches together.

LH Left-hand.

LT Left twist: with right-hand needle behind left-hand needle, skip one stitch and knit second stitch through the back loop; then insert RH needle into front of first stitch and knit it; slip both stitches from needle together.

M1 Make one stitch.

MC Main color.

oz Ounce(s).

p Purl.

p1-b Purl one stitch through the back loop.

p2tog Purl two stitches together.

pat(s) Pattern(s).

psso Pass the slipped stitch over the last stitch(es) worked.

rem Remain(ing)(s).

rep Repeat(s).

rev St st Reverse-stockinette stitch.

rib Rib(bing).

RH Right-hand.

rnd(s) Round(s) in circular knitting.

RS Right side.

RT Right twist: knit two stitches together, leaving stitches on left-hand needle; insert right-hand needle between the two stitches just knitted together, and knit first stitch again; slip both stitches from needle together.

sl Slip(ped)(ping). Slip stitches from left-hand needle to right-hand needle, as if to purl.

ssk Slip, slip, knit: slip two stitches individually, as if to knit; then knit them together through their backs.

st(s) Stitch(ed)(es)(ing).

St st Stockinette stitch: knit right-side rows and purl wrong-side rows.

tog Together.

wyib With yarn in back.

wyif With yarn in front.

yd Yard(s).

yo Yarn-over.

WS Wrong side.

Patterns not included in the main text

The four designs whose instructions follow appear in various chapters in the book. Since they are not Designer Notebook projects, their instructions have been placed here in order not to interrupt the text.

INSTRUCTIONS FOR HIROSHIGE-INSPIRED PULLOVER

A classic-fitting pullover (see p. 133) inspired by a Hiroshige print. For the experienced knitter.

Note: Specific instructions are given for the garment pieces and for finishing. However, space limitations preclude the inclusion of charts for branches and flowers, which are worked in duplicate stitch after the garment is complete. To design your own details, refer to the photos of the sweater on p. 133 and the Hiroshige print on p.123.

SIZE
To fit 32-34 (35-37)-in. bust, with a classic silhouette.

FINISHED MEASUREMENTS
(AFTER SEAMING)
Finished bust at underarm: 38 (42) in.
Length: 28 in.

MATERIALS
I combined a slightly grainy silk/wool blend and a soft lightweight 100% wool, using them together in a small, stranded "checkered" pattern. If you substitute other yarns, choose ones with similar yardage that will yield same gauge.
•Rowan's "Silkstones" from Westminster Trading (52% silk/48% wool; 1¾ oz = 200 m) in following colors and amounts (symbol used on charts and in instructions below is shown after each color, in parentheses):
    Chili #826: 3 skeins (no symbol, just open square).

Natural #5: 1 skein (N).
Blue Mist #832: 1 skein (B).
Marble Grey #833: 1 skein (G).
Woad (Indigo) #829: 1 skein (W).
•Rowan's "Lightweight Double Knitting" from Westminster Trading (100% wool; ⅞ oz = 67 m) in following colors and amounts (symbol used on charts and in instructions below is shown after each color, in parentheses):
    Cool red #42: 5 (6) skeins (O).
    Warm red #44: 5 (6) skeins (X).
    Ivory #2: 1 skein (+).
    Beige #84: 1 skein (*).
    Pale peach #401: 2 skeins (-).
    1 skein each of 7 shades of blue, ranging from light to dark: Blue #47 (1); Blue #63 (2); Blue #123 (3); Blue #122 (4); Blue #52 (5); Blue #53 (6); Blue #108 (7).
•For duplicate st, small amounts of lightweight yarns in following colors: brown for branches, and coral, salmon, orange and red for flowers.
•1 pair each knitting needles sizes 4, 6 and 7, or sizes to obtain gauge.
•1 blunt tapestry needle.

GAUGE
•24 sts and 24 rows equal 4 in. over checkered pat with size 7 needle.
•28 sts and 24 rows equal 4 in. over corrugated rib with size 6 needle.
•To save time later, take time to swatch and check your gauge.

PATTERN CHARTS FOR HIROSHIGE PULLOVER

Key
□ = chili
☒ = warm red
Ō = cool red
⊟ = a shade of blue
N = natural
+ = ivory

Corrugated rib

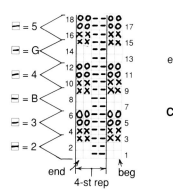

⊟ = 5
⊟ = G
⊟ = 4
⊟ = B
⊟ = 3
⊟ = 2
end   beg
4-st rep

Checkered pat, red version

end   beg
2-st rep

Checkered pat, moon

2-st rep

Red ribs are in St st: k RS, p WS.

Blue ribs are in rev St st: p RS, k WS.

Blue changes every 3 rows: shade shown at left of chart.

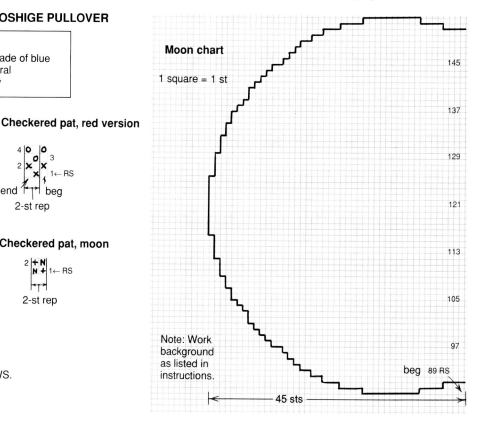

Moon chart

1 square = 1 st

145
137
129
121
113
105
97
89 RS

Note: Work background as listed in instructions.

beg

← 45 sts →

SCHEMATIC FOR HIROSHIGE-INSPIRED PULLOVER

1 square = 1 in.

PATTERNS

See pat charts (facing page) for corrugated-rib and checkered pats. Carry yarn not in use loosely across WS.

RED SECTIONS

Back, left front and left sleeve

With size 6 needle and chili, cast on number of sts indicated on schematic for corrugated rib. Beg chart for rib on next row. Work until chart is complete, inc necessary sts evenly on last WS row of rib. Change to size 7 needle. Beg red checkered pat on next RS row. Work to lengths shown on schematic (above), working shaping as indicated. For side-sleeve shaping, inc as follows: k1, M1,

work to last st, M1, end k1.

Right front with moon

Two different areas of color are knitted in: changing bkgrnd and moon (smaller flowers and branches will be duplicate st later). Each area is worked in checkered pat, with 2 different colors used for each section at all times. When changing colors, pick up new color from under last color used in previous section.

• With size 7 needle and *, cast on 79 (85) sts. Beg with a RS row, work in checkered pat, using colors listed for each row AS LISTED BELOW; AND AT SAME TIME, work even as est until row 88 is complete (piece should measures approx 15 in. long).

Next row, row 89 (RS): Work 45 sts of moon chart, using N and + in checkered pat for moon section, cont color sequence for bkgrnd as listed. Work even after moon chart is complete, shaping neck and shoulders as indicated on schematic.

COLOR SEQUENCE FOR BACKGROUND

Rows 1-6: - and *. **Rows 7-8:** - and N. **Rows 9-10:** - and *. **Rows 11-16:** - and N. **Rows 17-18:** * and N. **Rows 19-22:** - and N. **Rows 23-24:** * and N. **Rows 25-26 (beg right sleeve):** - and N. **Rows 27-29:** * and N. **Row 30:** N and -. **Rows 31-37:** * and N. **Row 38:** N and +. **Rows 39-45:** * and N. **Row 46:** N and +. **Rows 47-49:** * and N. **Row 50:** + and 1. **Row 51:** * and

N. **Row 52:** 1 and +. **Row 53:** N and *.
Rows 54-57: * and 1. **Row 58:** * and 2.
Row 59: 1 and *. **Row 60:** * and 2.
Row 61: 1 and *. **Rows 62-65:** 2 and 1.
Row 66: B and 1. **Row 67:** 1 and 2.
Row 68: 2 and B. **Rows 69-70:** B and 1.
Row 71: 2 and 1. **Rows 72-74:** B and 2.
Rows 75-76: 3 and B. **Rows 77-78:** 2 and
B. **Rows 79-80:** 3 and B. **Rows 81-82:** 3
and G. **Row 83:** B and 3. **Row 84:** 2 and B.
Row 85: G and 2. **Row 86:** 3 and G.
Rows 87-89: B and 3; on 89 — beg moon
chart. **Row 90:** 2 and B. **Row 91:** 4 and 2.
Rows 92-93: 2 and B. **Row 94:** 3 and 4.
Row 95: G and 3. **Row 96:** 2 and G.
Row 97: G and 4. **Row 98:** 4 and B.
Row 99: B and 2. **Rows 100-101:** 3 and B.
Rows 102-103: 3 and 4. **Row 104:** 2 and
B. **Rows 105-106:** G and 2. **Rows 107-
108:** G and 3. **Row 109:** B and 3.
Rows 110-111: 4 and B. **Rows 112-113:** 4
and 3. **Row 114:** 4 and G. **Row 115:** B and
4. **Row 116:** 3 and B. **Row 117:** 5 and 3.
Row 118: 3 and B. **Row 119:** B and 4.
Rows 120-121: 4 and 5. **Row 122:** B and
5. **Row 123:** 4 and B. **Row 124:** G and 4.
Rows 125-126: 5 and G. **Rows 127-128:** 5
and 4. **Rows 129-130:** 5 and B. **Row 131:**
5 and 4. **Row 132:** G and 5. **Row 133:** 6
and G. **Row 134:** G and 5. **Row 135:** 6
and G. **Rows 136-137:** B and 5. **Rows
138-41:** B and 6. **Row 142:** G and 5. **Row
143:** 6 and G. **Row 144:** 7 and 5. **Row
145:** 6 and 7. **Rows 146-147:** W and 5.
Row 148: 7 and 5. **Row 149:** W and 7.
Row 150: 6 and W. **Row 151:** 5 and 6.
Rows 152-153: 7 and 6. **Rows 154-155:**
W and 5. **Row 156:** W and 7. **Rows 157-
158:** 5 and W. **Rows 159-160:** 7 and W.
Rows 161-162: 7 and 6. **Rows 163-164:**
W and 5. **Rem rows:** W and 7.

RIGHT SLEEVE

With size 7 needle, cast on 55 (55) sts.
Beg with a RS row, work in checkered
pat beg with row 25 of color sequence
listed for right front. Omit moon chart on
sleeve, work only bkgrnd colors and
shaping as indicated on schematic.

FINISHING

Steam all pieces lightly. Sew front pieces
tog. Referring to photo of pullover on
p. 133 or Hiroshige print on p.123, baste
lines with large running sts to est a nice
arrangement of branches. Embroider
branches and small flowers in duplicate
st on front and sleeves. Steam lightly.
Neck edging: Sew front to back at
1 shoulder. With size 4 needle and chili,
pick up 114 (122) sts along entire neck
edge.
Work trim: Using a different red for each
row, k 1 row, p 1 row, bind off in k.

Left sleeve, lower edge: With RS facing,
size 4 needle and chili, pick up 1 st for
each cast-on st along lower edge of
sleeve. Work trim as above.
Body, lower edge: Sew 1 side seam. With
RS facing, size 4 needles and chili, pick
up 1 st for each cast-on st along lower
edge of body. Work trim as above.
Right sleeve, lower edge: With RS facing,
size 4 needle and chili, pick up 1 st for
each cast-on st along lower edge of
sleeve. With a different red for each row,
k 1 row, p 1 row. With a different light
blue for each row, p 1 row, k 1 row. With
chili, p 1 row, then with a different red
for each row, p 1 row, bind off in k on
next row. Sew rem shoulder seam.
Sew sleeves in armholes. Sew side and
sleeve seams.

INSTRUCTIONS FOR TRADITIONAL ARAN PULLOVER

A traditional Aran saddle-shoulder
pullover, with slightly oversized fit
(see the photo on p. 144). For the
experienced knitter.

SIZE

To fit 33-35 (36-38, 40-42, 43-45)-in.
bust/chest.

FINISHED MEASUREMENTS
(AFTER SEAMING)

Finished bust/chest at underarm: 41 (44,
47, 50½) in.
Length (from center of shoulder strap):
24½ (25, 25½, 26) in.
Sleeve width at upper arm: 19 (20, 21,
22) in.

MATERIALS

• 9 (10, 11, 13) skeins "Germantown
Knitting Worsted" from Brunswick
(100% wool; 3½ oz = approx 220 yd) in
color ecru #4000.
• Knitting needles sizes 5 and 7, or size to
obtain gauge.
• 1 circular knitting needle, size 5,
16 in. long.

GAUGE

• 20 sts and 28 rows equal 4 in. with size
7 needles over moss stitch.
• To save time later, take time to swatch
and check your gauge.

PATTERNS

See charts on facing page. Read all from
left to right on WS rows, and from right
to left on RS rows.

SCHEMATIC FOR ARAN PULLOVER

1 square = 1 in.

Key

- □ = k RS, p WS
- ⊟ = p RS, k WS
- Ọ = yo
- ◪ = k2tog
- ◪ = ssk
- ◪ = k1-b RS, p1-b WS
- ◪ = sl 1-k2tog-psso
- ◈ = make bobble: k into front, back and front of st, [turn and k these 3 sts] 3 times, then turn and sl 1-k2tog-psso
- = sl st to cn and hold in back, k1; then p1 from cn
- = sl st to cn and hold in front, p1; then k1 from cn
- = sl st to cn and hold in back, k1-b; then p1 from cn
- = sl st to cn and hold in front, p1; then k1-b from cn

ARAN PULLOVER PATTERNS

Key (continued)

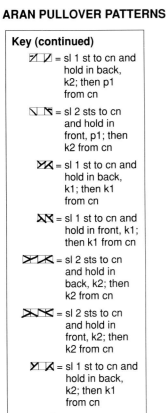

= sl 1 st to cn and hold in back, k2; then p1 from cn

= sl 2 sts to cn and hold in front, p1; then k2 from cn

= sl 1 st to cn and hold in back, k1; then k1 from cn

= sl 1 st to cn and hold in front, k1; then k1 from cn

= sl 2 sts to cn and hold in back, k2; then k2 from cn

= sl 2 sts to cn and hold in front, k2; then k2 from cn

= sl 1 st to cn and hold in back, k2; then k1 from cn

= sl 2 sts to cn and hold in front, k1; then k2 from cn

= sl 3 sts to cn and hold in back, k2; then k3 from cn

Left zigzag   Right zigzag

← 5 sts →   ← 5 sts →

Twisted tree

← 9 sts →

Border (multiple of 8 sts plus 1)

← 8-st rep →

Scotch cable

← 6 sts →

Spearhead and chain

← 24 sts →

1x1 rib

2 sts

Moss st

2-st rep

Eyelet and seed-st blocks

← 12 sts →

Diamond and chain

← 16 sts →

Two-textured rib

Version 1

← 8 sts →

Version 2

← 8 sts →

Open cable

← 15 sts →

BACK

With smaller needle, cast on 125 (139, 155, 171) sts.

Next row (WS): p2 (keep in St st); then work row 1 of following pats: 1x1 rib over 0 (7, 15, 23) sts; {twisted tree over 9 sts, 1x1 rib over 7 sts, left zigzag over 5 sts, 1x1 rib over 7 sts} twice; twisted tree over 9 sts; {1x1 rib over 7 sts, right zigzag over 5 sts, 1x1 rib over 7 sts, twisted tree over 9 sts} twice; 1x1 rib over 0 (7, 15, 23) sts, end p2 in St st. Work even until 41 rows are complete, end with WS row (rib measures approx 5½ in.). K RS row, dec 18 (26, 34, 42) sts evenly — 107 (113, 121, 129) sts. P 2 rows. Change to larger needle and p WS row.

Next row (RS): k 1 (4, 4, 4) in St st, work row 1 of border pat over center 105 (105, 113, 121) sts, end k 1 (4, 4, 4) in St st. Work even for 5 more rows. Change to smaller needle. P RS row. Change to larger needle. P WS row. K RS row, inc 31 (33, 33, 33) sts evenly — 138 (146, 154, 162) sts.

Next row (WS): p2 (keep in St st), then work Row 1 of following pats, unless noted: moss st over 5 (9, 13, 17) sts, k1 in rev St st, Scotch cable over 6 sts, diamond and chain over 16 sts, eyelet and seed-st blocks over 12 sts, 2-textured rib (version 1) over 8 sts, k1 in rev St st, Scotch cable over 6 sts, spearhead and chain over 24 sts, Scotch cable over 6 sts, k1 in rev St st, 2-textured rib (version 2) over 8 sts, Row 17 of eyelet and seed-st blocks over 12 sts, diamond and chain over 16 sts, Scotch cable over 6 sts, k1 in rev St st, moss st over 5 (9, 13, 17) sts, p2 (keep in St st). Work even until piece measures 22 (22½, 23, 23½) in.

SHOULDER AND BACK-NECK SHAPING

Keep in pat, bind off 17 (19, 20, 21) sts at beg of next 2 rows, then 18 (18, 19, 20) sts at beg of next 4 rows. Bind off rem 32 (36, 38, 40) sts.

FRONT

Work same as for back.

SLEEVE

With smaller needle, cast on 47 (51, 51, 55) sts.

Next row (WS): p2 in St st, then work Row 1 of following pats: 1x1 rib over 5 (7, 7, 9) sts, left zigzag over 5 sts, 1x1 rib over 7 sts, twisted tree over 9 sts, 1x1 rib over 7 sts, right zigzag over 5 sts, 1x1 rib over 5 (7, 7, 9) sts, end p2 in St st. Work even until 33 rows have been completed, end with WS row (rib should measure approx 4 in.). K RS row, inc 2 (4, 4, 2) sts evenly — 49 (55, 55, 57) sts. P 2 rows. Change to larger needle. P WS row.

Next row (RS): k 0 (3, 3, 0) in St st, work Row 1 of border pat over center 49 (49, 49, 57) sts, end k 0 (3, 3, 0) in St st. Work even for 5 more rows, so end with a WS row. Change to smaller needle. P 1 row. Change to larger needle. P 1 row. K RS row, inc 36 (30, 34, 32) sts evenly spaced — 85 (85, 89, 89) sts.

Next row (WS): p2 in St st, then work Row 1 of following pats: moss st over 3 (3, 5, 5) sts, diamond and chain over 16 sts, Scotch cable over 6 sts, 2-textured rib (version 2) over 8 sts, open cable with waved rib over 15 sts, 2-textured rib (version 1) over 8 sts, Scotch cable over 6 sts, diamond and chain over 16 sts, moss st over 3 (3, 5, 5) sts, p2 in St st. Work even for 2 more rows.

Next row, inc row (RS): k2, M1, work to last 2 sts, M1, end k2. Cont as est, rep inc row after 3 more rows, then every 4th row after for a total of 16 (19, 19, 21) incs each side — 117 (123, 127, 131) sts. Work incs into moss st, cont until sleeve measures 16 (17, 17, 17½) in., or to desired length, end with WS row. Bind off 42 (45, 47, 49) sts at beg of next 2 rows — 33 sts. Keep 1st and last st in St st, work even in pats until shoulder strap measures 7½ (8, 8½, 9¼) in. Bind off.

FINISHING

Sew bound-off edges at front and back shoulders to sides of shoulder straps. Sew side and underarm seams.

Neckline rib

With RS facing and circular needle, pick up 33 (37, 39, 41) sts evenly along back neck, then 28 (28, 27, 28) sts along shoulder strap, then 33 (37, 39, 41) sts along front neck, then 28 (28, 27, 28) sts along shoulder strap to beg — 122 (130, 132, 138) sts. Place marker and join. Note: Read all pat-chart rows from right to left when working in the round.

Next rnd: Beg with k1 work 1x1 rib over 61 (67, 69, 73) sts, work left zigzag over 5 sts, work 1x1 rib over 7 sts, work twisted tree over 9 sts, work 1x1 rib over 7 sts, work row 1 of right zigzag over 5 sts, beg with k1 work 1x1 rib over 28 (30, 30, 32) sts to end. Work even for 23 more rnds. Bind off.

INSTRUCTIONS FOR KNITTED "KIMONO"

A one-size-fits-all, slip-stitch-patterned silk "kimono" (see the photo on p. 165). For the experienced knitter.

SIZE

One size fits all, with an oversized, exaggerated silhouette.

FINISHED MEASUREMENTS (AFTER SEAMING)

Finished bust at underarm: 50 in.
Length: 30 in.

MATERIALS

I suggest a 100% silk yarn, to create a lustrous garment with drape. As an alternative, you may opt for a smooth, shiny cotton yarn. A smooth cabled wool would create a more durable, easy-to-knit garment, but it would lack the sheen of silk. If you substitute another yarn, choose one with a similar yardage that will obtain same gauge.
• 14 skeins "Xian" from Crystal Palace, (100 % silk; 1¾ oz = 135 yd) in mocha #2377.
• 2 skeins of "Xian" in black #2320.
• 2 skeins of "Xian" in cobalt blue #2311.
• 1 pair each knitting needles sizes 4 and 7.
• 1 circular knitting needle size 4, 36 in. long.
• 1 circular needle for picking up stitches, size 1 or 2, 36 in. long.

GAUGE

• 22 sts and 34 rows equal 4 in. over herringbone pat with size 7 needle.
• Maze pat, worked in a panel of 18 sts (16 sts in pat with an edge st on either side) with size 7 needles should measure approx 2½ in. wide.
• To save time later, take time to swatch and check your gauge.

PATTERNS

Left diagonal herringbone (multiple of 6 sts)
Note: All sts are sl as if to p with yarn in FRONT.
Row 1 and all other WS rows: P.
Row 2: * sl 3, k3; rep from *.
Row 4: k1, * sl 3, k 3; rep from *, end sl 3, k2.
Row 6: k2, * sl 3, k3; rep from *, end sl 3, k1.
Row 8: * k3, sl 3; rep from *.
Row 10: sl 1, * k3, sl 3; rep from *, end k3, sl 2.
Row 12: sl 2, * k3, sl 3; rep from *, end k3, sl 1.
Repeat rows 1-12.

Right diagonal herringbone (multiple of 6 sts)
Row 1 and all other WS rows: P.
Row 2: Same as Row 2 above in right diagonal herringbone.
Row 4: Same as Row 12 above.
Row 6: Same as Row 10 above.
Row 8: Same as Row 8 above.
Row 10: Same as Row 6 above.
Row 12: Same as Row 4 above.
Repeat rows 1-12.

"KIMONO" SCHEMATIC

Back

6 in.

30 in.

24 in.

24 in.
134 sts (1 + 132 + 1)

Left front

Right front

6 in.

24 in.

30 in.

12 in.

18 in.

6 in.

6½ in.
38 sts (1+ 36 +1)

6½ in.
38 sts (1+ 36 +1)

Blue side insert (make 2)

18 in.

30 in.

2 in.
14 sts
(1 + 12 + 1)

Center-front panel (make 2)

2½ in.
18 sts
(1 + 16 + 1)

Sleeve band (make 2)

32 in.

2½ in.
18 sts
(1 + 16 + 1)

Sleeve (make 2)   ⌐ Center sleeve

8 in.

32 in.
176 sts (1 + 174 + 1)

1 square = 1 in.

Key

▨▨▨ = right herringbone pat

▨▨▨ = left herringbone pat

⦀≣⦀ = maze pat

Maze pat (multiple of 14 sts plus 2)
Colors mocha (A) and black (B). Cast on with color A and p 1 row. Note: On all right-side odd-numbered rows, sl all sts as if to p, with yarn in BACK.
Row 1 (RS): With B, k1, * k7, (sl 1, k1) 3 times, sl 1; rep from *, end k1.
Row 2 and all other WS rows: P all sts worked on previous row, with same color; sl all same sl sts with yarn in FRONT.
Row 3: With A, k1, * sl 1, k7, (sl 1, k1) 3 times; rep from *, end k1.
Row 5: With B, k2, * sl 1, k7, (sl 1, k1) 3 times; rep from *.
Row 7: With A, * (k1, sl 1) twice, k7, sl 1, k1, sl 1; rep from *, end k2.
Row 9: With B, k2, * sl 1, k1, sl 1, k7, (sl 1, k1) twice; rep from *.
Row 11: With A, * (k1, sl 1) 3 times, k7, sl 1; rep from *, end k2.
Row 13: With B, k1, * (k1, sl 1) 3 times, k7, sl 1; rep from *, end k1.
Row 15: With A, k1, * (sl 1, k1) 3 times, sl 1, k7; rep from *, end k1.
Row 17: With B, rep row 1.
Row 19: With A, * k7, (sl 1, k1) 3 times, sl 1; rep from *, end k2.

Row 21: With B, k6, * (sl 1, k1) 3 times, sl 1, k7; rep from *, end last rep k3.
Row 23: With A, k5, * (sl 1, k1) 3 times, sl 1, k7; rep from *, end last rep k4.
Row 25: With B, k4, * (sl 1, k1) 3 times, sl 1, k7; rep from *, end last rep k5.
Row 27: With A, k3, * (sl 1, k1) 3 times, sl 1, k7; rep from *, end last rep k6.
Row 29: With B, k2, * (sl 1, k1) 3 times, sl 1, k7; rep from *.
Row 31: With A, rep Row 15.
Row 32: Same as Row 2.
Rep rows 1-32.

Ribbing (multiple of 5 sts plus 3)
Row 1 (RS): k3, * p2, k3; rep from *.
Row 2: p3, * k2, p3; rep from *.
Rep rows 1 and 2.

NOTES
• Using larger needles, cast on number of sts shown on chart for each piece. Since cast-on edge of body pieces will receive no further trim or edging, make sure cast-on edge is neat and firm. K 1st and last st of every row as an edge st, and work in designated pat over center sts.
• Work to lengths indicated. Change diagonal herringbone pat where

indicated, ending 1st section with a Row 12 of pat and beginning next section with a Row 1 of new pat. Steam fabric occasionally if necessary to see if your lengths are accurate.

FINISHING
Steam all pieces lightly. Sew a center-front maze panel to each front herringbone section. Sew fronts to back at shoulders. Sew blue side inserts to front and back. Sew a maze panel along bound-off edge of each sleeve.
Sleeve ribbing: With RS facing, very fine circular needle and blue, pick up 203 sts along edge of maze panel. Change to size 4 needle. Work ribbing as follows: With blue, k WS row. Change to mocha. Work in ribbing for 2½ in., then bind off loosely. Fold ribbing to WS and sew in place. Rep border on other sleeve.
Ribbing for fronts and neckline edge: With RS facing, very fine needle and blue, pick up 178 sts along right front to back-neck edge, then pick up 27 sts along back neck, then pick up 178 sts along left front to lower edge—383 sts. Change to size 4 needle. Work ribbing as for sleeve. Fold ribbing to WS and sew in place.

SCHEMATIC FOR SPIDERWEB LACE SHAWL
(WORK AREAS ① TO ⑦ AS INDICATED

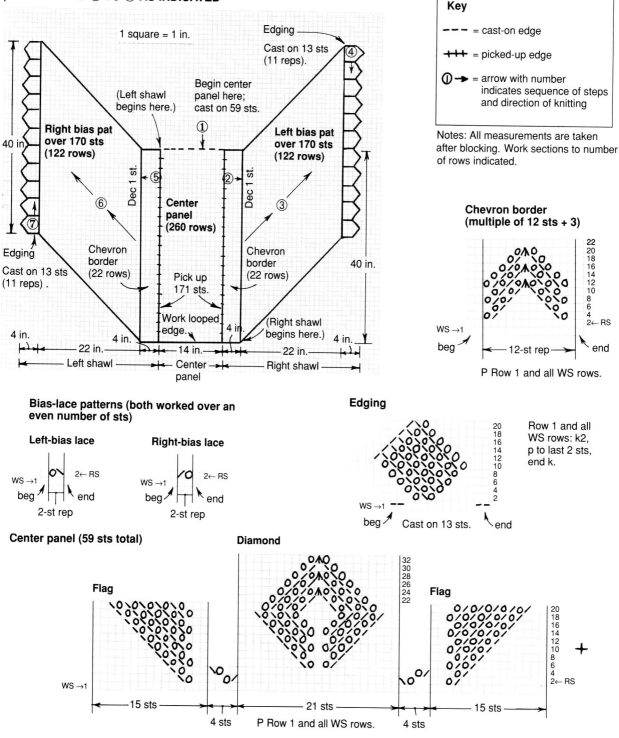

Key

--- = cast-on edge

+++ = picked-up edge

①→ = arrow with number indicates sequence of steps and direction of knitting

Notes: All measurements are taken after blocking. Work sections to number of rows indicated.

Chevron border (multiple of 12 sts + 3)

22 20 18 16 14 12 10 8 6 4 2← RS

WS →1 beg

12-st rep — end

P Row 1 and all WS rows.

1 square = 1 in.

Edging

Cast on 13 sts (11 reps).

Begin center panel here; cast on 59 sts.

(Left shawl begins here.)

Right bias pat over 170 sts (122 rows)

Left bias pat over 170 sts (122 rows)

40 in

Dec 1 st. ⑤

② Dec 1 st.

Center panel (260 rows)

⑥ ③

Chevron border (22 rows)

Chevron border (22 rows)

Pick up 171 sts.

Work looped edge.

(Right shawl begins here.)

⑦

Edging

Cast on 13 sts (11 reps).

40 in.

4 in. — 22 in. — 4 in. — 14 in. — 22 in. — 4 in.

Left shawl — Center panel — Right shawl

Bias-lace patterns (both worked over an even number of sts)

Left-bias lace

WS →1 beg — 2← RS end

2-st rep

Right-bias lace

WS →1 beg — 2← RS end

2-st rep

Edging

20 18 16 14 12 10 8 6 4 2

Row 1 and all WS rows: k2, p to last 2 sts, end k.

WS →1 beg Cast on 13 sts. end

Center panel (59 sts total)

Flag

WS →1

15 sts

4 sts

Diamond

32 30 28 26 24 22

21 sts

P Row 1 and all WS rows.

4 sts

Flag

20 18 16 14 12 10 8 6 4 2← RS

15 sts

Mark center of sleeve top. Sew sleeve top to body above blue side insert, matching center sleeve to shoulder seam. Sew sleeve side seams. Leave sleeve open at trimmed edge that is not joined to body.

I-cord ties (make 2): With larger needle and blue, cast on 3 sts, * k3, sl these 3 sts back to LH needle; rep from * until cord is 8 in. long. Bind off. Sew cords at front edges underneath ribbing.

INSTRUCTIONS FOR SPIDERWEB LACE SHAWL

A shawl with bias-lace patterns (see the photo on p. 198). For expert knitters.

SIZE

Approx blocked size and measurements are shown on schematic (above).

MATERIALS
•8 balls "Mohair Extra" from Lanas Margarita (100% mohair; ⅞ oz = 218 yd) in color pale grey #2341.
•Knitting needles size 6, or size to obtain gauge.

BLOCKED GAUGE
•Approx 18 sts and 22 rows equal 4 in. with size 6 needles over lace patterns.
•To test gauge, I suggest working a swatch of central border, then blocking it. If you want shawl to be denser or more open than blocked swatch, adjust needle size.

PATTERNS
On RS rows, read all charts from right to left. In most cases WS rows have been omitted from charts: p odd-numbered WS rows. Where WS rows are shown, read chart from left to right.

CENTER PANEL
Cast on 59 sts. Work center panel pats for 261 rows (8 reps of diamond pat, plus 5 rows), so end with a WS row.

TO FORM LOOPED EDGE
Next row (RS): k1 loosely, * sl this looped st back to LH needle, then k1 again; rep from * 3 more times: do not sl back to LH needle. K next st on LH needle, then pass 1st looped st over it. Rep from * until all sts have been looped. Do not cut yarn; leave last st on needle.

PICKING UP BORDER (RIGHT SHAWL)
With RS facing, pick up 1 st on adjacent edge, pass last looped st over it, then pick up 170 more sts along this edge (approx 2 sts for every 3 rows)—171 sts. Work border pat until 22 rows are complete, dec 1 st on last row row—170 sts. Work in left bias pat for 123 rows, so end with a WS row. Sl sts to holder.

ATTACHING EDGING
Cast on 13 sts. Work WS row of edging to last st, then k last st together with 1st st on holder. Work RS row. Then, on next WS row, k last st tog with next TWO sts on holder. Work RS row. Rep last 4 rows to attach edging as you knit.

LEFT SHAWL
Work as for right shawl, picking up sts and working edging from opposite direction, work right bias pat.

FINISHING
Wet-block severely (see p. 230). Allow to dry thoroughly.

Sources of supply

Yarns
Unless indicated as a mail-order supplier of yarn, the following yarn companies provided materials for projects in this book. Contact your local yarn shop or write or call the company directly for addresses of retailers near you who carry their yarns. Write to the mail-order suppliers to request information about their catalogs or price lists.

Berroco, Inc., Elmdale Rd., P.O. Box 367, Uxbridge, MA 01569; (800) 343-4948
("Glacé" and "Dante" novelty yarns used in shawl in Ch. 2)

B. Blumenthal and Co., Inc., 140 Kero Rd., Carlstadt, NJ 07072-2699; (201) 935-6220
(Satin-covered buttons and buttonloop tape for shawl in Ch. 2)

Brunswick Yarns, P.O. Box 276, Pickens, SC 29671; (800) 845-4788
("Germantown Knitting Worsted" for black and white pullover in Ch. 5 and for traditional Aran on opening spread of Ch. 6)

Classic Elite Yarns, Inc., 12 Perkins St., Lowell, MA 01854; (800) 343-0308
("La Gran," "Cleo" and "Sharon" mohair yarns for jackets in Ch. 3; "Cambridge" wool/cotton blend for guernseys in Ch. 4; and "Paisley Light" rayon/wool yarn for leaf sweater in Ch. 7)

Crystal Palace Yarns, 3006 San Pablo Ave., Berkeley, CA 94702; (800) 227-0323
("Xian" silk yarn for kimono in Ch. 6)

Evergreen Enterprises, 267 Burt St., Taunton, MA 02780; (617) 823-2377
(Handspun angora for "ermine" collar in Ch. 2)

Lanas Margarita, Inc., P.O. Box R, Island Heights, NJ 08732; (201) 929-3232
("Mohair Extra" for lace shawl in Ch. 7)

Lane Borgosesia, 16 Mahopac Village Center, Mahopac, NY 10541; (800) 431-1999
("Maratona" wool yarn for suit in Ch. 8)

Laninter Corp., Pingouin Yarns, P.O. Box 1542, Mt. Pleasant, SC 29465; (800) 845-2291
("1920" and "Fresque" novelty yarns for shawl in Ch. 2 and "Fleur de Laine" wool yarn for the two Aran variations in Ch. 6)

Reynolds Yarns, A Division of JCA, Inc., Scales Lane, Townsend, MA 01469; (800) 225-6340
(Paternayan "Persian" wool yarn for rainbow coat in Ch. 5)

Schoolhouse Press, 6899 Cary Bluff, Pittsville, WI 54466; (715) 884-2799
(Mail-order supplier, offering wool yarns, including authentic Shetland and Icelandic wools, an excellent list of books, knitter's graph paper, needles and other tools)

Tomato Factory Yarn Co., 8 Church St., Lambertville, NJ 08530; (609) 397-3475
(Retailer and mail-order supplier, with a wide range of yarns and books)

Westminster Trading Corp., 5 Northern Blvd., Amherst, NH 03031; (800) 445-9276
(Rowan's "Chunky Cotton Chenille" for shawl in Ch. 2 and "Lightweight Double Knitting" wool yarn and "Silkstones" silk blend for Hiroshige-inspired pullover in Ch. 6)

Buttons, beads, surface-embellishment & art supplies
The following companies supply materials for nonknitting techniques mentioned in the book. Call or write to request information about catalogs or price lists.

Cerulean Blue, Ltd., P.O. Box 21168, Seattle, WA 98111-3168; (206) 443-7744
(Mail-order supplier of dyeing and surface-design equipment)

Ornamental Resources, P.O. Box 3010, 1427 Miner St., Idaho Springs, CO 80452; (303) 567-4987
(Mail-order company, with a huge catalog offering all kinds of beads, feathers and jewelry findings)

Rupert, Gibbon and Spider,
P.O. Box 425, Healdsburg, CA 95448;
(707) 433-9577
(Mail-order company offering dyes,
tools, books and silk woven fabrics)

Shipwreck Beads, 5021 Mud Bay Rd.,
Olympia, WA 98502; (206) 866-4061
(Mail-order company whose catalog
shows a huge range of beads life-size
and in color)

Tender Buttons, 143 East 62nd St.,
New York, NY 10021
(Retail store only, offering a
remarkable collection of both old
and contemporary buttons; a must for
any visitor to New York City)

Dressmaker patterns and supplies
The major pattern companies—
Vogue/Butterick, Simplicity, McCall's
and Style—sell their patterns through
fabric stores.

Folkwear, The Taunton Press,
P.O. Box 5506, Newtown, CT
06470-5506
(Mail-order reproductions of vintage
and ethnic garments)

Newark Dressmaker Supply,
6473 Ruch Rd., P.O. Box 24488, Lehigh
Valley, PA 18001; (215) 837-7500
(Mail-order supplier of general
dressmaking equipment, including
premarked boards or cloths for
blocking surfaces)

Superior Model Forms,
545 Eighth Ave., New York, NY
10018; (212) 947-3633
(Dressmaker forms in a range of
commercial sizes used in the garment
industry and custom-made forms to
specific measurements)

Mail-order booksellers
These sources offer both current
and out-of-print books related to all
fiber arts.

Bette Feinstein Books, 96 Roundwood
Rd., Newton, MA 02164;
(617) 969-0942

Wooden Porch Books, Route 1,
Box 262, Middlebourne, WV 26149;
(304) 386-4434

Bibliography

The following list offers only a taste of the books that have inspired me. Due to space limitations, there are many omissions. I have included those that I think support the area of garment design. Also, although I have many, I have listed only a few museum exhibition catalogs, as they are printed in relatively small quantities and have short-lived availability. I have not listed many useful old embroidery or knitting leaflets, some from foreign countries, because they are out of print and/or rarely available.

For easy reference, the books are arranged in categories. For access to books that are no longer in print, check your library or contact a secondhand book dealer.

Basic knitting
Editors of Vogue Knitting. *Vogue Knitting*. New York: Pantheon Books, 1989.
(Inspiring, clearly illustrated volume of knitting techniques, with good beading and embroidery sections; small dictionary of pattern stitches; good design information and patterns for some traditional sweaters.)

Norbury, James and Margaret Agutter. *Odhams Encyclopedia of Knitting*. London: Odhams Books Ltd., 1957.
(A wonderful, now-rare volume, reminiscent of Mary Thomas's books, with some design-related material; also some classic sweater designs with instructions.)

Stanley, Montse. *The Handknitter's Handbook*. London: David and Charles, 1986.
(Good source, especially for different cast-on methods.)

Thomas, Mary. *Mary Thomas's Book of Knitting Patterns*. London: Hodder and Stoughton, Ltd., 1943. Reprint. New York: Dover Publications, Inc., 1972.
—. *Mary Thomas's Knitting Book*. London: Hodder and Stoughton, Ltd., 1938. Reprint. New York: Dover Publications, Inc., 1972.
(These two books look old-fashioned but, to my mind, have never been surpassed for straightforward technical information. Topics include beading, increases and decreases, and Shetland lace shawls.)

Pattern dictionaries
Abbey, Barbara. *Knitting Lace*. New York: The Viking Press, 1974.
(This is my favorite lace book, with an impressive collection of edgings and an intriguing system of symbols.)

Aytes, Barbara. *Adventures in Knitting*. New York: Doubleday & Company, 1968.
(Features the tied-bow patterns, a favorite of mine.)

Fanderl, Lisl. *Bauerliches Stricken*. Germany: Rosenheimer, 1975.
—. Bauerliches Stricken 2. Germany: Rosenheimer, 1979
—. Bauerliches Stricken 3. Germany: Rosenheimer, 1980.
(Excellent Bavarian pattern dictionaries, including knit/purl patterns, lace, and, most notably, intricate twist-stitch patterns.)

Mon Tricot Knitting Dictionary: Stitches, Patterns. Paris: Editions de l'alma, no date.
(Excellent source of both textured and colorwork patterns for both knit and crochet.)

Phillips, Mary Walker. *Knitting Counterpanes: Traditional Coverlet Patterns for Contemporary Knitters*. Newtown, Conn.: The Taunton Press, 1989.
(Not technically a dictionary but a great source for designers of some less familiar knit/purl, lace and embossed-leaf patterns that can be adapted for use in garments.)

Walker, Barbara G. *Charted Knitting Designs: A Third Treasury of Knitting Patterns.* New York: Charles Scribner's Sons, 1972.
—. *Mosaic Knitting.* New York: Charles Scribner's Sons, 1976.
—. *A Second Treasury of Knitting Patterns.* New York: Charles Scribner's Sons, 1970.
—. *A Treasury of Knitting Patterns.* New York: Charles Scribner's Sons, 1968.
(Barbara Walker is perhaps the most influential of all American knitting authors, and her treasuries, divided into families of patterns, are indispensable for knitwear designers. Her clearly presented system of charting (in *Charted Knitting Designs*) is my favorite. The exhaustive mosaic knitting book describes the techniques and includes many patterns, both allover and borders.)

Knitting garments

Duncan, Ida Riley. *The Complete Book of Progressive Knitting.* New York: Liveright Publishing Corp., 1968.
(May seem a bit dated but contains valuable suggestions for garment contruction and shaping.)

Mon Tricot Special, Knit and Crochet: The Knitters' Basic Book, volumes 1 and 2. Paris: Editions de l'alma, no date.
(Hard-to-find editions, originally published in France by the editors of *Mon Tricot* magazine. Designers will appreciate sections on sleeve types and collars in Volume 1, and darts, cuffs and pleats in Volume 2.)

Walker, Barbara G. *Knitting from the Top.* New York: Charles Scribner's Sons, 1972.
(Excellent guide to knitting seamless garments from the top down. Thorough description of all double decreases, with photo showing each. Familiar sweater shapes along with pants, capes, skirts, and more.)

Zimmermann, Elizabeth. *Knitter's Almanac.* New York: Charles Scribner's Sons, 1974. Reprint. New York: Dover Publications, Inc., 1981.
(Arguably the best book from this influential American knitwear designer. A must for enthusiasts of garter stitch, I-cord, and, of course, circularly knit garments.)

Traditional and ethnic knitted garments

Bohn, Annichen Sibbern. *Norwegian Knitting Designs.* Oslo: Grondahl and Son, Publishers, 1965.
Excellent charted colorwork patterns, including dancing ladies, snowflakes, reindeer and birds.

Compton, Rae. *The Complete Book of Traditional Guernsey and Jersey Knitting.* New York: Arco Publishing, Inc., 1985.
(Many historical photos and good charts of knit/purl patterns.)

Don, Sarah. *The Art of Shetland Lace.* London: Bell and Hyman, Ltd., 1986.
(A lovely book of Shetland lace patterns and motifs.)

Gibson-Roberts, Pricilla A. *Knitting in the Old Way.* Loveland, Colo.: Interweave Press, 1985.
(Covers a wide range of traditional garment shapes and types, including circularly knit yoke sweaters and a Cowichan pullover from the Pacific Northwest.)

Gottfridsson, Inger and Ingrid Gottfridsson. *The Swedish Mitten Book.* Asheville, N.C.: Lark Books, 1984.
(Wonderful charts, many of floral motifs.)

Gravelle LeCount, Cynthia. *Andean Folk Knitting: Traditions and Techniques from Peru and Bolivia.* St. Paul, Minn.: Dos Tejedoras, 1990.
(A truly inspirational book, with great charts for geometric patterns and wonderful animal motifs.)

Harrell, Betsy. *Anatolian Knitting Designs.* Istanbul: Redhouse Press, 1981.
(A superlative pattern book, with a wide range of unusual, often angular patterns taken from Turkish stockings.)

Hollingworth, Shelagh. *The Complete Book of Traditional Aran Knitting.* New York: St. Martin's Press. 1982.
(A lovely book, almost half devoted to useful background material and traditional patterns, with the remainder filled with fine Aran-inspired designs.)

McGregor, Sheila. *The Complete Book of Traditional Fair Isle Knitting.* New York: Charles Scribner's Sons, 1981.
—. *The Complete Book of Traditional Scandinavian Knitting.* New York: St. Martin's Press, 1984.
—. *Traditional Knitting.* London: B.T. Batsford, Ltd., 1983.
(The Fair Isle book is an excellent source for patterns. The book on Scandinavian knitting is full of interesting photos and a wide range of charted patterns. The third book has nice color photos of traditional garments and a short text, but no charts.)

Norbury, James. *Traditional Knitting Patterns from Scandinavia, The British Isles, France, Italy and Other European Countries.* New York: Dover Publications, 1979.
(A useful volume with a wide range of patterns, including unusual Arabic motifs and a Spanish Adam and Eve.)

Starmore, Alice. *Alice Starmore's Book of Fair Isle Knitting.* Newtown, Conn.: The Taunton Press, 1988.
(A good collection of pattern charts, plus fine color information and inspirational designs by the author.)

Thompson, Gladys. *Patterns for Guernseys, Jerseys and Arans.* London: B.T. Batsford. Reprint. New York: Dover Publications, Inc., 1971.
(The first knitting book I ever bought and still my favorite. Thompson gathered much of this information first-hand, visiting knitters in the British Isles. Great charts, truly inspirational Arans.)

Upitis, Lizbeth. *Latvian Mittens.* St. Paul, Minn.: Dos Tejedoras, 1981.
(Great mittens with charts. Interesting discussion of traditional shapes that occur in patterns and motifs.)

van der Klift-Tellegen, Henriette. *Knitting from the Netherlands.* Asheville, N.C.: Lark Books, 1985.
(Inspirational old photos of Dutch guernseys with charts for knit/purl patterns.)

Embroidery patterns

Cirker, Blanche. *Needlework Alphabets and Designs.* New York: Dover Publications, Inc., 1975.
(Many alphabets, with small to very large letters, some more suitable for knitting than others; some allover patterns too.)

Kiewe, Heinz Edgar, ed. Charted *Peasant Designs from Saxon Transylvania.* New York: Dover, 1964.
(An excellent source for complex embroidery patterns that can be adapted to stranded colorwork.)

Spinhoven, Co. *Celtic Charted Designs.* New York: Dover Publications, Inc., 1987.
(Interlocking maze-like patterns and intricated rounded motifs that could be adapted to stranded colorwork or mosaic-knitting techniques.)

Vinciolo, Federico. *Renaissance Patterns for Lace, Embroidery, and Needlepoint.* Paris: Jean Leclerc, 1587. Reprint. New York: Dover Publications, Inc., 1971.
(Delightful charted pictorial scenes and motifs.)

Drawing, dyeing and color

Birren, Faber. *Principles of Color.* New York: Van Nostrand Reinhold Co., Inc. Reprint. West Chester, Pa.: Schiffer, 1987.
(A classic text on color theory.)

Buchanan, Rita. *A Weaver's Garden.* Loveland, Colo.: Interweave Press, 1987.
(An excellent guide to natural dyes and the dyeing process.)

Edwards, Betty. *Drawing on the Right Side of the Brain.* New York: St. Martin's Press, 1989.
(An encouraging book on learning to draw that proves anyone can do it.)

Fassett, Kaffe. *Glorious Knits.* New York: Clarkson N. Potter, Inc., 1985.
(The book that took every knitter's breath away. Color foremost, with interesting motifs and patterns.)

McCann, Michael. *Artist Beware.* New York: Watson-Guptill Publications, 1979.
(A valuable guide to working with toxic art materials, including chemical dyes.)

Dressmaker fabrics and techniques

The New Vogue Sewing Book. New York: Butterick, 1980.
(Basic sewing techniques.)

Hageney, Wolfgang, ed. *Tartans.* Rome: Belvedere Co. Ltd., 1987.
(Includes all the tartan plaids of the clans of Scotland.)

Rohr, M. *Pattern Drafting and Grading.* Waterford, Conn.: Rohr Publishing, 1968.
(This book gave me my first taste of pattern drafting. Includes slopers and inspirational garment shapes, predominantly 1940, 1950s and 1960s in style.)

Fashion, past and present

De Osma, Guillermo. *Mariano Fortuny: His Life and Work.* New York: Rizzoli International, 1980.
(One of my favorite designers.)

Keenan, Brigid. *Dior in VOGUE.* New York: Harmony Books, 1981.
(A good overview of the designs that shaped the silhouettes of the 1950s.)

Lee-Potter, Charlie. *Sportwear in VOGUE, since 1910.* New York: Abbeville Press, 1984.
(An inspirational overview of this century's high fashion sportswear.)

Leymarie, Jean. *Chanel.* New York: Rizzoli International, 1987.
(Although Chanel is remembered primarily for her suits, this book shows the whole range of her designs.)

Lobenthal, Joel. *Radical Rags, Fashions of the Sixties.* New York: Abbeville Press, 1990.
(Great photos from this wonderful fashion period, including some knitwear.)

Martin, Richard, and Harold Koda. *Jocks and Nerds: Men's Style in the Twentieth Century.* New York: Rizzoli, 1989.
(Fascinating, heavily illustrated book categorizing the various "types" represented in men's fashions.)

Olian, JoAnne, ed. *Authentic French Fashions from the Twenties.* New York: Dover Publications, Inc., 1990.
(Good illustrations of typical fashions of the period.)

White, Palmer. *Elsa Schiaparelli.* New York: Rizzoli, 1986.
(Inspiring book covering the long and varied career of one of my favorite designers.)

Nonknitted ethnic clothing

Burnham, Dorothy K. *Cut My Cote.* Toronto: Royal Ontario Museum, 1973.
(Concise guide to ethnic garment shapes.)

Gilfoy, Peggy Stoltz. *Patterns of Life: West African Strip Weaving Traditions.* Washington, D.C.: National Museum of African Art, Smithsonian Institute, 1987.
(Good photos of West African woven cloths.)

Hail, Barbara. *Hau, Koa! The Plains Indian Collection of the Haffenreffer Museum of Anthropology.* Providence, R.I.: Brown University, 1980.
(Inspirational source for North American Indian graphics.)

Penn, Irving. *Issey Miyake: Photographs by Irving Penn.* A New York Graphics Society Book. Boston: Little, Brown and Co., 1988.
(My favorite contemporary "pushing-the-limits" designer. Includes some knitwear.)

Tilke, Max. *Costume Patterns and Designs.* New York, Rizzoli, 1990.
(An illustrated source for ethnic garment shapes from antiquity through the 19th century.)

Yamanaka, Norio. *The Book of Kimono.* Tokyo: Kodansha International, 1982.
(Guide to the styles and wearing of the kimono, with a brief history.)

Index

Page numbers in italics indicate photos and drawings.

Editor: Christine Timmons
Designer and Layout Artist: Deborah Fillion
Assistant Art Director: Jodie Delohery
Art Assistant: Cindy Lee Nyitray
Photographer, except where noted: Cathy Carver
Illustrator, except where noted: Deborah Newton
Illustrations on pages 18, 94, 108, 196 and 227: Marianne Markey
Copy/Production Editor: Ruth Dobsevage
Indexer: Pam Purrone

Typeface: Palatino
Paper: 70-lb. Influence Soft-Gloss Matte, neutral pH
Printer: Ringier America, New Berlin, Wisconsin